THE COLLECTED PAPERS OF PETER BIRKS

The Roman Law of Obligations

Peter Birks in the Old College library, University of Edinburgh (1980s)

THE COLLECTED PAPERS OF PETER BIRKS

The Roman Law of Obligations

Peter Birks

EDITED BY

Eric Descheemaeker

OXFORD
UNIVERSITY PRESS

OXFORD
UNIVERSITY PRESS

Great Clarendon Street, Oxford, OX2 6DP,
United Kingdom

Oxford University Press is a department of the University of Oxford. It furthers the University's objective of excellence in research, scholarship, and education by publishing worldwide. Oxford is a registered trade mark of Oxford University Press in the UK and in certain other countries

First edition published in 2014

Published in the United States of America by Oxford University Press
198 Madison Avenue, New York, NY 10016, United States of America

British Library Cataloguing in Publication Data
Data available

Library of Congress Control Number: 2014940439

ISBN 978-0-19-871927-4

Acknowledgements

I am grateful, first and foremost, to Jacqueline Birks and Alex Flach for their on-going help over the years in bringing this project to fruition; also to John Cairns and Ernest Metzger for their unstinting help and advice.

ED

Contents

Table of Legal Sources

I. Justinianic

Codex

Institutes

Digest

II. Other Roman Sources

Collatio legum Romanarum et Mosaicarum

III. Early Modern Sources

Stair, Institutions of the Law of Scotland

Table of Ancient Non-Legal Sources

Rhetorica ad Herennium

Aulus Gellius, *Noctes Atticae*

Cicero, *De Officiis*

Cicero, *Topica*

Seneca the Elder, *Controversiae*

Introduction

This *Roman Law of Obligations* comprises notes of lectures given at the University of Edinburgh in 1982 by Peter Birks, who was then Professor of Civil Law in the Scottish capital. These notes, his own, were found in his archives some years after his death and are now being published. The rekindled grief for all those who knew him when he was with us will not, it is hoped, overshadow the intellectual pleasure that this manuscript should bring, both to scholars of Roman law and to those interested in the writings of one of the greatest legal academics of his century.

The Collected Papers of Peter Birks

Before we introduce these lectures it is appropriate to mention the wider context of their publication. Some years after Peter Birks' sudden death, which took him away at the height of his academic career in 2004, a project was initiated among Oxford University Press (Alex Flach), Professor Birks' widow Jackie, and the present editor (who had been one of Peter's doctoral students) to make the entirety of his scholarly writings available to the legal community. The vision was to include not only his previously published work, with the exception of two self-standing monographs (The *Introduction to the Law of Restitution* of 1985 and the two editions of his *Unjust Enrichment* of 2003 and 2005), but also as much hitherto unpublished materials as would be deemed possible and worthwhile. The aim was threefold: to make readily available, both in print and online, works which although in the public domain were often difficult to access; to help legal scholars see the big picture of the honorand's intellectual development, in particular how the various bits of his multifaceted œuvre fitted together; finally, to complete this picture by contributing further materials which, for all manner of reasons, their author had not committed to the printing press during his lifetime.

This project will materialize over a number of years, one volume at a time. The present *Roman Law of Obligations* is the first in the series. Although there is no particular reason why it should come first, it is in fact an excellent illustration of what is hoped will be achieved through this project. Though these lectures were offered to undergraduates in a jurisdiction whose private law is still directly rooted, at least in part, in the Roman law library, one cannot help but bemoan, going through the pages, the waste it was to restrict the audience to them. They are a scholarly opus in their own right and should be of interest to all private lawyers, even non-Romanists. First, to students: Birks had this remarkable ability to make difficult facts and ambitious ideas accessible to the untrained, but keen, mind. These lectures are indeed accessible to the first-year student who is willing to move beyond the dumbed-down version of the law that so many introductory courses feed them on the somewhat patronizing assumption that the young cannot cope with complexity. They do not require much, if any, previous knowledge of either law, classical antiquity, or Latin: only a desire for understanding. But they will also be read with alacrity by more advanced scholars, for it is a rare reader who will not find here some fresh insights into the workings of the law, familiar though they might already be with the field. The two go hand in hand, this ability to achieve what O.W. Holmes called 'simplicity on the other side of complexity' being in fact a characteristic of Birksian scholarship. If we believe that simplicity is a hallmark of truth, it is an aspiration that we will want to share.

Indeed, that the significance of the Roman law of obligations goes much beyond the Roman law of obligations is a theme that permeates the pages that follow. Birks passionately believed, like many of his pupils, in the continued relevance of Roman law for twentieth and then twenty-first-century students of the law. Not only did it supply, in the institutional stream which introductory Roman law invariably follows, a 'map' of the law—something common lawyers, in particular, desperately needed—it also provided a form of universal grammar of the law which could be used to expound, understand, and evaluate the modern law. This introductory function of Roman law was not, to his mind, limited to Romanist jurisdictions; if anything, it might be *more* relevant to English lawyers and students of the common law. Whether to highlight features that are common to two systems—English and Roman—which cannot be understood apart from their actional dimension, or to understand better the workings of the common law by contradistinguishing it from the matrix of the civilian tradition, the importance for common lawyers to study Roman law is a theme—Birksian par excellence—which these lectures return to throughout. Their aim is to introduce not only the Roman law of obligations but, in many ways, obligations *simpliciter.* Just as past and present (indeed the future, as one ponders what lessons can be learnt from the study of what once was) are constantly intertwined, so low-level details are related to our jurisprudential understanding of law generally. This is training for the modern legal mind, not for the student of classical antiquity.

Crucial to this ambition are an emphasis on the centrality of taxonomy and a fascination for the less well-mapped areas of the law of obligations, those lying beyond contracts and delicts (torts). This is particularly titillating if one remembers that these lectures were written at the same time as the book which would define its author for the next twenty years in the English-speaking world, the *Introduction to the Law of Restitution*, was being shaped. Now, that Birks was *also* a Roman lawyer is something that naturally everyone knows; but quite the extent to which he was *primarily*—the term can be used both in a chronological and in an analytical sense—a scholar (and a lover) of Roman law is not necessarily appreciated by all those who came to know him and his works through the English law of unjust enrichment. There is no line to be drawn, not even a dotted one, between the Romanist of the 1960s–early 1980s and the restitution enthusiast who mostly took over afterwards. Though of course an ellipsis, it would hardly be an exaggeration to say that the twenty years he spent consumed by the desire to mould a law of unjust enrichment in its *mos anglicanus* were a long meditation on paragraph 3.91 of Gaius's Institutes.[1]

[1] Below, 17.

These Lectures

The present volume contains notes for a series of twenty-four lectures on the Roman law of obligations: two fifty-minute lectures per week over the long, twelve-week, Edinburgh term. Birks shared the teaching of Civil Law, as it is called here, with others and Obligations are the only part of the curriculum on which he is believed to have produced such notes.

The Lectures are not only organised around, but a constant reflection over the institutional structure of the law, so named after the Institutes of Gaius and Justinian, which (in a modified form) would become the backbone of the later civilian tradition. They approach the law of obligations, in the first instance, as a constituent part of this framework. '*Omne autem ius, quo utimur, vel ad personas pertinet vel ad res vel ad actiones*', as every student of Roman law learns early in their study: 'All the law we use has to do either with persons or with things or with actions.'[2] Obligations are concerned with the middle element, 'things'. From a modern perspective, we would probably want to say that the law of things comprises assets, that is to say, rights. These rights can be 'real' (in the sense of pertaining to a thing, in Latin *res*) or they can be 'personal' (residing in a *persona*): from this we derive our law of property—the study of rights *in rem*—and our law of obligations—the study of rights *in personam*.

That Birks believed this to be the map through which the common law too could best be understood is visible, in particular, from his attempt to produce Institutes of English law in the guise of *English Private Law*,[3] a double-decker he coordinated at the turn of the century. (This was later followed by an *English Public Law*,[4] which he spurred even though he did not contribute directly to it.) However, our modern version of the scheme, whether civilian or 'Birksian', is markedly different from the Gaian-Justinianic attempt, which itself was entirely at odds with the traditional mode of thinking of Roman lawyers. Quite how one moves from the actional materials to, first, Gaius and Justinian's scheme, and then onto the modern law, raises many difficult questions which are almost invariably taken for granted

[2] G.1.8; below, 5–6.

[3] Peter Birks (ed.), *English Private Law* (Oxford: OUP, 2000). Two subsequent editions were prepared under the editorship of Andrew Burrows (2007, 2013).

[4] David Feldman (ed.), *English Public Law* (Oxford: OUP, 2004), now in its second edition (2009).

when we discuss issues of structure today. Yet, as the first chapter of these Lectures demonstrates, Birks expected his first-year students to engage seriously with them.

The following ten chapters follow closely the Gaian order of Roman obligations. At the next level, obligations are divided according to their causative event, that is to say, the real-life event to which the law responds by creating a right vesting in Peter Plaintiff (in Latin, Aulus Agerius) and available against David Defendant (Numerius Negidius). These events are contracts, civil wrongs (delicts) and a miscellany which Gaius called 'a variety of types of causes'.[5] The identification and classification of these miscellaneous events poses redoubtable problems. Indeed, Gaius did not include them in his original Institutes and only mentioned them in a later work, known to us through excerpts in the Digest, the *Res Cottidianae*.[6] Though of particular interest to Birks, they are examined with comparative brevity in the third and final part of these Lectures.

The first two parts, Contracts and Delicts, are divided one level down into nominate *species* of their *genus*, such as sale and mandate for contracts or loss wrongfully caused and contempt (*iniuria*) for delicts. (Contracts, but not delicts, are arranged in clusters of like events into the four classes of contracts *litteris* [by writing], *verbis* [by words], *re* [by delivery of a thing], and *consensu* [by consent, *sc.* by consent alone]. There is on the other hand only one class of delicts.) The part on contracts is longer than that on delicts, although it is hard not to sense that Birks' heart is more in the latter, as indeed the rest of his career shows. What makes the contractual section of these Lectures especially interesting is precisely that the author published precious little on contracts, whether Roman or English, in his lifetime. In the hierarchy of his interests, the traditional order—contracts, civil wrongs, unjust enrichments—was clearly reversed: unjust enrichments, then civil wrongs, then contracts. Not that this should surprise us from a man whose appetite for intellectual order was insatiable; but these lectures give us at least some insight into his perception of the best-mapped province of the law of obligations, an area which is so central to it that, almost 2,000 years after Gaius, the French Civil Code could fail to

[5] D.44.7.1 *pr.* (Gaius, 2 *Nuggets*); below, 18.

[6] Below, 18, 248–50. In these Lectures, the *Res Cottidianae* are referred to as 'Nuggets', after their alternative Roman title, '*Aurea*'.

properly distinguish between 'obligations' and 'contracts' without raising much of an eyebrow in the legal community.[7]

As we move to delict, one noticeable feature is that Birks starts to engage with other scholars, the likes of Daube, Honoré, Jolowicz, and Kelly. The style is also different: less attention is given to the fine-tuning of the law as the Romans knew it, and more emphasis is laid on jurisprudential aspects. It is clear that Birks regarded delict as a more challenging subject and one more worthy of engagement on the part of the modern mind (the same premise which explains why, for several decades, the sole Roman law course on the Bachelor of Civil Law in Oxford was an advanced course in Roman delict). Indeed, it is well-known that writing a book on the Roman law of delicts was one of his main plans for the retirement he never had a chance to enjoy.

Within delicts, the attention of modern scholars has been disproportionately directed to the *lex Aquilia*, the action for wrongful loss that was the basis on which the civilian tradition gradually erected a general principle of liability for loss caused by fault, and which has so many echoes in the modern history of the English tort of negligence. Birks shared this fascination for the Aquilian action, on which he wrote at length, returning to it over the course of two decades.[8] But his interest was not limited to it, and these lectures contain extensive developments on the other two main civil wrongs of Roman law, on which he also wrote: *furtum* (a very wide form of theft) and the transversal delict of *iniuria*, which he liked to translate as 'contempt', for which Birks had a profound interest. This would resurface, in particular, in his John Maurice Kelly Lecture, given many years later in memory of his old Roman law tutor at Trinity College Oxford,[9] and which the present editor regards as one of the finest pieces of scholarship he ever produced.

[7] Title 3.3 of the Code is headed 'Of contracts, or of conventional [=contractual] obligations generally'.

[8] See list of related publications, below, 296.

[9] Peter Birks, *Harassment and Hubris: The Right to an Equality of Respect, Being the Second John Maurice Kelly Memorial Lecture* (Dublin: University College Dublin, Faculty of Law, 1996), later published as Peter Birks, 'Harassment and Hubris: The Right to an Equality of Respect' (1997) 32 *Irish Jurist* (NS), 1–45.

The Manuscript

It is Birks' views on these four topics—obligations in general, contracts, delicts, and other causative events—as they were put on paper for the benefit of undergraduate students in Edinburgh in the early 1980s, which are presented to today's readers. The new audience will undoubtedly have a very different profile from the original one; and it is the role of editorial work to facilitate the transition from one to the other without ending up rewriting the text.

In one sense, these notes are complete. They read remarkably fluently, and indeed the fact that a copy was deposited at the time in the law library of his institution indicates that Birks expected them to be read by others. This made the work of the editor, coming many years later and with no opportunity to ask questions of the author, much easier than it could have been. Nonetheless they were never intended for publication as a book, and so significant work had to go into preparing the manuscript for that purpose. The choice was made to intervene as little as possible: these remain lecture notes, written in an oral and informal style. At the end of the day nothing can, or for that matter should, change this fact. And so *caveat lector*. What the editor has done is simply try to polish the manuscript in such a way as to make the reading experience of the reader more like that of a normal book and less like that of the scholar diving in archives. Typos and evident mistakes were corrected; style of citations harmonized; references provided in footnotes; and tables and index compiled. In spite of this, it remains evident that these are notes that were meant to be read aloud to students, not the polished sort of work that the author would have produced had he decided to turn these lectures into a book himself.[10]

A difficult question that faces the editor of a text written by another is the extent to which he should mark out what is original and what is not. It was thought that a pious respect for the text, turning every intervention into marginal gloss, would make the book look exceedingly clumsy and user-unfriendly. At the same time, while the editor took the liberty to delete or change a few words when they did not make sense, he also chose not to insert anything of substance in the text: all—minimal—additions went into footnotes. Also, within

[10] Here it is difficult to resist the temptation to call to mind Gaius's Institutes and to be struck by the parallel.

citations of sources, round brackets were used to indicate alternative versions (for instance English and Latin), while square brackets were meant to signal Birks' own gloss on the original.

At the end of the book, the reader will find a list of questions followed by a translation of extracts from Gaius (and Justinian in the context of the 'quasi categories', which do not feature in Gaius's Institutes). These were extracted from a series of eight hand-outs prepared by Birks for tutorials associated with these lectures. The snippets were included despite the availability of modern English translations,[11] both because some questions refer to specific passages in them and also because the way Birks chose to translate these is a matter of scholarly interest in and of itself.

Finally, while Latin permeates these lectures throughout, which ought not to be tampered with because no serious study of a legal system can do without attention being given to the language in which it expressed itself, Birks had anticipated the tragic collapse of classical studies in British schools over the last 30 years: everything in these lectures is either translated or explained. A smattering of Latin helps greatly to follow, and the reader with such knowledge will hugely benefit from Birks' engagement with the original; but the one who is not so equipped should not find it a hindrance.

Eric Descheemaeker
Edinburgh
5 October 2013

Notes: (i) References to 'Lenel' are to Otto Lenel, *Das Edictum Perpetuum* (3rd ed., Leipzig: Bernhard Tauchnitz, 1927); (ii) all translations in the lectures are believed to be Birks' own unless otherwise specified.

[11] Peter Birks and Grant McLeod, *Justinian's Institutes, Translated with an Introduction, with the Latin Text of Paul Krueger* (London: Duckworth, 1987); William M. Gordon, Olivia F. Robinson, *The Institutes of Gaius, Translated with an Introduction, With the Latin Text of Seckel and Kuebler* (London: Duckworth, 1988). The two translations were very helpfully made to coordinate.

1

Obligations: The Conceptual Map

The subject called 'obligations' is mostly about contract and delict. There are some other heads to be considered, but the right impression is given if we say that contract and delict between them occupy about ninety per cent of the ground. Not that accurate measurement is really possible. It is not obvious on first hearing what 'obligations' and 'contract and delict' have to do with each other. How do they relate? Why is it possible to say so confidently, as though it were self-evident, that 'obligations' is mostly about these two events? That is one of those questions to which you can either see the answer at once or have to wait and kick yourself for not seeing. It is obvious, once you know.

Precisely because there are questions of that kind, there comes before the concrete topics a section on what might be called the jurisprudence of the subject or, even more trendily, aspects of its philosophy. There are three principal questions: 1. What is an obligation? 2. Where do obligations fit in the Roman view of the law? And 3. Inside the category, how are obligations organised? If you prefer headings to questions, you might say: 1. Definition. 2. Differentiation. 3. Internal Organisation. These, and the more detailed issues which they raise, together make up 'The Conceptual Map'.

Some people react against this kind of discussion. And they are right to the extent that there must not be too much of it. But as a general rule it is unsafe to get down to the nitty-gritty without stopping to think what you are doing. You are bound to have to use rather difficult words and ideas. If you plunge straight in you are likely to get in a muddle, probably without noticing until it is too late to see why; or to get out even if you can see. This matters. Because when lawyers are muddled ordinary people win and lose disputes for no good reason. More accurately, by mistake. In short because of intellectual pig-headedness injustice is done. And that is disgraceful. It is an entirely secondary consideration that well thought out law is elegant, economical, easy to learn. Do not despise jurisprudence. It is about knowing what you are doing. Sometimes, admittedly, it is difficult to find out.

1. Definition: What is an Obligation?

Justinian's *Institutes* bravely give a definition as soon as they begin to consider obligations. So J.3.13 *pr.* says this:

Nunc transeamus ad obligationes. Obligatio est iuris vinculum, quo necessitate adstringimur alicuius solvendae rei, secundum nostrae civitatis iura.
Now let us move on to obligations. An obligation is a bond of law, by which we are tied down to the necessity of making some performance, according to the laws of our state.

It is convenient to begin with the point which is made at the end: 'according to the laws of our state'. Whatever precisely an obligation is, lawyers are only interested when it is a phenomenon recognised by their legal system. If someone gives you a present, it makes sense to say that you are under an obligation to say thank you. Similarly, when you are far from home you are under an obligation to keep in contact with your family. You recognise it perhaps only in the breach, from mental energy spent in putting off the necessity which ties you down. But these are moral obligations. The law has nothing to say about their breach. In the conventional language of modern jurisprudence they belong to a different normative system, morality, not law. The word 'normative' and its noun, which is 'norm', come from the Latin '*norma*', which is a carpenter's T-square, just as a '*regula*' is his ruler. The metaphor is the same in both cases. The words which name the tools which guide the carpenter in giving shape to his material also serve to name the standards which guide people in moulding their behaviour. A norm is a rule or standard of that kind, used to mould behaviour. It tells you what you ought to do. And you have to see what kind of 'ought' is in question. There are different normative systems.

Morality is one. Etiquette may be another. Or perhaps it is only a department of morality. Law is yet another. It is the system of norms actually applied in the courts. That is in the nature of a working hypothesis. If you feel uneasy about it, well enough. What law is, what the relationship is between law and morality, are matters of incessant jurisprudential debate. But it is not disastrously misleading to say that law is the normative system applied in the courts. And, in the definition of obligation, what the words *secundum nostrae civitatis iura* signify is that for the purposes of legal study the only obligations which come into view are those recognised by law of the state.

That tells us nothing about the definition of obligation. It only says that, whatever it may be, we are not interested in any non-legal manifestation which the phenomenon may have.

The next words to be considered are . . . *iuris vinculum, quo . . . adstringimur*. First, *vinculum*. This comes from the family of words round the verb *vincire*, meaning 'to bind'. A *vinculum* is anything with which binding is done. Hence, a fetter, bond, chain or rope. In the translation which I gave I used 'bond' but I almost prefer 'rope' or 'chain'. Then *adstringimur*. This is another word of binding. *Adstringere* means 'to tie up tightly', 'to confine with bonds'. So the metaphor in the definition is a man tied down by a rope or chain. It is an image not confined to *vinculum* and *adstringimur*. For it is in *obligatio* too. You know words like 'ligament' and 'ligature'. They come straight from *ligare*. Less obviously, also the French *lier* and English 'liable'. *Ligare* means much the same as the other verbs, 'to tie' or 'to fasten'. The metaphor crops up in one other place as well, in the verb *solvere*. We will come to that in a minute.

So far we have this. An obligation is a rope . . . by which we are tied . . . Dwell on that image. Here am I with a rope around my neck. We must allow for the other end of the rope. You are holding that. I am under an obligation to you: the picture is of this rope between us, and you in control; the rope is round my neck but in your hand. But we have missed out the word *iuris*. The obligation is not said to be just a *vinculum* but a *vinculum iuris*. *Iuris* is the genitive of *ius*. It means 'of law'. So what does *iuris* add to *vinculum*? Two things. First it tells that all this rope business is only metaphor. There is no rope there. It is just the image of an idea. A rope of law. We might say 'a rope in law', meaning 'in the eyes of the law' or 'according to the law's way of explaining'. Second, it contains a forewarning of the point made in *secundum nostrae civitatis iura*. We have looked at that. It is not a bond of morality but a bond of law.

An obligation is a bond (rope, chain) of (in) law by which we are tied . . . according to the laws of our state.

The words missing are *necessitate alicuius solvendae rei*. The order jumps around because it is different in each language. In the first translation these words are 'the necessity of making some performance'. And they are joined into the sentence just given with the extra words 'down to'. The translation says that we are 'tied down to the necessity' and so on. This is not easy.

Start again with the phrase *alicuius solvendae rei. Solvere* is an astonishing word. The Oxford Latin Dictionary gives it twenty-two distinct senses. The beginning is 'to loosen', 'to untie', 'to release'. You can see how it completes the metaphor in *obligatio*, from the other end of the story. The rope is untied, released. *Obligationem solvere* is 'to discharge an obligation', the tie untied. But that sense is not immediately present in this sentence. It is no more than a deliberate overtone. For *solvere* also applies, not directly to the obligation itself, but to the performance which is the content of the obligation. That is, to the performance which will, when made, effect release from the *vinculum iuris*. The performance may be to pay money; to do or abstain from an act such as building a wall or not competing with X's business; or to render a thing (the cow Daisy) or a quantity of things (a thousand kilograms of butter). *Solvere* applies to all of these, paying money, performing work, finishing goods.

Alicuius solvendae rei is not the easiest construction. It is all in the genitive, because it depends on *necessitate*, and it means 'of some thing to be performed'. The word *res* (here *rei*) means 'thing' or 'matter'. So 'a thing to be performed' covers all the variety of performances just mentioned. It is only for the sake of greater elegance that the translation turns it round, into 'of making some performance'. And you need consciously to add in the overtone about release: 'of making some (rope-cutting) performance'.

Then there is *necessitate*. That is not difficult in itself. *Necessitas* is our 'necessity', and this is the ablative 'by (a, the) necessity'. The difficulty arises because the sentence makes us tied by two things at once. We are tied by the rope of law, and we are tied by the necessity of acting. This is a consequence of having in the one sentence the metaphorical force of the rope and the real compulsion of the law itself. The translation makes the transition from metaphor to reality by saying that we are tied down (by the rope) to the necessity of performing. Otherwise you have to go in for something much longer: 'An obligation is an imaginary rope of legal forces whose effect is to compel us to make some performance according to the laws of our state.'

Here are some examples. I promise, in the way which the law requires for a promise to be recognised and enforced in the courts, that on the first day of next month I will convey to you my farm, Blackacre. I am under an obligation to you to make that performance. Metaphorically, you can give the rope round my neck a good shake if I do not. In reality, pulling on the rope means going to court and putting the force of the law into operation. Again, suppose that you are standing waiting to cross the road and I carelessly drive my car over the raised pavement. And thus over your toe. I come under an obligation to repair your loss and suffering in money. Again there is the imaginary rope which is really a legal duty cast on me for breach of which the courts will give you redress. Or again, suppose you pay me money by mistake. You think I worked fifty hours for you at £2.00 per hour. In fact I only worked forty hours. £20 too much. I must repay the £20. The rope which the law sees is in your hands. If I pay I regain my freedom. I release myself.

Suppose we strip away all metaphor. What is left is a relationship between two people such that one is under a legal duty to make some performance and the other has a correlative right to claim that performance. The word 'obligation', at least in English, denotes that relationship as viewed from the standpoint of the duty.

There is more to be said about the nature of this two-ended relationship, but it is more easily done in the next section.

2. Differentiation: Where do Obligations Fit in the Roman View of the Law?

Let us start by assuming that 'the Roman view of the law' is the view of the Institutes of Gaius and Justinian. Both use the same means of dividing the whole mass and thus bringing it under control. The scheme is announced in the simple statement—'simple-looking' would be more fair, since it represents an immense intellectual achievement—at G.1.8 (repeated at J.1.2.12):

Omne autem ius quo utimur vel ad personas pertinet vel ad res vel ad actiones. Et prius videamus de personis.
All the law we use has to do either with persons or with things or with actions. And first let us consider persons.

I have left in 'And first let us consider persons' because it serves to reinforce the fact that this threefold division is indeed the basis on which Gaius intends to structure his exposition.

Obligations belong in the law of things. They hold their place there by virtue of the division between things corporeal and things incorporeal. This is Gaius at G.2.12–14. I give Zulueta's translation with some bits of Latin in brackets.

12. Further, things (*res*) are divided into corporeal and incorporeal. 13. Corporeal things are tangible things (*quae tangi possunt*), such as land, a slave, a garment, gold, silver, and countless other things. 14. Incorporeal are things that are intangible, such as exist merely in law (*quae tangi non possunt, qualia sunt ea quae iure consistunt*), for example an inheritance, a usufruct, obligations however contracted. It matters not that corporeal things are comprised in an inheritance, or that fruits gathered from land (subject to a usufruct) are corporeal, or that what is due under an obligation is commonly corporeal (*et quod ex obligatione nobis debetur plerumque corporale est*), for instance land, a slave, money; for the rights themselves, of inheritance, usufruct, and obligation, are incorporeal (*nam ipsum ius successionis et ipsum ius utendi fruendi et ipsum ius obligationis incorporale est*). Incorporeal also are rights attached to urban and rural lands (*iura praediorum urbanorum et rusticorum*). Examples of the former are the right to raise one's building and so obstruct a neighbour's lights, or that of preventing a building from being raised lest neighbouring lights be obstructed, also the right that a neighbour shall suffer rain water to pass into his courtyard or into his house in a channel or by dripping; also the right to introduce a sewer into a neighbour's property or to open lights over it. Examples of rights attached to rural land (*praediorum rusticorum iura*) are the various rights of way for vehicles, men, and beasts; also that of watering cattle and that of watercourse. Such rights, whether of urban or rural lands, are called servitudes (*Haec iura tam rusticorum quam urbanorum praediorum servitutes vocantur*).[1]

[1] Francis de Zulueta, *The Institutes of Gaius* (Oxford: Clarendon Press, 1946), vol, 1, 67, 69.

I have let this passage run on a bit because the job of fitting obligations in their place is not finished when one has said that they are in the law of things as '*res incorporales*'. It is also necessary to differentiate obligations from these other incorporeal things.

Nevertheless we have got some way already. All the law is about persons or things or actions. Things divide between corporeal and incorporeal. Incorporeal things divide between those which are not and those which are obligations. That is quite an elegant bit of map-making. Is there any obvious problem with it? There is one. An obligation is *prima facie* a burden. As we saw, it looks, at least in English, from the duty end of the relationship, not from the right or benefit end. How can it line up with land, slaves, garments, gold, inheritances, usufructs and all these other good things? They are all items of wealth. They suggest that a good translation of *res* would be 'asset'. But, according to the sense we want to give it, an obligation is not an asset. It belongs in the other column, a minus rather than a plus, a negative asset (if that is not nonsense).

There are two ways out of this difficulty. You either stick with the translation of *res* as 'asset' and adjust your view of the Roman understanding of *obligatio* or, *vice versa*, you revise 'asset'. This is not a small thing since it affects the whole way in which one sees the *ius rerum*, the second division of the tripartite institutional scheme. What adjustment is possible for the meaning of *obligatio*? To make the word sit happily in a list of 'assets', you have to change the angle of vision from the burden end to the benefit end of the rope. Or, at the very least, you have to make the word neutral as between the two points of view. Suppose you have received a mistaken payment from me. You are under an obligation to pay it back. To make the obligation an asset it must be possible for the words 'my obligation' to be used by me as well as by you. By me to denote my right against you that you should pay. For only if that usage is possible (*obligatio* = right, claim) is an obligation an item of wealth. What adjustment is possible to *res*? If it is not 'asset' or 'item of wealth', it must be just 'thing'. 'Thing' is very vague but it can be firmed up a little in two ways. First, by opposition. Many legal terms only become clear when you look for their opposites; or, more accurately, for what they are meant to exclude. So here 'thing' acquires boundaries by opposition to persons on the one hand and actions on the other. Secondly, by a core case. Again, many legal terms depend for their intelligibility on their having, so to say in their centre, an example or some examples about which nobody would disagree that they are properly described by the word in question. So here *res* can take meaning from the core at its centre, undoubtedly the corporeal item of wealth (land, garment, gold ingot), without being required to be free of uncertainties and instabilities in its periphery. More accurately, without being required to have no periphery of less certain cases. If *res* is no more than 'thing' in that way it can reach *obligatio* even without the need to turn the word round from duty to right. Because, given the acceptance of incorporeal things in the first place, this imaginary rope can be a 'thing' even as a negative asset, a burden or, non-metaphorically, a duty owed to someone else.

As between these two ways out of the difficulty I myself incline to the second. The other is the one generally adopted. The issue is genuinely uncertain. I have not myself seen any convincing example in which *mea obligatio* or *obligatio* with a genitive indicates right rather than duty.

Subject to this doubt, it remains true that obligations belong in the law of *res* as one species of *res incorporalis*. The next question is: how do obligations differ from the other incorporeal things? At this point it is very easy to slip into a not quite Roman form of explanation. And if we are going to do that, at least we ought not to do it without knowing what is happening.

The other *res incorporales* as Gaius gives them are inheritance (*hereditas*), usufruct and praedial servitudes (*iura praediorum*). He does not call usufruct a servitude but it came to be described as a personal servitude, and there were others in the same category, all in the nature of reduced or cut down usufructs. Just as praedial servitudes are, in Latin, rights *of* landholdings, so personal servitudes are rights *of* persons, *iura personarum*. The reason for setting out this terminology is that it provides the basis for asserting, as we shortly shall, that there is all the difference in the world between *iura personarum* and *iura in personam* (rights *of* persons and rights *against* persons). A right *of* a person may be *in rem* (*against* a thing). For the moment this will seem merely muddling. It had better not do later. For the difference between *in rem* and *in personam* is of fundamental importance. They are analytical tools which no lawyer can do without.

Take just one of these other incorporeal things. How is usufruct different from obligation? What is true for usufruct will be true for the others too. I think the Roman answer would have been that the difference would show up when it came to pleading. If you had to go to court, the words of your claim would be quite different if you were claiming a usufruct from what they would be if you were trying to claim the performance of an obligation. For the usufruct (just as for a corporeal thing, the cow Daisy) the words of your claim (your *actio*) would be focused on and directed against the *res* itself and would not mention any person at all or at least not till much lower down in the pattern of words. You would not be litigating at all if there were no opponent; but, in the form of words which claims a usufruct (or Daisy) the defendant's name does not figure in what is called the *intentio*, the plaintiff's primary contention; only later, in the *condemnatio*, the clause which says who is to be condemned or absolved. In simplified form, what the plaintiff says is 'This *res* is mine' and in the programme for adjudication (the *formula* which carries the issue to the judge) it comes out as 'If the *res* is the plaintiff's, condemn the defendant; if not, absolve him.'

By contrast, when the *res* is not Daisy or a usufruct but an obligation, the action always takes a form of words directed against a person. And the *res* which is the obligation itself is not mentioned at all. Its existence is a matter of inference from the words which are used. What the plaintiff says, again in the simplified equivalent of the example in the last paragraph, is 'You ought to convey Blackacre to me.' And this comes out in the *formula* as 'If it appears that the defendant ought to convey Blackacre to the plaintiff, for as much as Blackacre shall be worth condemn the defendant to the plaintiff; etc.' The primary contention of the plaintiff is that the defendant ought to do something. The words are directed against that person. There is no such pleading as can be boiled down to this, 'I say the obligation that you should . . . is mine.' Or to this *formula*: 'If it appears that the obligation that the defendant should convey Blackacre to the plaintiff belongs to the plaintiff. . .' The incorporeal *res* 'obligation' is never itself mentioned in any claim. It is an abstract conception inferred from the verbs used in the *actio*. If I claim that I have a usufruct in such and such a piece of land, it is easy to say that the *res* I am talking about is this abstract right of taking the enjoyment and yield of the land. But if I claim that you ought to convey a piece of land to me it is not so obvious what the *res* is about which I am talking. It is not the land, because the land is one step away. It is an 'ought to convey the land'. But what is the thing which exists—or, in other words, what is the substantive abstract conception—when it is the case that one ought to convey to another? '*Obligatio*' is the answer. There is no doubt that the words of these actions, of the 'defendant ought . . .' kind, existed long before anyone came up with the idea that such actions supposed the existence of an abstract *res* capable of being coordinated in the mind with rights to use and take fruits, rights of light, rights of way, and so on.

The 'defendant ought' actions (all based by inference on obligations) are directed against a person rather than a thing. They do not name the abstract thing which they seek to realise, the *obligatio* itself. Those two sentences are correct. But it is incorrect to go further and say that such actions do not name any *res* at all. They say what the defendant ought to do. And since the content of his obligation will often be the giving of, or some other doing to, a thing (whether corporeal or incorporeal), saying what he ought to do will often mean naming a thing. 'You ought to convey Blackacre to me.' Blackacre is named. But the words of my claim hit you first and then bounce back on Blackacre. Contrast 'Blackacre is mine'. Here the words dive straight down into Blackacre.

The question was, How would the Romans have seen the difference between usufruct and obligation? The answer has been that they would have said it was a matter of different patterns of action. Usufruct was claimed by an action *in rem* (a pleading immediately directed against the *res*); an obligation was enforced by an action *in personam* (a pleading immediately directed against a person).

At this point I want to underpin what has just been said by looking at the opening passage of Gaius's treatment of the third of his main divisions, namely actions. This is G.4.1–5. Again the translation is Zulueta's.

1. It remains to speak of actions. Now, to the question how many *genera* of actions there are the more correct answer appears to be that there are two, *in rem* and *in personam*. For those who have maintained that there are four, counting the *genera* of *sponsiones* (i.e. of actions *per sponsionem*?), have inadvertently classed as *genera* certain *species* of actions. 2. An action *in personam* is one in which we proceed against someone who is under contractual or delictual obligation to us, an action, that is, in which we claim 'that he ought to convey, do, or answer for' something (*cum intendimus* DARE FACERE PRAESTARE OPORTERE). 3. An action *in rem* is one in which we claim either that some corporeal thing is ours, or that we are entitled to some right, such as that of use or usufruct, of foot- or carriage-way, of aqueduct, of raising a building or of view. On the other hand an action (*in rem*) denying such rights is open to our opponent. 4. Having thus distinguished actions (*sic itaque discretis actionibus*) we see that we cannot sue another for a thing belonging to us using the form of claim 'if it appears that the defendant ought to convey (*dare*)'. For what is ours cannot be conveyed (*dari*) to us, since obviously *dari* means the giving of a thing to us with the effect of making it ours [obviously? *scilicet*]; but a

thing which is already ours cannot be made more so. It is true that out of hatred of thieves, in order to multiply the actions to which they are liable, it has become accepted that, in addition to the penalty of double or quadruple, they are also liable in an action for the recovery of the thing in the form: 'if it appears they ought to convey' [SI PARET EOS DARE OPORTERE], notwithstanding that the action claiming ownership of the thing lies against them as well. 5. Actions *in rem* are called *vindicationes*; actions *in personam*, claiming that there is a duty to convey or do [DARE FIERIVE OPORTERE] are called *condictiones*.[2]

You can see from this passage, first that claims are divided between those which are framed against a thing (*in rem*) and those which are framed against a person (however they may also be about a thing) and, secondly, that the two types are kept contentually separate by the technical interpretation of *dare*. It is not nonsense to say, if you have my cow, that you 'ought to give it to me'. But that common sense would allow the claim to express two fundamentally different ideas, 'owning' and 'being owed'. The understanding of *dare* as 'convey' stops that happening. The case of thieves is the exception which proves the rule.

At this point we should regroup. The proposition was that obligations hold their place in the institutional scheme by virtue of being 'things' and, in particular, 'incorporeal things'. The immediately foregoing discussion has been about the difference between obligations and other incorporeal things, inheritance, usufruct and praedial servitudes. It has been exploring the question, How would Gaius himself have expressed that difference? One reason why that question is difficult is because we now express the difference in a way which itself (despite Latin labels) is not quite Roman. The next few paragraphs are intended to give the modern way of putting it.

We say that the difference turns on the nature of the right held by the plaintiff, and we do not talk in terms of forms of words used in making claims. The distinction is between rights *in rem* and rights *in personam*. And the distinction between obligations and the other incorporeal things is then that (looking from the benefit end of the rope) obligations connote rights *in personam* and the others are rights *in rem*.

i. The difference between rights in rem *and* in personam

A right *in rem* is one which depends for its exigibility on the location of a thing. A right *in personam* is one which depends for its exigibility on

[2] Zulueta (n. 1), 233. The author uses the English forms 'vindications' and 'condictions'.

the location of a person. 'Exigibility' means 'ability to be demanded'. And when it comes to exacting rights of either kind there is always a person at the receiving end of the demand.

Consider rights *in rem* first. Ownership is the instantly recognisable example. Suppose that I own the cow Daisy. She somehow comes into the possession of another person. 'Somehow' means 'by some series of events other than a transfer of my title'. Let us say that she just wanders off to your field or was driven there in the dead of night. So long as I do not know where she is I cannot effectively demand my right in her. It is true that I can go from place to place and person to person saying 'Daisy is mine.' But I cannot achieve very much by doing so. I cannot realise my right unless I find out where Daisy is. On the other hand when I do find out where she is her location determines the identity of the person from whom I can exact my right. Her possessor, even though I have never encountered him before and had no dealings with him, is the person against whom I can effectively assert 'This cow is mine.' It is sometimes said that a right *in rem* is one which can be enforced against the whole world. This is what that means, the location of the *res* determines the person from whom the right can be exacted. Until I know who has her I can do nothing; when I know who has her I know who must be confronted. Notice what happens when the cow ceases to exist. My ownership becomes a thing of the past: 'I did own Daisy.' It is nonsense to say 'I own' of something which has ceased to exist. The same of something which has not yet come into existence. This is all part of the statement that exigibility depends upon the location of the thing. You cannot locate a thing which does not exist.

Two points need special mention. First, the definition turns on exigibility, not on alienability. Usufruct is a right *in rem*. If I have a usufruct in the cow Daisy I can demand that right against anyone in possession of Daisy. Her location determines the identity of the defendant. But usufruct in Roman law was an inalienable right. If my father's will made me usufructuary of a farm or a herd or just of Daisy, I could not transfer that right to anyone. I could hire out the enjoyment of the things but I could not assign the *ius utendi fruendi* as such. That is why usufruct is numbered among *iura personarum*, rights of persons. It is a *ius personae* but *in rem*, annexed to a person (unlike praedial servitudes) but (like praedial servitudes) *in rem*, exigible against anyone in possession of the *res*. That is not a difficult statement. It merely shows that the analysis *in rem/in personam* has nothing to do with the question, Can the right be alienated? Many systems, though as it happens not the Roman, have no difficulty with the notion of alienating rights *in personam*.

The second special point is this. Nothing that has been said implies that a right *in rem* must necessarily remain exigible so long as the *res* can be found. Some event may have intervened to extinguish the right. For example by the time I find Daisy in your hands you may (if all the facts are right) have acquired title by *usucapio*, extinguishing all that went before. You bought her from X and kept her for a year. X did not steal her. She was never stolen. It was a story of muddles and mistakes, not of dishonesty. Now I find her, but my right has gone. The moral of this is that one needs to say that a right *in rem* is one whose exigibility, so long as the right continues to exist, depends on the location of the *res* to which it relates.

By contrast rights *in personam*, though they may relate to a *res*, depend for their exigibility on the location of a person. Suppose that you have promised to convey Daisy to me but have not yet done so. Daisy wanders off to a third party. It is against you that I must demand my right. And if Daisy dies it does not follow that my right against you must be extinguished. That is to say, it does not follow from the nature of the right. For even when Daisy is lost or has ceased to exist it is not nonsense to affirm that you are under a legal duty to convey her to me. A right *in rem* cannot exist after the *res* has been extinguished, but a right *in personam* can. On the other hand just as a right *in rem* may be cancelled while the *res* still exists so a right *in personarum*, though capable of surviving its *res*, may be discharged if the *res* ceases to exist. It will depend on the law relating to the particular circumstances. In the case of rights *in personam* problems arise when the person against whom the right first arises meets his death. That is the equivalent to the destruction of the *res* subject to a right *in rem*, and the extinction of the right *in personam* can only be avoided by contemplating a successor as stepping into his shoes, a substitute for the original person subject to the right.

This distinction between rights *in rem* and *in personam* can be conveniently represented by the metaphor of a legal rope or chain. Where the right is *in rem* the rope in your hand (the benefit end) is attached at the other end to a thing. When the right is *in personam* the rope in your hand is attached at the other end to a person. Whichever you have, what you actually want is likely to be a *res*. With the right *in personam* you come to the *res* indirectly. You give the rope a good tug to get him to give it to you. The rope represents this: he is under a duty to do something, to make some performance. Giving a *res* is one example. Doing work of some kind is another, as for instance building a house. Warranting, or ensuring that a state of affairs comes about or stays the case, is a third. In Latin *dare*, *facere* and *praestare* are the key verbs for the content of personal duties correlative to what we call rights *in personam*.

These ropes *in rem* and *in personam* are invisible. They are ways of representing the operation of the law, images of real forces. This leads to one final observation. Rights *in rem* have to be kept under close control because when people buy *res* they must be able to know what invisible ropes to look for. I am buying a herd of cows and you are selling. I know that I risk disappointment and trouble. I may get home and find that the cows belonged all along to X or that X had (and therefore still has) a usufruct in them. So long as there are not too many of these dangers my life as a buyer will be tolerable. But it would quickly become intolerable if effects *in rem* were a matter for the free operation of parties' intentions. Suppose that the owner before you wanted to be sure that the herd was never used for beef or never crossed with other breeds. If he could give himself rights *in rem* of that kind just as he pleased, I as buyer would have an impossible task. On the other hand if that kind of aspiration is kept off the *res*, the danger to commerce is avoided without completely outlawing the pursuit of such ends. He can make you promise not to sell without taking a promise from your buyer not to slaughter, not to cross-breed and so on. He thus gets a right *in personam* against you that you should take such a promise on re-sale. If you do not, he can tug the rope attached to you; but the *res* remains free. So commerce is not impeded.

The need to keep rights *in rem* under control is particularly strong in relation to movable property. The purchase of land is so important a transaction that the buyer can accept the need and burden of making inquiries. But even in relation to land the kinds of adverse rights *in rem* which he must look for are not left completely to the whim of earlier owners. For example the general characteristics of praedial servitudes constitute limits on the variety and scope of such rights. 'A servitude cannot consist in having to do something' means that I cannot be surprised by the discovery that my newly bought farm owes forty days' ploughing to a powerful neighbour. That restriction forms a bulwark against dependent tenure on the feudal model.

This section has been about the difference between rights *in rem* and rights *in personam*. Obligations connote rights *in personam*. Indeed if we give 'obligation' its English sense, in which it takes the point of view of the person subject to a duty, obligations not only connote but correlate with rights *in personam*. That is, right *in personam* is the rope viewed from one end, obligation (or duty) the rope viewed from the other. One way of saying how obligations differ from the other incorporeal things is therefore to say that while obligations correlate with rights *in personam*, the other incorporeal things are all rights *in rem*. But this, as was said at the beginning, is not quite the Roman way of seeing it. It is truer to Gaius's perception to say that usufruct and so on were 'things' (like slaves, garments and so on) for the reason that, though incorporeal, they were protected by actions *in rem* (pleadings directed at *res* rather than at persons) while obligations by contrast were the things, not mentioned as such in any actions at all, about which actions *in personam* were brought. The coordination of obligations with other incorporeal things was a brilliant intellectual feat. We have no reason to believe that it was not Gaius himself who achieved it.

ii. Differences between Gaius and Justinian

The threefold pattern remains the same in both: persons, things and actions. And obligations remain in things as before. But the reformed and simplified law of actions, no longer based on set patterns of claim, takes up less space in the Justinianic version. This has an effect which is less important than it might at first seem.

Gaius divided the law of things into two books, not for conceptual reasons but more to suit the book technology of his time. The threefold division thus stretched over four books. Obligations belonged in the latter part of book III. Actions had book IV to themselves. In Justinian, obligations spill over into book IV and take 5 of the 18 titles in that book. This is only a mechanical difference. On the other hand within the law of actions a change of conceptual importance has happened, though one which cannot be pursued here. In Gaius an *actio* was a claim. Literally a form of words expressing a demand. The patterns of words having been displaced in favour of an omni-purpose method of claiming, what has an *actio* become? An action has become a right, a right of going to law to get one's due. J.4.6 *pr.* says: '*Superest, ut de actionibus loquamur. Actio autem nihil aliud est quam ius persequendi iudicio quod sibi debetur.* (It remains to speak of actions. An action is nothing other than a right of pursuing by a trial something which is due to oneself.)' We use the same not very satisfactory transferred sense. 'Smith has an action on these facts' now means that Smith has a right which a court will uphold. It does not mean that there is a list of propositions proposable by plaintiffs, one of which will fit Smith's case.

iii. Outside the institutional scheme

You should not imagine that the threefold division of all law used by Gaius and Justinian in their Institutes recurs in all Roman legal literature. The pattern of the Institutes no doubt retained a grip on the minds of all those who came to their knowledge of law by that route. But practitioners' stuff was less elegantly ordered. In particular the Edict as stabilised by Salvius Julianus under Hadrian retains the disorder to be expected of a document built up pragmatically over centuries. The matter of obligations is scattered through it. The Digest of Justinian follows an order discernibly derived from the Edict. So it too lacks a coherent pattern and does not keep obligations in one place.

3. Internal Organisation: How Are Obligations Arranged?

We have been talking about the category of obligations as a single lump and looking at its place in the whole law. At this point we pass inside the category itself and look to see how it was divided into manageable parts.

It is useful to say at the start that there are several different ways in which obligations can be classified. The Roman experience, and also the Scottish and the English, show signs of a competition between two in particular. One is classification by reference to the content of the obligation. According to this, obligations to give a certain thing or certain quantity of things can form a distinct class—*certum dare* obligations. Another class in the same series might be all obligations 'to do' as opposed to 'to give' (*facere* rather than *dare*). But of course the fact that one decides to classify obligations by content does not immediately determine what the divisions shall be, for content itself can be divided in different ways and at different levels of generality. The other system of classification is by causative events. That is, by the events which bring the obligation into being. Again there are choices to be made within such a system: How shall the events be classified?

i. The classification of obligations used by Gaius

He starts with a simple dichotomy, which soon gets into trouble. G.3.88:

Nunc transeamus ad obligationes. Quarum summa divisio in duas species diducitur: omnis enim obligatio vel ex contractu nascitur vel ex delicto.
Let us now move on to obligations. The principal division of these puts them into two species: for every obligation arises either from a contract or from a delict.

This is obviously a classification by causative events: *omnis obligatio . . . nascitur*. The question, literally, is, How are obligations born? And they are divided according as they come into existence by virtue of a contract or a delict.

This neat proposition encounters the proof that it is not exhaustive, and that it is therefore wrong, within three paragraphs. At G.3.91 Gaius encounters the obligation, undoubtedly recognised by the law of his time, to repay money received from one who mistakenly believed that he owed it. The event in question is receipt of a payment not due, *non debitum* (or *indebitum*) *accipere*. Of the obligation arising from that event Gaius rightly observes:

Sed haec species obligationis non videtur ex contractu consistere, quia is qui solvendi animo dat magis distrahere vult negotium quam contrahere.
But this type of obligation appears not to exist by virtue of contract. For one who pays with the intent to release himself wishes to discharge a deal rather than to sew one up.

He does not say that the obligation also does not arise from wrongdoing (delict) but that is quite obvious. So it follows that the event *indebitum accipere* is a non-contractual and non-delictual event which falsifies the simple dichotomy between contract and delict. And as we shall see there are others which also do not fit the two-term classification.

Gaius later adjusted to this difficulty. Before seeing how, it is useful to ask one more question about G.3.91. Why was Gaius brought into contact so quickly with the awkward case of mistaken payment? Often people look away from the deficiencies of their expositions. Gaius was not like that. But it was not merely intellectual honesty which led him to confront this difficulty. He was drawn into it. The reason was this. His classification in terms of causative events was, at one point at least, in conflict with the classification instinctively or inarticulately adopted in the list of actions. Actions *in personam* on sale, hire, theft, contempt, for example, all constituted packets of law focused on events, completely in harmony with the classification which Gaius wanted to use. But one very important action *in personam* was not. The Roman action of debt, the *condictio*, was based on a different unity. A unity of content, irrespective of event. The *condictio* lay wherever the plaintiff could say that the defendant ought at civil law to give him something (*certum dare*). Before the praetor he would make reference to no event at all. Before the *iudex* he would have to adduce some event which did at civil law serve to substantiate the abstract proposition made before the praetor. Amongst others, events which were held to do so included loan for consumption (*mutuum*) and mistaken payment (*indebitum accipere*). Confining attention just to these two we can see that within the longstanding category formed by the *condictio*, contractual and non-contractual events lived side by side without apparent contradiction. Because the unity was differently based. Only if someone insisted, as Gaius did, on a thorough-going classification by events would the *condictio* begin to look uncomfortably miscellaneous. As soon as Gaius turned from his division between contract and delict to a consideration of contract, the first contract he mentioned was *mutuum* (loan for consumption). That is at G.3.90. According to the traditional, actional classification the natural congener of loan was mistaken payment. Hence mention of *mutuum* drew him into contact with *indebitum accipere*. Having, so to say, stepped into the *condictio* he could not avoid seeing the non-contractual (and non-delictual) section of the spectrum of events for which that action lay. In the Institutes Gaius noted the difficulty and moved on without adjusting the two-term classification between contract and delict. But in a later book he cured the defect.

Digest 44.7, 'Concerning obligations and actions', begins with an excerpt from a book called *Res Cottidianae* ('Everyday Things'). 'Day to Day Law' might better capture the sense of its name. It is also called *Aurea* ('Golden Law', or 'Nuggets').

D.44.7.1 *pr., Gaius libro secundo aureorum. Obligationes aut ex contractu nascuntur aut ex maleficio aut proprio quodam iure ex variis causarum figuris.*

D.44.7.1 *pr.* (Gaius, 2 *Nuggets*). Obligations are born either of contract or of wrongdoing or, by virtue of some particular law, from a variety of types of causes.

That last bit, not so easy to translate, is really just adding 'other miscellaneous events' as an exhaustive third category after contract and wrongs. And that is not only wonderfully honest but also wonderfully useful. It takes the pressure off the two nominate terms and allows them to be defended even though they do not cover between them all the causative events from which obligations arise. The ground gained by the dichotomy in the Institutes is thus not lost. But nor is it retained at the cost of sacrificing truth, running away from known error. That never does any good. Notice that the word for wrong has changed too, no longer *delictum* (from *delinquere*) but *maleficium* (from *malum* + *facere*, bad doing).

We are not going to chase on through D.44.7. If we did have time we would find that Gaius seems to do to the residual miscellany something which is done to it in Justinian's Institutes. It may have been done by Gaius or it may have been attributed to him by interpolation. We will go straight on to Justinian's statement.

J.3.13 is Justinian's introduction to obligations. We have seen it begin with the *vinculum iuris* definition. Then it says, at J.3.13.1–2:

1. Omnium autem obligationum summa divisio in duo genera deducitur: namque aut civiles sunt aut praetoriae. Civiles sunt, quae aut legibus constitutae aut certe iure civili comprobatae sunt. Praetoriae sunt, quas praetor ex sua iurisdictione constituit, quae etiam honorariae vocantur. 2. Sequens divisio in quattuor species deducitur: aut enim ex contractu sunt aut quasi ex contractu aut ex maleficio aut quasi ex maleficio. Prius est, ut de his quae ex contractu sunt dispiciamus . . .

1. The main division between all obligations puts them into two *genera*: for they are either civil or praetorian. The 'civil' ones are those set up by statutes or indeed recognised by the *ius civile*. The 'praetorian' ones, also called 'honorarian', are those set up by the praetor in the exercise of his jurisdiction. 2. The next division makes four species: for they are either from contract or as though from contract or from wrongdoing or as though from wrongdoing. And we must look first at those which arise from contract . . .

This passage does two things. First, it asserts that there is such a thing as a praetorian obligation. Gaius had simply assumed that *obligatio* was a *ius civile* phenomenon with which praetorian forms of action had nothing to do. Without wanting to push the analogy too far, this is rather like, in England, aligning the linguistic usage of common law and equity, driven apart by centuries of separate development. Then it turns the threefold classification with which we left Gaius into a division by four.

It resolves the miscellany into two *quasi* categories. As we shall see the obligation to repay an *indebitum* becomes a central example in the category *quasi ex contractu*. But I am not going to discuss the rest of the content of these *quasi* categories here. They will have a section of their own right at the end. We can do contract and delict safely so long as we remember that they do not exhaust the whole category of obligations. We do not need to think about ordering the miscellany, if miscellaneous the residue really is.

ii. The classification of obligations in Stair

I want to finish by looking at Stair's partial departure from the Roman scheme. Stair based himself on the pattern of Justinian's Institutes, but not in the sense of borrowing it lock, stock and barrel. He accepted it with a characteristically critical and rational independence. In the result the pattern of the Institutes is often departed from, for good reasons given. This is the subject of Professor A. Campbell's David Murray Lecture for 1954, 'The Structure of Stair's Institutions'.[3] This is not the place to look at all the differences. Only at obligations. The nature of the relationship with the Roman material is immediately apparent. Stair, *Institutions of the Law of Scotland* (1681), 1.3.1–2:

1. The same right, as it is in the creditor, it is called a personal right, but as it is in the debtor, it is called an obligation, debt or duty, which is retained as the more proper name, *Inst. de obligationibus in prin.* [Author's note: This is Stair's mode of citing J.3.13 *pr.* and is, I think, forward looking to the following sentence, notwithstanding the punctuation.] Obligation is a legal tie by which we may be necessitate or constrained to pay, or perform something. This tie lieth upon the debtor; and the power of making use of it in the creditor is the personal right itself, which is the power given by the law, to exact from persons that which they are due.
2. Obligations by the Romans are distinguished in four kinds: in obligations *ex contractu, vel quasi ex contractu, ex maleficio, vel quasi ex maleficio.* Which distinction insinuates no reason of the cause or rise of these distinct obligations as is requisite in a good distinct division; and therefore they may be more appositely divided, according to the principle or original from whence

[3] Archibald Hunter Campbell, *The Structure of Stair's* Institutions. *Being the Twenty-first Lecture on the David Murray Foundation in the University of Glasgow, delivered on the 24th of February, 1954* (Glasgow: Jackson, 1954).

they flow, as in obligations obediential, and by engagement, or natural and conventional.

Pausing there we can see that Stair's main classification, his *summa divisio*, is between obediential and conventional. 'Natural' is offered as a synonym for 'obediential' as is 'conventional' for 'by engagement'. The contrast is between obligations imposed willy-nilly and obligations incurred because willingly accepted.

Whether Stair's criticism of the four Roman categories is thought fair depends to some extent on whether it is understood as focusing on the *quasi* categories or on all. It is certainly true that the two *quasi* categories have no explanatory force in the names which they bear. The same is not true of contract and wrongdoing.

The *summa divisio* does not indicate the extent of Stair's departure from the Roman scheme. It is slipped in at a high level. Below it comes a line of sub-categories represented by Titles 4–9 and Titles 11–17 of Book I. Titles 4–9 are the species of obediential obligations: '4. Conjugal Obligations; 5. Obligations between Parents and Children; 6. Obligations between Tutors and Curators, and their Pupils and Minors, between Persons Interdicted and their Interdictors; 7. Restitution; 8. Recompense or Remuneration; 9. Reparation, where of Delinquence, and Damages thence arising'. Then follows Title 10, which is a general introduction to conventional obligations, called 'Obligations Conventional, by Promise, Paction and Contract'. Titles 11–17 then run through the species of conventional obligations: '11. Loan, or *Mutuum* and *Commodatum*, where of Bills of Exchange; 12. Mandate or Commission, where of Trust, etc.; 13. Custody or *Depositum*, where also of Pledge and Hypothecation; 14. Permutation and Sale, or Emption and Vendition; 15. Location and Conduction, where of Annualrent and Usury; 16. Society, where of Co-partnery; 17. Accessory Obligations, where of Transaction, Caution, Oaths and other Accessories.'

All this looks very different from the Roman classification, but what is really different is exaggerated by the inversion of the Roman order. If one goes backwards the Roman picture comes back into focus. Thus Title 10, from which hang Titles 11–17, is, with its dependencies, the category of obligations *ex contractu*. Title 9, the last species within obediential obligations, is, in its second name, 'of Delinquence'. And its content shows that it is indeed the category *ex delicto*. So Stair's scheme brings together, albeit in inverse order, the two main Roman categories, contract and delict. Then, proceeding further from back to front, Titles 8 to 4 contain much of the matter which the Roman scheme put into the miscellaneous residue, later broken into quasi-contract and quasi-delict. So it is not unfair to say that beneath a different *summa divisio* Stair uses a scheme which goes (i) miscellaneous, (ii) delict, (iii) contract, exactly the Gaian order in reverse. And one way of summing up his intention is to say that he was aiming at a better, more rational treatment of the miscellaneous group. Better, that is, than Justinian managed with his two quasi categories.

This short comment on Stair's scheme requires two modifications to save it from having misrepresented the picture. First, his five heads of the miscellany are not identical in content to the Roman matter. The chief difference is that he brings in obligations based on marriage and parenthood, matters which the Roman scheme dealt with in the law of persons. Stair dispenses with 'persons' as a separate division of the law. Secondly, Stair's category of delict is so named only secondarily. Its full name is 'Reparation, where of Delinquence, and Damages thence arising'. It is reparation first and then delict (delinquence). And reparation forms the last of a run of three—restitution, recompense (or remuneration), reparation—in which the unity is made to depend on the content of the obligations: obligations to make restitution, to make recompense, to make reparation. But in this run reparation at least turns out to be a category with two unities. It is not all obligations to make reparation however arising, but obligations arising from delict which concurrently are obligations to make reparation.

We saw that Stair adapted the Roman scheme to try to improve it and we began with criticisms made by him. At this point we may venture two criticisms of his attempted improvement. First, he allows himself to do something which a perfect classification should always avoid: he varies the basis of his categories, some contentual (restitution, recompense), some contextual (between parents and children, between tutors and pupils), some causal (contract). There are dangers in this. Just as there would be dangers for a naturalist who started by classifying animals as mammals, reptiles, birds and carnivores. That is an obvious case. It serves to show what disasters are likely to happen when a classification turns a corner. All the worse when it is not obvious. The other criticism is of categories with double unities, like delict/reparation. They can lock you into a view which may be wrong. The category seems to affirm that necessarily at all times and places delicts give rise to reparatory obligations. That particular affirmation is certainly incorrect at least in the sense that it is not universal. It may have been true for Stair's own time. But the fact that Roman delicts give rise to obligations variously measured shows that it is unsafe (at all times and places) to assume a bond between one kind of event and one measure of liability.

We can end with a criticism of the Roman scheme which Stair did notice and which was picked up more seriously by Austin, the first professor of jurisprudence at London University. He held the chair from 1826 to 1835. In his *Lectures*, he observed that the dichotomy between contract and delict was defective.[4] Quite apart from the fact that it fails to exhaust the category of obligations as a whole, it is unsatisfactory because it fails to cope with breach of contract, an obligation-creating event quite distinct from contract (i.e. the making of a contract). Stair had encountered this problem in *Institutions* 1.9.3. Austin's professed scheme was to make a distinction between 'primary' and 'secondary' (or 'remedial') obligations. In this scheme breach of contract and delict stand together on the secondary tier because they trigger obligations to remedy wrongs, the wrongs being breaches of anterior primary obligations. Contract and, for example, receipt of a mistaken payment belong up on the primary level, since they are events which trigger obligations without themselves being breaches of anterior obligations. If you promise to pay me money or receive a mistaken payment from me your obligation cannot be seen as a remedy or sanction for any other pre-existing obligation, though in its turn it may need such a remedy or sanction itself. That is why it is called primary as opposed to secondary. This Austinian distinction has lasting value. I think Gaius would have said that on the Roman material itself the primary/secondary distinction was not strictly necessary. But I think he would have agreed that a classification should, ideally, have validity independent of the accidents of time and place. And on that basis he would perhaps have incorporated a *summa divisio* between primary and secondary before coming to contract (primary) and delict (secondary).

[4] John Austin, *Lectures on Jurisprudence* (5th ed. by Robert Campbell, London: J. Murray, 1911), vol. 2, 769ff.

PART I

Contracts

2

The Organisation of Roman Contract

There are different ways or organising a law of contract. That is as much as to say that there are different ways of responding to the central tasks which contract has to perform. So the right starting point is not the mode of organisation adopted by one system but those central tasks which have to be addressed by all. What are they?

To start with, leave the law out of it. In ordinary life we are continually trying to get other people to rely on us. We do it in different ways. At the seaside children call to their parents, 'Come on in. It isn't cold. Really it isn't. I promise.' The invitations to rely are stacked up. A straight statement ('It isn't cold'). Then an emphatic statement, excluding playfulness or deceit ('Really it isn't'). And finally super-emphasis by the use of a conventional word for 'You can rely on me absolutely' ('I promise'). The parent enters. The water is freezing. The child gets ducked. It was bound to end in that. These are pretended invitations to rely, the ritual prelude to a ducking which itself is only simulated anger. But the game would be no good if the structure were not real. The ducking is an expression of love and admiration. How is it made to happen? Because invitations to rely always contain the implication 'You can get me, and if you are any good you will get me, if I let you down.' And 'get me' covers a range of sanctions reasonably proportionate to the event. At the least and most general, it will be proper for you to complain. You will have a right to complain, which may manifest itself in something more than moaning. The seaside game of broken faith is focused on the moment at which the parent thinks 'Now I've got to get you.' And the child thinks 'Yes, now you've got to get me.'

That is a simplified story about a game played according to real rules. The word 'promise' is not essential, but the idea of promising is. 'Will you meet me at the theatre at 7.00?' 'Yes, I won't be late.' No promise as such, but plenty of moaning if lateness happens. 'Will you lend me your book till tomorrow?' 'Yes, here it is.' Here the work is all done by the language and idea of lending and borrowing. 'Will you lend?' means 'You can rely on me to give back.' If we say that invitations to rely consist in promises, undertakings, agreements, covenants, guarantees (or warranties, which is the same word), we must not be understood to mean that any of these particular words must be used. They only assist. People use them to rub the message in.

An invitation to rely can be expressed thus: 'I want you to regard me as bound.' That is what it comes down to. 'Regard me as under an obligation.' In whatever language it is actually done, that is the idea of a promise. The promissor puts himself under an obligation. He wants to incur the obligation, and he uses language (together with conduct and circumstances) to impose the obligation on himself. Notice, 'I promise (or "vow") to smoke no more cigarettes.' Or, on a desert island, 'I promise (or "swear" or simply "I must") to remain cheerful.' These are specially difficult because, though I try to impose the obligation on myself just as in the case in which I make the promise to you, there is nobody but myself (in the metaphor of binding) who can pull the rope. A vow to God helps with this problem.

The last paragraph shows that invitations to rely and the means of putting oneself under an obligation are not co-terminous. I put myself under an obligation to get you to rely on me, but I sometimes put myself under obligations for other purposes. There is room for a prolonged discussion. Which comes first? But no room here. It is safe to say that in human society the reason why people put themselves under obligations is, overwhelmingly, to engender reliance.

Where does the law come in? We have been talking about an extra-legal phenomenon. The law's first task in the area is to say what has to be done if one wants to incur a legal obligation. One, that is, which will be recognised in the courts in such a way that 'You can get me' will mean 'You can get me by process of law.' A simple version of the question is, Which promises (undertakings, agreements, etc.) are binding at law? What does a man have to do to impose an obligation on himself when he wants to induce reliance or bind himself for some other purpose? The work of answering this question can be contrasted with the work which produces the law of delict and indeed of quasi-contract and quasi-delict. They are all categories of obligations imposed by law, involuntarily. Remember Stair's division between obediential obligations and conventional obligations.[1] Obediential obligations are those which are imposed willy-nilly, without an act of choice. As where you run over my toe and have to pay compensation, or receive a mistaken payment and have to make restitution. Their question is, What obligations are imposed on people by the direct operation of law? By contrast the law of contract has to address the question, When a man wants to put himself under an obligation, what must he do?

There is a second major task. And it is not in complete harmony with the first. A given promise, using that word in the widest sense, will induce a given reliance. But the reliance will not be explicable solely in terms of any words used. 'Will you look after my suitcase till tomorrow morning?' 'Yes, it will cost you 50 pence.' This is a common enough transaction. He has undertaken (promised) to look after my case and I am relying on that promise. But what exactly am I expecting of him? Must he stay up all night with a gun across his knees? What happens if the station burns down and my case with it? What if he gives it to another customer by mistake? The point is, the exchange of words is only a brief shorthand. It does not cover every eventuality. Even if there is a sheet of 'small print' there will always be questions unanswered by the words used or their logical implications. 'Will you take £500 for that painting?' 'Yes.' Nothing has been said about, for example, the case in which it turns out that the painting has been stolen from Lord X by the person who sold it to you. But I will want to say that the reliance engendered by your 'Yes' extended to your ownership: in short, I took you to be affirming that it was yours to sell.

This second task derives from the laconic nature of undertakings. It is intending to build up packages of obligations inherent in transactions and, in particular, in ones which commonly recur. Reference is often made to 'implied terms'. I much prefer *natura contractus*, the nature of the contract. The business is, to settle a version of what reasonable men would say if they set out to specify all the rules of, say, sale or hire or pledge and so on. That package states 'the nature of contract'; and then, subject to more or less restriction according to the needs of the age,

[1] Above, 21.

people can exclude or extend it as suits their circumstances and the nature of their bargain. 'Implied terms' would be innocuous were it not that it leaves no separate language for terms genuinely intended but not expressed. The *natura contractus* is the law's version of the deal. It embraces matters which the parties themselves will never have thought of and whose inclusion in the contract cannot realistically be referred to the actual but tacit intent of the parties.

The reason why this second task is not completely in harmony with the first is touched on at the end of the previous paragraph. In fleshing out the skeletons of commonly recurring deals, the law imposes obligations which are reasonably incidental to the parties' intents but which cannot be referred directly to their agreement. If I sell a car I can say afterwards that I never agreed to assume any obligation in respect of quality; and when I have to pay damages in respect of a latent defect I may maintain that the obligation is as much 'imposed by law' as the obligation to compensate for negligent injury inflicted in the course of driving. It is true that the particular package on which the law settles is not the package on which A or B or C would have agreed, and certainly not what he would say with hindsight that he would have agreed. But that should not obscure the fact that around every promise there is a penumbra of unexamined assumptions, qualifications and undertakings. The seller who says no more than 'Yes' is genuinely opting into a complex bundle of obligations. In examining the unexamined and settling points on which individuals might differ, the law necessarily goes beyond what was agreed to and accepted by the one or demanded and expected by the other.

We have identified two major tasks which a law of contract has to perform. It has to answer these questions: (i) What promises are binding at law? (ii) What package of unmentioned rules does a given promise carry with it? These are short versions of the questions, not intended to vary the sense of what has been said already.

The second of these tasks exercises a very definite influence on the organisation of contract. It favours the identification of specific contracts, the formation of a list of commonly encountered transactions in which people make and receive promises. Because a list is ideal for working out standard packages of law suitable for different contexts. On the other hand, the first (Which promises are binding in law?) pulls rather in a different direction. It invites a general answer, free of specific content, an answer in terms of mode as opposed to content. As, for example, when they are seriously intended; or, when they are in writing; or, when they are followed by a hand-shake. The reason why this question favours this kind of answer is that it takes little imagination to perceive the potentially infinite diversity of content. Hence, an answer in terms of content instantly meets the objection that the list would have to be too long. It would be unmanageable. Or, if it were short, it would simply fail to meet people's reasonable needs.

The last paragraph supposes two possible principles of organisation. One based on a general test: all promises, whatever their content, are legally binding if... The other, specific rather than general, based on content: promises are binding if they are promises to sell, buy, lend, borrow, pledge deposit and so on. On the other hand, if it is right to say that the law of contract has to perform both the tasks which have been identified, and if both pull in different directions, it will be difficult for a system to settle exclusively on one or the other pattern. Some sort of compromise will be necessary. It is an important difference between Roman law and the common law that, though both compromises, Roman law puts the emphasis on specific contracts and the common law on general modes of contracting.

The Roman law of contract was dominated by eight specific contracts: sale, hire, partnership, commission (*mandatum*), loan for consumption (*mutuum*), loan for use (*commodatum*), deposit and pledge. This list covers the whole range of commercial and social life. But it is in the nature of any such list to be less than completely comprehensive. The contractual figures in the list rise like islands in the sea, an archipelago not a single continent.

The need for a general mode of contracting, free from specific content, was met in two ways. First, from earliest times the contract of *stipulatio* could be adapted to any content. To refer to it as 'the contract of *stipulatio*' is to align it with sale, hire and so on. That is safe enough, once the difference has been observed. *Stipulatio* depended on promising in a particular manner, by the exchange of question and answer and probably using particular words. The spirit of the thing is captured if we imagine one person saying 'Do you solemnly swear to...?' and receiving the answer 'I solemnly swear it.' It is, quite literally, a form of words. So, strictly, it is a mode of contracting, not a type of contract. Secondly, there developed, by way of long-stop, a doctrine of contracts without a name, innominate contracts. According to that doctrine any agreement involving reciprocal performances became actionable by a party who had done his part. The roots of the doctrine are classical. As definitions were tidied up, something had to be done for those whom only the need for tidiness squeezed out. Barter, a horse for a kingdom, was taken out of sale by the requirement of a money price. And you will not find it in the list. We may be sure though that there never was a time when barter was remediless. Ad hoc, the gap was filled. The question is whether the ad hoc solution of this kind of problem by actions *in factum* or actions *praescriptis verbis* gave way during the classical period to a general doctrine. Perhaps only much later.

There should be questions in your minds as to why, if *stipulatio* was old and flexible, there ever was a need for actions on particular transactions and then, later, a need for another general doctrine. I shall deal with that in the context of *stipulatio* itself.

1. Arrangement of the List in Gaius's and Justinian's Institutes

There is a grouping of the contracts into four classes. The differentiation is based upon the way in which the contract is made. That is, upon the nature of the event which brings it into being. It is a classification which continues from the division by contract and delict and so on. Even within contract, the focus is still on the events from which the consequences arise. On this Justinian (J.3.13.1) follows Gaius, G.3.89:

Et prius videamus de his quae ex contractu nascuntur. Harum autem quattuor genera sunt: aut enim re contrahitur obligatio aut verbis aut litteris aut consensu.
First let us consider those that arise from contract. Of such there are four *genera*: for an obligation by contract arises either *re* [by delivery of a *res*: real contract], by words [verbal contract], by writing [literal contract] or by consent [consensual contract].

You will see from Zulueta's translation that the class of contracts '*re*' does not slip easily into English. That will be considered in more detail later. The others are clear enough. By Justinian's time, the membership of the category '*re*' had slightly changed and the literal contract had barely any existence. Of the eight contracts mentioned as dominating the entire picture, sale, hire, partnership and commission (mandate) are grouped as consensual, requiring only agreement in order to become binding; and loan for consumption, loan for use, deposit and pledge are Justinian's contracts '*re*', requiring the delivery of a thing to become binding. *Stipulatio* on its own accounts for all but the whole of the category *verbis*, requiring oral words. The contract by writing has not found a place in this introduction. It was never important. That is not the same as saying that writing itself was never important, as we shall see.

This fourfold division of contracts makes no mention of some praetorian additions to the list which were stable enough to have names or of the doctrine of innominate contracts which has already been mentioned.

The common law has nothing to do with this fourfold list—*re*, *verbis*, *litteris*, *consensu*—and at first sight seems to reject entirely the approach through specific contracts identified by content. It certainly starts on the other foot. If you ask it, Which promises are binding at law?, the answer comes in two parts, both of which are content-free: either you put your promise in writing and, having sealed it, deliver the sealed writing as your deed; or you promise in exchange for some consideration. What is a 'consideration'? Something—anything—asked for and given as the price of the promise, a counter-promise, a giving or some other doing or not doing. This two-part answer is beginning to look shaky. Perhaps it is time to add a third part: or you promise in such a way as to induce detrimental reliance, in which case you will be bound, on the ground of estoppel, after there has been some such reliance. But even this third addendum still speaks in general terms, of a mode of becoming bound rather than of a promise binding by reason of its specific content. The picture remains all of one piece: promises, generally, become binding when made by deed, supported by consideration or followed by detrimental reliance.

If one wanted to challenge the smoothness of this, the way would be to say that the doctrine of consideration is not really a general test at all but merely a rather wide 'specific contract' test. For what it says is that 'bargains' are binding. The nit-picking answer is that, even so, that has no reference to the content of the undertakings, which remain infinitely various. The more liberal answer is that the line between general tests and specific tests is admittedly not clearly marked, and that there is something to be said for the view that a 'bargain' could be described as belonging to the specific contract approach, though it certainly includes far too much matter to be useful in working out the incidents of particular transactions. Admitting this, I still prefer to see consideration as a general test.

Common lawyers are educated to believe in the generality of this law of contract. And that is not wrong. So far as concerns parol contracts it has all been worked out, at least since the early seventeenth century, in one action, the action of *assumpsit*, in which, boiled down to essentials, the plaintiff's allegations were that in consideration of such and such the defendant promised such and such (*assumpsit*) but wickedly broke his promise. The text of the one action structured the whole development. The deed was a survival from an earlier time, useful for making gratuitous promises binding but peripheral to the main business. And promissory estoppel is a newcomer, still peripheral and indeed hardly at cross-purposes with the established core.

But this picture of one central and two peripheral tests all of the same 'general' kind is partly misleading. The common law has also had to generate packages of rules for specific contracts. The obvious case is sale of goods, which has a little code to itself. But Volume II of *Chitty on Contracts* reveals that sale is only the most prominent example. The chapter headings there closely resemble the Roman list. Agency and bailment need special mention. The contract of employment has become a specialism. Hire-purchase has its own rules. Statutory control has accelerated what the common law was already doing. The result is that the general law which is still learned under the heading of contract is hardly more than an introduction, an indispensable foundation of principle but nothing like the whole story.

For all this it remains true that the basic orientation of the two systems is different. The Roman way was to throw up an archipelago of contractual islands in the sea and then to wonder what to do about people left in the water. The common law of contract rose out of the sea in one piece, or one large and two small, but was then too flat and had laboriously to build its high places.

2. Formal and Informal Contracts

Nothing so far has turned on the difference between formal and informal, a distinction which cuts across the division between general and specific tests. A form sometimes provides a mode of contracting, as with the deed: any promise can be made binding with the use of that formality. But even in a list of specific contracts formal requirements can be insisted upon, either across the board or piecemeal. It would be inconvenient but not impossible to say every contract in the list must be made in writing. More plausible is something more selective: sales shall be in writing; or, sales of land, or sales of subject-matter worth more than £100. Moreover, writing is not the only possible formality. A requirement that you should clap your hands in the air before promising, or stand on one leg while promising, would count as a requirement of form. But writing is the most prominent modern example, whether to be sealed or merely signed.

What is meant by formality? It is not always easy to say whether a given requirement should be regarded as a requirement of form. You have to ask yourself what the 'natural' or informal way of doing the thing in question would be. Then a formal requirement will be one which either adds to what would be 'naturally' done or restricts the modes in which it could so be done by excluding some which would seem to work just as well if the law would let them. The requirement of a seal is a super-added formality: nobody's natural vision of a promise would include it. A general requirement of writing would be a restrictive formality. In the natural version you can alter a promise by word of mouth or semaphore or writing; in short by any manner of communication.

By this test, stipulation must count as formal whether or not special words had to be used. For the insistence on spoken words is in itself an artificial restriction, exactly on a par with the insistence on writing contemplated in the last paragraph. By contrast, the contracts '*re*' (real contracts) do not count as formal. The law sees the contractual bond as coming into existence only when the *res* is delivered by the lender (of either kind), the depositor or the pledgor. But, subject to a sophistication which we will encounter in the case of pledge, this cannot be said to constitute a formal requirement. For, if you contemplate the natural or commonsensical versions of these deals, lending for consumption or for use and deposit and pledge, you see that they do all involve the delivery of a thing. So the law is not adding to what has to be done or restricting the modes in which it can be done. These contracts are not formal.

The relativity of formality (which is just shorthand for the observation that the decision to call something a formality depends sometimes on your view of the natural phenomenon in question) is well illustrated by the common law's doctrine of consideration. If you take the view that the natural phenomenon which the common law is looking for is 'the bargain' or 'the non-gratuitous promise', there is nothing to say for the view that the requirement of consideration is a requirement of formality. For the consideration is the very element of reciprocity which 'naturally' indicates a bargain or shows the promise to have been bought at a price, however trivial. But if you think that what the common law is really looking for is the seriously intended promise, the promise meant to bind, then you may well begin to see the insistence on consideration as something super-added to the commonsensical phenomenon by the courts. By taking literally the doctrine that the adequacy of consideration is not to be inspected, the law has made it possible for parties to behave as though this latter view were right. How do you make a gratuitous promise binding? Either put it in the form of a deed or exact some nominal consideration. The nominal consideration, a peppercorn or a rose at midsummer, here becomes as much a formality as the red sticker which now replaces a seal.

What is the point of formality? It serves to concentrate the mind. That is, the person about to incur the obligation (or trigger the other legal consequences, whatever they may be) knows exactly when it is going to happen. He has the opportunity therefore to give it his serious consideration. Nowadays it is a familiar device for consumer protection to insist that the consumer be given a written document and a set time in which to contemplate its finality. Whenever you execute a deed (or make a will) you cannot help being aware that you are taking a serious step. So formality warns.

It also militates against fraud and uncertainty, though not all formalities are equally effective or operate in the same way. Writing obliges people to make themselves clear and provides good evidence, especially when all other evidence of the act in question is excluded. The ceremony of *mancipatio* made acts public and well-witnessed.

The assertion that formal requirements have these good purposes should not close our eyes to the fact that they may also get built into the law by accident or may outgrow the purposes for which they were introduced. And, further, they can have bad side-effects. Where the law insists on formality, people sometimes go on following commonsense. And that can be an engine of fraud. If the law says I can only give you my house in writing, what if I take your money and let you in without the trouble of any document? The obvious Roman version of this is the case in which I am selling a *res mancipi* but decide to skip the *mancipatio*. Something had to be done to stop me treacherously taking advantage of the technical effects of ignoring the formal requirements.

Formal requirements always carry this kind of difficulty, an in-built overkill.

Is this section on formality a digression? The topic is the organisation of Roman contract. So how does formality come in? Neither Gaius nor Justinian makes anything of the division between formal and informal. They do not divide the four groups (*re*, *verbis*, *litteris*, *consensu*) in this way. But it is convenient to do so and as it happens it can almost be done simply by changing the order. The categories *verbis* and *litteris* are categories of formal contracts. The others are not. So by taking verbal and literal contracts first, one can deal with the whole topic of formality. But there is a snag. It is not quite so neat as that.

The snag is that Justinian imposed a requirement of writing on all contracts, to an extent which remains controversial. And, even before that, writing was for purely practical reasons very important right across the board.

This means that a division between formal and informal contracts cannot be neatly slipped over the groupings used in the Institutes. But even so this division remains useful. Nor will the coherence of the Roman categories be disturbed by bringing into a discussion of formal contracts the consideration of the rôle of writing in the whole law of contract. For that can conveniently be done in connexion with the contract *litteris*. The treatment of contracts in these lectures will comprise two chapters on formal contracts (*litteris*, *verbis*), followed by two on informal contracts (*consensu*, *re*).

3

The Contract *Litteris* and the Rôle of Writing Generally

The key to this is the distinction between the dispositive and the evidentiary use of writing. A dispositive use of writing occurs where the law specifies the written word as the means by which a legal effect is achieved, here the making of a contract. The effect is triggered by the document as such, precisely because of the writing. Not because the writing evidences something else, some other event from which the consequence in question flows.

Evidentiary use of writing occurs where a document is drawn up not for its own sake but to prove that some other dispositive event has happened.

Take the case of the conveyance called mancipation. The law specifies that *dominium* over Italic land cannot be passed from one person to another except through this ceremony with bronze, scales and witnesses. Suppose, however, that in order to avoid a journey we just write out that the mancipation of the land took place on such and such a day before such and such witnesses. As alienee you may be perfectly happy with that. If the document, duly authenticated, says that the mancipation happened, it will be difficult for anyone to say it did not. A layman may say that the document itself has the effect of transferring *dominium*. But a lawyer will say that that analysis is obviously wrong. The dispositive event is the mancipation. The document obtains its utility because it is very good evidence of the mancipation having happened. Even if the mancipation had happened the documentary record would probably have been made. That is only sensible. You always need to be sure of having good and convenient evidence.

If the document seems to work on its own, that is only because people are exploiting the practical realities of the relationship between written evidence and the dispositive ceremony. The document itself is only evidence.

This example is taken from outside the field of contract, mancipation being a conveyance rather than a contract. But it serves to illustrate the relationship between matter which is dispositive and matter which is evidential. Notice that the contrast, quite clear in principle, can be blurred in two ways. If the law makes a document the only acceptable evidence of the event, that is tantamount to saying that the consequence attaches to the writing itself. Or, if the law makes the inference from the writing irrebuttable, or rebuttable only in limited ways, the statement that the writing takes its effect only from the event behind it again begins to look unreal. Rules of this kind narrow the gap between dispositive and evidentiary use of writing. The subtleties of the relationship should not be underestimated.

The category of contracts *litteris* should not have anything to do with the merely evidential use of writing. Just as contracts *verbis* are those made by word of mouth and contracts *consensu* are those made by agreement however reached, so contracts *litteris* should be contracts made by writing, those for which writing is the dispositive event.

It is almost true that classical Roman law knew no such contract. That is, that its law of contract made no use at all of dispositive writing. Under the heading of contracts *litteris* Gaius puts forward only one tiny figure, already obsolescent if not obsolete. And his most important statements are negative. These negative statements are at G.3.134 and G.3.131–2. G.3.134 reads:

Praeterea, litterarum obligatio fieri videtur chirografis et syngrafis, id est, si quis debere se aut daturum se scribat, ita scilicet si eo nomine stipulatio non fiat. Quod genus obligationis proprium peregrinorum est.

Besides, an obligation based on writing seems to be made by chirographs and syngraphs. That is, where (supposing the case to be one in which no stipulation is made for the matter) one writes that he owes or will convey. But that type of obligation is peculiar to peregrines.

This is negative from the point of view of the Roman law. Gaius is obviously very conscious of the Hellenistic practice of treating documents as dispositive. So much so that he introduces these Greek writings as though he is going to admit them. But then at the end he curtly expels them as *proprium peregrinorum*, a non-citizen matter only. Notice the bit in brackets. What is the purpose of emphasising the fact that no stipulation has been made? It is that where a stipulation has been made it does not even seem that the contract arises *litteris*. Why not? Because the writing is then obviously evidential, deriving its effect from the stipulation which it evidences. Such writings are not even candidates to be considered contracts *litteris*.

In G.3.131–2 he is making a similar point about genuine cash-book entries (*nomina arcaria*). Suppose I take £10 from my cash-box (*arca*) and lend it to you. And I enter the loan in my cash-book. Does the writing put you under an obligation? No. There is no obligation unless you receive the money and if you do receive the money your obligation is 'real' (*re*). These entries should be said *nullam facere obligationem sed obligationis factae testimonium praebere* (to create no obligation but to evidence an obligation already created). And then he goes on to say that you cannot therefore maintain that *peregrini* are here bound by written entries (*nomina*) since they are bound only by the paying out of the loan, a contract indubitably *iuris gentium*. Again you detect a theme on these lines: can the Greek attitude to documents be explained within the Roman framework? If they regard themselves as bound by these *nomina*, they will be bound but not by the writing, only by the *ius gentium* contract *re* evidenced by the writing.

We are working backwards and so come last to the things which Gaius does present as true examples of contracts *litteris*. As well as genuine *nomina* recording loans, there are also what are called *nomina transcripticia*, transcriptive entries. The transaction involving these entries is also known as *expensilatio*, which might be translated 'debit' or 'entering a debit'. We do not know very much about it. It is only a way of transforming an existing obligation, not of creating a new one *ab initio*.

Gaius (G.3.128–30) says there are two types of transformation depending on whether the transcription is 'from a matter to a person' or 'from a person to a person'. The former, *a re in personam*, happens where for instance you owe me the price of goods sold to you or hired to you. In my ledger I carry this to your debit, presumably only with your consent. What change is thus effected? I get a stricter form of action, for *expensilatio* gives rise to the old *condictio*. It is one of the traditional causes of strict *ius civile* debt. Sale and hire by contrast give rise to claims based on good faith, giving you more room to manoeuvre. Then the latter, *a persona in personam*, happens when, with the agreement of my debtor, I enter to your debit the sum which he owes me. And the effect of this implementation of an arrangement made between all three of us is to give me the *condictio* against you in place of him. In both these versions what seems to happen is that, without any money actually passing, a position is reached exactly as though the first obligation had been discharged by payment and the money had then been lent out again, either back to the payor (*a re in personam*) or to someone else, the new obligee (*a persona in personam*). I have spoken of the first obligation's being 'transformed'. The technical term for such transformations—extinctions and renewals—is 'novation'.

There are several puzzles about *expensilatio*. One reason why we know so little is that it was at best obsolescent in Gaius's time. No detailed discussion has survived. One question is whether the written entries really took their force from the paying out which they seem to simulate. Was the writing really effective only as evidence of an actual discharge and new loan? It is likely that that was the beginning of it. But probably the question was raised at some point, whether a defendant could resist liability by showing that the payments in and out had never in fact been made. If so, the holding must have been that he could not: if the written entries had been made with the intent of novating an existing obligation, proof that the underlying story was untrue was immaterial. At that point it became fair to say that the writing itself had dispositive effect. If this is right, the dispositive effect grew out of an earlier evidential rôle, the acid test being as to the consequence of proving the non-existence of the facts supposed to be evidenced. Once the real facts ceased to matter the writing was dispositive.

We have already seen that so far as concerns *nomina arcaria*, where the entry evidences an actual loan and there is no element of novation, Gaius scrupulously ascribes to the writing only evidential force: *in his enim rei, non litterarum obligatio consistit; quippe non aliter valent quam si numerata sit pecunia* (G.3.131): for in these the obligation arises *re* not *litteris*; since they are not valid except in the case in which the money has been paid out.

It looks as though, faced with a plaintiff relying on *nomina* (ledger entries), the defendant could escape by showing there had been no actual paying out to him, unless the plaintiff could show there had been a transcription of one of the two kinds. Within the scope of that 'unless' the writing had ceased to be merely evidential.

There is a vivid example of a *transcriptio a re in personam* in Cicero, *De Officiis*, 3.58–60. According to our way of naming cases this would be *Pythius v. Canius*, an action by a seller for the price of the thing sold, brought not on the sale itself but on the basis of *expensilatio*. Canius was looking for a holiday house near Syracuse. Pythius asked him to dinner at his own seaside villa. He persuaded the fishermen of the district to do their fishing on that day within view of the house, and he told Canius that the place was a centre of the fishing industry. Canius agreed to pay a fancy price.

The contract of sale rests on good faith, as we shall see. Pythius could not therefore have sued by action on that contract. His *mala fides* would have given Canius a defence. But this deal had been transformed *litteris* as soon as made. Hence Pythius's claim lay by the strict *condictio* and not by the *actio venditi*. Canius had no defence, for the date was before the introduction of the *exceptio doli* by Aquilius Gallus. Pythius had, by his *transcriptio a re* (from the sale) *in personam*, acquired an action immune from the effects of his own dishonesty. The trick would not have worked once the defence of fraud had been introduced into the *condictio*. That praetorian innovation went far towards eliminating the difference between the *stricti iuris* and the *bonae fidei* actions.

1. Justinian's Contract *Litteris*

Though *expensilatio* had long since disappeared, Justinian retained the category of contracts by writing. But he did not put much in it. The document to which he refers in J.3.21, *De litterarum obligatione*, is one in which the defendant has acknowledged a debt. There are, he says, certain circumstances in which such a writing can be regarded as having dispositive effect. He gives the impression of having leaned over backwards to discover them. What are they?

The normal rôle of such an I.O.U., in Justinian's time and before, was evidential. The document evidenced the making of a loan. Against the document it would be difficult to disprove the making of the loan. But not impossible, either in fact or law. An inveterate malpractice of lenders is to overstate the amount of the principal sum lent. The documentation of the loan says 100 were lent but only 80 are actually paid over. The effect is to give the lender a premium, something over and above any interest he may arrange. Against this practice imperial constitutions, starting in Caracalla's reign, introduced the protective mechanism called the *querela non numeratae pecuniae*. This had two elements. First, a defence obliging the lender to prove that he had paid over the full amount of the loan. Second, a claim by which the borrower could recover the false document. These were subject to a time-limit which varied. Justinian took it down from five to two years: J.3.21; C.4.30.14.

Suppose that the time for the *querela non numeratae pecuniae* has passed. The plaintiff has a document acknowledging a loan which was never in fact made. Further, the document cannot be viewed as evidence of the making of any other contract and, in particular, not of a *stipulatio*. Here the defendant is going to be caught by the document itself. It is in these circumstances that Justinian says that 'even today' one can be bound by a writing.

This looks like a trick. The writing evidences the loan. It derives its force from the practical difficulty of rebutting the evidential inference which it purports to support. We know, because we have been told, that the loan was not made. But in court the document will work because that crucial fact will not be known. It can be said with reasonable certainty that the defendant's difficulty is practical, not legal. He can try to rebut the document. If he could show the loan had not been made he would be exonerated. Only it is difficult to prove without the onus-shifting *querela*.

So it seems that Justinian has elevated a mere practicality of evidence so as to pretend that there still is a contract *litteris*. Why? Part of the answer may be that he did not want to depart from the classical pattern. But I do not think that goes the whole way. Equally or more important is the fact that in practice Justinian himself had done much to enhance the rôle of writing in the making of contracts. This had been done without technically adopting the position that the writing was dispositive. Nevertheless in practice he had made documents so important that, of all the classical categories of contract, none would have been more oddly or incongruously omitted from those 'by writing'. It would have been stranger to omit it, a more striking misrepresentation, than to retain it with doubtful content.

2. The Rôle of Writing Outside Contracts *Litteris*

It is obvious that, since the contracts *litteris* do by definition form the category in which the writing is dispositive, or can be said to be by stretching a point, the use of writing in the rest of the law of contract is to provide evidence. Everyone knows that if it comes to a dispute it is useful to have the terms in writing. And that is true even before the argument gets as far as litigation. Without a writing there is room both for genuine doubts and for evasion. Hence the wise man documents both the fact of the agreement and its terms.

This sensible instinct can manifest itself in agreements not to be bound until the documentation is complete. The parties say in effect 'Yes, now we are agreed on everything but let us postpone the legal bond till the agreement has been written out.' This is essentially what is meant by the English practice of buying land 'subject to contract', for that phrase has been construed as putting off all legal effects until the exchange of finalised documents. English law allows a contract for sale of land to be made informally so long as it is supported by a written memorandum signed by the party to be charged. But English practice invariably postpones the legal bond by using the tag 'subject to contract'.

We have seen how Gaius, writing before the extension of the citizenship by Caracalla (by the *Constitutio Antoniniana* in AD 214), had to keep pointing out that according to Roman law writings were, for the most part, evidentiary and not dispositive. In the Hellenistic east the law was different. That is what Gaius says: these chirographs and syngraphs are peculiar to peregrines, to non-citizens. The Greek law is obviously very close to the surface of his readers' minds. When the citizenship was extended, with the effect that everyone fell under the same Roman law, the only way you could go on behaving as though nothing much had happened would be, if you were really Greek, to agree to postpone the legal consequences until the Greek moment. That is, till the writing. There may have been very difficult questions. What is sufficiently a complete writing? And, worse, what is sufficiently an agreement to postpone the legal effects? After all agreements can be tacit, and people following the Greek way might reasonably say that they should be taken impliedly to have intended only the writing to bind.

Justinian legislated on this matter. The principle which he operated was this. Even if your contract was of a kind which could in theory be concluded without writing, if you agreed that it should be done in writing, then only a document of utmost finality should have any legal effect. C.4.21.17 (from AD 528):

In the case in which it is proposed that there should be made in writing a contract for sale, exchange, non-registrable gift, *arra*-giving or for any other purpose whatsoever, and similarly in the case in which it is proposed to reduce a compromise to writing, we ordain that the contract or compromise shall have no force at all unless the documents have been put in their final form and confirmed by the subscription of both parties or, if written by a notary, finalised by him and released to the parties: so that henceforth nobody shall be allowed, till these steps have been concluded, to claim any right from such a contract or compromise, neither from a draft (even in the writing of one or both parties) nor from a final copy not yet executed or delivered. And this shall extend even to the point, in sales of this kind, of excluding the proposition that the fixing of the price compels the vendor to complete the contract or, failing that, to make good in money the buyer's interest in his performance.

This is clear enough. An agreement to contract in writing means that nothing whatever can be made either of the mere fact of mutual assent or of any preliminary memoranda or drafts. So in the period up to the final documentation either party can get out or gazump. There is a pre-contractual phase unknown to the unimpeded operation of classical law.

This legislation is recited in an abbreviated version in the Institutes, at J.3.23 *pr.* Justinian is talking about the contract of sale. He begins with the rule '*Emptio et venditio contrahitur simulatque de pretio convenerit quamvis nondum pretium numeratum sit ac ne arra quidem data fuerit.* (Sale is contracted as soon as the price is agreed, though the price has not been paid and no *arra* has even been given.)' And then he explains that that rule has been changed for contracts agreed to in writing, an observation which leads into the paraphrase of the legislation.

3. *Arra*

Several times we have encountered this word. It means 'deposit', in the sense of 'earnest' as opposed to the sense of a deposit for safe-keeping. The account of Justinian's legislation in relation to documents is incomplete without some description of his use of *arra*. For he also laid down provisions as to *arra* which were supposed to complement or extend his rules on writing. There is a considerable dispute as to exactly what he meant. It is one of those problems about which every Romanist feels obliged to have his say.

What is the matter in dispute? It is convenient first to be able to draw on a phrase which will still be unfamiliar: 'the *arra* rule'. The *arra* rule, derived from Greek law, is that where a party deposits an *arra* and subsequently withdraws from the transaction which the deposit was to sanction, he forfeits all claim to its return; and, from the other side, where a party has received such an *arra* and subsequently withdraws, he must return the *arra* twice over, so as to put him in the same position as he would have been in had he been depositor rather than depositee. In short, the *arra* rule is: in case of withdrawal, depositor forfeits, depositee repays double. The question in dispute is whether Justinian intended to introduce the arra rule solely to cover the pre-contractual stage which he created, for written contracts, between agreement and final documentation. Or did he mean the *arra* rule to displace the normal regime for sanctioning executory contracts even after the moment at which, according to the classical rules as modified by his reform in relation to writing, they acquired legal effect? The narrowest view: he said that, where the contract was to be in writing, if you wanted a sanction at the pre-contractual stage between agreement and writing, you could give and take *arra* and rely on the *arra* rule. The largest view: he said that if you wanted any sanction at all in respect of performances still to be made, i.e. in respect of executory contracts, you had better give and take *arra* and operate the *arra* rule.

The cause of this dispute is a clash between what is said in the Codex and what is said in the Institutes in relation to the contract of sale. It arises in relation to the part of Justinian's enactment which follows that which we have already looked at. So far as there is a clash, we ought not to forget that the Institutes is an elementary textbook. That is, we should not give it primacy in resolving the difficulty. Nevertheless I shall give the passage from the Institutes first. For it is that passage which seems to do something drastic, to support the larger of the two views set out earlier. I will put my own cards on the table. I think the right view is the narrow one. J.3.23 *pr.*:

> . . . *Donec enim aliquid ex his deest, et poenitentiae locus est et potest emptor vel venditor sine poena recedere ab emptione.*
>
> . . . For as long as any of these are lacking there is both a *locus poenitentiae* [time for changing one's mind] and the possibility for either buyer or seller to withdraw from the purchase without sanction.

So far so good. There is no doubt at all that 'any of these' which may be lacking are the steps required to make a written contract final, for this passage follows on from the description of the way in which a document is finalised. There is a bit of a puzzle as to why it was thought necessary to say 'both *locus poenitentiae* and possibility of withdrawal *sine poena*' which repeats the same point twice. But this is hardly more than an infelicity. Perhaps it is due to the need to emphasise. For there is a problem in the offing. What if, while the documents are being drawn up, one party withdraws and then, after the notary has released them, the other says that they have retroactive effect? 'Now we have final documents your attempt to withdraw is no help to you'. Justinian scotches this line of argument: before finalisation the parties are quite free to withdraw. There is no doubt that to this point Justinian is only talking of the space between agreement and final writing in a contract which is to be *in scriptis*. J.3.23 *pr.* (continued):

Ita tamen impune recedere eis concedimus, nisi iam arrarum nomine aliquid fuerit datum: hoc enim subsecuto, sive in scriptis sive sine scriptis venditio celebrata est, is qui recusat adimplere contractum, si quidem emptor est, perdit quod dedit, si vero venditor, duplum restituere compellitur, licet nihil super arris expressum est.

However, we allow them to withdraw without sanction only if nothing has already been given by way of *arra*. If there is an *arra*-giving behind the transaction (*hoc enim subsecuto*), then, whether the sale has been celebrated with or without writing, the one who refuses to complete the contract loses what he gave if he is buyer and is obliged to restore double if he is seller. And this rule applies even if nothing is said about what is to happen about the *arra*.

There are no surprises in the first part. The absence of sanction for withdrawal before final documentation is qualified: there will be a sanction if there has been *arra* given. If the second part went on to give shape to that sanction and no more, there would be no problem. For contracts *in scriptis*, between agreement and final writing: withdrawal *sine poena*, subject to the *arra* rule if *arra* is given.

But the second part is not so simple. It undoubtedly says that the *arra* rule is to apply *sive in scriptis sive sine scriptis venditio celebrata est*, whether the sale is 'celebrated' in writing or not. For example, the text does certainly contemplate that if *arra* is given under a straightforward sale by word of mouth (binding by the classical rules and unaffected by Justinian's intervention in written sales) the *arra* rule is to apply.

Similarly in a written sale already finalised (binding under Justinian's own rule). So, even in contracts apparently effective in law according to any rule we have so far met, if *arra* is given, the *arra* rule applies.

That is all right. It is inelegant in that it suddenly reaches beyond the particular problem in the reader's mind—the space before the final writing in contracts *in scriptis*—but it does not do any substantive damage to the larger picture to which the reader has to re-focus. For the *arra* rule can be grafted on to the normal regime for sanctionary contracts, an extra sanction if *arra* happens to have been given.

Then the bombshell. Taken as a whole, does not the passage say that withdrawal *impune* is always possible so long as *arra* has not been given? Does it not say that in sales written and unwritten the only sanction is the *arra* rule if *arra* has been given? If so, that is something quite incompatible with the 'normal regime'. Suppose an unwritten sale. We meet in town. We agree that I will sell and you will buy the 10,000 litres of wine in my vats for £5,000. The normal regime says that we are now bound and can only 'withdraw' on pain of paying damages. Does this text say that we can *impune recedere* (withdraw without sanction) if only I have not insisted on your paying over an *arra* of, say, £2,000 so as to attract the sanction of the *arra* rule?

It all depends on that wretched colon, which in the English I changed into a full-stop. The punctuation of the Latin is modern. It is not to be relied on. What is the effect of the colon? It makes everything which comes afterwards, hence the very wide statement of the *arra* rule for all kinds of contracts *in scriptis* and *sine scriptis*, seem to be an expansion of what comes before. And what comes before is 'We allow withdrawal without sanction if *arra* is not given.' So the expansion is all about the system which can provide a sanction, against the background of *impune recedere*. The effect of the colon is to make free withdrawal the general rule.

Without the colon the *impune recedere* just looks back to the pre-contractual space before the finalisation of documents. The rest of the passage does inelegantly enlarge the range of its comment but says nothing about sanctionless withdrawal in cases in which *arra* is not given. This seems the best way to understand the passage.

If we now turn back to the enactment in the Codex we will not find anything which supports the wider interpretation of what is said in the Institutes. We have already seen Justinian providing that, when the contract is to be in writing, nobody is to claim any right from any preliminary document and then going on to rub in the change in *huiusmodi venditionibus* (in sales of this—i.e. written—type). He goes on (C.4.21.17, continued):

Illud etiam adicientes ut et in posterum si quae arrae super facienda emptione cuiuscumque rei datae sunt sive in scriptis sive sine scriptis, licet non sit specialiter adiectum, quid super isdem arris non procedente contractu fieri oporteat, tamen et qui vendere pollicitus est, venditionem recusans, in duplum eas reddere cogatur, et qui emere pactus est, ab emptione recedens, datis a se arris cadat, repetitione earum deneganda.

And we also add this, that hereafter if, in relation to a purchase which is to be made of any *res* whatsoever, some *arra* has been given whether in *scriptis* or *sine scriptis*, then, even if it has not been expressly said what should happen in relation to the *arra* if the contract fails to go forward, yet he who has promised to sell shall on repudiating the sale be compelled to restore double, and he who has agreed to buy shall on withdrawing from the purchase forfeit the *arra* given by him, its recovering being refused.

The last part of this just lays down the *arra* rule. It raises no problems. The first part expresses the range of the provision. It does contain some puzzles. The order is odd. What does 'whether in writing or not in writing' go with? It might be linked to the *facienda emptio cuiuscumque rei* or to the *arrarum datio*. It is closer to the latter, except that the notion of *dare in scriptis* is a bit strained. And then, if the *emptio* is *facienda* (still to be made, not made already) can it be described as 'in or not in writing', since if there is to be no writing at all the sale is complete and not about to be completed when the *arra* is given? All the same I incline to the view that 'whether in writing or not in writing' does go with the purchase, not the giving of *arra*.

If that is right, the provision is about the case in which *arra* is given in *emptio-venditio* (written and unwritten) and it says that the *arra* rule is to apply. It does not say that without *arra* there is no sanctioning regime at all. On the other hand, if I am wrong and the clause goes with the *arra* giving, then the provision is about 'purchases to be made'. Nothing turns on the use of 'purchase' instead of 'sale'. If '*facienda*' is taken in a loose lay sense, the scope is simply 'all and any case of *emptio-venditio* in which an *arra* is given'. And then the effect of the provision is very much as before, with the addition of the careful statement that once the *arra* is given it does not matter whether it is given in writing or without writing. However, lastly, if '*facienda*' is taken technically so as to mean strictly that the *emptio* is still imperfect, still to be made binding, then the scope of the provision is only 'contracts of sale about to be made' and that would certainly suggest that it was intended to focus only on those which, though to be made in writing, are, pending finalisation, still in their pre-contractual phase. So on this view the scope of the provision would be narrower than appears from its re-telling in the Institutes. But I think this third possibility is the least likely. '*Emptio facienda*' seems to me to indicate a purchase 'to be performed' rather than one 'to be concluded'. However, even if this third view were right, what would be the result? It would open a gap between Codex and Institutes, but it would do nothing to support the view that the sanction for an executory contract had become *arra* or nothing.

The simplest summary seems to be this. Justinian introduced a rule which said that if a contract was to be in writing it had no force till finally written. And he said what 'finally' meant. To cover the period up to that finalisation you could rely on *arra* if you chose to. Also, you could rely on *arra* after the finalisation, or indeed in unwritten contracts. If you did, the *arra* rule would apply to you. If you did not, the normal regime of damages would sanction the contract. Presumably, in a case in which *arra* had been given under a binding contract, breach of which would give damages, you could only recover damages if and so far as they exceeded what you obtained by virtue of the *arra* rule.

4. Writing and Stipulations

We have met the contract of stipulation briefly, enough to know that it was a contract *verbis*. That is, it depended on word of mouth, an exchange of question and answer between parties in each other's presence. The details of what was required will be considered later.

The practice was to write out the terms and put at the bottom a little clause indicating the exchange of question and answer, 'X put the question; Y promised'. The document was evidential only, but no doubt people often skipped the oral exchange. Almost any document which made some reference to a promise having happened could be used as evidence of a *stipulatio*, even without a full stipulatory *clausula* of the kind just illustrated. A writing which said 'I promise to pay you £20' would not do, because no inference can be drawn, given the use of the present tense, of any previous oral promise. But a document saying 'I promised to pay you' would support an inference of a promise made orally and in response to a question. Again, a document using the present tense, though useless in itself, would help if you could show independently that it was drawn up *inter praesentes*. In that case it could be reasonably inferred that the writing reflected an oral exchange. All this follows straightforwardly enough from the fact that the document took its force from the oral form. Any document which supported the inference would be useful, the most unequivocally the better.

Justinian's enactment on contractual documents which we have been looking at does not mention stipulations expressly, though it does refer to 'contracts . . . for any other purpose' which is in principle wide enough to reach stipulations. However, it is a nice question whether it is logically possible 'to agree to make a stipulation in writing' since in theory the writing cannot be more than evidential. I am not sure what the answer to that is.

At all events, Justinian bolstered the effect of stipulatory writings in another way. He made it well nigh impossible to rebut the inference that the parties had met and exchanged question and answer. The consequence of putting obstacles in the way of that rebuttal must have been to make the document dispositive in all but theory. The constitution is at C.8.37.14. Its effect is set out in the Institutes thus (J.3.19.12):

> An obligation *verbis* which has been framed *inter absentes* is also void (*inutilis*). But this used to provide litigious men with material for their litigation. For instance they would advance such allegations after time had passed and would maintain that either they or their adversaries had been away. It was for this reason, to meet the need to speed up the resolution of law-suits, that we wrote the *constitutio* which we sent to the advocates of Caesarea. We laid down that writings of a kind which show that the parties were present are entirely to be accepted (*omnimodo esse credendas*) unless the party who relies on such unmeritorious allegations adduces the very clearest proofs either in writing or through witnesses of substance, and thus proves that for the whole day on which the document was completed either he or his adversary was away in another area.

You can see that the burden put on the party faced with such a document is almost impossible to discharge. This is not unreasonable. For it is quite true that if separation of the parties is the only objection to the other's claim, it does constitute a discreditable and technical defence. The technique of reinforcing the document is twofold. First, he must prove separation for the whole of the relevant day.

Secondly, he must prove it in a special way, with the utmost clarity and by writing or men of substance (*idoneos*).

It is evident that the writing is regarded as all important. And this is further revealed by a little logical slip at the beginning, repeated at the end more understandably. Early on, Justinian complains that parties wriggle out by saying that either they or their adversaries were absent. That form of words supposes something from which to be absent, and that something can only be the drawing up of a writing. From an oral exchange it is impossible for one party or the other to be absent: they are either both present or both absent.

4

Contracts *Verbis*

These are the contracts which are made by word of mouth. Much the most important is *stipulatio*, but it is convenient to mention and put aside the two others, both highly specialised. Gaius mentioned them but they were obsolete by Justinian.

1. *Dotis Dictio* (Declaration of Dowry)

Dotis dictio (declaration of dowry) was a means of promising a fiancé or husband that a given dowry would be certain. It was open only to the woman's *paterfamilias*, to herself if she were *sui iuris* and to her debtor with her authority. Anyone else wanting to promise a dowry would have to use the *stipulatio*, and these three could also do that if they wished. It was no extra trouble. The difference was that in *dotis dictio* there was no need for the promise to be made in response to a question put by the promisee.

2. *Iusiurandum Liberti* (Freedman's Oath)

This was the promise made on manumission by which the slave acquiring freedom swore to do works for or confer benefits on his patron, the former owner. This could also be done by *stipulatio*, and also differed from *stipulatio* in being a one-sided declaration, 'with only one person speaking and no question put' (G.3.96).

Why did these specialised tiddlers survive beside *stipulatio*, at least into classical law? It would have been so easy to merge them. The answer is probably no more mysterious than that the law harmlessly respected the etiquette of these two social contexts. It is indelicate to stipulate for a dowry. One does not care to put such a gross question to a future father-in-law, not even with his prior consent. It strikes the wrong note. So also with freedmen, though the shades of feeling are different. A patron does not ask for his *operae*. They are offered.

3. *Stipulatio* (Stipulation)

This is a very ancient contract. It goes back to the time of the Twelve Tables, at least in the form of the *sponsio*, which is the version of the *stipulatio* using *spondere* as the word of promising. The basic idea is simple: 'Will you promise . . . ?' answered by 'I will promise'. Subject to one qualification, the contract does not have an action of its own. It is one of the grounds which a plaintiff can adduce to substantiate the abstract *intentio* of the *condictio*: 'If it appears that the defendant ought (*sc.*[1] at civil law) to give the plaintiff £20 (or Daisy, or 200 kilos of corn), . . .' The qualification is that a stipulation for a service would not fit the *condictio*, whose unity was *certum dare*. On a stipulation for a service an *actio ex stipulatu* lay: 'Whereas the plaintiff took a stipulation from the defendant for such and such a thing to be done, whatever on that account the defendant ought (*sc.* at civil law) to do for the plaintiff, for so much . . . etc.'

The first two questions are: What precisely was the formality required? And, what stopped *stipulatio* developing into a general and complete law of contract in itself, displacing the need for the rest of the list?

i. What was the formality?

For the classical law the only real doubt is whether the oral exchange of question and answer had to use special words or could use any words which sufficiently expressed the agreement of the parties. This is what Gaius says (G.3.92–4):

92. An obligation *verbis* is made by question and answer, in this way (*veluti*): '*dari spondes? spondeo* (Do you warrant to convey? I do warrant),' '*dabis? dabo*

[1] *sc.* (*scilicet*) = namely.

(Will you convey? I will convey),' '*promittis? promitto* (Do you promise? I do promise),' '*fidepromittis? fidepromitto* (Do you give your word? I do give my word),' '*fideiubes? fideiubeo* (Do you guarantee? I do guarantee),' '*facies? faciam* (Will you do? I will do).' 93. The obligation *verbis* which is made using the form '*dari spondes? spondeo*' is peculiar to Roman citizens. But the rest are *iuris gentium* (part of the law of all peoples) and are valid between all men whether Roman citizens or foreigners, and even if they are expressed in Greek, as in this way (*veluti hoc modo*): [There follow four words in Greek, with *spondeo* omitted, obviously for the reason given, and no word for *fidepromitto*.] And these words are also valid for Roman citizens so long as they understand Greek. And, the other way round, if Latin is used even foreigners are bound if they understand the Latin language. But the obligation *verbis* '*dari spondes? spondeo*' is so particularly confined to Roman citizens that, even though the verb *spondeo* is said to come from Greek, it cannot be given any Greek equivalent. 94. Hence it is said that there is only one case in which a foreigner can also use this word to put himself under an obligation, as (*veluti*) where our emperor stipulates for peace from the ruler of a foreign people, with this question: *pacem futuram spondes* (Do you warrant that there will be peace)? Or alternatively the emperor may be put the same question. But this is too sharp a way of finding an example, since any breach of such an agreement gives rise not to an action on the stipulation but to a determination by the law of war.

The question is whether Gaius's list of words is exhaustive or merely illustrative. The word *veluti* is capable of introducing either kind of list. If there was only this passage to go on, I would still incline to the view that the list is exhaustive. The reason is that if you are merely illustrating questions and answers you do not go on quite so long and, much more important, you do not give exact equivalents in another language. In particular I do not think the statement outlawing any equivalent for *spondeo* is intelligible unless the list is closed.

If such formality seems unreasonable, only recall the difference between a signed document and a deed in modern law. The vestigial seal makes all the difference. Yet in itself it is as unreasonably fussy as insistence on specified words in the Roman contract. Also if *dare* and *facere* seem too light-weight and colloquial, the answer may be that they are hallowed by their use in litigation, as for instance in *formulae*.

Justinian's Institutes certainly support the view that the classical law did not allow a free choice of words. Having set out the Latin list they explain that Greek can be used, or Greek by one and Latin by the other. They then say (J.3.25.1):

But these solemn words were used in former times (*haec sollemnia verba olim in usu fuerunt*). Later a *constitutio* of Leo was enacted which, having abolished solemn requirements as to words (*sollemnitate verborum sublata*), looks only to the meaning and common understanding of the parties in whatever words expressed (*sensum et consonantem intellectum ab utraque parte solum desiderat, licet quibuscumque verbis expressus est*).

The *constitutio* of Leo to which this refers is given in the Codex, C.8.37.10 (from AD 472):

Omnes stipulationes, etiamsi non sollemnibus vel directis, sed quibuscumque verbis pro consensu contrahentium compositae sunt, legibus cognitae suam habeant firmitatem.
Let all stipulations known to the law take effect even though composed not in solemn or ordained words but in any words whatsoever fitting the agreement between the contracting parties.

This provision is easily understood as eliminating the need for set words. Those who take the other view are driven to more difficult positions, as that it was aimed only at the written evidence of the stipulation or that it abolished the need for question and answer altogether, so that a stipulation became any agreement and, in practice, any written agreement.

The debate about the classical requirement is conducted against a background in which stipulation is, for the evidentiary reasons discussed earlier, customarily and probably almost invariably backed up with a written *cautio*. Already in the pre-classical period Cicero described the contract as something done by writing (*Topica*, 26.96). And we have already seen how Justinian made the writing virtually conclusive evidence of the meeting of the parties and the exchange of question and answer. Does the practice of writing make set words more or less likely? No certain answer can be given. But I think the relationship of writing and oral formality helps to explain how the theory of a set list of words could have survived till as late as 472. Against a writing raising an inference that question and answer had been exchanged, there would in practice be little room for a defence based on the assertion that the wrong words had been used. After all, there would not be much scope for a defence denying the meeting and exchange themselves. So the oral words would remain unexamined, and the theoretical requirement of specific words could survive without causing any actual inconvenience. In what event might it begin to cause trouble? If defendants began to draw the oral theory down into the writing, trying to get themselves off the hook by suggesting that the document itself should use a listed word, that might spark off a reform. The medicine could be of two kinds. Re-affirmation that the writing, as evidence, did not itself have to use the formal words. Or, more radically, Leo's measure aimed at the theory itself. If the oral exchange could be in any words, *a fortiori* the document evidencing that exchange would be set free.

Justinian might have taken the step of turning stipulation into a written contract in theory as well as in practice. But he did not take that option. He strengthened the evidentiary weight of the *cautio*. But, subject to re-affirming Leo's abolition of fixed words, he preserved the classical explanation of why the document worked. That is, he affirmed that the *cautio* drew its efficacy from the oral form which it evidenced.

The most dramatic indication of the orality of stipulation even in Justinian's law is the survival of the rule imposing a specific incapacity on those who could not speak or hear the words. J.3.19.7:

> A mute obviously cannot be either stipulator [the one who puts the question] or promissor. And the same rule has been accepted for the deaf. For the one who stipulates must hear the words of the promise, and the one who promises must hear the stipulator's question. This reason shows that we speak only of those who cannot hear at all, not of those who have difficulty in hearing.

Less dramatic but also indicative of the survival of the classical formality except as concerns the *sollemnia ac directa verba* is Justinian's continued insistence on perfect congruence between question and answer. Congruence, that is, of substance. The promissor must not add to or take away from the substance of the question put to him. J.3.19.5:

> Further, a stipulation is void (*inutilis*) if one fails to answer to the question as put (*ad ea quae interrogatus non respondeat*). As where the stipulator asks for ten *aurei* to be given and you promise five. Or vice versa. Or where the stipulator puts the question unconditionally and you promise subject to a condition. Or vice versa. The void case is that in which you express a

divergence, as where you answer to a conditional or postponed stipulation 'I promise now this very day'; but if you just answer 'I promise' then you are understood implicitly to have promised subject to the same condition or postponement. For it is not necessary when giving the answer to repeat everything expressed by the stipulator.

ii. Why did stipulation not develop into a general law of contract complete in itself?

The question implies that it might have done. On all views the formalities were simple to comply with. What need therefore of separate actions for sale, hire, partnership and so on?

There can never be simple answers to questions which ask why things did not develop differently. But certain factors can be identified which made *stipulatio* less serviceable than first appears. Most obviously, formality is irksome, however slight and simple. The need to meet (or at least to appear to have done so) constitutes an inconvenience. But this does not explain much since the form would have been eroded away if the potential for generalisation had not been impeded in other ways.

The second factor is that *stipulatio* was *stricti iuris*, judged according to strict law. This does not mean much until one makes the contrast with *bonae fidei iudicia*, trials based on good faith. In trials of the latter kind the *iudex* had to ask himself, according to the terms of the *formula*, what was owing *ex fide bona*. In trials based on *strictum ius* he had to ask what was owing (*sc.* according to the *ius civile* unsupplemented by good faith). A number of consequences followed, of which two are important in the context of this question.

Bona fides provided a basis on which to build up those packages of obligations which fill out the unspoken aspects of common transactions. We said earlier that a party's reliance goes beyond the words used. The evolution of packages of 'implied' obligations is necessary if that reliance is not to be repeatedly let down, creating a sense of injustice, an area in which the law appears deficient. In trials based on *strictum ius* that springboard was missing and there was no other obvious substitute. You had what the parties had actually said. You could construe the letter of their utterances but you could not easily find a way in for the spirit.

Suppose by *stipulatio* I promised to build you a boat and then when it was finished it was not well built but altogether badly built. What could the *iudex* do unless you yourself had stipulated for a particular standard of workmanship? The letter of my agreement required me to build a boat. If it was a boat, that was that.

It is not to be thought that sets of 'implied' obligations could not have been developed without the introduction of *bonae fidei iudicia*. It might have been done. But the problem was aggravated by the fact that *stricti iuris* actions were ancient and acquired their character before it seemed possible to launch out from the safe shores of what was said and done into the depths of tacit expectations. So *stipulatio*, despite being adaptable to any content, remained tied to conservative and skeletal interpretation. It never offered much protection beyond express terms.

The other important consequence of its *stricti iuris* character was the absence until late in the Republic of equitable defences. This is the other side of sticking to the letter of the agreement. A plaintiff cannot add terms, but a defendant cannot escape from the terms to which, even by fraud or pressure, he has agreed. This is a distinct advantage from the plaintiff's point of view. But, taking the large view, it adds to the picture of a contract not suited to ordinary commercial life. Too rigid and inflexible. The introduction of the *exceptio doli* and *exceptio metus* went much of the way to eliminating this deficiency and redressing the imbalance in this respect between *stricti iuris* and *bonae fidei* actions. But by then the pattern had been set. The *bonae fidei* actions had already been called into being, and the chance, if ever there had been one, of developing all the law of contract within *stipulatio* had been lost.

It is an interesting fact of comparative legal history that the common law also began life with a contractual action—covenant—which looked well fitted to deal with all the business. 'Covenant' is *conventio* in Latin, and the writ of covenant simply directed the sheriff to command the defendant to keep his agreement with the defendant in such and such a matter (*Praecipe X quod iuste et sine dilatione teneat conventionem suam*). At the end of the twelfth century you might have guessed that all the common law of contract would develop under that text, as the scope of the writ was defined. But that did not happen. The common law also found its law of contract so to say at the second attempt, pushing covenant to the sidelines. But the common law's second attempt produced, as we have seen, another 'general' law of contract. Roman law, choosing not to maximise the potential of *stipulatio*, embarked instead on the business of exploring specific transactions. And this choice was made early. The *bonae fidei iudicia* may have started to emerge as early as the third century BC.

iii. What limits were there on the scope of stipulation?

The limits on *stipulatio* were, subject to some special adaptations for this particular figure, the same as are placed on contract generally. The Institutes take the opportunity, under the head of 'void stipulations', to state some of these boundaries. The main heads are impossibility, illegality and privity.

(a) *Impossibility*. There is a distinction between factual and legal impossibility. Legal impossibility is not very easy to distinguish from illegality.

A stipulation to do what is factually impossible at the time of the promise is void. So if I promise to give you a dragon, or fly to Crete, I cannot be sued. The same if I promise to give you Stichus who unknown to me is already dead, for it is impossible to convey a dead slave (J.3.19.1). What if the promise is factually possible but subject to an impossible condition? Such conditions offer a choice, whether to ignore them or to suspend the obligation permanently (i.e. render it void). In relation to legacies there was a school dispute, with the Sabinians in favour of validity (G.3.98). But stipulations so conditioned were void. Gaius gives the example 'if I touch the sky with my finger' (G.3.98). A negative impossible condition, 'if I do not touch the sky', leaves the obligation immediately valid (J.3.19.11).

Subsequent impossibility is a more complex topic. There is no general logic to the effect that the obligation must be discharged. It depends on the law relating to the particular transaction, and, since the commonest cause of supervening impossibility is destruction of the subject-matter, on the rules relating to the case to be shown by the party seeking to be released. Logic allows him to be strictly liable however careful or, at the other end of the spectrum, liable only if he deliberately brought about the impossibility. In stipulations the question was whether he was in any way at fault. If he was then the supervening impossibility would not save him: he would be liable as though he had refused to perform.

Legal impossibility is exemplified by promises to convey to the promisee something which is already his. Or to convey to him something which is incapable of or removed from private ownership. As, to convey a man who is free, not a slave; or to convey land dedicated to the Gods (*locus sacer vel religiosus*). These are all void. And you cannot promise to convey a free man if and when he becomes a slave (J.3.19.2).

(b) *Illegality*. Stipulations to perform immoral or illegal acts or to pay for such acts were void. Justinian gives the simple example of a stipulation to commit homicide or sacrilege (J.3.19.24).

(c) *Privity*. There are two aspects to this. Attempts to put third parties under obligations, to impose burdens on them. And attempts to benefit third parties, to give them rights. The general rule is that neither is possible. I cannot promise that another will do something, and I cannot promise you to confer a benefit on another. Both these negatives can be circumvented, not contradicted, by the use of penal stipulations. 'I promise to give you 10 if X does not send you 5.' And 'I promise to give you 10 if I do not give X 5.' This circumvention only worked because Roman law did not regard penalties as unlawful.

The ban on imposing burdens on third parties needs little explanation. The obligation generated by contract is generated by consent, and if the third party has not consented to the burden, that is an end of it, at least in the absence of some strong policy operating on the relationship between promissor and third party. It is more difficult to explain the ban where the third party does consent and is actively seeking to use the promissor as an agent. The Roman attitude to agency will be considered in relation to mandate.

The ban on creating rights in a third party is more difficult to explain. If I promise you that I will benefit X, there is a general difficulty in giving X an enforceable claim. What would be the relationship between his right to claim against me and your right to control the promise made to you? Suppose that you wanted to let me off and he wanted to sue. It is your promise, even if his disappointment. This clash can explain why a system may turn its back on the third party. But it does not quite explain the nullity of a stipulation in favour of a third party (G.3.103; J.3.19.19). Nullity is a bit much. Why should you not sue me if I break my promise to benefit X? Cutting off his claim does not logically mean cutting off yours.

This nullity gave rise to a problem in relation to promises to pay 'X and Y' and 'X or Y', where X is promisee and Y is third party. 'X or Y' is all right. Y can be paid but cannot sue. 'X and Y' divided the schools. The Sabinians said X could claim the whole sum. Justinian adopted the Proculian rule: X could claim half the sum, Y nothing.

The explanation of the nullity may have to do with a difficulty of pleading. The *formula* in the classical procedure directed the *iudex* to ask himself if the defendant ought (at civil law) to give the plaintiff whatever it was. Answer invariably negative if the promise had been for a third party. On the other hand this reasoning only applies to the *condictio*, not to the *actio ex stipulatu*.

This approach may explain how Justinian is able to uphold stipulations for third parties (with respect to the promisee, not the *tertius*) when the promisee has an interest in the performance to the third party, even though he subscribes to the nullity doctrine (J.3.19.20). The view may have emerged even during the classical period that a promise to benefit a third party (even to *dare* to a third party) could be regarded as a service for the promisee, allowing the *actio ex stipulatu* to go, so long as the promissor had some pecuniary interest capable of being assessed. At all events the end result is sensible. The promisee can sue so long as he has an interest, notwithstanding assertions of nullity.

There is one major exception to the rightlessness of a named third party. A stipulation for performance to one's *paterfamilias* or owner was good. But this only reflects the concentration of rights in the person of the *paterfamilias*. We will recur to this in the discussion of agency, under the contract of mandate.

One further special case needs to be mentioned. Rights acquired by stipulation are transmissible to your heir. He steps into your shoes. That does not break the principle of privity. He is you, by succession. On the other hand you could not obtain a promise in favour of your heir. You could not validly propose a stipulation 'Do you promise to convey to my heir?' Gaius says (G.3.100) *inelegans esse visum est* (it has seemed offensive to principle) for an obligation to take effect first for the person of the heir. There were odd consequences, because different words could have the offensive effect. So you could not take a promise for payment 'after my death'. That is obvious. But you also could not have one for payment 'the day before I die'. Because only after death would the day before become apparent. 'When I am dying' or 'as I die' were all right. But the logic of that looks odd, since again only death would show that I was dying. But perhaps 'the day before' is more difficult, because of the precise timing. The general drift may be apparent before the event, though not the hour and day.

At all events Justinian changed the rule and allowed the obligation to begin in the person of the heir, sweeping away all this *scrupulosa inquisitio* (J.3.19.13; C.8.37.11). It is arguable, all the same, that he meant to leave invalid for impossibility promises which plainly envisaged giving and receiving after death: 'Do you promise to give me 10 after I am dead?'

iv. Special applications of stipulation

Subject to these general inhibitions, anyone could use stipulation for anything. But there were one or two special contexts which need to be noticed. There is a great deal of law here. This will only serve to point at it, not to explore it.

(a) *Stipulations in litigation.* In a number of situations you could apply for a compulsory stipulation, i.e. a stipulation imposed on your adversary by the court, either praetor or *iudex* according to the circumstances. And, not very dissimilarly, the praetor would sometimes impose a stipulation as a condition of offering some other relief or to regulate the business of litigation itself. A party who refused risked further sanctions, often *missio in possessionem* (a decree authorising the other to seize his property). On the other hand, once the promise had been given the promisee then had a remedy against the promissor just as though an ordinary formal contract had been made between them.

A good example comes from the touchy subject of relations between neighbours. Suppose your neighbour's house was in such a state that you expected that you might soon suffer loss yourself if he let the trouble go unattended. Or suppose he started up some new operation such as a smoky factory which injured the amenity of your land. In these cases you would apply for a formal promise to pay for loss (the *cautio damni infecti*) or to undo the new work so far as unlawful (the *cautio ex operis novi nuntiatione*).

(b) *Personal security.* If you propose to lend or otherwise give credit to someone, or to extend an existing credit, you may want security. If you take a right against a thing, say a house or a ship or a ring, that is called 'real security', with 'real' used in its *res* sense. The mortgage is the universally familiar modern example. We will encounter real security in the discussion of the contract of pledge (*pignus*). On the other hand you may take a right against a person, some friend or supporter of the principal debtor willing to make himself answerable for the same debt. We call such secondary debtors 'sureties' or 'guarantors'.

Stipulatio was the main but not the only Roman way of taking personal security. The technique was to put a question to the guarantor asking him whether he would promise *idem*, the same performance as the principal debtor. Making that promise, the guarantor would become a co-promissor with the principal. Generically, all stipulatory guarantors are thus called *adpromissores.*

The importance of the subject is marked by an unusually high degree of legislative interference, and the picture is made still more complex by the fact that the consequences of suretyship were regulated differently according as the sureties assumed their liability using the verb *spondeo*, *fidepromitto* or *fideiubeo*. *Sponsors* and *fidepromissors* were the oldest types, applicable in support only of obligations *verbis* while *fideiussors* could validly guarantee any kind of obligation. By Justinian only *fideiussio* survived. And, in accord with the post-Leo stipulation, the actual word used was immaterial.

The main practical questions which arise for the law are these: Can the surety be sued before the principal? If the surety pays, can he recover from the principal? If there are two or more sureties, can one be made to pay and, if so, can he turn against the others?

The order of attack In the classical law there was no formal reason why the creditor should not demand performance from a surety even before approaching the principal debtor. The only restraint was imposed by the law of delict. A creditor who turned unnecessarily to a solvent debtor's guarantors risked having to pay the debtor damages for contempt-*iniuria* for the injury to his personality inflicted by the imputation of insolvency. If it came to actual litigation on the debt the creditor had to proceed carefully because (there being but one obligation) joinder of issue against one party, whether principal or surety, would extinguish everything but the right to carry that issue to trial. But this extinctive effect of *litis contestatio* did not mean that the creditor had to go against the debtor first. He would be a fool to do so if the debtor were insolvent. Justinian changed this. He first abolished the rule that joinder against one released all and then, in a Novel, introduced for the sureties the 'right of correct order (*beneficium ordinis*)' by which they could insist on the debtor's being sued first.

Indemnity from principal debtor There was an ancient action, the *actio depensi*, given to sponsors by a *lex Publilia*: if the sponsor was not reimbursed in six months he could sue in such a way as to get double damages if the principal denied liability and lost. For other guarantors the normal recourse was by *actio mandati*. They would have become guarantors at the request of the debtor, and that request or commission will itself have amounted to a contract of mandate between the debtor and his guarantor. Hence the guarantor's contractual action for reimbursement. A rare case is not covered by this. Suppose the creditor approached the guarantor himself or the guarantor came forward spontaneously. These facts negative any mandate between debtor and guarantor. But there is a way in which such a guarantor can get a remedy. He has a 'right of cession of actions (*beneficium cedendarum actionum*)' by which before paying he can demand that the actions which the creditor has against the debtor, and indeed all other remedies, be assigned to him. Standing in the creditor's shoes he could then sue the debtor despite the absence of any legal relation directly between them.

Sharing the burden: contribution This is a problem which only arises when there is a plurality of guarantors. The Roman technique was not to introduce rights of contribution between co-sureties but to limit the liability of each to his *aliquot* share of the whole principal debt. The history goes back to three Republican *leges* in the early second century BC, the *lex Appuleia*, *lex Furia* and *lex Cicereia*. But it was reformed and generalised by a rescript of Hadrian. Gaius says that despite the earlier legislation *fideiussors* remained bound each for the whole sum but that *ex epistula diui Hadriani* (by an epistle of the now deified Emperor Hadrian) the creditor came under compulsion to sue each for his own share, the share being determined by dividing the debt by the number of solvent sureties (G.3.121). The application of this 'right of division (*beneficium divisionis*)' was facilitated by the extension in practice of a system introduced by the *lex Cicereia* for *sponsors* and *fidepromissors*, by which the creditor was bound to give the surety notice of the number of sureties he was taking (G.3.123). A surety was bound to claim this *beneficium* if sued. If he did not he could not afterwards complain. But if he obtained cession of actions on payment of the whole sum without litigation, it seems that he could then sue the other sureties (*qua* creditors) and that it would then be for them to claim the right of division.

5

Contracts *Consensu*

All contracts involve agreement. On close inspection that simple-looking statement can be made to suffer from historical, semantic and analytical difficulties. But it manages to survive them, at least in a rough and ready way. Contracts *consensu* differ from the rest only in requiring nothing else. They do not require the agreement to be expressed in any particular way or acted upon up to a certain point. They become binding in law when the agreement is complete. In other words the conclusion of the agreement is one and the same with the conclusion of the legal contract. The label was attached in the classical law. We have already discussed the extent to which Justinian imposed a requirement of writing and made their enforceability depend on the giving of *arra*. On views more extreme than the one taken here, 'consensual' had become a misnomer for the law of his time.

There are four contracts in this category: *emptio-venditio* (sale), *locatio-conductio* (hire), *societas* (partnership) and *mandatum* (commission, or agency). As well as being consensual, these contracts also share another important characteristic. They were all enforced by, and thus all developed within, actions which referred the 'ought' not to *strictum ius* but to *bona fides*. The question sent to the judge was, What ought the defendant to give or do *ex fide bona* (in, or on the basis of, good faith)? This characteristic of the actions worked back into the contracts themselves, decisively influencing the shape of each package of implied obligations.

1. *Emptio-Venditio* (Sale)

Sale is the commonest contract and, in that sense at least, the most important. I propose to deal with it quite fully, at the cost of cutting down the space available for the others. The jurists themselves did the same.

If you were a buyer and were driven to sue your seller, this is the *formula* which you would use:

Quod Aulus Agerius de Numerio Negidio hominem quo de agitur emit, qua de re agitur,
Whereas Aulus Agerius bought the man who is the subject of the action from Numerius Negidius, which matter is the subject of the action,

quidquid ob eam rem Numerium Negidium Aulo Agerio dare facere oportet ex fide bona,
Whatever on account of that matter Numerius Negidius ought to give to or do for Aulus Agerius in good faith,

eius iudex Numerium Negidium Aulo Agerio condemnato; si no paret absolvito.
for the value of that let the judge condemn Numerius Negidius to Aulus Agerius; if it does not appear, let him absolve.[1]

The pattern of this, the *formula* of the *actio ex empto*, was given in the edict. All you had to do was to accommodate it to your own facts, putting your own and your seller's name instead of the characters N.N. and A.A. ('Numerius Negidius' and 'Aulus Agerius': names made up from *negare*—'to deny or defend'—and *agere*—'to plead or claim') and your own *res* for the slave here supposed to have been bought. If you were seller your *formula*, now of the *actio ex vendito,* would be exactly the same with the parties turned about and 'sold' used for 'bought'.

You can see that this programme reflects a claim, in direct speech, on these lines: 'I bought the slave from you and you ought in good faith to ...' Before the *iudex* the party will have to establish the fact of the purchase and then show that, according to the implications of good faith as settled by juristic interpretation, something or other is indeed owing. It is convenient for us to abide by that division. It corresponds to the distinction between the formation of the contract and the consequences of its having been formed.

[1] Lenel, §110(111).

i. The demonstratio

'Whereas X bought the *res* from Y.' This is a pruned down version of the clause which in the language which describes the syntax of *formulae* is called the *demonstratio*. What facts have to be the case before it can be said that one person has bought something from another? What would the plaintiff have to prove? This is the same as asking, What is the legal definition of *emptio-venditio*?

The short answer is that there must have been an agreement to exchange a *res* for a price. There are four elements in that statement. I hope it is not merely perversity which makes me take them in reverse order: (i) price, (ii) *res*, (iii) to exchange, and (iv) agreement.

*A. Price (*pretium*)* Before the judge you show that you agreed to give your horse for the slave. Does that show that you bought him? In other words, is barter within the definition of sale?

This was a point disputed between the schools. The Proculians maintained that barter and sale had to be different contracts, because in sale different obligations lay upon the parties. Only by insisting on a money price could the law distinguish the buyer from the seller for the purpose of distributing these different incidents. The difficulties start with the action itself. 'Whereas he bought'—who should say that? This seems an irresistible argument. Nevertheless the Sabinians maintained the contrary. And Caelius Sabinus seems to have thought that the necessary discrimination between buyer and seller would be achieved by asking which had offered something for sale and which had bid.

Gaius states this dispute in the present tense, as though the point was still unsettled. And he loyally gives prominence to the Sabinian position. But the rule he propounds at G.3.141 is actually that of the other school: *pretium in numerata pecunia consistere debet* (the price must consist in money). The word *numerata* disappears in the translation. It does not signify that the money must be paid out. *Pecunia numerata* is just an idiom for 'cash'. The Proculian position here favoured by Gaius was also adopted by Justinian.[2] In the Digest, Paul also seems to speak of a continuing debate, but he too comes down in favour of a money price.[3]

[2] J.3.23.2.
[3] D.18.1.1 (Paul, 33 *On the Edict*).

Even those who take this position accept that sale finds its origin in barter. In D.18.1.1 (Paul, 33 *On the Edict*) Paul speaks of the inefficiency of barter as being the stimulus for the invention of money as a medium of exchange. His account seems to assume that coined and minted money is the first step, whereas the Roman evidence indicates an intermediate stage in which uncoined bronze served as the universal medium of exchange. Whence the survival of scales in formalities '*per aes et libram*'.

The decision to insist on a money price was not pushed further than necessary to achieve the discrimination for which the Proculians argued. What we call 'part-exchange' (my car plus £1,000 for a new vehicle) remained within sale. There is a hint of doubt about the transaction which is really an exchange into which one party injects a few pounds as a makeweight. Perhaps the safest thing is to say that the price had to be in money but need not be wholly in money, so long as the non-money element did not bulk so large as to destroy the money's power to distinguish buyer from seller.

Final commitment to a price naturally comes last in the negotiations for a sale. For other matters, for example the question as to who must answer for defects or repairs, will be reflected in the price. The more responsibility accepted by the seller, the higher the price. So the fixing of the price seals the entire deal. The Romans took that as the moment at which the contractual bond was formed. G.3.139:

Emptio-venditio contrahitur cum de pretio convenerit, quamvis nondum pretium numeratum sit, ac ne arra quidem data fuerit. Nam quod arrae nomine datur, argumentum est emptionis et venditionis contractae.
Sale is contracted when there has been agreement on the price even though the price has not been paid over and even if no *arra* has been given. For what is given as *arra* is evidence of sale contracted.

Then D.18.1.2.1 (Ulpian, 1 *On Sabinus*):

Sine pretio nulla venditio est: non autem pretii numeratio, sed conventio perficit sine scriptis habitam emptionem.
There is no sale without a price: and it is not the payment of the price but the agreement on the price which perfects a sale (made without writing).

Mention of *arra* in the passage from Gaius and the interpolation of *sine scriptis habitam* in the bit from Ulpian remind us of the discussion we have already had, about Justinian's innovations.[4] No need to go into that again. It is all very well to say that agreement on the price concludes the contract. But when is agreement on the price itself complete? The answer is, when the price is *certum*. G.3.140: *Pretium autem certum esse debet* (But the price must be certain).

What amounts to sufficient certainty? The requirement of certainty does not mean that the price has to be ascertained in figures, only that a *formula* must have been agreed which will yield the figures without further negotiation. There is a maxim which expresses this, though it makes circular nonsense if you look at it too carefully: *certum est quod certum reddi potest.*[5]

If I buy the sweets in a jar at 1 penny per sweet or 20 pence per quarter, weighing and counting will have to be done to reveal the price in figures. But that is all right so far as making the contract is concerned. An aunt gives you Walker's *Principles of Scottish Private Law* for Christmas, just after you had bought it for yourself. I might say 'I'll give you as much as she paid for it' or '. . . as much as you paid for yours' or '. . . half as much as she paid for it' and so on. These too are *formulae* impressed on the price which fix it sufficiently according to the Roman rules. But some of these can throw up a problem. Suppose we agree that I shall have your Christmas Walker 'for as much as your aunt paid for it' and then it turns out that she got it for nothing, a review copy. Must you give it to me for nothing? No. That would offend the rule that there can be no sale without a price. You may say that there is no substantial difference between a zero price and a very low price. Law suffers from in-built insensitivities, not to be accepted without a struggle but not worth getting too upset about. Perhaps this is one. If the *formula* yields no price, the sale is off as though upon a condition which failed. If the *formula* yields a tiny price you get no second chance. You have to go through with it.

Suppose the agreement was that you would sell at a price to be fixed by a third party: *quanti ille aestimaverit* (for the sum set by X's valuation). This caused trouble to the classics and Justinian settled the argument by one of his Fifty Decisions, C.4.38.15. There is a shorter version at J.3.23.1. He makes the sale conditional. If X names the price the

4 Above, 44–9.
5 i.e., 'is certain what can be rendered certain'.

contract becomes operative; if he fails to do it then the sale is a nullity as though no price had ever been agreed. A *decisio* supposes a contrary view. What was it? The version in the Codex reveals that some were prepared to argue that if the named X failed to act, the *formula* pressed on the price might be construed as 'a reasonable price', as though not X had been intended (one given person) but simply a representation of reason, X as a reasonable man. C.4.3.15 says, towards the end, that what had to be got rid of was 'guesswork as to whether the parties agreed the term with an eye to one certain person or to *boni viri arbitrium*, a sound man's judgement'.

The view overridden in this legislation has interesting implications for agreements to sell 'at a reasonable price', 'at a fair price'. The difficulty with the named third party was whether he should be construed to have been named as a representative of reason. The exercise of construction was difficult. But suppose the appeal to reasonableness was direct and open. The inference is that that would be certain enough to make the contract binding. These are difficult texts which seem to treat 'as much as *you* think reasonable' as indistinguishable from 'as much as you like' which clearly is too uncertain. But 'for whatever you (one of the parties) think reasonable (or fair)' may have had its defenders in classical law. If not, it does not follow that 'for whatever is reasonable', free of a party's subjectivity, would have been tarred with the same brush. Willingness to appeal to *boni viri arbitrium* in cases of third party valuation does show that open-textured stability based on such notions as reasonableness, fairness, sound judgement probably was thought sufficient. Test it this way. Would a judge have had to substitute his own ideas for those of the parties if he had to determine the price? Would he have been floored as to what they meant? I do not think so.

Classical law knew nothing of control of prices by any doctrine which required the price to be fair, the exchange of value roughly equal. The price had to be *verum*, genuinely intended to be demanded as opposed to merely colourable, pretended. A transaction dressed up as a sale but actually a gift would be void. But a genuine sale for a very cheap price or a very expensive price would be upheld. Only in very late law, in an attempt to curb exploitation of the weak by greedy *potentes* (magnates), did there emerge a doctrine of *iustum pretium* based on what was called *laesio enormis*. The object was to protect the weak who were being bought out of their land. They could set aside the contract if the price was less than 50 per cent of the market rate.

B. Res *(subject-matter, or thing)* At D.18.1.8 *pr.*[6] Pomponius says '*Nec emptio nec venditio sine re quae veneat potest intellegi* (You can never make out a purchase or a sale if there is no thing being sold).' This principle must be approached with caution. Sale is always of something. It must have a subject-matter. But if you read the requirement of a *res quae veneat* too literally and concretely you can go wrong. A carpenter can sell 'the next chair I make', and the contract is good even though the *res* is as yet only a twinkle in his eye. And it is possible, if an exercise of construction shows that the parties so intended, for the subject-matter to be no more than a chance or speculation. 'All the gold in your land.' None is found. You should not conclude that the sale is necessarily void.

Just as the price, so the *res* had to be certain. If you complained that the defendant had sold you 'part of his field' or 'some of his wine' you would merely reveal that your negotiations still had some way to go. But what counted as sufficiently certain? Alternatives were all right. If you showed you had bought 'Daisy or Buttercup' the sale was valid and, if nothing was said to the contrary, the seller could pick which to give. And selections from a given stock were all right: 'Twenty litres of olive oil from your vat' or 'A thousand bricks from the clay on your land'. But what about descriptions which failed to state the *corpus* from which the *res* was to come? Suppose we agree a price for 10,000 kilos of Egyptian grain, or just of top quality grain. Is this sale? The dominant view is that it is not. If your *formula* said 'Whereas A. A. bought from N.N. such and such a quantity of grain', Numerius Negidius would be able to object that the sale was generic and as such no sale at all in the law. No *emptio generis*. The argument is chiefly *e silentio*. Respectful scepticism is perhaps the best position. If I take cloth to a tailor to have made up into a suit, that is hire; but if I order the suit and do not myself provide the cloth, that is sale. But it is not said that he must have the cloth at the time of the order. So the contract for the suit is, in its own way, by generic description. And where is the line between '100 litres of Bordeaux Supérieur', '100 bottles of Château Cissac 1975' and 'a litre from your vat'?

[6] Pomponius, 9 *On Sabinus*.

Suppose the *res* on which the parties focused their attention never comes into existence: 'The yield of this olive tree's next harvest', 'This girl's baby when it's born', 'the next catch of fish'. There is no fixed answer. It depends on the right construction of the deal. Did they mean 'the yield if there is one' or 'the hope of a yield'? If the former, *emptio rei speratae*, the sale is conditional on there being some *res*; if the latter, *emptio spei*, the *spes* (the hope, or gamble) is the *res*, so that the contract binds even if no yield ever happens. If the seller interferes with the risk, as for example if he will not till the soil, he becomes liable for that. Hence, if you buy next year's crop and I refuse to sow or tend it, I become liable *ex empto* notwithstanding there being no *res*.

What if the *res* never existed? You sell me your sunken treasure ship out in the bay. There is no such ship. You have confused it with another case, without dishonesty. The easy answer is to say 'no *res*, no sale', but the solutions applied to *emptio spei* and *emptio rei speratae* suggest an exercise of construction. Did I buy an adventure, including in the gamble even the existence of the ship? If yes, I must pay, and can claim nothing for my expenses. If we assumed the existence of the ship, outside the gamble, either its existence was a neutral condition or you undertook responsibility for its existing. If the latter I must be able to sue you, for interfering with the risk. I will say 'whereas I bought the ship . . .' even though the ship never was there at all. This is a bit of a guess. The texts are not clear.

What if the *res* existed but perished before the contract was conducted? The sale appears to be void. D.18.1.15 *pr.* (Paul, 5 *On Sabinus*):

Et si consensum fuerit in corpus, id tamen in rerum natura ante venditionem esse desierit nulla emptio est.
Even if there is agreement on the physical identity of the thing, the purchase is void if it ceases to exist before the sale.

There are two kinds of difficulty about this proposition. What constitutes 'ceasing to exist'. Some cases are easy. A book which has gone up in flames no longer exists. Homes leave the land behind. Fruit which goes bad is still there though suitable for the compost heap not the table. The Roman texts do not come up with any very satisfactory test. We will recur to this under 'risk'. Secondly, what is the status of the proposition? Is it an inflexible dogma? Or just the commonest construction, in the absence of contrary intents? If it were a dogma it would be impossible within the contract of sale for the seller to warrant the continued existence of the *res*. So probably nullity simply reflects the normal case. If you sell me the horse at home in your field, the usual construction will be that our deal is conditional on the existence of the horse. Only in exceptional circumstances will I gamble on its existence (i.e. agree to pay whether it is alive or dead) or you warrant its existence (agree to pay my losses arising from your non-delivery).

Suppose the slave you bought turns out to be free. Or the land turns out to be dedicated to the Gods, as for example a burial place. These things exist but they are removed from commerce and ownership. So in a sense they do not exist, not for business purposes. Can you substantiate the *demonstratio* of the *actio ex empto* so as to get a remedy that way, or will the defendant be able to answer that the sale is void? The original position seems to have been that the rule was void if the *res* was *extra commercium*. But that reduced the range of remedies. At least in the case of the free man the classics therefore favoured making the sale valid and the seller liable. The position of other *res extra commercium* was later assimilated to that of the free man, probably only by Justinian. The assimilation is not perfect, though the Institutes assert that it is intended to be (J.3.23.5):

Loca sacra vel religiosa, item publica, veluti forum, basilicam, frustra quis sciens emit quas tamen si pro privatis vel profanis, deceptus a venditore, emerit, habebit actionem ex empto, quod non habere ei liceat ut consequatur quod sua interest deceptum non esse. Idem iuris est si hominem liberum pro servo emerit.

Knowingly to buy sacred and religious places, or public ones such as a forum or basilica, is merely to beat the air. But if you are misled by the seller and buy them as private or secular you will have an action *ex empto*. The ground of the action will be, that you are not being allowed to possess, and the measure of recovery is your interest in not having been misled. The same law applies where you buy a free man as a slave.

What this does is to treat sales of *res extra commercium* on the model not of *res extinctae* but *res alienae*. That is, the analogy of non-existent things is given up, and the analogy of things belonging to third parties is followed instead. We have not looked at *res alienae*.

Suppose you sell me a cow belonging to your neighbour. Even if you mancipate her to me she will still belong to your neighbour, though if all the circumstances are right maybe I will usucapt her after a year has passed. During the year he reclaims her, as is his right. I must come against you. Can you say the sale was void? No. D.18.1.28 (Ulpian, 41 *On Sabinus*):

Rem alienam distrahere quem posse nulla dubitatio est: nam emptio est et venditio: sed res emptori auferri potest.

There is no doubt at all that anyone can sell something belonging to another. Indeed there is then purchase and sale: but the *res* can be taken away from the buyer.

So the buyer cannot keep the *res* but does have his contract to rely upon against the seller. We will recur to the nature of the contractual remedy when we consider the obligations generated by the contract described in the *demonstratio*.

By way of summary, note that we have considered a series of, as it were, special cases or problem cases in relation to the *res vendita*. These labels will serve to call them to mind: (a) *emptio generis*, (b) *emptio spei* and *rei speratae*, (c) *emptio rei extinctae*, (d) *emptio rei extra commercium*, (e) *emptio rei alienae*.

C. Exchange We said that sale is an agreement to exchange a *res* for a price. At this point the focus falls on 'to exchange'. In 99 cases out of a hundred what happens is that the seller gives up ownership of the *res* and gets the price instead. Is it completely safe therefore to substitute for 'to exchange a *res*' the words 'to give ownership of a *res*'? Technically it is not quite right.

First, the Roman seller is not understood as undertaking to make the buyer owner. It is not part of the definition of sale that ownership must pass and it is not part of the seller's package of obligations that he must make it pass. After all we have seen that sale of a *res* belonging to a third party is valid.

The seller's part is to convey the thing. That is, to do what is necessary to transfer such ownership if any as he has, by *traditio* or *mancipatio*. These conveyances are subject to the maxim *nemo dat quod non habet*. They cannot constitute new titles in alienees. If the alienor is owner, they serve to carry that ownership across. If not, nothing happens. Conveyance is not necessarily successful. Bearing that in mind, we can say that for 'to exchange a *res* for a price' we should say 'to convey a *res* in exchange for a price'.

Secondly, it still counts as sale if the buyer is already owner and the transaction is intended only to obtain possession or to obtain release from a condition under which his ownership is threatened (D.18.1.34.4;[7] D.18.1.6.1).[8] These holdings are made against the background of the rule that purchase of one's own property is a nullity (D.18.1.6 *pr.*)[9] These rare cases make it unsafe to say even that the seller must do what he can to divest himself of ownership.

The negative proposition is certainly true, that the transaction cannot be sale if the seller is to retain ownership, though he may retain a lesser interest such as a usufruct. There is nothing wrong with a sale of a farm or flock *deducto usufructu*, with a usufruct reserved for, say, three years.

Perhaps it is safe to say that the seller's part is so to convey the *res* to the buyer so that he retains no interest in it, save such interest less than ownership as is reserved to him. This is what one is driven to by the need to avoid unintended exclusions and distortions. The common sense version is always too narrow. The artificial version is repugnant in other, less dangerous ways.

If I give £20 for one week's use of your car, that is hire, not sale. Similarly if I hire your services as a mechanic. We do not say that I buy the slice of time in your car or your own labour-over-time. If we wanted to compress sale and hire into one we could take that line. But we do not. And nor did the Romans. The two are kept apart by declining to see enjoyment-over-time or labour-over-time as an independent *res*. All the same the line between the sale and hire could be very tricky. The difficult cases are most conveniently kept till we come to *locatio-conductio* itself.

D. Agreement Before the judge your opponent may say that, though you have described a transaction within the notion of sale, he never agreed to it. If that is true he never sold and you never bought. We need not deal with the simplest versions of this. For example, he may maintain that he never dealt with you at all or that he flatly rejected the terms which you say he accepted. The subtler versions of the same

[7] Paul, 33 *On the Edict*.
[8] Pomponius, 9 *On Sabinus*.
[9] Pomponius, 9 *On Sabinus*.

thing are those where he says he was mistaken or that the agreement was only conditional. I shall take conditions first.

(a) *Conditions*. Suppose we agree to the sale of a horse at such and such a price 'if he wins the race next Tuesday'. Before Tuesday I tell you that I have changed my mind. And then he wins, and you sue me. There are two views of the matter: no contract until the outcome is known, or contract binding but suspended till the outcome is known. On both views if the condition fails there is no contract: once the horse has lost, the deal is off. The difference is as to the situation in the run-up to the fulfilment of the condition. If there is no contract the parties can get out; if there is a suspended contract they must abide the event.

There are traces of the first view but it did not prevail. In the classical law a conditional agreement was binding. The presence of the condition had an effect on the rules about risk but did not allow the parties to change their minds. They were bound, at least in the sense that only failure of the condition would release them. What if a party took steps to make sure that the condition failed? For example, I refuse to allow the horse to run in the race. There is a doctrine, usually labelled *pro impleta*, whereby a condition can be regarded as having been fulfilled if frustrated by one party. But this only works when the condition can be waived by the plaintiff without damaging his own interest. 'I will buy if you redeem the mortgage.' Clearly I am never going to waive that condition, should you refuse the redemption. If the construction of the transaction is such that you are taken to have promised to race the horse or redeem the mortgage I can have an action for breach of that term.

Not all conditions are suspensive. In that sale of the horse we might have used words, the proper construction of which would be that the sale was to come into immediate effect subject to being resolved if the horse lost the race. The business of unpicking the legal consequences in that event is complex, and the details are disputed. But it is more obvious in the case of a resolutive condition that there is no question of withdrawal *pendente condicione*: the contract is pure, subject to a question for the future.

(b) *Mistake*. This is always a difficult topic, chiefly because the inclination to offer relief to the mistaken encounters a fear that people generally will abuse such relief, concocting mistakes *ex post* and upsetting all kinds of transactions as soon as they begin to feel disappointed. And, distinct from this, there is another fear peculiar to commercial life, namely that the market will not work if those with bad judgement are not driven to the wall. The premise being, that the avoidance of mistakes is precisely the quality which marks the successful and efficient businessmen. So there are pressures both ways, for and against relief, and that is what makes for puzzles and artificialities in the law.

Sale requires agreement (*consensus*) in order to come into being. It follows that a party who can show that there was still disagreement between him and the other (*dissensus*) shows that no contract was made. If he is saying 'You know perfectly well that I never agreed to sell for £20,' he does not seem to be raising an issue of mistake. But if he is saying 'Though I see you thought differently, in fact I never did agree to sell for £20,' then words such as 'mistake', 'misunderstanding', 'error' and so on do appear to be appropriate. But *dissensus* is more exact. The word does not matter, so long as the idea is right. Which is, 'We differed,' 'We had different views of the matter.' And this must be contrasted with vitiated *consensus* where one party says 'I thought so too.' It is the reaction of the second party which distinguishes *dissensus* from flawed *consensus*. 'Well, I didn't!' makes it *dissensus*. 'That was my view too!' makes it *consensus* on the basis of a shared mistake.

The Roman approach made the contract void if there was *dissensus* as to *res* (I meant Daisy, you were thinking of Buttercup), price (I meant £100, you thought £50) and *negotium*, the nature of the deal (I meant to sell, you intended to hire). But difficulties were felt when there was *dissensus* as to qualities of the *res* (I thought it was fire-resistant, you did not). It is here that relief for mistake can threaten bargains and also here that mistake can present itself as flawed *consensus* as well as *dissensus*. The opinions of the jurists seem to have varied from a determination to give no relief at all to a willingness to avoid the contract for a very fundamental mistake. Ulpian appears to have favoured relief for fundamental mistake of quality, subject however to the spongy notion of fundamentality being crisped up by a mechanical test, itself not very satisfactory: was there *error in substantia*, mistake as to the materials? The leading text is D.18.1.9–15, part of which is D.18.1.9.2 (Ulpian, 28 *On Sabinus*) which reads as follows:

If there is no error as to the thing itself (*si in ipso corpore non erratur*) but rather a mistake as to *substantia*, is there *emptio-venditio* or not? As where vinegar is sold for wine, bronze for gold or lead, or something else similar to silver, for silver. Marcellus in book 6 of his *Digesta* says the sale holds good, because there is *consensus* as to the thing itself though error as to the *materia*. I myself agree as to the wine since the essence is the same, at least if the vinegar was indeed soured wine. Yet if it was not sound wine but vinegar *ab initio*, one thing would seem to have been sold for another. For the rest I think the sale is void as often as there is a mistake as to material.

It seems that he took the view that the same test should apply to cases of flawed *consensus* as to *dissensus* (D.18.1.14).[10] That seems sensible. There is only one reason for handling flawed *consensus* differently, namely that relief is somewhat less contrary to the nature of bargaining when both share the same mistake. On the other hand it is difficult to make much of that since it lies too easily with the other party to choose whether to say he shared the mistake or knew the truth all along.

When is it in a party's interest to try to avoid the contract for mistake? Usually it is a ploy used by a buyer to defeat an action for payment and non-acceptance. After he has found out the truth. Sometimes a seller will want the contract void so as to keep silver he thought was lead; or to resist a possible claim for damages if silver turned out to be lead. This all happens within the actions on the sale. There are other contexts. There may be a question of recovering a price already paid by *condictio* or of arguing in a *vindicatio* that property in the *res* never passed.

ii. The intentio

'Whatever in that account Y ought to give to or do for X in good faith . . .' This is the *intentio* of the *formula*, the part which expresses the plaintiff's principal contention. Up to now we have been talking about the *demonstratio*. The question has been, What facts serve to substantiate the assertion that a sale has happened? Now we are concerned with the consequences of that fact. For the moment we will retain the viewpoint of the buyer's action rather than the seller's. What is it that a seller ought on account of a sale to give or do in good faith? Or, What is the package of obligations on which a buyer can rely?

A. Before delivery The seller's obligations are to take care of the *res* till delivery and to deliver it. Suppose I buy a horse from you. Knowing that you are going to give it up to me in a day or two, you mistreat it. You make it gallop for miles and miles. Until it drops. Of course, you did not mean that to happen. You just stopped taking care. And now

[10] Ulpian, 28 *On Sabinus*.

you will be liable for non-delivery, just as though you had wantonly changed your mind.

It is always unhelpful to talk of an obligation to take care unless mention is made of a standard. Does he have to be very careful (to take all the precautions that can be taken) or moderately careful (to take such precautions as are taken by the generality of mankind)? And so on. There are many ways in which standards can be expressed. The common law continually invokes 'the reasonable man' and, slightly less prominently 'the prudent businessman'. One standard used by the Romans was that of the *bonus paterfamilias*. Literally he is a 'good head of the family', but 'prudent property-owner' probably catches the idea better. And in fact the modern reasonable man is taken to behave much in the same way as the notional *paterfamilias* who set this Roman standard.

The Roman seller certainly had to show before delivery of the *res* the care which would have been shown by a *bonus paterfamilias*. He would be liable if damage or destruction happened for want of that standard of care. Just possibly the classical law expected even more of him. He may have had to answer for *custodia* (safe-keeping). If so he would have been liable, whether actually careless or not, if damage or destruction happened, unless they happened because of *vis maior* (irresistible force) such as flood, earthquake, robbery. For example, one who had to answer for *custodia* remained liable if the *res* was lost by theft (as opposed to robbery, which is theft with violence) even if he had taken such precaution against thieves as a prudent proprietor would have taken.

Suppose that a disaster occurred despite the seller's having discharged his obligations of care. The horse was struck by lightning. Can the buyer sue for failure to deliver? He cannot. To say otherwise would make the obligation to deliver absolute and the obligation of care strict. For events of this kind the buyer has no more cause for complaint than if he caught measles. It is just bad luck. He will have to pay and get nothing. Just as though his own horse had been struck rather than a horse destined by contract to become his. But there is a qualification. The disaster must have happened after the point at which the risk (*periculum*) passes to the buyer. In most cases the moment at which the risk passes is the same as the moment at which the contract becomes binding. But not in all. An excursus on the risk of accidental damage would unbalance the discussion at this point. I shall deal with it as a separate topic later.

Suppose that the disaster occurs outside the seller's area of responsibility but is also not an act of God. As, for instance, if a third party robs the seller of the horse. Here the buyer has no claim against the seller for his failure to get the horse, but he will want to sue the third party. The seller is therefore put under an obligation to assign the actions against the third party. He has, so to say, to deliver the actions instead of the horse. And he will be liable *ex empto* if he does not.

One way of summarising this is to say that the seller is liable if he fails to deliver the *res* and/or actions arising in relation to its damage or destruction; and, on the other side of the penny, is not liable despite failure to deliver either *res* or actions if disaster overtook it even though he discharged his obligation to look after it between contract and delivery.

B. *After delivery* There are two things that a buyer chiefly fears. A bad title. And latent defects. Suppose the horse I bought from you turns out to belong to a third party. Or suppose it has a sickness which weakens it and stops it being able to work.

Before dealing specifically with these it is convenient to distinguish two different bases of complaint. There is the fault (or *mala fides*) basis and the warranty basis. The fault basis of complaint rests directly on the words of the *formula* which suppose that the seller must behave with good faith. The judge is actually asked what the seller ought to do *ex fide bona*. And this means that there is a general liability for *mala fides* as settled and explained by the jurists. Further, this liability is non-excludable. Because of being built into the action. Broadly speaking, the basis of complaint means establishing shabby, unconscientious behaviour on the part of seller, usually by showing that he knew that the buyer was in for trouble.

By contrast the warranty basis of complaint is not dependent on proof of fault. It simply saddles a seller with responsibility for a given state of affairs without imputing any disreputable conduct to him. For example, if a modern seller promises that his carpets will survive under normal condition of fair wear and tear for five years, the reason why he is made liable when they have to be replaced after two is not that he dealt shabbily (though he may have done) but that he promised to answer for their durability. Express promises are the easy case of no-fault liability, but the *natura contractus* may also be understood to impose the same kind of liability on sellers who do not expressly undertake it.

In one respect the contrast between these two bases of liability is false. For both are referable to the *bona fides* on which the action is based. That is, where a warranty liability is recognised the reason is that in those circumstances the defendant 'ought in good faith' to accept responsibility irrespective of fault. One way of putting this is to say that that 'ought in good faith' always requires the defendant to make good the effects of actual bad faith but sometimes requires him to honour liabilities whose origin does not lie in unconscientious behaviour.

(a) Bad title

The seller who knows he is selling a *res aliena* is liable for his *mala fides*. For the rest a warranty liability did develop, but not in the form of a liability specifically for failing to make the buyer owner. It was not a warranty of title but a warranty against eviction. Suppose you discovered that the horse which I sold and mancipated to you was not mine and hence not yours. If I knew, you could sue me at once, for my bad faith. If I did not know, you could not make me liable unless you were evicted from possession by the third party.

The history of the warranty against eviction seems to go like this. The conveyance of *mancipatio* carried a built-in warranty. At least from the Twelve Tables the alienee by *mancipatio* could bring a special action (*actio auctoritatis*) for double the price if he was evicted. Then, during the Republic, the practice developed of imitating the regime for *mancipatio* by taking stipulations against the danger of eviction. These would only be necessary where *mancipatio* was not used. And in the event of eviction the action brought would be on the stipulation, not on the sale. Then, the early classics drew on the general liability for bad faith in this way: they affirmed that good faith required the giving of these stipulations, so that a seller who did not enter into the conventional undertakings was by that fact itself guilty of a breach. Finally, but before the end of the classical period, the conventional undertakings were regarded as having been given unless there was an agreement between the parties to the contrary. If there was a *pactum de non praestanda evictione* (a pact against answering for eviction) the buyer was remitted to the fault-basis of complaint. Without such a pact the seller was liable if eviction happened.

(b) Latent defects

By Justinian's time the picture is of a general warranty against serious latent defects. But the development is a good deal more complex than in the case of eviction.

There is a preliminary problem about the meaning of the phrase 'latent defects'. 'Latent' is the easier part. It means 'hidden' or 'not discoverable by such inspection as a buyer could reasonably be expected to make'. But 'defect' is not so easy. Corn which is contaminated may still be fit for animals to eat. A spear which is brittle may serve very well as a clothes prop. Cloth which is useless for making clothes may be all right as rags or stuffing for furniture. And so on. These are extreme cases. The wine-snob may class as undrinkable bottles which others drain with pleasure. The Rolls Royce mentality regards the ordinary version of everything as vicious. So what is a defect? It is not safe to say that it is a bad quality which, if known, would have reduced the price. Too many sales could be upset if it were a ground for complaint that in use the cooking-pan or pot showed less well than on the seller's shelf. You are driven towards the notion of merchantability. Is the bad quality such that, declared openly, it would prevent the thing's being bought and sold under the description and categorisation under which it was sold? Does the defect take the thing out of the commercial category in which it was sold? There is no general test in the texts.

The problem addressed in the last paragraph concerns the case in which no special qualities are ascribed to the *res* by the seller. If by contrast he says that the slave is literate or skilful as a painter, or that the timber is suitable for boat-building, or that the pots are fire-resistant, then there can be no argument but that the thing is defective if it lacks the quality ascribed to it.

(i) *Warranty liability*. You will remember that this term is being used to denote liability independent of bad faith or fault of any kind. What was the position in classical law under the *actio ex empto*? That question implies two exclusions for the time being: the aediles' jurisdiction and the law of Justinian. Suppose two concrete cases: corn which, contaminated by poison, kills all the buyer's chickens, and a chair which, badly glued up, becomes wobbly after a few days' use.

The first question is, Did the seller undertake to be answerable for the quality in question? Did he give a warranty that the corn was suitable for chickens or that the chair was well made? If he agreed to be liable he will be liable. D.19.1.11.1 (Ulpian, 32 *On the Edict*):

The first thing to have in mind is that it is the liabilities agreed by the parties (*quod praestari convenit*) which above all are passed upon in this trial [*sc.* under the *actio ex empto*]. For it is a trial based on good faith. And nothing agrees better with good faith than that there should be fulfilled whatever was intended between the contracting parties (*quam id praestari, quod inter contrahentes actum est*). But in the absence of agreement the liabilities will be those which the nature of the transaction puts within the scope of this trial (*quae naturaliter insunt huius iudicii potestate*).

So the position of the seller who accepted liability for the quality is clear. The only difficulty will be in deciding whether he did accept it. There is a line between affirming the existence of a quality and accepting liability for it. But it seems that the practical difficulty of deciding which the seller had done (if he had done either) became less by the end of the classical period. For the high classical jurists seem to have been prepared to treat a seriously intended representation, as opposed to mere puffery, as a warranty. They reached this position by developing the notion of fault-based liability to the point at which fault was inferred from the making of the representation, that is, by so denaturing the requirement of fault that the liability became warranty-based. D.19.1.13.3 (Ulpian, 32 *On the Edict*):

But what if the seller did not know that the slave was a thief and asserted that he was of good character and trustworthy and sold him for a high price? Is he liable *ex empto*? And I would think that he is (*et putem teneri*). But he did not know! Yet he ought not to have been so quick to make assertions about something outside his knowledge (*sed non debuit facile quae ignorabat adseverare*). Thus, there is not much difference between this seller and one who knows but keeps quiet: for the one who knows ought to warn the buyer that the slave is a thief while this seller ought not to be quick with rash ascriptions.

Also D.18.1.43 *pr.* (Florentinus, 8 *Institutes*):

Things which sellers say to commend their wares do not put them under any obligation provided they are obvious (*si palam appareant*). As where the seller says the slave is fine-looking or the house is well built. But if he says the slave is literate or has some skill, he ought to answer for those qualities. For by reason of these statements he sells for more.

Here Ulpian is cautious, arguing from the stronger case of fault-based liability represented by the seller who knows he is selling a thief. Florentinus, who may actually have been rather earlier than Ulpian, is more firm: the seller must make good statements which enabled him to sell for a higher price. It is not completely clear whether the 'obviousness' which he says lets a seller off is as to the quality or the nature of the statement as mere blurb. *Domum bene aedificatam* suggests the latter. It might be difficult to see the quality of the work. But nobody takes any notice of the rubbish in estate agents' advertisements.

So the seller is liable if he accepts liability. And, by the late classical period, he was taken to accept liability if he asserted the existence of a quality in circumstances calculated to induce reliance and raise the price. But what if he said nothing at all about the quality? Did the *natura contractus* impose any liability on him, independent of fault?

Now we are concerned with the case in which the seller said nothing about the corn or the chair. The buyer just came and said he wanted twenty measures of 'that corn' or that he would give so much money for 'that chair'. And the seller obliged. This is difficult and uncertain. There is virtually no doubt that the texts have been managed, in order to give effect to Justinian's views. If you take an extreme view of the degree of interpolation you can come quite respectably to the conclusion that the classical position, outside the aedilician jurisdiction, was *caveat emptor*: 'let the buyer beware', and 'let the buyer insist on express terms'. On the other hand there is some evidence of a doctrine to the effect that goods must conform to the description under which they were sold. It is possible that the owner of the poisoned chickens could have maintained an *actio ex empto* on the warranty principle while the buyer of the wobbly chair could not. On the ground that poisoned feed is not feed at all while a chair which quickly goes wobbly is nonetheless a chair despite being a bad one. In short, the seller ought *ex fide bona* to answer for the goods being what he held them out to be. A great deal depends on whether one accepts as genuine what is said about Labeo's opinion in D.19.1.6.4 (Pomponius, 9 *On Sabinus*):

If you have sold me a certain container (*vas aliquod*) and have said that it takes a certain amount or holds a certain weight, I shall sue you *ex empto* should it prove smaller (*si minus praestes*). But if you have sold me a container with the assurance that it does not leak (*ita ut adfirmares integrum*) then, if it does leak, you will be answerable to me even for what I thereby lose. On the other hand if the intention behind the agreement was not that you should provide a sound container (*si vero non id actum sit, ut integrum praestes*) you must answer only for bad faith [according to Sabinus] (*dolum malum dumtaxat praestare te debere*). Labeo thinks the opposite. He maintains that the only correct approach is that, unless there is an intention expressed to the contrary, the container must be sound (*nisi in contrarium id actum sit, omnimodo integrum praestari debeat*). And that is right.

Here the square brackets round Sabinus show that he does not figure in the Latin. There is an accusative and infinitive construction which in commentaries *ad Sabinum* usually indicates an opinion of Sabinus unless the contrary appears. And then there is the opposite view of Labeo which meets with Ulpian's *et est verum*. Labeo seems to be saying that in a sale of a vessel or container (*vas aliquod*) the seller must answer for its not being leaky unless the opposite intention can be inferred from the conduct of the parties, as for instance by the buyer's making clear that he only wanted it for its ornamental value or only to store apples in. Which is as much as to say that, absent such an intention, a vessel must be able to hold liquids in order to come within that description. If you believe that Labeo held that view you can infer that he would have said that corn is also not corn if it is contaminated with poison.

Similar to *The Leaky Container* is *The Not So New Clothes*. This text runs into deeper problems as it proceeds, but the first few lines appear to confirm what we have seen of Labeo's views. D.18.1.45 (Marcianus, 4 *Rules*):

In his book called *Posteriora*, Labeo writes that, in the case in which a man buys, as new, clothes which are actually '*interpola*', Trebatius's opinion was that so long as the buyer was unaware that the clothes were '*interpola*' the seller must make good the buyer's interest.

'*Interpola*' is left in Latin because it is difficult to translate. It may just mean 'second-hand'. But more likely it means 'made up from cloth cut from discarded clothes'. In which case the nearest analogy in our experience is buying tyres which turn out to be retreads. Either way, the trouble is much the same. The buyer finds worn patches, the life already gone out of the cloth. And again it is Labeo who favours liability.

This is only part of the evidence and, as you will see, even this is not unequivocal. Perhaps the safest summary is conditional. If there was any implied warranty liability in classical law, it was on these lines: the seller was bound to answer for the *res* being what it purported to be, having the characteristics and qualities definitively necessary for it to qualify for its description. Vessels must hold liquids in order to be vessels, unless proclaimed to be 'for dry goods only'; and clothes must be made of new cloth unless proclaimed to be cast-offs or re-makes.

(ii) *Fault liability*. Obviously, the less warranty liability you are able to believe in, the more important becomes the fault liability. People do not embrace the burden of proving bad faith unless they have to or unless there is some considerable advantage in doing so. If there was no warranty liability, or none except such as was accepted by the seller, then clearly buyers had to turn to fault liability. Even if there was a warranty liability there may have been advantages in proving bad faith. Even in classical law the damages may have been higher, as they certainly were under Justinian. And it may have been possible to reach defects less fundamental in character than those within the warranty liability. Also conformity to good faith was non-excludable.

In the previous section we dealt first with the seller who ascribed qualities to the *res* and then with the one who said nothing but simply held the *res* out as having a particular identity or description. The same division can be made here.

The seller who knowingly makes false statements of quality is liable unless they are obvious puffery. This follows *a fortiori* from what will be said about knowing silence. And we have already seen that in D.19.1.13.3 Ulpian argues towards a warranty liability for innocent statements from the case of statements made in bad faith.[11] The objection he puts to his cautious conclusion for liability is 'But he did not know!' It is obvious that had he known, there would have been no hesitation.

If it is right that only the late classics managed to assimilate misrepresentations and warranties (i.e. mere statements and statements accepting liability for what was said), the only recourse in all the earlier period

[11] Ulpian, 32 *On the Edict*; above, 83.

for misrepresentation will have been by proof of fraud. In other words, there will have been no liability for misrepresentation as such. Only a liability for *mala fides*, one way of incurring which was to make knowingly false statements about the goods being sold.

Fraudulent silence is the more interesting case. This happens where the seller knows that the buyer is going to suffer a disappointment in the *res* but does not speak out to warn him. There is no doubt that this kind of reticence did give rise to liability. But there is great difficulty in making out the scope of the duty of disclosure. The reason is obvious. On an extreme view the duty would oblige the seller to undo all the advantage of his bargain. You never met a shopkeeper who thought he had to tell you that you would get the same thing cheaper and better round the corner. Clearly a line has to be drawn. And it is not at all clear where it was drawn.

The operation of this liability for non-disclosure is illustrated in sales of land when legal defects appear after conveyance. Suppose you buy land from me and find afterwards that there is a right of way over it. You can bring the *actio ex empto* if you can show that I knew of the adverse servitude and did not tell you. D.19.1.1.1 (Ulpian, 28 *On Sabinus*):

A seller will not escape the *actio ex empto* if he has concealed a servitude when he knew it was owed, provided only that the buyer did not know of it. For everything done contrary to *bona fides* comes into the *actio ex empto*.

On the other hand if I myself was innocent you can only complain if I accepted liability for the land's being clear of servitudes, which I probably would have done, if at all, by using the conventional phrase '*optimus maximusque*'. D.18.1.59 (Celsus, 8 *Digest*):

When you sold farm land, you did not say '*ita ut optimus maximusque*' (subject to the term 'best and greatest'). It is correct, as Quintus Mucius held, that the land must be made over as it actually is and not free from burdens (*non liberum sed qualis esset*). And the same applies to urban holdings.

The picture here is this: the buyer's only hopes of redress lie in an express warranty or, failing that, in fault-based liability. There is no implied warranty-liability.

From a much earlier period Cicero gives an example which has a modern flavour. It concerns the sale of a house subject to a demolition order. Only the reason for the order is antique. Cicero, *De Officiis*, 3.66–67:

Titus Claudius Centumalus had a house on the Mons Caelius. Its height obstructed the auspices. The augurs wanted to conduct an augury on the citadel and therefore ordered him to demolish the house. He then advertised it for sale and it was bought by Publius Calpurnius Lanarius. The augurs served the same notice on him. Calpurnius demolished the house, but when he discovered that Claudius had advertised it after getting the augurs' demolition order he took Claudius to law on the formulary issue 'whatever he ought to do for him in good faith'. Marcus Cato . . . pronounced this judgement as *iudex*: 'Since, in the course of selling, the seller knew of this matter and did not reveal it he ought to make good the buyer's loss.' Hence his opinion was that good faith required that the buyer should be told of a *vitium* known to the seller.

How far did this liability for *mala fide* non-disclosure go? That is, what limits were put on it to stop the erosion of every advantage in a bargain? There seem to be three possibilities. First, that it applied only to legal defects in land. Second, that it applied within the *actio ex empto* to the same defects as were covered, within the aediles' jurisdiction, by the aedilician edict. Third, that it applied to all cases in which, according to prevailing commercial morality, suppression of the truth would have been regarded as immoral. This third possibility is loosest and leaves most to the judge, but I incline to the view that it may be the right answer. We have seen, in the case of *The Leaking Container*, that Sabinus thought, contrary to Labeo, that the seller should be liable only for *dolus malus*, and one can infer that he meant that the seller would be liable if he knowingly sold a leaky container to a customer who expected one which did not leak. If that is what he thought the first and second possibilities must be wrong. On the other hand it is difficult to imagine Sabinus saying that the seller of a not very well made chair must explain to his buyer that it would probably not last very long. This is much spongier that it should be. But undeniably the position is unclear.

(iii) *An overview*. This is by way of summary of the last two parts, making the picture clearer than it really is. How should the dissatisfied buyer phase his inquiry? Perhaps in this way. First, did the seller ascribe qualities to the *res*? If so, he may have warranted or merely represented.

If he warranted, he is liable without fault. If he merely represented, he will be liable if he knew that his statement was untrue (unless it was obvious puffery); and towards the end of the classical period he became liable as though he had warranted, irrespective of fault. Because warranties and misrepresentations were assimilated. Until then the innocent misrepresentation triggered no liability as such, i.e. unless the seller would have been liable even if he had not uttered it. Second, if the seller ascribed no qualities to the thing, he may yet be liable in one of two ways. Either he may fall within the doctrine of dishonest silence, incurring fault-liability for dishonest non-disclosure, or he may fall within an implied warranty liability for defects so serious as to deprive the *res* of the identity under which it purported to be sold. Both these doctrines are of uncertain scope. Dishonest silence certainly applies to legal defects in land and may find its limit merely in prevailing notions of commercial morality. The implied warranty applied only to defects essential to the description of the thing, few of which would not be patent.

(iv) *The aediles' edict.* This edict supported an action superintended by the aediles themselves, not by the praetor. Its life was thus separate from that of the *actio ex empto*.

The scheme of the edict was to impose a warranty liability for undeclared defects. For slaves, the seller was to declare all disease or defect (*morbum* and *vitium*) and certain listed non-physical vices (fugitive, wanderer, noxally liable, capital offences, sent into arena, suicide attempts). Then, if the slave turned out contrary to what had been declared, or to what had been *dictum promissumve* in circumstances such that the *dictum* or *promissum* ought to be made good, two remedies were available. Within six months, an action for redhibition, a giving and taking back; and within twelve an action for reduction of the price. Then, in relation to beasts of burden (*iumenta*), similar provisions for disease and defect. The edict is said to be designed to counter fraud. But liability under it is not a fault liability. The plaintiff buyer only has to prove that the *res* was not as declared. So fraud was countered by giving a remedy against fraudulent and innocent alike. Patent defects and very trivial defects were ignored. For slaves the defects within the edict were those which interfered with his work and service (*usus et ministerium*).

(v) *Justinian's law.* He merged the *actio ex empto* and the aediles' edict into one body of law, making the aedilician principles apply throughout, even to property other than the slaves and animals originally contemplated. This was achieved by interpolation. Which means that we cannot easily see what, if anything, had already been done by his time. It is this interference in the texts which makes the whole topic so difficult. It may yet be demonstrable that the absorption of aedilician principles into the *actio ex empto* was largely achieved well before Justinian.

The effects of the merger were to introduce a general liability for *dicta* other than puffs. On the remedial side, the aediles' actions for redhibition and reduction of price were made available alongside the normal damages under the *actio ex empto*, subject to this innovation. Normal damages covering the buyer's whole loss were retained for the case in which the seller had been guilty of bad faith while redhibition and reduction were made available against the innocent seller. In this way a distinct advantage developed for those who were willing to prove bad faith.

It is often said that the law relating to latent defects is easier to understand if one starts from Justinian and works backwards. It is then a question of disentangling the strands which contributed to the general warranty. On the one hand the warranty liability under the aediles' edict; on the other the limited warranty liability under the *actio ex empto* and the liability for *mala fides* under the same action. The confluence of these streams will remain the pattern of the historical development even if it turns out that they met a good deal earlier than in Justinian's time.

iii: The action against the buyer

The seller's action is the *actio ex vendito*. The *formula* is the same with the parties turned round and 'sold' put in the *demonstratio* instead of 'bought'. And of course the facts to be proved to substantiate the *demonstratio* would be the same.

Emptio-venditio is bilateral, and we have seen that it was differences between the obligations of the two parties which forced *permutatio* (barter) into a separate compartment. What could the seller sue for? From the other side, what were the obligations of the buyer? The buyer's side is more straightforward, chiefly no doubt because the problem of latent defects is not found in relation to money.

The *actio ex vendito* lies above all for the price, which the seller can claim so long as he himself has performed or is ready and willing to do so. Whereas the seller is only obliged to warrant against eviction, the buyer must make the seller the owner of the coins. Hence if he pays over money belonging to a third party he is immediately in breach, even before the third party himself takes action.

Though there must be money in the price in order to identify the buyer there may be other elements too. And the seller's action lies for them. D.19.1.6.1,2 (Pomponius, 9 *On Sabinus*):

1. If I have sold you an apartment block for a fixed sum of money and an undertaking to repair another block of mine, I will have the *actio ex vendito* to enforce the repair. But if the agreement charged you only with the repair it would not amount to *emptio-venditio*, as Neratius also wrote. 2. But if I have sold and conveyed a plot of land to you for a fixed price on the terms that you are to build a block on it and then re-convey a half part to me, it is right that I can bring the *actio ex vendito* both to enforce the work of building and to get you to execute the reconveyance of the block once built. For it is clear that so long as there remains with you something attributable to the *res vendita* I retain my *actio ex vendito*.

Though more various than simple payment of coins, all this can be summed up in the one duty to pay the price.

The buyer's other principal obligation is to take delivery. The seller must make *traditio* or, originally and where necessary, *mancipatio*. But that does not mean that he has to seek out the buyer or send the *res* to him. The terms of the contract may impose that obligation but if they do not then the buyer must come to take the *res* from the seller. D.19.1.9 (Pomponius, 20 *On Sabinus*):

If someone who has bought stones from an estate will not take them the *actio ex vendito* can be brought against him to make him remove them.

See also D.18.6.1.3 (Ulpian, 28 *On Sabinus*):

The seller of wine can even pour it away if he specified and made available a time for it to be measured out and it was not measured out. But he will not be able to pour it out at once, before giving the buyer notice before witnesses to fetch the wine away or leave it in the knowledge that it will be poured off. However if having the right to pour it away he abstains from doing so, that is praiseworthy and for that reason he can demand payment for the vessels, so long at least as he had an interest in their being emptied of the wine in them, as for instance if he was going to hire them out or needed to hire in others for himself...

iv. Risk (periculum)

The Latin *periculum* is more familiar as 'danger'. We are all exposed to danger all of the time. That is what insurance is about. And social security too. Leaving those safety schemes aside, we can say that if disasters do materialise there either will or will not be someone to sue. If you drive into my car negligently I can sue you for compensation and thus shift the loss to you. If my car is swept away in a flood or overturned by a whirlwind there will almost certainly be nobody to complain against. So the disaster will be all my own. Just like catching measles.

The dangers to which property is exposed are destruction (including loss) and damage (including deterioration). It is convenient to divide these even though in practice it is sometimes difficult to say whether the damage is so bad as to count as destruction. If property never changed hands the danger of damage and destruction would simply be borne by the owner. Sale does involve a change of hands. So there is obviously a question to be faced. In the story of a sale when exactly does the burden of bearing these risks pass from the seller to the buyer? That is the question when. But there is also a question what: What is involved in the passing of the risk?

A. What is involved? It is much easier to start by concentrating solely on destruction. Think of a horse which dies or a vase which smashes into pieces. Once the risk of destruction has passed to the buyer he falls into the same position as an owner has in relation to goods which he has no notion of selling. And that is true even though he, the buyer, may not yet be owner. For it is not to be assumed that risk and title pass together. So once the risk has passed the buyer has to ask himself what if anything he can do about the loss which he has suffered. Can he sue anyone? Was it through someone's want of care that the horse died or was killed, or the vase shattered? He may be able to maintain a claim or he may not. What he cannot do once the risk has passed is to shift the loss on to the seller by calling the contract off and refusing to pay the price or, if it has been paid, demanding it back.

Suppose the poor horse is struck by lightning a year after I bought him. It is obvious that I cannot go to the seller and say I want the sale reversed. And equally obviously if I still have not paid I must pay. And the same is true from the very moment after the risk passes. The year only makes the point seem too plain for argument. The sooner the destruction happens the more it seems as though the buyer has to pay for nothing. And if the risk passes before he obtained possession it may also materialise before he obtains possession. In which case he must pay even though he gets nothing at all, in the sense at least that he gets not even one second's enjoyment. Suppose I buy the horse which from your window we can see standing in your field. Let it be given that the risk of destruction passes. As we walk out to the field a storm breaks and the horse is struck. I must pay. The modern moral is that the time from which to insure is the moment at which the risk passes.

All this can be summed up thus. If destruction happens after the risk of destruction has passed, the buyer cannot shift the loss back to the seller by refusing or reclaiming the price. His only hope of shifting the loss is that the circumstances may be such as to make someone, perhaps even the seller, liable for the disaster.

What if the destruction occurs before the risk passes? Then the seller cannot shift the loss to the buyer by claiming or retaining the price. It is his affair, just as though there had been no sale in view. It is strictly speaking a separate question whether he might, in addition to bearing the loss of his *res*, also have to pay damages for non-delivery. The answer is that he will not, because the contract will be aborted by the disappearance of its subject-matter. The only doubt is whether that is an invariable rule or a rule of construction which holds good in 999 cases out of a thousand.

Damage is rather more difficult. Once again the best approach is to start by asking about damage which happens after the risk passes. Suppose the horse is lamed or the vase chipped. The seller can shrug his shoulders. It is none of his business, unless it happens that it was his fault. Suppose that the buyer has insisted on a term in the contract that the *res* shall be in perfect condition. It does not make any difference, because, whatever the contractual standard, deteriorations happening after the risk passes are the buyer's affair. If the vase was perfect when the risk passed the loss from the chip must be approached in the same way whether it happens one second or a year later.

What about damage before the risk passes? This is where there is a problem. Suppose a system in which there is no implied liability for quality and a contract in which there is no express term about it. Here damage which happens 'before the risk passes' is a contradiction in terms. For the quality of the thing is at the buyer's risk throughout. Let him insert a contractual standard. Say, specifically that the horse shall not be lame. Now the notion of risk of damage, or at least of risk of lameness, begins to make sense. The contractual standard requires no lameness, and the lameness has supervened before the risk passed to the buyer. So the seller will be liable for breach of the standard laid down in the term against lameness. There is no ground for suggesting that the sale is void because of the lameness, though that result could be reached by the use of conditions.

The thrust of the last paragraph is that, for damage, the notion of a transfer of risk is a virtually meaningless concept. To gain meaning it requires 'damage' to be understood as 'deterioration below the contractual standard set by terms as to quality'. If there is no such standard there is no time during which, once a sale has been agreed, it can be said that the risk of deterioration was on the seller. And contrary-wise, to affirm that the risk of damage is on the seller is to affirm that there is indeed a contractual standard in relation to quality, set by express, implied or imposed terms.

B. *When does the risk pass?* The first rule is that this is something within the power of the parties to choose. Failing express agreement, the risk passes on conclusion of the contract. J.3.23.3:

> When *emptio-venditio* is contracted (which we have described as happening as soon as there is agreement on the price when the business is done without writing) the risk in the thing sold immediately attaches to the buyer, even if the thing still has not been delivered to the buyer.

So the risk passes where the agreement is complete, not when the *res* is delivered. Hence, before ownership. The maxim *res perit domino* (when property is lost, it is the owner who suffers) does not apply. The reason must be that it is from the moment of being bound to give the thing up that the owner loses his economic interest in it. From then its value and potential belong to the buyer, whatever the technical location of title.

This statement in the Institutes is a simplification. It covers the common case. More accurately it should be said that the risk passes at the point of 'perfection', which can come later than conclusion of the contract. If there is a condition to be fulfilled or if there needs to be weighing or measuring to identify the *res* (20 gallons from this vat) or to ascertain the price in figures (all this vat at £20 per gallon), the contract is binding but 'imperfect'.

In such cases, where there is an imperfect phase between contract and perfection, there is sometimes room for an argument that the sale can become perfect even though the *res* is destroyed. For example, you buy this foal subject to the condition that its mother wins tomorrow's race. The foal dies and the mother wins. Or you buy all the wine in this vessel at £1.00 per litre. The vessel is punctured and the wine spills out, but I mend the hold and, filling the vessel with water, measure the contents at 10 litres. This argument leads to the suggestion that the risk of destruction might pass retroactively from the notional perfection back to the making of the contract, so that you would have to pay. But that argument did not prevail. The sale was avoided with the destruction of the *res*. However, the contrary position appears to have been taken in relation to deterioration in the imperfect phase. But this is not certain.

In all cases in which *traditio* does not follow instantly upon perfection of the contract, there is a phase during which the buyer bears the risk though the seller is in possession. It should not be thought that the buyer is unduly vulnerable during that time, for the seller is subject to a high standard of care and will be liable to the buyer for losses inflicted for want of that care. Also, an entirely different kind of mitigation of his difficulty gives him an entitlement to fruits and other enhancements which accrue during the period when he bears the risk. J.3.23.3 (continued):

And so if the slave has died or been harmed in some part of his body, or the house has been wholly or partly consumed by fire, or the land has been wholly or partly swept away by a torrent or has become worse or smaller by far through flood or the destruction of trees by a gale, the loss lies on the buyer. He will have to pay the price even if he does not get the thing. For whatever happens without deceit or fault (*sine dolo aut culpa*) on the part of the seller, as regards that the seller will be safe. But if after the sale anything accedes to the land by fluvial accretion (*per alluvionem*) that advantage goes to the buyer. For whoever bears the risk of disaster should also enjoy the hope of advantage (*nam et commodum eius esse debet cuius periculum est*).

v. The passing of property

The outline is as follows. First, the agreement itself did not transfer ownership: contract and conveyance were separate events. Second, sales of *res mancipi* required mancipation or cession *in iure* if *dominium* was to pass. Otherwise the buyer would just be put in *via usucapiendi*, with praetorian protection till *dominium* accrued by *usucapio*. Third, for *res nec mancipi*, and in Justinian's law for *res* of all kinds, *traditio* was necessary. In classical law the *traditio* following sale was sufficient in itself, without payment of price. G.2.20:

And so if I deliver to you some clothes or gold or silver on the basis of sale or gift or some other such cause, the *res* immediately becomes yours, if only I myself am owner to start with.

However, Justinian introduced a new rule, which he said was an old one. J.2.1.41:

If *res* are delivered by *traditio* on the basis of gift or dowry or any other cause there is no doubt that they are alienated. But things sold and delivered by *traditio* do not become the property of the recipient buyer unless he has paid the price to the seller or given him some other satisfaction as by surety or pledge. And this is laid down even by the Twelve Tables, though it is right to say that it is also part of the *ius gentium* (i.e. of the *ius naturale*). But it is also true that if the seller grants credit to the buyer the *res* immediately passes to the buyer.

This same rule is stated in the Digest, attributed to Pomponius at D.18.1.19.[12] But at D.18.1.53,[13] Gaius is made to say that either payment or security is necessary if title is to pass, with no mention of the granting of credit. There seem to have been last minute vacillations on the part of Justinian's commissioners. It is not clear what they were aiming at. The old rule, if it existed, applied to *mancipatio*. The provision about the granting of credit comes very near to short-circuiting the whole change, since there must be few cases in which the price is not paid and credit is not given. But the effect of the rule is to give the seller the security of continuing ownership in the one case in which he had made no arrangements of that kind with the buyer.

Ad hoc reservation of title by way of security for payment can be troublesome. Subsequent buyers are in danger of getting no title. It may have been considered more convenient to reserve title in every case, thus putting all subsequent buyers on notice to ask for proof of price paid or some arrangement made. But this is a guess.

12 Pomponius, 31 *On Quintus Mucius*.
13 Gaius, 28 *On the Provincial Edict*.

2. *Locatio-Conductio* (Hire)

Suppose I get a car for a week from Avis or Hertz or another such firm. According to the colloquial usage of our language the word 'hirer' does not unequivocably mean me or them. And it is the same with the verb. We tend to add 'out' for what the firm does. Hertz 'hires out' the car and I 'hire' it. To make matters worse the noun 'hire' can denote not only the transaction between us, the contract of hire, but also the sum to be paid by me, the rent for the car. 'Rental' is becoming more common. 'Rent' we keep for land.

In Latin, Hertz is the *locator*, and the sum to be paid is the *merces*. I am the *conductor*. The same language can be used in relation to land as well as movables. Literally the word *locator* means 'placer out'; and *conductor* means 'leader with'. A *merces* is a reward. So, a mercenary is for us a soldier who fights for anyone who will reward him. It is convenient to have stable terminology. Let us keep the Latin *locator* and *conductor*. They are not difficult. And let us say that Hertz, the *locator*, 'lets' the car to me; that I 'hire' it and am *conductor*; that what I pay, the *merces*, is simply the 'reward'. This terminology will run into some sticky ground, but I will abide by it. The transaction itself can still be called 'hire'.

Gaius (at G.3.142) and Justinian (at J.3.24 *pr.*) both start by saying that *locatio-conductio* resembles sale. This is true. And it allows our treatment to follow the same pattern, though much more shortly. There is less law on hire in the sources anyhow. But, beyond that, we now have to speed up.

Under the formulary system the *locator*'s pleading went like this:

Quod Aulus Agerius Numerio Negidio fundum quo de agitur locavit qua de re agitur,
Whereas Aulus Agerius let the land which is the subject of this action to Numerius Negidius, which matter is the subject of this suit,

quidquid ob eam rem Numerium Negidium Aulo Agerio dare facere oportet ex fide bona,
whatever on that account Numerius Negidius ought in good faith to give to or do for Aulus Agerius,

eius iudex Numerium Negidium Aulo Agerio condemnato; si non paret absolvito.
for the value of that let the judge condemn Numerius Negidius to Aulus Agerius; if it does not appear let him absolve.[14]

14 Lenel §111(112).

If the *conductor* rather than the *locator* needed to sue,the pattern was the same. But the 'whereas' clause said *conduxit* (hired) instead of *locavit* (let). The *locator*'s action was called 'the action of letting', *actio locati* or *ex locato*. In the same way the *conductor*'s action was the *actio conducti* or *ex conducto*.

i. The demonstratio

'Whereas the plaintiff let (or, hired)': What facts would substantiate this allegation? In other words, what fell within the definition of hire? My transaction with Hertz is right in the centre of the picture. But there are two other cases less to be expected according to our notion of hire.

Suppose I have a slave who is trained as a carpenter. If you pay me to let you have him for a month, that is exactly the same as the case of the car. At least it is once you have adjusted to the fact of slavery. Hire of a slave, hire of a thing, it is all one. But suppose I am a carpenter, and you employ me for a period as your carpenter. Nowadays that contract of employment would be put in another category as something quite different from hire of a thing. The Roman conception makes hire of services the same as hire of a thing. The services (*operae*) are the 'thing' hired: you are *conductor* of my carpentering services. And I am *locator*, just as though I was letting a plough or a horse.

The next case is more surprising. Suppose you have a broken chair to be mended. You come to me, still a carpenter, with this job to be done. You do not want to employ me as your carpenter, just to have this carpentering task done. This is hire too. You are *locator* of a chair to be mended. Or it might be wine to be transported, rubbish to be burned, sheep to be tended. And I am *conductor* of these jobs to be done. This is *locatio-conductio operis faciendi*. What is remarkable is that in this case the reward passes from *locator* to *conductor*. The *locator* lets the job to be done and pays for it. The *conductor* (according to our convention set at the start) hires the job to be done and gets paid. This is where the terminology on which we settled gets sticky.

The threefold division between *locatio rei* (hire of a thing), *locatio operarum* (hire of services) and *locatio operis faciendi* (hire of a job to be done) is not made in the Roman texts. The Roman perception simply makes the thing a unity. That means no fuss has to be made to explain how three different looking animals could be put together. We see them as different. They did not. It is difficult to catch their standpoint. Obviously the money, or more accurately the direction of money passing, was not essential to the way they saw it. Something like control for a purpose for a time, with that party paying who happened to agree to pay. If I want to go for an early morning ride on your horse I will agree to pay you, say, £10 for an hour's riding. If you want your horse to be exercised and I would much prefer to stay in bed you will pay me £10 for the same hour's riding. Either way you locate your horse to me: control of a horse for riding for an hour. It is the same with fields to be cultivated for a season. There is the control for a purpose for a time. But only the agreement will reveal the direction in which the reward must pass. *Locatio* of services fits in this picture by saying it is the *locator* himself who is under the *conductor*'s control for a purpose (carpentering) for a time, or, more respectfully, not himself but his work-capacity, his labour. But there is no denying that the unity is elusive.

A. The reward There must be one. Otherwise the transaction will be something else. A car for a week without any price is not what Hertz does. It will be a loan-for-use, not hire. Loan-for-use is called *commodatum*; as opposed to loan-for-consumption, which is *mutuum*. And if the car is handed over not for use but for safe keeping ('Will you keep my car in your garage while I am away in France?') that will be *depositum* if gratuitous. And if you accept an unpaid commission to perform some task for me ('Will you book my flight and obtain my foreign currency?') that will be *mandatum*.

Must the *merces* be in money? We saw that in sale, after dispute, the price had to be. To distinguish buyer and seller. The equivalent case here is loan against loan: I lend you my horse for ten days in return for your lending me your horse for the following ten days, as for instance so that we shall both have a pair with which to plough. Gaius leaves the question open (G.3.144). Justinian says this is not hire. And not *commodatum* either since not gratuitous (J.3.24.1). It is covered by a gap-filling *actio praescriptis verbis*. But this leaves room to count as hire the case in which I give a sheep for ten days' use of your horse, or a quarter of my crop for hire of your land. The parties are sufficiently distinguished, since one, here you, gives a temporary control and the other makes a final surrender.

Like the price in sale, the reward had to be fixed (*certum*). And its being fixed was taken as the moment at which the contract was made. Justinian applied the same solution as in sale to the case in which the parties agreed to abide by the decision of a third party (J.3.24.1): the sale was conditional on his making known his valuation. We saw that behind this problem lay the question whether reasonableness could be understood as the measure really intended by the parties and, if so, whether reasonableness provided a sufficient standard of certainty.[15] The same question underlies another problem. What if I go to a cleaner with clothes to be cleaned or to a tailor with clothes to repair and arrange the job to be done but without fixing the price? This is not the case where he has a tariff to which I assent impliedly. The construction of my intent is that I will pay as much as shall be agreed afterwards. Gaius (at G.3.143) says this makes a question whether hire is contracted (*quaeritur an locatio-conductio contrahatur*). Justinian says the answer is no and he pushes this transaction into the gap-filling *actio praescriptis verbis*.

B. Liberal professions Even if the definition of hire appeared in all respects to be satisfied, nonetheless some services were regarded as removed from its scope. To save their dignity. Advocacy, surveying, philosophy and the law provide examples. Presumably a defendant could therefore maintain before the judge that the facts did not amount to hire because his service was of a kind which it was not usual to hire. But there is a complication which makes the picture unclear. Some kinds of work, as for instance curing the sick, were done at different levels of society, from slaves upwards. The exemption from *locatio-conductio* seems not to consist solely in the nature of the work but in a combination of type of work and status of its practitioner. What is exempt is the genteel version. Complex psychology underlies this. And there is nothing particularly Roman about it. The dark side is pretence in the quest for dignity: the would-be superior pretends that he does not need money and, the other way about, can be relied on to meet his liabilities extra-legally, as matters of honour. But that is not the whole story. The nobler part is that man really is at his best when working for his work's sake, not for money. Nowadays we find it difficult to recognise this higher life, unless perhaps we first identify the person in view as a musician or an artist. If a lawyer claims it, we suspect humbug. Things change, and change back.

C. Three old chestnuts

(a) Work and Materials

If I take a cup to be engraved, or jewel to be cut, into a shop to have the work done, there is no doubt that the contract is hire. I locate the

[15] Above, 70.

job-to-be-done. It is the case in which the *locator* pays. It is the same when I take a lump of gold to a goldsmith to have it made up into rings. But what if I simply go in and ask for rings to be made to a given specification? In more general terms what if the worker provides not only labour but also the material to be worked upon? G.3.147:

... *Cassius ait materiae quidem emptionem venditionemque contrahi, operarum autem locationem et conductionem. Sed plerisque placuit emptionem et venditionem contrahi.*

... Cassius holds that in respect of the material there is a contract of sale, in respect of the labour a contract of hire. But most authorities consider that the contract is sale.

The difficulty is that where the worker provides the material the property in the thing made must in the end pass to the customer. And that is contrary to the nature of hire. On the other hand there is some awkwardness in contemplating an action of sale to compel the doing of labour, and also in drafting the pleadings. For what is it that must be said to have been sold? The ultimate solution, making the whole contract sale, shows these hesitations to be superable. Cassius took a fussier line. But its inconvenience is obvious. Nobody wants to have to litigate about one transaction under two heads.

Suppose that I want a block of flats built on my land in the city. You now win the contract. You will provide all the materials. Is that sale or hire? It is hire. Because I am providing the land. Property in your materials will pass to me, but not by virtue of the contract. The fixture accedes to the land as it is built.

(b) Gladiators

This is best taken *verbatim* from Gaius himself (G.3.146):

Again, suppose I deliver gladiators to you on these terms: twenty *denarii* are to be paid me for the sweat of each one who comes off unharmed, one thousand *denarii* for each one killed or weakened. Is the contract sale or hire? And the preferred view is that there is hire of the ones who survive intact and sale of those killed and weakened. The uncertainty is resolved by what happens, as though there was a conditional sale and hire of each one. For there is no longer any doubt that things can be sold and hired subject to a condition.

There are loose ends. First there are events in which litigation can happen before events resolve the uncertainty. How should the transaction then be described? Suppose non-delivery. Presumably hire. But that means the solution should be described as hire of all subject to conditional transformation into sale. Secondly, there is an assumption that the *debilitati* (the weakened as opposed to killed) pass into the ownership of the impresario. Otherwise the fact of their injury, and the consequent increase in price, is no reason for taking the contract over into sale. Lastly, there is a problem, in the case of the *occisi*, in seeing a condition fulfilled by the destruction of the subject-matter. This awkwardness arises from the rule or guideline 'no sale without a *res* sold'. But it can be met by insisting that the existence of the *res* while the condition is pending is sufficient; or, alternatively, by saying (insisting that the rule is only a guideline) that the intentions of the parties determine whether the sale survives the destruction of the *res*.

(c) Heritable Hire (*Emphyteusis*)

Gaius observes (at G.3.145) that, without transferring ownership, municipalities sometimes deal with their land in such a way as to produce results *de facto* much the same as if a sale had happened and *dominium* had passed. That is, they let the land at a rent on the terms that so long as the rent is paid the land will stay in the family. He speaks of the original recipient and his heir. But their right was or became assignable, *inter vivos* and by will. The person entitled had, by virtue of a praetorian action, an interest *in rem* as well as contractual rights *in personam* against the landlord. Gaius says the preferred opinion was that this was hire, not sale. The argument to the contrary is apparent: the effects are tantamount to transfer of *dominium*; and, if you can once view the long or perpetual hire as creating a right *in rem*, then the transaction looks technically very like the sale of a servitude, as for instance a right of way, except that the 'price' is to be paid in perpetual instalments.

This case was settled in the fifth century by Zeno. He put *emphyteusis*, which by his time had extended into private law as a transaction between individuals, into a compartment of its own, neither sale nor hire.[16]

[16] J.3.24.3.

ii. The intentio

'Whatever the defendant ought on that account to give to or do for the plaintiff *ex fide bona*': Now the *demonstratio* has been substantiated. So it is given that there is a contract of hire between the parties. What follows? Good faith is again the basis on which the obligations are worked out.

A. The locator*'s action* The *actio locati* asks the judge what the *conductor* ought to do. That is, it is concerned with the *locator*'s rights, the *conductor*'s duties. The *locator*'s main concern is that the *conductor* should look after and return whatever is entrusted to him. And if he is a locator who is to be paid he will want his money. That is a matter for the express terms.

The position is summed up very briefly by Justinian in the Institutes (J.3.24.5):

The *conductor* ought to do everything according to the terms of the hiring (*secundum legem conductionis*). And where the terms are silent he ought to answer for whatever is good and fair (*ex bono et aequo debet praestare*). A *conductor* who has given or promised a reward for the use of clothes or of silver or of an animal is required to show such safe keeping (*custodia*) as the most attentive owner shows to his own things (*qualem diligentissimus paterfamilias suis rebus adhibet*). And if he fulfils that standard and nonetheless by some accident (*aliquo casu*) he loses the thing he will not be liable for its return.

The careful *locator* would protect himself carefully with express terms. Here are two examples. First, D.19.2.29 (Alfenus, 7 *Digest*):

In the contract it had been written (*In lege locationis scriptum erat*): '*Redemptor silvam ne caedito neve cingito neve deurito neve quem cingere caedere urere sinito*: the conductor shall not cut, strip or burn the woodland; nor shall he allow anyone to strip, cut or burn it.' The question was put: was the conductor's obligation to prevent these things happening if he saw anyone doing them, or was it so to guard the wood that nobody could do these things? I gave this *responsum*: the word *sinere*, 'to allow', can bear both meanings, but the sense which the locator is taken to have intended is that the conductor should not only prevent someone cutting whom he happened by chance to see but that he should also see to it that nobody did cut.

Second, D.19.1.11.1 (Ulpian, 32 *On the Edict*):

Suppose that the hiring agreement has this term '*Ignem ne habeto*: [the *conductor*] shall have no fire'. And then he does have one. He will be liable if mere mischance (*fortuitus casus*) causes a blaze. Because he should have had no fire at all. It is different where the term is for *ignem innocentem habere*, having a harmless fire. For that allows him to have a fire so long as it is not dangerous.

In the absence of express provisions, good faith required the *conductor* to exercise a high degree of care. He would be liable if he failed to keep to the standard of the very careful owner. Some *conductors* may have been subjected to that very severe liability called *custodia* under which only violence and natural disasters would excuse them. But the general standard was 'everything the most careful owner would do'. D.19.2.25.7 (Gaius, 10 *On the Provincial Edict*):

Suppose a *conductor* hires the job of transporting a column (*columnam transportandam conduxit*). If while it is being lifted, carried or set down it is broken, he must answer for that disaster (*ita id periculum praestat*) in the case in which blame (*culpa*) attaches to him and the men whose labour he uses. But there will be no blame if everything was done which every very careful man would see to. And we will certainly understand the law to be the same where the hire is of jars or timber to be transported. The same can be applied to other things.

Also D.19.2.13.6 (Ulpian, 32 *On the Edict*):

If a cleaner accepts clothes for cleaning and mice eat them he is liable *ex locato*. For he ought to have taken precautions against that event. And a laundry which muddles up sheets and gives the wrong one to the wrong customer will also be liable *ex locato* even if it is done unawares.

Again, if the *res* is damaged while under the *conductor*'s control, the question can arise whether the *conductor* himself is liable if either a slave or free employee did the damage. This next text answers that the *conductor* himself is liable if he was at fault in employing such people or otherwise giving them the opportunity to cause the trouble. D.19.2.11 *pr.* (Ulpian, 32 *On the Edict*):

Must a *conductor* answer for the fault of his slaves and such other people as he brings in? And to what extent? Noxally, with the option of surrendering his slaves, or directly on his own account? And against those whom he brings in must he assign such actions as he has or must he himself answer as for his own fault? In this I hold that he himself must answer even for the fault of those whom he brings in and even in the absence of express agreement provided only that he is guilty of fault in having such people either in his employ or as his guests: and Pomponius takes the same position in the sixty-third book of his commentary on the edict.

In the next two examples the subject-matter is carriage. In the first though the facts are not fully given. I think we have to imagine a taxi accident, with a passenger killed. The victim is a slave. In the second it is carriage by water. Both might have happened yesterday. They have the same familiar ring as that contract we looked at, so precisely and economically phrased against the *conductor*'s abuse of woodland. D.19.2.13 *pr.*-1 (Ulpian, 32 *On the Edict*):

What if a cab-driver . . . overturns his cab when trying to overtake others and shakes up a slave or kills him? For he ought to have kept to a moderate speed (*tempere enim debuit*). But there will also be an action on the policy of the *lex Aquilia* (*utilis Aquiliae*) against him. 1. Suppose a boatman takes on the task of shipping a cargo to Minturnae. Then, when his boat proves unable to go up the river at Minturnae, he transfers the cargo to another ship. And then that ship is lost in the mouth of the river. Is the first boatman liable? Labeo says that he is not liable if he lacks *culpa* (blame, fault). By contrast if he does it against the owner's wishes (*invito domino*) or at a time when he ought not to have tried it or on to a less suitable boat then the *actio ex locato* is to be brought.

The theme here, not without some intriguing difficulties of detail, is that the *conductor*'s liability turns on *culpa*. The question is always: was he at fault? That in turn rests ultimately on the contractual duty to observe good faith.

B. The conductor*'s action* The *actio conducti* or *ex conducto* directs the *iudex* to the *locator*'s obligations, the *conductor*'s correlative rights. What is the *conductor* chiefly concerned about? He wants to get the temporary control and advantage which the agreement holds out to him. That car I hired at the beginning. My main worry is that it will break down.

I shall lose two days of my week. Worse still if it spits oil over my clothes. As *conductor* I want from the deal the advantage or enjoyment which a hirer may reasonably expect. In the same way a garage which takes on a motor mechanic pays him to put his labour at its disposal for the while. In the Roman terms the garage is also a *conductor* of his labour. It wants to be sure of competent motor-mechanical *operae*. That is the anticipated 'enjoyment' equivalent to my expectation of trouble-free motoring. 'Enjoyment' is not quite right for the *conductor* who takes on a job to be done, a roof to be repaired, shirt to be washed and so on. He is being paid. What he wants is trouble-free access to whatever *corpus* he is to work on. It is a kind of enjoyment, necessary to his livelihood. But we do not usually think of opportunities to work and earn quite in the same way as temporary access for which we pay.

As with the *locator* the *conductor*'s first line of protection is the express contract. The *locator* must abide by all the express terms exacted from him when the agreement was made. Suppose that he is letting agricultural land. If he warrants that the estate will support a thousand sheep then he must honour that warranty. Fault does not enter into it. Where the term is express the only doubts are doubts of construction. Did he promise that the land was capable of carrying so many sheep or that it would at all events remain so capable for a five year period? And did he really warrant absolutely that it had, or would retain, this capacity, or did he only promise that it was as certain as reasonable care and skill could establish that it had or would retain that capacity? The exercise of construction is not often easy. But the subject of the exercise is intelligible: what was it that he undertook?

What are the *locator*'s liabilities independent of express terms? He must put the *res* at the disposal of the *conductor*. And that means not only the bare *res* itself but also any equipment which customarily goes with it to allow the expected user. If the *res* is a vineyard or olive orchard then wine-making and olive-pressing gear must be included. There are standard lists.

Once the *conductor* has the *res* at his disposal, the questions will arise from defective or interrupted enjoyment. The land is infertile. The vessels leak. And so on.

The *locator* who knows that the *res* has a defect which will impair the expected enjoyment must make good the whole interest of the *conductor*. That is, he must pay the full damages to make good loss suffered.

This fault-based liability is evidenced in D.19.2.19.1 (Ulpian, 32 *On the Edict*):

... si saltum pascuum locasti, in quo mala herba nascebatur: hic enim si pecora vel demortua sunt vel etiam deteriora facta quod interest praestabitur si scisti, si ignorasti pensionem non petes.
...if you have let pasture in which poisonous weeds were growing: for here, if farm animals have died or suffered harm, full damages will be payable if you knew; if you were unaware, you will not be able to claim the rent.

This is incomplete. We will come to the bit which precedes it in a minute. The liability for the harm to the cows is limited to the case in which *scisti*, you knew of the danger. Then there is a lesser consequence for *si ignorasti*, if you were unaware. We will come back to that.

The preceding lines show that Ulpian also envisages a liability to pay full damages at least in some cases in which the *locator* was ignorant of the defect. D.19.2.19.1 (Ulpian, 32 *On the Edict*):

Si quis dolia vitiosa ignarus locaverit, deinde vinum effluxerit, tenebitur in id quod interest. Nec ignorantia eius erit excusata. Et ita Cassius scripsit. Aliter atque si ...
If he lets defective vessels unawares and then wine pours out he will be liable for the full interest of the *conductor*. And his ignorance will not be excused. And so Cassius wrote. It is different if... [and here follows the case of poisonous weeds].

The contrast between *Defective Vessels* and *Poisonous Weeds* is much debated. It may be right, I incline to think it is, to say that the former indicates a warranty liability against latent defects which render the thing unfit for the enjoyment to be expected from it. That is, unfit for its ordinary purpose. A pasture with poisonous weeds is not unfit. Much as a Christmas pudding is not unfit if it has lumps of metal in it (silver charms or coins). Looking for them is part of the user.

This text is dealing with initial defects which impair the enjoyment. But interruptions can supervene when all seems to be going well. Starting from fault liability, there is certainly an obligation on the *locator* to abstain from fraudulent and malicious schemes to deprive the *conductor* of his enjoyment. That is the elementary outwork of the *bonae fidei* character of the contract. Harassment to get a tenant out would be caught by this. So also a concocted tale of trouble in the foundations with the same end in view, emptying the building on the pretence of major repairs. Further, the *locator* was liable if he failed to keep the *res* in repair for its ordinary use. This liability seems to be based on *culpa*. That is he must do what is reasonable to maintain the *res*. Liability is for unreasonable failure. There is a warranty liability for eviction. That is, if the *conductor* is excluded because, as it turns out, the *locator* let out something which did not belong to him and then the owner came forward and asserted his right. D.19.2.9 *pr.* (Ulpian, 32 *On the Edict*):

Somebody buys a house or farm in good faith and lets it to me. Then he is evicted, without there being any fraud or blame (*dolus* or *culpa*) on his part. Pomponius holds that he is nonetheless liable *ex conducto* (on the contract of hire) to the *conductor* on the ground that he is bound to ensure that he is allowed to enjoy that which he hired (*ut ei praestetur frui quod conduxit licere*).

This text actually contains a suspect addendum which asserts that the *locator* should be excused if he is prepared to provide an equivalent substitute. It then goes on to consider the special position of hire by a usufructuary who reveals that he has only that limited interest. If the *locator*-usufructuary dies (thus ending the usufruct) during the agreed term and the *dominus*, his title now cleared of the limited interest, excludes the *conductor*, the usufructuary's heir is not liable for the premature exclusion. Because termination of the usufruct is a foreseeable risk in such transactions.

We have been considering the *locator*'s liability to pay full damages. Even where he is not so liable he may have to give the disappointed *conductor* something less, namely a remission of the *merces* (reduction of the reward). This is hinted at in the concluding words of *Poisonous Weeds*, considered earlier. This lesser remedy is conveniently considered under the head of payment.

C. Payment It is easiest to take this topic out, though strictly obligations to pay or to remit payment belong within the actions whose range we have just been considering. The reason for separating it out is that, as we saw, it depends on the particular contract whether payment falls on the *locator* or the *conductor*. Hence it comes within now one and now the other action.

The general observation is that, quite apart from the question of liability for damages, there are circumstances in which the party expecting payment cannot have it or, if he has already been paid, cannot retain it. Where payments are by instalments over time this remission may apply only to portions of the whole time. The starting point is this. He cannot have the reward if the other does not get the enjoyment reasonably to be expected.

Hence if flood or earthquake or drought destroys a harvest the *locator* of the farm must remit the rent for the year, for productive cultivation is the user to be expected. There is no warranty against exceptional disasters. So no damages. But the *locator* bears the loss in the sense that he cannot take the rent. (If a very good year follows he is allowed to make up the remission.) Not every disappointment leads to the *conductor's* having this remission. Every expected user carries, so to say, its own internal risks. The dangers of his own operation (*ex ipsa re*) have to be borne by the *conductor*. The line is not easy to draw. Weeds in his corn, wine which comes out sour. Such things are within the normal risks of cultivation and viticulture. The case of *Poisonous Weeds* is problematic in this respect and may here be distorted by interpolation or gloss. It says that the *locator* must remit the rent if *mala herba* of which the *locator* was unaware kill the cows. But this looks like a risk *ex ipsa re*, from the thing itself, which ought to mean that the *conductor* has to put up with it and bear the loss. Just possibly a difference was taken between a defect present *ab initio* and one which supervened.

The proposition that payment could not be demanded unless the party to pay got the enjoyment reasonably to be expected needs to be adapted to fit *locatio* of labour and of tasks-to-be-done. The worker letting out his labour had to put himself at the disposal of his *conductor* but he was entitled to his whole wage 'if it was not through him that he could not perform his work (*si per eum non stetit quo minus operas praestet*)' (D.19.2.38 = Paul, *Rules*). One would want to know more about this. The bricklayer on site unable to build because of the pouring rain is no doubt covered. I am less sure about the one who is prevented from even turning up, as by being run over on his way to begin a week's employment. Nevertheless Paul's statement is widely put. Compare D.19.2.19.9 (Ulpian, 32 *On the Edict*):

A secretary let out his labour. Then the *conductor* died. The Emperor Antoninus in conjunction with the Deified Severus wrote this rescript in reply to the petition of the secretary: 'Since on the facts as you give them it was not through you that you could not perform your services for Antonius Aquila, then, if you did not receive wages from someone else in that same year, it is right that the contractual expectation should be fulfilled.'

So far as payment for a task to be done is concerned, payment to the *conductor* for building a house, repairing a river-bank and so on, it is necessary to go very carefully. The difficult question is, What happens if, after a great deal of time and effort has been put in, the product of the labour is destroyed without fault on either side? The half-built house is burned down, an earthquake shakes away a nearly complete scaffolding, a painting is destroyed by a flood just as the finishing touches were going to be applied. The *locator* does not get the product which he was after. Does he have to pay? If the work had been complete he would have had to bear the risk in all respects. If payment was to be made stage by stage the same applies as each stage is finished. If approval is needed before payment then if it can be shown that all was complete except approval and, further, that approval would not have been withheld, he must pay. That leaves the case in which the work, or a stage of it if it is so divided, is unequivocally incomplete. Some texts speak of the 'risk' (*periculum*) being on the *locator*. But it is not clear that this means that he has to pay for the work done. It may mean only that nobody is going to make good the destruction of his property (D.19.2.59,[17] D.19.2.62).[18]

3. *Societas* (Partnership)

One usually meets *socius* first in warlike contexts. There it means 'ally'. But here 'partner'. The words 'society' and 'association', and the family of adjectives and verbs which go with them, come from this Latin. Also 'dissociate'.

The action's name is *pro socio*. *Actio pro socio* just means 'action for a partner'. Under the formulary system the pleading was on these lines:

Whereas Aulus Agerius entered into a partnership with Numerius Negidius in respect of all their property (*omnium bonorum*), which matter is the subject of this action,

whatever on that account Numerius Negidius ought to give to or do for Aulus Agerius in good faith,

[17] Javolenus, 5 *From the Posthumous Works of Labeo*.
[18] Labeo, 1 *Plausible Views*.

for the value of that, not exceeding the capacity of Numerius Negidius to pay (*dumtaxat quod Numerius Negidius facere potest*), let the judge condemn Numerius Negidius to Aulus Agerius; if it does not appear let him absolve.[19]

i. The demonstratio

What facts would substantiate the allegation that a partnership had been entered? The specimen *formula* in the edict used the example reproduced here, the partnership of all goods. This betrays origins other than in the field of commerce. But in practice most partnerships would ordinarily be much more limited and would be commercially motivated. The content of the partnership could be some line of business, narrowly or widely defined: importing wine, manufacture of pottery, retailing food, and so on. Or it could embrace all the commercial activities of the partners: a partnership in commerce generally. Or, at the other extreme, it could focus on just a single operation: selling one house, or buying a piece of land.

Whatever the scope, the making of the partnership consists in an agreement to join together so as to contribute resources to the venture. There is no reason why the contributions should be equal or all of the same kind. One party may have money, another goods, another a skill as a salesman, another good contacts among possible customers.

Partnerships hope to prosper but risk losses and lean times. If the agreement is that one party shall bear the risk of loss but be excluded from the hope of profit, the contract is void (*societas leonina*: partnership with a lion). Apart from that, shares can be fixed by the agreement and deal differently with profit and loss. It is possible for one partner to have two thirds of *lucrum* (profit) and one third of *damnum* (loss) while the other is entitled to one third of the *lucrum* but risks having to bear two thirds of any *damnum*. It is even possible for a partner to be exempted entirely from the risk of *damnum*. It is only where a partner is excluded from the hope of gain that the lion mischief comes in.

An arrangement by which one is to take a fixed sum first and then the other is to take all the rest of the profit, if any, is accepted as valid. Thus D.17.2.52.7 (Ulpian, 31 *On the Edict*):

Papinian in book 3 of his *Responsa* reports this answer which he gave when consulted on a case: There was an agreement between Flavius Victor and

[19] For the Latin, see Lenel §109.

Bellicus Asianus that premises would be bought with Victor's money for the manufacture of monuments through the skill and labour of Asianus; further that from the sale of the monuments Victor would receive money up to a fixed sum and Asianus, contributor of labour to the partnership, would have the rest. On these facts the *actio pro socio* will lie.

If the parties do not quantify their shares the contract does not fail for uncertainty. Presumptions come into play. If they say nothing they are presumed to have intended equality. If they fix only the shares in profit they are presumed to have intended the same shares in loss. And *vice versa*.

The flexibility in departing from equivalence in gain and loss was not arrived at without hesitation. Another sign of origins outside the cut-throat world of commerce. Gaius notes the dispute (G.3.149):

There was a great debate as to the validity of a partnership in which a party takes a larger share in profit and a smaller share in loss. Quintus Mucius [consul in 95 BC] thought that contrary to the nature of partnership. But Servius Sulpicius [praetor in 65 BC, murdered in 43 BC], whose opinion has prevailed, was so firmly of the view that there could be such a partnership that he even held that one partner could be validly exempted from loss but allowed a share of profit if only (*si modo*) his contribution seems so valuable as to make it fair to make him a partner on that basis.

It is impossible for a partnership to be enlarged except with the agreement of all partners. If ten people are partners and seven admit an eleventh they only succeed in making him a member of a new or sub-partnership between themselves and him. D.17.2.19 (Ulpian, 30 *On Sabinus*):

Someone admitted as partner is only partner to the person admitting him. And that is good law, since partnership is created by agreement and nobody can become my partner whom I do not want. What then if my partner has admitted him? He is just his partner.

This is then summed up in D.17.2.20 (Ulpian, 31 *On the Edict*) which serves to show that Ulpian and the compilers liked tongue-twisters: '*nam socii mei socius meus socius non est*: my partner's partner's not my partner.'

Sometimes partnership intent is all that distinguishes another transaction from *societas*. D.17.2.44 (Ulpian, 31 *On the Edict*), for example, looks to offer a choice between *emptio-venditio* and *aestimatum* (sale or return) which is covered by one of those supplementary actions *praescriptis verbis*:

I give you a pearl to be sold. The agreement is that if you sell it for ten I shall receive ten but if you sell it for more you keep the rest. It seems to me that if this was done with partnership intent (*animo contrahendae societatis*) the action *pro socio* lies. If not, then the *actio praescriptis verbis*.

A similar example is provided by *locatio-conductio* of, say, a field for cultivation. At least in the case of *locatio partiaria* where the *merces* is paid in the form of a share in the yield (a transaction which in appropriate economic conditions can reduce the share-cropper to near slavery) an intention to treat the transaction as a joint venture between equals will turn into partnership what otherwise seems to belong clearly with hire.

ii. The intentio

What obligations flow from partnership? This question is best addressed by asking first what the general function of the action is.

It has nothing to do with relations between the partnership and the outside world. The *intentio* directs the judge's attention to the obligation owed, internally, by one party to another. There are indeed no relations between the partnership and the world outside. Suppose my partner in buying pictures goes off to an auction. As between the auctioneer and my partner the partnership is irrelevant. We can refer to the partnership as though it were an entity different from its members, much as we refer to a club or society or a flock or a herd as a distinct collectivity. But the law does not follow the ordinary usage of the language. It does not endow every collectivity with legal personality so as to enable it to own, owe and sue. If we say that the Butterfly Society owns premises and equipment we probably mean its members do, unless the Society has done what is necessary to turn itself into a body corporate. So with a Roman *societas*. It had no legal identity. Rights and duties vested in its individual members, the partners themselves. Hence, as a matter of logic, there could be no relations, externally, between partnership and persons dealing with one or other partner.

But this goes one stage further. Not only was the partnership not a legal person in itself but, further, the transaction of one partner did not vest rights in or impose duties on another partner. Selling a picture to my partner you could not later sue me or be sued by me. My *societas* with him was irrelevant to your *emptio-venditio* with him.

So this is the first point. The *actio pro socio* is concerned with the internal regulation of the partnership. The second is that joinder of issue terminates the contract: the partnership is finished. The need for litigation shows that the mutual trust and commitment (the *fraternitas*, 'brotherhood') between the parties has broken down. So the action's rôle is to wind up the partnership. If things are going well then the settling up which the action brings about should proceed amicably from accounting period to accounting period. The action comes in at the breakdown. The analogy of divorce is not far-fetched.

The fundamental principle is one with which the other *bonae fidei* contracts have now made us familiar. Good faith is the basis of the partners' mutual obligations. D.17.2.52.1,2 (Ulpian, 31 *On the Edict*):

> 1. What is taken into consideration in this trial for a partner is good faith (*Venit autem in hoc iudicium pro socio bona fides*). 2. The question arises therefore whether a partner must answer only for fraud or also for fault (*ultrum . . . tantum dolum an etiam culpam praestare socium oporteat*). And in book seven of his *Digesta* Celsus writes: partners must in their relations answer for both fraud and fault (*socios inter se dolum et culpam praestare oportet*).

What are the central concerns? What does a partner chiefly have to worry about? In the action, and for that matter in every accounting period, his overall aim is to have a true account of the partnership's finances. These anxieties arise from routine human temptations. Disloyalty and laziness. The law makes partnership viable by imposing legal obligations in respect of these worries, where reliance might otherwise be withheld. So the general obligation to abstain from fraud, and fault here bites in practice chiefly on secret profits and improper expenses (disloyalty) and opportunities missed or botched (laziness).

People who join together to gain are nevertheless tempted to try to keep opportunities to themselves and so to prevent this or more profit from showing up in the partnership account. The law therefore has to have techniques of definition, for saying whether a given profit is or is not within the scope of the partnership. Then, if it is, the partner must bring it in.

Sometimes the partner just tries to keep the matter quiet. Another manifestation of the same disloyalty is the tactical renunciation of the partnership. Withdrawal is permitted: no partner is obliged to maintain the relationship when the will and wish to has gone. But tactical withdrawal to take a profit leaves you still under an obligation to bring the gain into the account. G.3.151:

... Clearly, however, if someone gives up a partnership in order to take for himself the opportunity of a gain which is coming his way, he will be compelled to share that gain. As, for example, where I have a partner *totorum bonorum* (of all goods) and he withdraws with a view to keeping to his own profit an inheritance which he has been left.

D.17.2.52 *pr.* (Ulpian, 31 *On the Edict*) is another example. The text has been managed to some extent in the Digest, probably just abbreviated. One sign is that the parties seem to change over in the middle. In this translation I have smoothed that out:

A piece of land is for sale. It adjoins that of two neighbours, A + B. A asks B to buy it on the basis that the part next to A's land will then be conveyed over to him. Then, without B's knowledge, A buys the plot himself. Question: Does B have any action against A? Julian writes that it depends on the facts: If what was intended was only that B should buy and then share with A then B has no action against A who did the buying; but if what was intended was that the deal should be a joint venture (*ut quasi commune negotium gereretur*), then A will be liable to B in the trial on partnership to make over all the land less that part he commissioned to be reserved for himself.

First you have to decide that you are looking at a partnership. Once you are, then no partner can be allowed to go it alone, even if on second thoughts or perhaps because of a new source of finance he suddenly sees that he can do better without co-operation. This same temptation is encountered outside partnership whenever one is placed in a position to perceive opportunities which are not entirely one's own, as for instance as agent for a principal, trustee for a beneficiary or in any other case in which one is managing the affairs wholly or partly of another.

Another form of disloyalty is fiddling expenses. That is, attributing to the partnership account an outgoing which is not properly incurred in the pursuit of partnership business. No partner may do that. The same goes for losses incurred outside the scope of the partnership. He must not impute these private minus quantities to the partnership account. If he has he must make good the sum. This involves an exercise of definition to establish a line between what is inputable and what not. Thus D.17.2.52.4,15 (Ulpian, 31 *On the Edict*):

4. Some people made a partnership dealing in clothes. One partner travelled to buy in. Bandits (*latrones*) attacked him. He lost his money, his slaves were wounded, and he lost his personal effects. Julian says the loss is to be shared and in the *actio pro socio* the other partner must acknowledge a half share of it in respect of the money and the other things which he would not have had with him unless he had set out on a journey to buy supplies on the partnership's account. And Julian quite rightly approves of the proposition that the partner must also acknowledge a share of anything spent on doctor's bills. It is the same if something goes down in a shipwreck when it is not usual to have the goods carried otherwise than by ship. There both must bear the loss. For just as profit, so such loss must be shared as does not arise from a partner's fault (*culpa*) . . . 15. If one partner sets off on partnership business, as to buy supplies, he will impute to the account only those expenses which he lays out on that business. [The text then lists travel, hotel, stable and storage expenses for himself, his men and the goods].

The next text, D.17.2.60 *pr.*-1 (Pomponius, 13 *On Sabinus*), combines reference to the duty to bring in partnership profits and the duty not to impute extra-partnership losses. It is Pomponius, citing Labeo. And the tone and substance is strict.

A partner makes a profit from the partnership. He delays repaying it and uses the money himself. Labeo says he must pay interest too. But not really as interest but to make good what the partnership loses by his delay. But if he does not use the money or if he does not delay the opposite conclusion applies [i.e. no interest]. Also, after the death of a partner no such calculation is to be made on the basis of his heir's conduct, because partnership is dissolved by the death of a partner. 1. Partnership slaves were up for sale. They made a break for freedom. One partner resisted and was wounded. Labeo says he cannot obtain his medical expenses in an *actio pro socio* because that expense was incurred not in but only on account of the partnership, just as if a partner on account of his partnership was cut out of a will, lost a legacy or was inattentive to the management of his own affairs. For it is the same with an advantage which comes to him because of his partnership. He does not have to bring in an inheritance or gift which comes to him merely because of the partnership.

We have been considering disloyalty, the temptation to keep a profit to oneself or to impute a loss to the partnership account which ought to be borne by oneself. To handle the obligation of loyalty the law has to draw a line round the partnership, to define its scope.

Now laziness or other forms of inattention and carelessness. An event may be *prima facie* within the scope of the partnership but still a partner may wish to and be able to complain. Suppose I am to buy land for grazing and I make no inquiries about the behaviour of a river running nearby. It turns out that for much of the year the land is under water. I have paid far too much and, besides, I have failed to meet our needs for pasture which means we must hire a field from someone else. All because I did not look before my leap. Or suppose we were selling and I wanted to get the business done quickly. I was to sell our wheat at the local market and settled for the first offer without ever discovering the strength of the day's demand. It cost the business hundreds of pounds.

In such cases the partner responsible for the loss or the failure to profit is obliged to make good the consequences of his own *culpa*. The question is, What standard applies to determine blame in a partner? Justinian says that it has to be remembered that people choose who to team up with and should therefore not expect more than their partner is normally capable of in relation to his own affairs. This makes the standard 'the care shown in his own affairs' (*quam in suis rebus*). The kind of fault for which a partner must answer is 'concrete fault' (*culpa levis in concreto*) as opposed to 'abstract fault' (*culpa levis in abstracto*) measured by the standard of a hypothetical reasonable man, the *bonus paterfamilias*.

The text in the Institutes largely reproduces D.17.2.72 (Gaius, 2 *Nuggets*); it can be found at J.3.25.9:

There has been a question about this: are partners liable to each other in the *actio pro socio* only for what they do fraudulently (*dolo*), as in the case with a man who allows a deposit to be made with him? Or are they also liable on the ground of *culpa*, that is, for their laziness or inattention? The view which has prevailed is that they are liable even for *culpa*. But the blame is not to be measured by the very most demanding standard of care (*non ad exactissimam diligentiam dirigenda est*). For it is enough that the partner shows on the partnership affairs (*in communibus rebus*) such attention (*diligentia*) as he usually shows on his own. In fact someone who takes on a partner who is not careful enough ought to hold himself to blame. That is, he should put it down to his own account.

iii. The condemnatio

Hitherto the difficult questions about the actual measure of the condemnation directed by the *formula* have been omitted. This third section is added here only to take note of one special feature. The *formula* limits the *condemnatio* by a *taxatio*, a claim which sets a maximum. The maximum is expressed as 'what he can meet'.

This is the *beneficium competentiae*. It prevents the condemnation running higher than the sum of the defendant's worldly wealth at the time of the judgement and thus saves him from processes by way of personal execution. He does not escape liability for the balance, for the judge compels him to enter into a *stipulatio* to pay the rest later.

This *beneficium* (privilege, indulgence) is a further indication of the non-commercial character of the contract. That is, on the assumption that commerce is supposed to be naturally cut-throat. Just possibly the restriction was in classical law confined to the very un-commercial, more commune-like, partnership of all worldly wealth (*societas omnium bonorum*). Contrary to one's first thoughts this seems to have been the original case, modelled directly on the relationship arising by operation of law between co-heirs or, more accurately, on the artificial creation of that relationship by a formal act (*certa legis actio*) before the praetor (as to which, see G.3.154–154b).

4. *Mandatum* (Mandate, Commission or Agency)

Nowadays we hear of mandates chiefly between constituencies of various kinds and their spokesmen. As for instance in national politics, industrial relations, or in university politics. And more often than not there is the implication that the spokesman was meant to have no discretion. He was to do as he was told, a delegate and not a representative. 'He was mandated to vote for the miners' leader' means that he was to vote, and for nobody else. The terms of his mandate were tightly drawn. An older political usage leaves wider margins. When new developments raise a question whether some drastic measure is within the government's mandate, the doubt is not about precise instructions. The electorate issues none. It gives a general authority to govern, limited in some debatable degree by the issues canvassed at the time of the election. Its mandate is wide. The truth is, modern usage aside, that the scope of a mandate depends upon the construction of its terms, against the background of the circumstances in which it was given.

The Latin verb *mandare* comes from *manus* (hand) and *dare* (to give). It means 'to entrust' or 'to commission'. Other translations also serve. But the root idea is plain: putting something into someone else's hands. More particularly, putting some task into someone's hands. Buying a house for me, extending credit to my friend, pursuing a claim against my enemy.

In the language of agency the person who gives a mandate is a 'principal'. And its recipient is the 'agent'. As we shall see there are differences between mandate and modern agency. In token recognition of those differences it is as well to say *mandator* rather than 'principal'. But on the other side 'agent' is more convenient than *mandatarius*, itself not used by the Romans, and certainly more familiar than 'factor'. So I shall say that a *mandator* gives 'a mandate' to 'an agent'.

The action of the *mandator* was the *actio mandati directa* (the main action on mandate); and the agent had the *actio mandati contraria* (the counter action on mandate). Subject to changing the parties over the wording was the same in either case:

Whereas Aulus Agerius mandated Numerius Negidius to . . . , which matter is the subject of this action,
whatever on that account Numerius Negidius ought to give to or do for Aulus Agerius *ex fide bona*,
for the value of that let the judge condemn Numerius Negidius to Aulus Agerius; if it does not appear, let him absolve.[20]

i. The demonstratio

What facts would substantiate the allegation that a contract of mandate had been made between these two parties? The defendant agent must

[20] For the Latin, see Lenel §108.

have agreed to do something at the plaintiff mandator's request. The dots in the *formula* represent the task to be done. That gerundive construction (a house to be sold, a slave to be bought) is common in the texts on mandate. But it should especially recall hire and, in particular, *locatio operis faciendi*.[21]

The most obvious way of getting something done is to pay. But the most striking feature of mandate is that it must be gratuitous. If the agent is paid or otherwise rewarded the contract cannot be mandate but must be hire or something else. It follows that we have to adjust our image of the contract.

The model on which some texts draw is founded on friendship, *amicitia*. Friendship entails, and indeed feeds on, reciprocal duties. The *mandator* is one who makes a call on the friendship of another. His mandate so to say cashes a credit on this non-commercial plane. This is the right picture, so long as the rôle of *amicitia* is not exaggerated. The law's intervention in and around gratuitous services needs some explanation. Why should a man be liable at all if unrewarded? The answer is the need for mutual solidarity, the same good which friendship also promotes. In this way *amicitia* is the ideal which provides the explanatory peg on which the contract hangs. But it is not necessary to think of every mandate as arising directly out of an established friendship.

The line between mandate and hire depends on the presence or absence of reward. There are also lines between mandate and other gratuitous figures. Among obligations *quasi ex contractu* we will find those arising from uninvited intervention in another's affairs (*negotiorum gestio*).[22] Here the word 'uninvited' is crucial. If you mend my roof when it springs a leak while I am away on holiday there is no contract between us. That is *negotiorum gestio*, an uncommissioned service, the content of mandate without the mandate itself. Suppose I had asked you to meet all such emergencies. That would be enough to turn it into mandate. Or suppose that you stand surety for me and I know but do nothing to forbid you. By hanging back I tacitly request the intervention; and that is enough to make it mandate (D.17.1.6.2 = Ulpian, 31 *On the Edict*).

If I deposit a case with you and pay you, that will be hire. If I do not pay it will be deposit, another gratuitous contract. The titles on deposit

[21] Above, 98.
[22] Below, 259.

and on mandate (D.16.3 and D.17.1) both contemplate the line between mandate and deposit. They do not say that every deposit is also a mandate, which would release the tension. But no satisfactory distinction is propounded. It is certainly difficult to say why a deposit should not be regarded as a mandate to keep, and pleaded as such. Down this path lie quite awkward questions about the need for an independent contract of deposit.

There is obviously a difference between advice and encouragement on the one hand and mandate on the other. If I say, knowing that you have £5,000 in your bank doing nothing, that you could do much better to have it on deposit or in a building society, I would not take myself to be mandating you to invest. We will see that one effect of mandate is to give the agent a right to an indemnity. That is, though not to be rewarded he was to be held free from loss. So if this advice could be turned into a mandate you would be able to invest risk-free, since I would have to indemnify you if things went wrong.

The commonest case in which my communication to you should be construed as mere advice and no mandate is where only your own interest is at stake, which your own judgement should assess. But there may have been a less sensitive time, namely that there could never be a mandate if the agent had any interest at all in the performance. This is what Gaius says (G.3.155–6):

155. There is a valid mandate in both the case where we give a mandate in our own interest (*nostra gratia*) and the case in which we do it for a third party's interest (*aliena gratia*). Hence if I give you a mandate to conduct my business or the business of another, the obligation of mandate is contracted. The result is that we are bound one to another to make good to each other whatever we ought in good faith to answer for . . . 156. If in fact I give you a mandate in your own interest, the mandate is futile (*supervacuum*). For if you are going to do something in your own interest (*tua gratia*) you ought to do it on your own judgement (*de tua sententia*) and not in reliance on a mandate from me (*ex meo mandatu*). So if I encourage you to lend at interest money which you have idle at home you will not have an action on mandate against me even if you lose your money to a dud borrower. Or again, if I encourage you to buy something which turns out to be no use to you, I will not be liable in mandate. And this is carried to the point at which there is a question whether someone is liable in mandate if he mandates you to lend to Titius at interest. Servius said no. He thought there could no more be an obligation in this case than where the commission was to lend out generally. But we

follow the opinion of Sabinus who held the contrary view, on the ground that you would not have lent at interest to Titius but for the mandate given to you (*quia non aliter Titio credidisses quam si tibi mandatum esset*).

The reason given at the end is horrible. For it is equally true of both cases that my intervention may have been the decisive factor. That is, if your strong preference is for keeping your money under your bed, it can as a matter of fact be true, whether I say 'Lend it out' or 'Lend it to Titius', that you would not otherwise have lent it.

One way out of this problem is on these lines. The original objective was to stop people trying to shift responsibility for losses by turning advice into mandates. A test was advanced which made the inquiry of fact into an inquiry of law: was the alleged mandate in the interest of the agent himself? If it was then (whether or not the advice had been decisive as a matter of fact) there could be no legal mandate. As a matter of law a person was under a duty to proceed in matters affecting his own interest on the basis of his own judgement (*id de tua sententia facere debes*). This raised a question. What if the agent had some interest but that interest was mixed with an interest on the part of either or both the *mandator* and a third party, as where the *mandator* wanted money lent at interest to a third party? Servius kept to the rule of law: no mandate where the agent had an interest. Sabinus said the rule of law gave way where the interests were mixed, but left the question of fact whether it was the mandate or the attractiveness of the venture which moved the agent. That is, where the interests were mixed, there could be a valid contract of mandate so long as on the facts it was as an instruction and not as advice that the alleged mandate was perceived.

This pattern of development is partly speculative. It goes some way towards explaining the complex divisions of mandate according to the interests involved, as at D.17.1.2 (Gaius, 2 *Nuggets*) and J.3.26.1–6. And it also seems compatible with what is said in the last cited passage from Justinian's Institutes.

These difficulties are best sealed up by citing one clear and vivid example which shows the Sabinian view (that there could be a mandate where the interests were mixed) in application. This is D.17.1.16 (Ulpian, 31 *On the Edict*):

This question has been put. If someone mandates me to do something on my own property and I do it does the *actio mandati* lie? Celsus, in bk. 7 of his *Digesta*, says that he gave a *responsum* to this effect: Aurelius Quietus's doctor had a garden estate at Ravenna to which Aurelius used to adjourn every year. When he was staying with the doctor it is said that Aurelius gave him a mandate to build a gym and a sauna bath and to do other works to provide health-giving facilities, all at Aurelius's expense. On these facts the *actio mandati* lies for the recovery of the outlay, subject to a deduction allowing for the improved value of his own buildings.

Here it is obvious that the old rule supported by Servius would have led to the opposite conclusion because the doctor agent had an interest in the improvement of his estate. But the interests were mixed. Aurelius enjoyed the air at Ravenna and wanted his host's facilities improved. And in the classical period Celsus had no difficulty in saying that the action would lie to reimburse the agent.

ii. The intentio

What could the plaintiff claim as owing in good faith on account of the mandate? In the *actio directa* (the main action) the *mandator* was concerned with the performance of the mandate and the render up of all that was acquired in the performance. It is convenient to take the render up first.

It is obvious that the agent must make over the very *res* he was told to get once he obtains it. So, if the mandate is to buy a house and the house is conveyed to him, then he in turn must convey it over to the *mandator*. But it does not stop there. He must also make over any actions he has against the vendor or against third parties as for example for damage done to walls or trees. And he must restore any produce of the land which he has taken during the period of his possession.

An agent who finds himself in possession of his principal's money is easily tempted to put it to work by lending it out at interest for a short term or by putting it to his own purposes, as into his own business. Either way he will have to account for the profit, either what he actually received or interest *in lieu*. D.17.1.10.3 (Ulpian, 31 *On the Edict*):

If my agent has money of mine he will certainly have to pay interest in case of delay (*mora*). But also if he puts my money out at interest and receives the instalments of interest, we shall have to draw the conclusion that he must make over whatever profit comes his way whether within the scope of my mandate or not. For this is a principle of good faith: not to make a profit from other people's wealth (*quia bonae fidei hoc congruit, ne de alieno lucrum sentiat*). But if he does not put the money to work but applies it to his own uses, he will nonetheless be liable for interest at the statutory rate prevailing in the district.

A variation on this theme is provided by the agent who, instructed to lend *gratis*, in fact lends at interest. Even though the interest is outside the terms of the mandate yet, in accordance with the principle set out by Ulpian in this passage, the agent must give it up. That case is reached a few paragraphs later, at D.17.1.10.8.[23]

So far as concerns performance the first principle is that the *mandator*'s claim for failure to perform extends only to his financial interest. If he has none, no claim. From the agent's side one way of putting that is to say that his obligation is not to cause loss by non-performance. Thus he can withdraw *re integra*. That is, if the *mandator* has time to rearrange the affairs without financial prejudice, he must accept the agent's renunciation of the mandate.

Once the *mandator* has an inextricable interest in the performance the agent must make good any loss from non-performance. And he must take care to keep within the terms of the mandate. For if he is told to buy peas and yet buys beans he will still be liable for non-performance in regard to the beans. And small deviations can produce dramatic effects. If I mandate you to sell 'for 100' (not 'up to 100' or 'as near to 100 as possible') and you sell for 90 I shall be able to vindicate the *res* from your purchaser and he will attack you for his eviction, and you will have no remedy against me. D.17.1.5 *pr.*–3 (Paul, 32 *On the Edict*):

Diligenter igitur fines mandati custodiendi sunt (Therefore the limits of a mandate are to be carefully observed). 1. For one who goes outside his terms is understood to make a quite different performance and is liable if he fails to fulfil the task which he undertook. 2. And so if I mandate you to buy Seius's house for 100 and you buy Titius's house, much more valuable, for 100 or even less, you will not be taken to have fulfilled your mandate. 3. Again, if I mandate you to sell a farm for 100 and you sell it for 90, then if I bring a *vindicatio* for the farm (*si petam fundum*) no defence will impede my claim unless you make up to me what is lacking from my mandate and hold me free from any loss arising.

[23] Ulpian, 31 *On the Edict*.

What about bad performance which causes loss to the *mandator*? Suppose the agent fails to take care of the *res* he has bought or defends an action so dilatorily that the case is lost. There is no doubt that if this kind of prejudicial performance resulted from *dolus* the agent would be liable. According to the principle that is applied in deposit which excludes liability for *culpa* where the defendant is to perform a gratuitous service, one would expect liability to be confined to *dolus* at least where the agent has no interest. But some texts do speak of a *culpa* liability, and it is certainly not impossible that the fundamental principle of adherence to good faith could have been developed to produce a liability for unreasonable behaviour short of *dolus*.

The main business of the *actio contraria* (the counter-action on mandate) was to obtain reimbursement of the outlay. We have seen one example in the case of *Aurelius Quietus* who evidently would not pay his doctor for the works done to improve his country retreat. Another is D.17.1.12.9 (Ulpian, 31 *On the Edict*):

If you have mandated me to buy something for you and I have bought it out of my own money, I shall have the *actio mandati* to recover the price. But even if I buy with your money I shall have the counter-action for anything *bona fide* spent on the purchase of the thing. And I shall also have the action if you will not take the *res* off me. And the law is the same in other mandates which involve me in expense . . .

Here too the need to attend to the limits of the mandate was brought home to the agent. If he exceeded the mandate he would lose his action for expenses. There was a school dispute on the question whether if the agent exceeded the authorised outlay he might voluntarily bear the extra himself. The Proculian view prevailed. G.3.161 (see also J.3.26.8):

I give you a lawful mandate. You exceed the terms. I have an *actio mandati* against you, provided you could have performed, for the amount of my loss from not having the mandate fulfilled. But you have no action against me. For example if I mandate you to buy a farm for 100 sesterces and you buy it for 150 sesterces you will not have an *actio mandati* against me even if you are willing to give me the farm at the price at which I mandated its purchase. This opinion was very strongly held by Sabinus and Cassius. But if you buy for less you will have your action against me without a doubt. For one who mandates a purchase at 100 impliedly mandates it to be bought cheaper if possible.

However in the Digest (D.17.1.4)[24] an extract from Gaius's *Nuggets* affirms that Proculus correctly thought the agent should have the action, carrying the excess himself. That view is said to be *benignior*, milder or less fierce. Justinian's Institutes say the same.

The contract was discharged by death of one or other party. What would happen then if the agent brought the *actio contraria* for expenses against the heir of the *mandator* and it appeared that the outlay had happened after the death of the *mandator*? Logically he should lose. For the expenses so incurred were not referable to any mandate. But logic did not prevail. The kind of argument which we call sensible or expedient (as opposed to logical) the classics referred to as *utilitas* (as we might say to 'sound policy'). So Gaius says (G.3.160; see also J.3.26.10):

> ... *sed utilitatis causa receptum est* (but it has been accepted on the basis of sound policy) that, where I perform a mandate after, and in ignorance of, the mandator's death, I can bring the *actio mandati*. Otherwise reasonable and demonstrable want of knowledge will cause me loss.

iii. Special applications

There are two special contexts which need to be mentioned and in fact deserve extended treatment though they cannot have it here.

A. Mandate and suretyship There are two ways in which the contract is crucial in the picture of personal security. First, it is the chief means (leaving aside the old *actio depensi* based on the *lex Publilia*) by which a surety obtains an indemnity if he has to pay up. In all but rare cases a surety takes on his rôle as a result of a mandate from the principal debtor. 'Will you guarantee my loan?' is a typical approach. So, when the guarantor agrees and enters into his contract with the creditor he does it under a mandate. And he has the action to recover his expenses. That is, if performing the mandate involves him in an outlay, he has the action to get it reimbursed. And being made to pay up is a guarantor's most obvious expense. He turns on the principal debtor under the contract of mandate between them.

Secondly, mandate can displace *stipulatio* as the means of giving a guarantee. That is, it can establish the relationship between guarantor and creditor as well as between guarantor and principal debtor. 'Lend

[24] Gaius, 2 *Nuggets*.

to Titius' or, thanks to the victory of the Sabinian view, 'Lend to X at interest' makes the lender to X my agent acting under my mandate. If he, the lender, fails to recover his loan then that is an expense under the mandate which he can recover from me. From there it proved possible to develop an informal contract of guarantee of no less importance than the stipulatory forms which we have already looked at.[25]

B. Mandate, litigation and agency At G.4.82–7, Gaius describes the law's attitude to representation in litigation. And it is remarkably relaxed. This has nothing to do with legal support but with substitution of one party for another. You can sue out my claim or defend a claim against me. You can do it by appointment—you will be a *procurator ad litem* or *cognitor ad litem* depending on the mode of appointment—or by uninvited but *bona fide* intervention, a common example of *negotiorum gestio*. Standing in my shoes, you will have to make over to me the product of the litigation and I will have to keep you free from loss. Once again the chief vehicle is the contract of mandate, though the actions for intervention in another's affairs (*actiones negotiorum gestorum*) have to do the work if the substitution is unauthorised.

This contractual representation makes it possible in effect to assign a claim. I want you to have my claim against X. I appoint you to represent me in the litigation. You recover. I do not insist on the accounting over to me. Indeed if the agreement was such that in substance the matter became yours I would not be able to claim the account even if I wanted to. Formally a representative of me, in substance about your own business, you would be called a representative *in rem tuam*, a representative in your own affair.

This same device of transferring the action through representation in litigation arranged by mandate served to supply the omission of any perfect law of agency. By 'perfect' is meant a system of agency in which the agent creates legal relations between his principal and the third party in such a way as himself to drop out: Principal tells Agent to order goods from Wholesaler; Agent does it; Principal has a contract with Wholesaler. Roman law could see that being done where the middle man was only a messenger, a *nuntius*, but not where he had to do the bargaining and fix the terms.

[25] Above, 62–4.

The Roman scheme was for Principal-Mandator to mandate Agent to contract with Wholesaler. Result: Wholesaler in contractual relations with Agent who in turn works under mandate from Principal. But by a simple litigation-mandate, Agent can put Principal in a position to sue Wholesaler *in rem suam*, as a representative about his own business. Principal appears in the action as his own agent's agent under the mandate back to himself. But that is an analytical, not a substantial truth. In substance he is suing on his own affair. And the double mandate (to the agent to bring, back to the principal to sue) only looks complicated. It is easily done.

This mechanism of double mandate only works as a means of allowing Principal to sue on Agent's contract. If Wholesaler wants to sue he has still to sue Agent, who has to rely on his right of indemnity against Principal. In this matter of suing through to Principal the only direct route was provided by the Praetor and then only in those circumstances covered by the 'additional liability actions (*actiones adiecticiae qualitatis*)'.

To give a complete picture of Roman mechanisms which substitute for perfect agency it is necessary to put together three pieces: the law relating to contracts made by those in power, including slaves, the law of mandate and in particular of the device of double mandate just described; and finally the law of these praetorian actions with an additional liability. The praetorian actions deal both with family agents and outside agents. Their business is to bring liabilities home to the principal, rights being accessible to him more easily either as *paterfamilias* or as representative *in rem suam*.

6

Contracts *Re*

The first group of informal contracts were those *consensu*, four of them. This second group also has four members. The apparent symmetry is deceptive. The numbers balance but the weight does not. Sale, hire, partnership and mandate between them cover most of commercial life. The four contracts *re* are much smaller fry. The four members of the group are *mutuum* (loan for consumption), *commodatum* (loan for use), *depositum* (deposit) and *pignus* (pledge).

All these involve the delivery of a *res* by one person to another. And it is from the moment of that hand-over that the obligations come into being. If you want to be able to rely on borrowing tomorrow or giving in your case to be stored the next day, you must arrange it by stipulation or in some other way, perhaps by mandate. These four contracts *re* having nothing to do with such executory obligations. They are only concerned with the consequences after the making of the loan, deposit and so on: not agreements to do them but obligations born of having done them. So the delivery of a *res* is an important marker and one common to them all.

Perhaps that is what *re* is meant to mean. The books all say so. But another view is possible, though at first sight less attractive. I think *re* here means 'by conduct'. If it means 'by the thing', the *res* in question is not the coin or the case or the sheep but the business of lending, depositing, pledging and so on. The thing denoted by the names *mutuum*, *depositum* and the others. 'By the event in the name' and hence 'by conduct', 'by the conduct of lending'.

This is not madly important. But we might look at some difficulties which arise if we say *re* means 'by delivery of a *res*'. I will not labour the point beyond two examples. First, Justinian coming to wrongs says this (J.4.1 *pr.*):

In the previous book we have dealt with obligations from contract and *quasi* from contract. The next thing is to deal with those which arise from wrongdoing. As we explained group by group, those contractual obligations are divided into four types. These delictual obligations by contrast are all of one kind. For they are all born *ex re*, that is *ex ipso maleficio* (from the wrongdoing itself) as from *furtum* (theft), from *rapina* (robbery), from *damnum* (loss), from *iniuria* (contempt).

How shall *ex re* be rendered? Obviously not 'from the delivery of a thing', which does not happen in these stories. 'From the thing itself' in the sense of 'the event described in the name' is all right: 'from theft,' 'from contempt' and so on. More generally 'from conduct' is also all right, making the same point less explicitly.

The next example is also from delict and may not yet be completely intelligible. The delict *iniuria* is very diverse in content. Contempts need to be classified in order to be made intellectually manageable. D.47.10.1.1 (Ulpian, 56 *On the Edict*) gives part of Labeo's plan:

Iniuriam autem fieri Labeo ait aut re aut verbis: re quotiens manus inferuntur: verbis autem quotiens non manus inferuntur convicium fit.
Labeo says that contempt-*iniuria* is committed either *re* or by words: *re* as often as a blow is struck, by words as often as no blow is struck but offensive words are shouted.

There are good reasons for thinking the expansion of the first division, either *re* or *verbis*, is textually unsound but that need not detain us here. *Re aut verbis*: what does *re* mean? It can mean 'by the event itself', it being understood that verbal events are in the other class. Or it could mean 'by conduct'.

There may be a way around this kind of evidence. But such as it is it points away from the contract *re* as a contract 'by delivery'. 'By conduct (*scilicet* the conduct in the name of the contract)' seems to me better. And the Institutional scheme '*re*, *verbis*, *litteris*, *consensu*' reads well and sensibly as 'by conduct, by words, by writing, by (mere) agreement'.

1. *Mutuum* (Loan for Consumption)

Actions with single causal events, such as sale, hire and so on, fit easily into the non-actional classification dominated by contract and delict. Each event fits into the category of contract or of delict or of miscellaneous other causes, and it carries its actional regime with it. The abstract, multi-causal *condictio* does not fit into this classification. The list of events, proof of which substantiates its allegation, has to be distributed between contract and the miscellaneous residue.

This is what the *condictio* says:

Iudex . . . esto. Si paret Numerium Negidium Aulo Agerio sestertium decem milia dare oportere,
Let . . . be judge. If it appears that Numerius Negidius ought-at-civil-law to give Aulus Agerius ten thousand sesterces,

iudex Numerium Negidium Aulo Agerio sestertium decem milia condemnato; si non paret absolvito.
for ten thousand sesterces let the judge condemn Numerius Negidius to Aulus Agerius; if it does not appear, let him absolve.

The claim here is for the render of money. For a *certum* in kind there had to be a slight change in order to get the condemnation into money. So if 'ten measures of best African grain' replaces the money in the *intentio*, the *condemnatio* has to become:

as much as that matter is worth for so much in money let the judge condemn Numerius Negidius to Aulus Agerius; if it does not appear let him absolve.

The *formula* puts the burden on the plaintiff to prove before the *iudex* some event which as a matter of law does amount to an 'ought-at-civil-law to give . . .'. He has to prove some acknowledged cause of indebtedness. We have already seen that *stipulatio* and *expensilatio* are events in the contractual part of the spectrum of such causes. The non-contractual part of the spectrum will be considered in connexion with the quasi categories and the miscellaneous residue of events beyond contract and wrongs.[1] *Mutuum* is the third and last event in the contractual part of the spectrum. If you prove a *mutuum* before the *iudex*,

[1] See Ch. 11.

you establish the ought-at-civil-law-to-give, the old *ius civile* obligation which the words of the *condictio* assert.

'Lend' and 'borrow' in our usage cover two transactions. 'May I borrow your pen?' This leads to a temporary transfer of the pen. The pen itself is to be returned, and there is no suggestion that the borrower acquires ownership of the pen. While I am writing with it, it remains yours. That is *commodatum*, loan for use. 'May I borrow £50?' Quite different. Now the £50 will be permanently transferred in the sense that the lender will never see those coins or notes again. There is to be returned, not the original receipt, but its equivalent, another £50. And here ownership does pass. This is not confined to money. 'May I borrow six eggs and a pint of milk?' Just as with the £50, these eggs and this bottle of milk must become mine. I will give back substitutes. This second type of loan is *mutuum*. We translate it as 'loan-for-consumption'. Not very elegant and not quite accurate, in the sense that money is not naturally 'consumed?', and if I borrow eggs I do not necessarily mean to 'consume' them. Perhaps I want to give them away or sell them or throw them at a politician. It makes no difference. So 'for consumption' is an approximation. Its rôle is to set up the contrast between the two kinds of loan. Is there a better translation? It is more exact to say 'loan where repayment is to be made by way of exchange in kind'. But that is cumbersome. 'Exchange-loan' might be acceptable but is not self-explanatory.

Paul says that the word *mutuum* is used because in this kind of loan the lending is such that *de meo tuum fit* (because what was mine becomes yours): D.12.1.2.1 (Paul, 28 *On the Edict*). Justinian repeats this: J.3.14 *pr.* This assertion that *mutuum* is really *meo-tuum* (mine-thine) makes a good point but is bad etymology. The word really belongs with the family based on the verb *mutare* which one learns first as 'to change'. A slightly more sophisticated list would include 'to exchange, replace, substitute'. The borrower, whose act is *mutuum sumere* or *mutuum accipere*, and the lender, whose act is *mutuum dare*, receive and give what must be given back by substitution. That seems to be where the ideas in *mutare* come in. Possibly also in the reciprocation between the parties.

Things which are normally handled by number, weight or measure and which if lent are therefore lent for return in kind and not *in specie* (money, apples, cloth) can in a rare case be lent the other way, for specific return. The play you are putting on may need among its props a bottle of whisky and a basket of apples. Coins and stamps may be exhibition-worthy. It is perfectly possible to borrow things usually returned in kind on the understanding that they shall be returned *in specie*. The intent of the parties, not the nature of the *res*, determines the character of the transaction. If the parties intend specific return the loan will not be *mutuum* but *commodatum*. This has important consequences. If you bring the *condictio* and the greengrocer shows that the deal was *commodatum* you will lose since *commodatum* does not give rise to a *certum dare oportere*. That is a pleading point and one which ceases to be relevant after the abandonment of the formulary system of litigation. But there are substantial points too. If the apples you borrowed went next minute under the wheels of a cab the whole pattern of inquiry will be different according as your borrowing was *mutuum* or *commodatum*. We will come back to that.

Mutuum always involves an exchange of exact equivalence in kind and quality. If the agreement is that I shall give back something different, the transaction will be barter (*permutatio*) or even sale. *Nam si aliud genus, veluti ut pro tritico vinum recipiamus, non erit mutuum*: For if a different genus [is involved] as that for corn we should get back wine, it will not be *mutuum* (D.12.1.2 *pr.* = Paul, 28 *On the Edict*).

This discussion resembles the treatment of the *demonstratio* in relation to the *formulae* of actions on sale, hire and so on. What is a *mutuum* and what is not quite a *mutuum*? But the *condictio* has no *demonstratio*, no 'whereas' clause stating the event from which the obligations are supposed to have arisen. The word 'abstract' is used to indicate this absence of grounds stated. We only re-create the pattern of the earlier discussions by concentrating on one particular ground, here *mutuum*. Having done that can we turn, as previously, to 'What follows?' Not really. Because only one thing follows. The single consequence is that which the *formula* describes in its fixed and abstract *intentio*. Slipped back into direct speech, the *formula* is asking 'Does it appear that the defendant ought-at-civil-law to give £20 (or 20 kilos of apples)?' When the *mutuum* is proved—or any other ground—that is what follows: it does appear that he owes the £20. And then the *condemnatio* follows up in exactly the same terms.

This means that you should not really approach *mutuum* by asking first what it is and then what follows. You should always be asking what amounts to this obligation to pay £20. What is the totality of the event which supports that conclusion? Take the issue of interest. It is elementary that interest cannot be recovered under *mutuum*. But the truer way (that is, truer to the classical eye) to perceive that is to suppose a *formula* in which the defendant is said to owe £110. And then to ask whether the plaintiff can recover if he shows that one year ago he lent the defendant £100 with a pact annexed for the payment of 10 per cent interest. And the answer is found in the fact that the *formula* puts the question on the basis of the letter of the *ius civile* unsupplemented by a reference to good faith. *Strictum ius*, deriving from ancient juristic interpretation, did not give effect to informal pacts. If the plaintiff wanted to show that he was entitled to his 10 per cent he could do it by proving a loan of 100 and a formal contract, a *stipulatio*, for interest. In practice if he had taken a formal promise for interest he probably would have taken it for the principal sum too, thus effecting his whole transaction by *stipulatio*.

Under the same *formula* asserting an obligation to pay £110, what happens if the plaintiff did lend that sum but ten seconds later all the money went, literally, down the drain? Or suppose the claim is for a bottle of wine, and he says that he dropped it before he could drink it. The defendant remains liable. There is no need to ask any questions about fault or standards or care. What is lent under *mutuum* becomes the property of the borrower. All the risks are on him. That is, as any owner he can look for someone to sue for causing him loss but he cannot use the existence of his contract of loan to shift the loss to the lender. Even if the money was lost by violent robbery or natural disaster (a sudden whirlwind) the lender must repay. What the borrower does once the loan is his is nothing to the lender. Neither bad luck nor good. If the borrower of 10 buys a trinket which turns out to be a treasure worth 10,000, the lender has no hope of a share.

There is one problem which arises when the loan is not of money. Take the standpoint of a *iudex* who finds himself handling a *formula* which says that the defendant owes wine in a given quantity. If it says nothing about quality, how can he condemn for the value of very good wine even if very good wine was lent? I am not sure how this problem would have been dealt with. The judge's difficulty may have been eased by the fact that the plaintiff was allowed to put a value on his claim under oath. But the proper way out was not to be vague in the pleading. You should say in your pleading what quality you lent within the *genus* which you lent. The model *formula* said 'best of African grain'. Narrow interpretation characteristic of *strictum ius* did not prevent there being an implication that the obligation was to repay the same quality as was lent. D.12.1.3 (Pomponius, 27 *On Sabinus*):

When we give something by way of *mutuum*, even if we fail to provide expressly for a return of the same quality, the debtor may not give back something worse albeit of the same genus, as new wine for old: for in contracting what is intended is to be taken as provided for, and what is intended here is understood to be that the repayment should be both of the same genus and of the same quality as what was given.

2. *Commodatum* (Loan for Use)

First a general comment, on leaving *mutuum* behind. The remaining three real contracts have much in common and stand somewhat apart from *mutuum*. *Mutuum* is *stricti iuris*, unilateral, entails transfer of ownership, and torn from the *condictio* is the founder member of the category of contracts *re*, its only member in Gaius's Institutes. By contrast the next three are *bonae fidei* (though all acquired their *bonae fidei* actions after they had been founded first on *actiones in factum*), are bilateral (though unequally so in the sense that one party's obligations are much less than the others), do not entail the passage of property, and evidently become real contracts only on second thoughts, though perhaps of Gaius himself (D.44.7.1 = Gaius, 2 *Nuggets*). So this transition marks the fact that the category of real contracts is made up from two historical traditions of quite different character. This makes it a brave category, insisting on a new unity.

The basic idea of *commodatum* has already been introduced: the loan of a pen, a knife, a horse, something to be returned *in specie*. The word itself is quite slippery. The simplest thing is to say that the noun *commodum* means 'an advantage, a profit, a favourable opportunity'. Then, the adjective *commodus* means 'pleasing, advantageous, suitable'; our 'commodious' is horrible now, abused by estate agents. The verb *commodare* thus means 'to put (something) at (someone's) convenience' and hence 'to lend for his use'. The main action (*actio commodati directa*) lay against the borrower to enforce his obligations to keep safe the *res* and to return it. In its *bonae fidei* version the action had this *formula*:

Whereas Aulus Agerius commodated the . . . to Numerius Negidius, which matter is the subject of this action,

whatever on that account Numerius Negidius ought to give to or do for Aulus Agerius *ex fide bona*,
for the value of that let the judge condemn Numerius Negidius to Aulus Agerius; if it does not appear, let him absolve.[2]

However, Gaius tells us (G.4.47) that *commodatum* is one of the events for which the praetor published model pleadings both *in ius concepta* (framed on the law: the one just given) and *in factum concepta*, framed so as to do more than tell the story, without asserting any legal inference about an *oportere* (an 'ought'). Gaius actually gives the *formula in factum* for deposit but the one for *commodatum* must have been much the same, with the important omission of any reference to fraud. G.4.47 (continued):

If it appears that Aulus Agerius commodated the . . . which is the subject of this action to Numerius Negidius and that it has not been returned to Aulus Agerius,
for as much as it shall be worth for so much let the judge condemn Numerius Negidius to Aulus Agerius; if it does not appear let him absolve.

The existence of both types of *formulae* and the active survival of the almost certainly older *actio in factum* is precious evidence for and, at the same time, a puzzle in the story of the development. It also raises interesting questions about the relationship between law resting on praetorian *imperium* and the non-praetorian *ius civile*. However these large questions have to be laid aside in favour of a brief account of the contract itself. I shall use the *formula in ius concepta* and shall stick to the method which deals separately with *demonstratio* and *intentio*.

i. The demonstratio

'Whereas AA commodated the . . .': There is not much that needs to be said. Ulpian thought the same. Expounding the words of the edict, not here the *formula*, he observes '*Huius edicti interpretatio non est difficilis*: the interpretation of this edict is not difficult' (D.13.6.1.1 = Ulpian, 28 *On the Edict*). And the one point he feels constrained to take is that the word *commodatum* is strictly apt only for movable things. He says Labeo's view was that *utendum dare* (to give for use) was the genus

[2] For the Latin, see Lenel §98.

with *commodare* the species peculiar to movable goods. If that was right as a matter of nice linguistic usage the edict was given the generic scope, to include land too. Ulpian cites Cassius and Vivianus for that.

The exercise of differentiation has mostly been done under other contracts. If the recipient gives a reward (*merces*) for the benefit of borrowing the plough the contract is hire, not *commodatum*. This contract is always gratuitous. Obviously there can be distinct loans which cancel each other out: last week I lent you my plough, today as it happens you lend me yours. But if the two are limited in one agreement—'In return for my lending now, you will lend next week'—the contract is neither hire nor *commodatum*. Not the latter because not gratuitous, not the former because in the same relation to *locatio-conductio* as is *permutatio* to sale. So the deal which looks like linked counter-loans has to be dealt with as an innominate contract by the gap-filling *actio praescriptis verbis*. Finally, what might otherwise be *commodatum* becomes *depositum* if the *res* is to be kept, not used. *Commodatum* is always for the convenience and advantage of the borrower, a horse for a journey or some other task. A horse to be kept for its owner is not lent.

ii. The intentio

What obligations follow? The lender's main concern is to get the thing back at the end of the loan. This shows up well in the *formula in factum concepta* in which the complaint is precisely that the *res* has not been given back: *eam rem redditam non esse*. Return is thus the borrower's main obligation.

But there is also the question of care during the period of user. What if the thing is given back but in a bad state? And this bears back on to the obligation to return. For what if the *res* has been destroyed or taken away by theft and cannot be returned for that reason?

This is a difficult matter. It turns on that warranty liability for safe-keeping called in Latin the liability *custodiam praestare*: to answer for security (but both words are difficult). There are two questions about this security-liability: What did it entail? and, When did it apply? The texts have been interfered with to a degree which remains exceptionally controversial.

It is a good policy when one sees a horrid instability approaching to say first whatever can be said with certainty. That way the doubt can be penned in. Otherwise more seems unintelligible than really is. What is certain in relation to this borrower is that his liability extends beyond *dolus*. He cannot escape by showing he did not mean to lose the *res* or to damage it. The other side of this same certainty is that he remains liable if he is at fault when judged by the standard of the reasonable man, the *bonus paterfamilias*. If there is any uncertainty there it is in the description of the standard by which the *culpa* (fault) is to be judged. But the question whether the *bonus paterfamilias* and our man on the Clapham omnibus are anthropomorphic conceptions of the same standard need not detain us. There are many texts which clearly endorse this assertion that the borrower's liability does extend to *culpa*, e.g. D.13.6.5.2–4 (Ulpian, 28 *On the Edict*):

2. Now we must ask what is caught by the action on *commodatum*. Is it *dolus* (hostile intent), *culpa* (fault) or *omne periculum* (insurance liability for every disaster)? Under contracts we sometimes have to answer for *dolus* only and sometimes for *culpa* too. In the case of deposit, it is *dolus* only. That is quite right, because no advantage (*utilitas*) accrues to the depositee . . . But where advantage accrues to both sides, as in sale, hire, dower, pledge and partnership, there the liability is for both *dolus* and *culpa*. 3. In *commodatum*, however, the advantage generally accrues solely to the borrower. Which is why the opinion of Quintus Mercius is the more correct. His view was that the borrower must answer for *culpa* and must therefore show *diligentia* (care, attention); and further that in a case where the *res* is handed over subject to a money valuation he must also answer for *omne periculum* in that he will have undertaken to make good the money value at all events. 4. On the other hand nothing is to be put down to the borrower's account where the *res* is overtaken by old age or by disease or dragged off by robbers, or if something else of that kind happens, so long as no fault is found on the borrower's part. In the same way if a blaze or the collapse of a building or some other fate-destined loss is the cause of some disaster, then the borrower will not be liable. Not unless, for example, when he could have made the borrowed things safe he carried out his own first.

The next pair is interesting because the first gives an extract from one jurist, Julian, and the second shows a later writer, Ulpian, citing and qualifying the earlier utterance. D.13.6.19 (Julian, *Digest*):

People who hire the job of keeping something or borrow something for use (*qui servandum aliquid conducunt aut utendum occipiunt*) do not, and this is far from being in doubt, have to bear the consequences arising from *damnum iniuria datum* (the delict of 'loss wrongfully caused') committed by another: for by what care or attention can we make sure that nobody commits wrongful loss against us?

Then D.19.2.41 (Ulpian, 5 *On the Edict*):

But Julian holds that you cannot sue him in respect of loss inflicted by another: for by what safe-keeping could you ensure that nobody did you wrongful loss? But Marcellus says it sometimes can work out like that. As where he could have arranged a guard or the guard he arranged himself did the wrongful loss. And this opinion of Marcellus ought to be followed.

These texts and others not dissimilar may have been tampered with. But if we use them to support the proposition that the borrower's liability went beyond *dolus* and extended to *culpa*, we will be safe. It is only when we ask whether they show that the borrower could not be liable without at least the proof of *culpa*, i.e. show also that there was no strict liability, that we have to treat what they say with *exactissima diligentia* (the most exacting attentiveness).

One more thing can be said with confidence. If the borrower went outside the scope of the contract, as by putting a slave to work up a scaffolding when he was lent for gardening or by taking a horse into battle when lent for an ordinary journey, he would have to answer for every disaster, *omne periculum*, irrespective of *culpa*. Furthermore, though this is a separate matter, even if no disaster supervened, he would face a delictual liability for theft if he had dishonestly extended the use he had been allowed. For liability in theft did not depend on an intention permanently to deprive the owner of the *res* itself.[3]

This brings us to security-liability (*custodiam praestare*). First, what was it? Second, did it at any time apply to the borrower by *commodatum*?

Security-liability was a species of strict liability; that is, liability independent of fault or, more accurately, of the proof of fault. But it was not an absolute liability; that is, it was not imposed totally without regard for the circumstances. A person subject to security-liability would be liable without proof of fault but not if the disaster occurred through an event beyond the power of any man to prevent, as death by old age or disease, earthquake, enemy action, incursion of armed bands. These forces are summed up in the phrase *vis maior* (too great

[3] Below, 161.

force, 'act of God'). Another way of looking at it is to say that one who, either expressly or by implication from the nature of the contract, warrants the security of the thing is understood to guarantee its safety not absolutely but so far as human means can achieve it.

You may say that this amounts to the same thing as fault liability. In nine out of ten cases it will produce the same result. If the disaster was an act of God outside the scope of the warranty, the warrantor will also be free of fault; if the disaster was not from act of God and therefore was caught by the security-warranty, the warrantor will have been at fault. In nine out of ten cases. In the tenth the conclusion will be different. I do everything that a *bonus paterfamilias* would do. I set two men to guard your plough. Nobody would do more. By an ingenious plan thieves nevertheless get the plough. Let it be that they lure the guards away with false messages apparently from myself. Anybody would have been taken in. Non-violent theft is not *vis maior*. So if I am under security-liability I must pay up. But I was not at fault. If my liability had been for *culpa* I would have escaped. It is an interesting question whether it is possible to construct an example the other way about. One, that is, in which I would be liable on a *culpa* basis but escape when the liability is for *custodia*. I think it is not. Because security-liability is something super-added to *culpa* liability. But this is historically, and analytically, more difficult than it seems.

This account is consciously coy about the kind of disasters within security liability. There is room to take one of two positions. The larger is that the warranty for security extended to all harm to the thing (damage and destruction) as well as loss, i.e. disappearance, typically by theft. The narrower view is that only loss, in the sense of disappearance, is in question, while harm is left to the *culpa* liability. I think the larger view is probably right. This doubt is an instability within the scope of security-liability. That is, whenever we say that security-liability did or did not attach to such and such a bailee (temporary transferee) we are not completely sure whether we mean a qualified strict liability for inability to produce the *res* or for both that and for damage apparent in the *res* as produced.

Did the *custodia*-liability attach to *commodatum* at any time? There is a good, though complex, argument to the effect that the compilers meant the liability to be limited to *culpa* except where more was expressly undertaken by the borrower. One way of undertaking *omne periculum* was to agree to take the *res* at a valuation, a sum to be restored at all events. But special arrangements between the parties aside, the

Justinianic law made liability turn on *culpa*, fault. In other words, no security-warranty was implied into *commodatum*.

On the other hand it is almost certain that in classical law the borrower did have this security-liability unless he expressly excluded it. In this connexion the exact words of the *formula in factum* would be decisive. Did it say just 'If it appears that the . . . was not returned . . .'? Or did it include some reference to a reason or qualification, as 'If it appears that the . . . through the defendant was not returned . . .'? Sadly we do not know, though Lenel gives the unqualified version. If Gaius had not chosen the formulae of *depositum* to be his full example of doubling up pleadings *in ius* and *in factum* we would have had the *commodatum* formulae spelled out in full. And the *commodatum* case is much more interesting. The liability in *deposit* is uncomplicated.

However, Gaius himself does provide the best evidence for the *custodia*-liability of the classical borrower. It is in his discussion of theft. His question is, Who may sue for theft? The general answer is, whoever has an interest in the safety of the thing. But this means, turned about, that sometimes an owner cannot sue because the safety of the thing is of no interest to him. When can that be? When he has the benefit of a contract under which there is a security-guarantee. For then whatever happens he cannot lose the value of the thing by reason of theft. G.3.205–7:

205. Also, suppose a cleaner receives clothes to be laundered or treated, or a tailor get clothes for mending and they do this for a fixed reward. Then they lose the clothes by theft. They, not the owner, have the *actio furti*. Because the owner has no interest in the clothes not being lost. For in the trial on hire he can obtain his whole interest from the cleaner or tailor, so long at least as the cleaner or tailor has the money to answer for the goods. In fact, if the worker is insolvent then the owner himself has the *actio furti*. Because, unable to get the value of his interest by that route, he has in this case an interest in the safety of his goods. 206. Everything we have said about the cleaner and tailor applies across to the person to whom we have lent something for use. Those two have to warrant the security of the thing because they earn a reward (*merces*) from it. In the same way this borrower has to bear the same warranty, because he too takes the profit of its use. 207. What of the depositee? He does not warrant the security of the thing. And he is only liable in respect of it if he himself does something *dolo malo* (with malicious intent). It follows from this that if the thing is snatched away from him he cannot bring the *actio furti*. Because, having no liability in the action on

deposit in respect of the restoration of the *res*, he lacks an interest in its safety. So the *dominus* has the *actio furti*.

The emphasis on theft comes from the context of the discussion. The inference however is quite clear: the liability of the borrower is such as to make the lender safe without inquiring into fault. That is the whole point.

There remains the *actio contraria*. What can the lender owe the borrower when the loan is gratuitous and in the borrower's interest? Paul points out, at D.13.6.17.3,[4] that as in *negotiorum gestio* what starts as a kindness becomes a duty once begun. If the lender gives something for a purpose and then leaves the borrower high and dry by recalling the *res* before the purpose is complete, he must pay his loss. As for example if you lend me a scribe to take down a contract or some scaffolding for building repair, and then, once I am relying on the loan to meet my need, you take the *res* back. If the *res* needs special attention, the lender should pay, as where a slave becomes ill and needs medical care. The borrower must meet daily and ordinary expenses, as for instance food. But not exceptional impositions. Again defective *res* can be more trouble than none at all. Vessels which leak or contaminate the contents cause loss, not *commodum*. And the lender must answer for it. This liability is referable to the good faith on which the action *in ius* is built. It appears not to be confined to *dolus*, despite the lender's lack of material interest.

3. *Depositum* (Deposit)

The word is clear. It comes from *deponere*, which produces more instantly recognisable forms in the past and passive (*deposui*, *depositum*). At its simplest *deponere* just means 'to put down' or 'to set aside' and from there it reaches 'to commit to (someone's keeping)'. The actions had *formulae* of two types. This has been explained in relation to *commodatum*.[5] The *formula in factum concepta* (drafted on the facts) ran as follows:

If it appears that Aulus Agerius deposited with Numerius Negidius a table made of silver and that by the *dolus malus* of Numerius Negidius it has not been returned to Aulus Agerius,

[4] Paul, 29 *On the Edict*.
[5] Above, 135–6.

for as much as it shall be worth, for so much money let the judge condemn Numerius Negidius to Aulus Agerius; if it does not appear, let him absolve.

As to the *formula in ius concepta* (drafted on the law), it read:

Whereas Aulus Agerius deposited with Numerius Negidius a table made of silver, which matter is the subject of this action,
Whatever on that account Numerius Negidius ought to give to or do for Aulus Agerius *ex fide bona*,
for the value of that let the judge condemn Numerius Negidius to Aulus Agerius; if it does not appear let him absolve.[6]

The edict over these model *formulae* is also useful to set out. It is preserved complete by a full quotation at the beginning of Ulpian's treatment of the topic. Only by weird punctuation can a translation approach the beautiful economy of the original. D.16.3.1.1 (Ulpian, 30 *On the Edict*):

Praetor ait:
Quod neque tumultus neque incendii neque ruinae neque naufragii causa depositum sit, in simplum,
earum autem rerum quae supra comprehensae sunt, in ipsum in duplum, in heredem eius quod dolo malo eius factum esse dicetur qui mortuus sit, in simplum, quod ipsius, in duplum,
iudicium dabo.

The praetor says:
On the ground that a deposit has been made other than by reason of riot, fire, collapse or shipwreck: for the simple value;
in the excepted cases here above described, against the depositee himself: for double value; against his heir: on the ground of what shall be said to have been done by the *dolus malus* of the deceased, for the simple value; on the ground of what shall be said to have been done by his own *dolus malus*, for double value, I shall grant a trial.

i. The demonstratio

The definition of deposit has already been encountered in differentiating other contracts from their nearest neighbours. The difficulty of

[6] For the Latin, see Lenel §106.

distinguishing deposit from mandate was considered in connexion with mandate.[7] Though deposit easily brings to mind a left luggage office, the transaction with British Rail would be *locatio-conductio*, because not gratuitous. The line between *commodatum* and deposit is clear enough, because deposit excludes user.

There is an awkward boundary with *mutuum* (loan for consumption), though in principle there ought to have been no blur. Money is the root of the problem. There is nothing wrong with a deposit of coins whether in a bag or loose, so long as the intention is that the depositee shall keep and return the very coins which are handed over. If the intention is that he shall use the money and return the equivalent that ought to be *mutuum*, with the property in the coins passing to the recipient. The motivation for the transaction ought not to be relevant. Hence the fact that the recipient was not soliciting a loan but being asked to accept one should not have the effect of drawing the transaction out of its natural category. Nevertheless, once you accept the validity of a deposit of coins to be returned *in specie* there are obvious practical difficulties in holding the line between that and the transaction in which the coins may be turned over. For example it is difficult to decide whether coins are being returned *in specie* or not. And if you cannot decide whether they are, it is better to say it does not matter. This practical problem joins forces with an advantage in allowing the development to happen. For if the 'deposit' which could be turned over could be litigated as a deposit rather than as *mutuum*, then the action would be based on *bona fides*. One consequence would be that informal pacts for interest could be annexed. At some time this departure from principle was achieved and 'irregular deposit' was accepted as deposit. This may have happened in the classical period. But that is doubtful. At all events this next text, D.16.3.24 (Papinian, 9 *Questions*), seems to be resisting the change though, arguably, it gives in at the end in lines very probably not from Papinian's pen:

'Lucius Titius sends greetings to Sempronius. I declare to you by this letter written in my hand that you should take knowledge of the fact that I now hold one hundred coins commended to me this day by yourself and paid over by Stichus your slave-accountant; which coins where and when you will I shall immediately repay.' On this a question is put about increase by

[7] Above, 120–1.

interest. My *responsum* was: The action which lies is the *actio depositi*, for what does 'commend' mean if not 'deposit'? Yet this is only so if what was intended was that the very same coins should be returned. But if it was agreed that the equivalent value should be given back the matter lies outside the very well-known limits of *depositum*. And in this question if the *actio depositi* does not lie because it was agreed to return the equivalent and not the same coins, then it must not lightly be said that an account of interest can be taken. It has indeed been laid down that, so far as interest is concerned in trials based on good faith the discretion of the judge can do as much as a *stipulatio*. Yet it is contrary to good faith and to the nature of the contract of deposit to seek interest for a time before *mora* (delay) from one who has done a kindness in undertaking to take in money. However, if from the beginning the agreement was that interest should be paid then the terms of the contract will be upheld.

This is thoroughly unhappy. It allows an action for agreed interest without ever saying quite what action it is to be. There is a very similar vacillation in D.16.3.26.1 (Paul, 4 *Replies*). There, however, the action to be given is clearly the *actio depositi*. Despite these difficulties some scholars believe that the interest-bearing generic deposit of money was classical.[8] It merits a sizeable question-mark. On the other hand D.16.3.28 (Scaevola, 1 *Replies*) contains a case which looks like a stratagem. The recipient writes that he himself has decided (without being asked) to put the other's money out to work. Scaevola allows a *bonae fidei iudicium*, presumably deposit. It is difficult to see how any other conclusion would be reached: since a secret profit would have to be accounted for, *a fortiori* once revealed. The contract is deposit, the depositee confesses he has misbehaved. Such admissions could do the trick.

ii. The intentio

The main action (*actio directa*) lay to recover the *res*. The obligation to return it has been sufficiently considered in connexion with *commodatum*.[9] The *depositee*, who receives nothing for his kindness, is liable only for *dolus*. Express terms can be agreed to oblige him to take care of the thing as well as to abstain from *dolus*.

[8] For an overview of the relevant literature, see Reinhard Zimmermann, *The Law of Obligations: Roman Foundations of the Civilian Tradition* (Oxford: Clarendon Press, 1996), 216ff and references cited.

[9] Above, 137–9.

The counter-action lay to the depositee for him to claim an indemnity against the incidental expenses of the deposit, if any. As for example the feeding of an animal or the carriage costs of a deposit agreed to be rendered up at another place. He could also use the action to obtain compensation for any loss inflicted by the deposit if good faith required the depositor to make it good.

Very often, but not always, the depositee would by the same *dolus* as made him liable in the *actio depositi* also incur liability for theft. Not always. Fraudulent denial would not in itself be theft without handling of the *res*. Malicious destruction of the *res* would not be *furtum* but *damnum iniuria datum* (loss wrongfully caused). When this separate question of delictual liability is allowed into the picture, there is a certain artificiality in saying that the depositee could only be liable for *dolus*. For in some fact situations he would incur liability for *damnum iniuria datum* on the basis of mere negligence.

4. *Pignus* (Pledge)

In the centre of the picture you can safely put the transaction with the pawnbroker. The rise of the High Street banks, which give relatively easy access to credit, has pushed pawnbroking into a smaller and ever seedier segment of the money-lending market. It has not disappeared. And times change. It may come back. At all events you know what is involved. I go in to borrow £10 and I leave my watch behind. When I pay I get my watch back. There is no need for the moment for a more careful legal analysis. This is *pignus*. You can see how it fits in with *commodatum* and *depositum*. It is instantly recognisable as a sort of specialised deposit, a bailment with a particular rôle and purpose.

There is one danger in starting from this point. So far as we create a gulf between pawning a watch and mortgaging a house or an aeroplane, that division is foreign to *pignus*. Gaius would secure a loan or other credit by pledging his silver cutlery or his farm. *Pignus* would serve equally for both.

In connexion with *stipulatio* we met the distinction between personal and real security.[10] There is personal security where a creditor before granting credit or giving more time insists on having a recourse

[10] Above, 62.

against a person other than the principal debtor. There is real security when the creditor insists on a recourse against a *res*. 'Recourse' is deliberately vague. It has to comprehend a number of different possibilities. Before going further into *pignus* itself it will help first to take a grip on the basic structure of real security.

There are two separate legal relations involved: (i) between the debtor and the creditor, and (ii) between the creditor and the *res*. To this for completeness should be added (iii) between the creditors themselves if and when there are more than one with recourse against the same *res*. But this third set can be ignored as factually not always present and legally not possible until a certain degree of sophistication is achieved.

The relationship between debtor and creditor is contractual, no different from the relationship between depositor and depositee, lender and borrower. There are reciprocal rights and duties founded on actual agreement or on the law's interpretation of the *natura contractus*, the nature of the contract. This is the part with which *pignus* is concerned. That is, the actions based on *pignus* (*actiones pigneraticiae*) deal with the contractual duties of the parties *inter se*. The direct action on *pignus* lies against the pledge-creditor; the counter-action lies to the pledge-creditor against the debtor. The symmetry with *depositum* and *commodatum* is evident.

The relationship between the creditor and the *res* has two aspects, practical (or, factual) and analytical (or, legal). These terms are not technical but just labels adopted for the purpose of exposition. It is often said that there are and can be many different kinds of real security. Even in Roman law itself there existed concurrently two kinds, *pignus* itself and *fiducia* (of which some mention will be made at the end of this chapter). The kinds of real security are differentiated chiefly in the nature of the legal aspect of the relationship between the creditor and the *res*. Differences in the legal aspect carry over into the practical aspect of the relationship.

The practical aspect is concerned with the physical whereabouts of the *res* during the period in which it is the creditor's security. Who is to keep the ring or occupy the farm? The simple case is that the debtor gives it up and does not see it again until he discharges his debt. More sophisticated and involving more faith in the force of law is the arrangement whereby the debtor is allowed to retain the *res* at least until the repayment becomes overdue. Most of us live in mortgaged houses. The practical aspect of the relationship between the creditor-mortgagee and the *res* (the house) is the sophisticated version: the creditor looks on while the debtor remains in occupation. It is different with the pawnbroker. He keeps the watch.

The legal or analytical aspect of the relationship between creditor and *res* is concerned with the question whether the creditor has any right *in rem*. That is, whether he has a right in the *res* such as allows him to demand it from anyone else who has it. And if he has such a right, how should it be described? In short, if it comes to litigation, is his only claim the contractual one *in personam debitoris*, against the person of the debtor? Or has he also an exigible right against the *res*? If so, what right?

There is a spectrum of possibilities. At the heavy end, it may be that the creditor becomes owner of the *res*. In that case the debtor's only claim to get it back will rest on the contract: the creditor's obligation to re-convey if paid off. The early common-law mortgage was like this. I convey my land to my creditor. He promises to convey it back if I pay my debt on time. Meanwhile the legal relationship between him and the land is that he owns it. *Fiducia cum creditore* has the same structure.

At the other end of the spectrum, it is possible to suppose a species of real security in which the creditor has no exigible interest in the *res* at all. Necessarily this would mean that from the practical standpoint he would have to hold the thing, because if he had no legally exigible right and no physical control he would have nothing at all. But the simplest form of real security is precisely this, that the creditor merely holds some *res* as a sort of hostage against payment and has no interest in it. Meaning that if the *res* falls into other hands he can do nothing. He loses his security. He can of course fall back on his personal claim against his debtor. But that is what he wanted not to have to do. He took the *res* for extra protection. The trouble with this crude version of real security is that it is not very secure. It will not encourage much lending. Creditors want an exigible right, something more than mere factual detention. And without that there never can develop, on the practical level, the sophisticated arrangement whereby the debtor can retain the enjoyment of the *res* so long as he pays punctually.

So there are intermediate points on the spectrum, between the creditor owning and the creditor having no right *in rem* at all. A system which has a list of rights *in rem* less than ownership can accord the creditor one of those already in wider use. So the creditor can be given a lease. Or a special right can be developed having its own tailor-made characteristics: a pledge-interest, a 'charge by way of legal mortgage'. There is no need to enter into further detail. *Pignus* belongs in this middle range. The creditor has exigible rights *in rem*, as we shall see.

He is not owner of the *res*. Nor, at the other end of the spectrum, does he have mere physical detention.

In the relationship between creditor and *res* there is one more element which needs to be mentioned because often a surprise. It is not a necessary part of any scheme of real security that the creditor's right, whatever it is, must ultimately allow him to sell the thing. That commonly is what the law permits, but it need not. Where the creditor becomes owner he may be restrained from sale, either by the general law directly intervening in an owner's rights or by his contract with the debtor. Where he does not become owner, *prima facie* he has no right to sell, unless the law or the contract confers the power on him.

i. The contract of pignus*: the relationship between pledgor and pledgee*

There were formulae *in ius* and *in factum conceptae*, though there is in this case a doubt because they are not either preserved *verbatim* or easily reconstructed. The *formula in ius* will have conformed exactly to the pattern already familiar in the other *bonae fidei* contracts. I shall not set it out. Lenel's reconstruction of the *formula in factum concepta* is:

If it appears that Aulus Agerius gave the *res* which is the subject of this action to Numerius Negidius as a pledge for money owed,
and that that money has been paid or some other satisfaction has been accepted on its account,
or in the alternative that it was through Numerius Negidius that the money was not paid,
and that that *res* has not been returned to Aulus Agerius,
for as much as it shall be worth, for so much let the judge condemn Numerius Negidius to Aulus Agerius; if it does not appear, let him absolve.[11]

The *res* would of course be named, and there could be a variation from *ob pecuniam debitam* (for money owed). Because a *pignus* could be given to secure obligations other than money owed. For example I could give a *pignus* to secure a promise to convey land or indemnify a person about to stand surety for me.

[11] For the Latin, see Lenel §99.

A. The demonstratio Little more needs to be said about the definition of pledge because the special nature of the transaction means that there are no fine lines to draw between *pignus* and other contracts. Typically *pignus* involved a delivery of the *res* to the creditor with the intention that it should be a pledge. And the action was only concerned with what happened after that, as in all contracts *re*. But developments towards the more sophisticated practical arrangement which allows the debtor to retain the enjoyment ultimately blurred this requirement, so that D.13.7 now opens with Ulpian apparently asserting that pledge is a consensual contract: 'Pledge is contracted not only by delivery' (D.13.7.1 *pr.* = Ulpian, 40 *On Sabinus*). These developments will be looked at in the next section, on the relationship between *creditor* and *res*.[12] It is safe to take it that in classical law the plaintiff had to show that the *res* had been handed over.

Another case which does not fit the picture of a *res* actually handed over, but for which special praetorian protection was made available, was the pledging of a debt. I say that my claim against my debtor shall be a *pignus* for you. 'This agreement is to be protected by the praetor' says Paul (D.13.7.18 *pr.*).[13]

Suppose I hand over land to you and then you allow me back in. And then I build a ship from the wood growing there. Is the ship bound by the pledge? Land added to the pledged estate by *alluvio* is added to the pledge, but the ship is not. For the ship and the timber are different things. Paul observes that the answer is different if the pledge of woodland is made on the term that it shall include '*quaeque ex silva facta natave sint*: whatever may have been made from the wood or may have originated in it'.[14]

B. The intentio The direct action lies against the pledge-creditor. The debtor's chief concern is to get the *res* back. He can bring his action once he has paid all he owes or settled in some other way with the creditor. The *formula in factum concepta* sets out the conditions on which the praetor held he should have the pledge back.

In addition to the obligation to return the *res* the creditor must exercise care during the keeping of it. D.13.7.24.3 (Ulpian, 30 *On the Edict*):

[12] Below, 151–4.
[13] Paul, 29 *On the Edict*.
[14] D.13.7.18.2 (Paul, 29 *On the Edict*).

The trial on *pignus* makes the creditor liable for any bad treatment of the *res*, as for instance if he weakens slaves. Obviously it must be said that he is not liable in the action if it is for their wrongdoing that he punishes them, puts them in fetters or hands them over to the prefect or governor. A pledge of a slave-girl is instantly terminated if the creditor prostitutes her or makes her do some other disgusting thing.

This shows the creditor liable for *dolus* and *culpa*. And there is some evidence that he may have had at some stage to meet that security liability (*custodia*) discussed under *commodatum* (cf. D.13.7.13.1).[15] But that is unlikely.

Where the creditor had and exercised a power of sale, this action lay to make him pay over the amount he received over and above what was due to him from the debtor. Security was not to be an oppressive source of profit. D.13.7.24.2 (Ulpian, 30 *On the Edict*):

Suppose the creditor sells the pledge for more than he is owed but has not yet exacted the price from the buyer. Can he be sued by action on the pledge for recovery of the excess? Or must the debtor wait till the buyer pays? Or must he, the debtor, take on the actions against the buyer? I do not think the creditor is to be pressed to pay. The debtor ought to be patient. And if he is not, the actions against the buyer should be mandated to him. But in that case the risk will be on the seller. However, once the creditor has received the money he has to hand over the excess.

The creditor could bring the *actio contraria* to recover expenses necessarily incurred in keeping the *pignus* and also to be compensated for losses brought on him by the debtor's *culpa* in relation to the pledge. If the *pignus* turned out to belong to a third party who would not ratify the pledge the debtor was liable whether he knew or not that the *res* was not his (D.13.7.16 = Paul, 9 *On the Edict*).

ii. The relationship between pledgee and res

Earlier we distinguished between the practical and the legal aspects of this relationship. The main question here is about the legal aspect. What claims, if any, did the law give the creditor vis-à-vis the *res*? The

[15] Ulpian, 38 *On the Edict*; above, 139–42.

practical aspect—where would the *res* actually be?—is the day-to-day background behind the analysis.

The praetor protected possession by means of interdicts. Anyone who was in possession even without title could, under conditions spelled out in the interdicts themselves, obtain one of these remedies if he lost control to someone else. The only real weakness of interdict protection was that you had to ask for them quickly. They remained available only for a short time, marked out in different ways. This, for example, is the interdict most commonly available for *res mobiles*. It is called *utrubi*, from its opening word:

Utrubi vestrum hic homo, quo de agitur, nec vi nec clam nec precario ab altero fuit, apud quem maiore parte huiusce anni fuit, quo minus is eum ducat vim fieri veto. With whichever of you this slave, the subject matter of this claim, has been for the greater part of this past year (discounting time obtained from the other by violence, through secrecy or on sufferance), with his taking the slave I forbid all forceful interference.[16]

The interdict is complex. But you can see that it is only any use to someone who can tot up more non-excepted time than his opponent. So he would have to move fairly fast.

The interdictal protection of possession has nothing peculiarly to do with *pignus*. But once the pledge creditor had received delivery of the *res* he had this protection. Because the pledge-creditor was understood to be more than a mere ministerial holder (with unprotected *detentio*). He was a *possessor*. So suppose he was given a cow by way of *pignus*. If the cow wandered off to X, then he could still use the interdict so long as he had more months than X in the calculation. Moreover, he could (having once received *possessio* by delivery) suffer the pledger to take back the cow to hold *precario* because that excepted holding would not cancel or endanger his own ability to turn to the interdict. Not only was the 'precarious' holding excepted: the possessor, and here therefore the pledgee, was considered to continue to possess through his tenant at will. So, if the cow went off to a third party, the pledgee would still have the interdict.

So the ordinary interdicts not peculiar to *pignus* allowed two things. First, they gave the pledgee at least short-term protection against all

[16] Lenel, §264.

comers. Second, they allowed the beginning of a more sophisticated practical arrangement under which if the pledgee only once received *possessio* he could then put the pledgor back into day-to-day control of the *res*.

The next step was to enable the creditor to be secure without the need to take possession at all until the debtor defaulted. This could not be done within the scope of the ordinary interdicts. During the Republic a special interdict was introduced, the *interdictum Salvianum* allowing a landlord to take possession of his farm tenant's equipment and other property. This was backed by an *actio Serviana* introduced to reach beyond the tenant to anyone else in possession of the tenant's movable property. These remedies were based on agreement that the movables should be security for rent, without more. That is, without any transfer of possession.

This development specifically between landlords and agricultural tenants was generalised in the Principate by the introduction of a modified *actio Serviana*, called *actio quasi-Serviana*. This could reach any *res* agreed to be pledged. It was an *actio in rem* available against anyone into whose hands the *res* which had been charged came. The action is no more than the manifestation in pleading of a substantive proposition which says that a base agreement to charge a *res* as security for some debt itself creates between the creditor and the *res* a special right *in rem*, a pledge-interest. It is not ownership. Analytically it aligns with other *iura in re aliena*, rights *in rem* owned by others. The wording of this claim went like this:

If it appears that Aulus Agerius agreed with Lucius Titius that the *res* in dispute should be a pledge for Aulus Agerius for money due,
and if that *res* was at the time of that agreement a belonging of Lucius Titius,
and if the money due has not been paid and no other satisfaction for it has been accepted and it is not through Aulus Agerius that the money has not been paid,
then, unless under the discretion of the judge the *res* is restored to Aulus Agerius,
for as much as the *res* shall be worth, for so much money let the judge condemn Numerius Negidius [note that this is the first mention of the defendant] to Aulus Agerius; if it does not appear let him absolve.[17]

[17] For the Latin, see Lenel §267.

This action is still about something called '*pignus*' but its availability creates a phase before the specialised bailment which we looked at in the contractual relation between debtor and creditor. The duties of care, redelivery, repayment of *superfluum* and so on are relevant only to the phase after the creditor has obtained possession. The picture might have been kept clearer if the vocabulary had remained unified. But in fact the executory version without immediate delivery of possession came to be called 'hypothec' rather than *pignus*.

The creditor-*res* relationship can be recapitulated in this way. At first he had to have delivery in order to have any protected relationship at all. That would give him interdictal *possessio*. Then a special interdict (*Salvianum*) and the *actio Serviana* as extended protected him against all comers on the basis of agreement to charge the *res* in question. This allows us to say that in the Empire the creditor had a security interest *in rem* which allowed him to stay out of possession until default. Agreements conferring that interest were known as hypothecs.

The final aspect of this relationship is the power of sale. Up to the late Principate the basis of the power to sell was agreement between the parties. Without a term for such a power the pledgee could only hold the thing. By the end of the classical period the power to sell had begun to be implied. It was there unless expressly excluded. Justinian imposed more detailed regulations.

A Note on *fiducia*

Fiducia resembles a trust. Where property is conveyed by *mancipatio* or by *in iure cessio* the alienor can come to an agreement with the alienee that the transfer of ownership shall be for some limited purpose and that the alienee shall be under a duty to re-convey when that purpose is fulfilled. Gaius, in his discussion of *usucapio*, distinguishes between *fiducia cum amico* and *fiducia cum creditore* (G.2.60). 'Trust with a friend' is really a heavyweight form of deposit for safe-keeping, with the 'depositee' becoming owner of the thing. Similarly 'trust with a creditor' is a heavyweight real security, the creditor becoming owner with a promise to re-convey on payment of the debt. Both versions drive the alienor back to rights *in personam* enforced by a *bonae fidei iudicium*. *Fiducia* is not, but might easily have been, treated as a contract. One explanation for that would have been that it became obsolete. But despite being attached to ancient formal conveyances it survived into the classical period, alongside the contracts *re*. The reason for its not being counted as a contract is probably that it presents itself as a secondary incident of *mancipatio* and *in iure cessio*. They are not contemplated as generating obligations; and *fiducia*, which does generate obligations, cannot conveniently be separated from them.

PART II
Delicts

7

Furtum (Theft)

People desire wealth. There are different ways of trying to get it. Since those of which the law approves are slow, uncertain and laborious, the temptation to take short-cuts is universal. 'Thou shalt not steal' is a commandment against that material impatience. At its widest theft is the wrongful reallocation of wealth obtained by others. Within this general idea, certain in the centre but blurred at the edges, the law has many choices to make. And as they are made the legal version of the wrong quickly becomes technical, differently in different systems. But the central case, the one of which all men agree that it is theft, stays the same. Dishonest, secret removal. The Romans thought *furtum* might be derived from *fraus* (fraud), which captures the element of dishonesty. Or from *furvus*, a word for 'black' or 'dark'. That catches the secrecy. Or from the verb *ferre*, meaning 'carry'. Modern etymologists accept this last derivation. It shows that the archetype is taking away. That is a statement about the layman's perception, from a time before lawyers had been thought of. There is no reason why it should make professional lawyers feel uneasy. However much the law is made to twist and turn, the typical image of a thief is likely to remain the same for ever.

1. The Action

There was more than one action, as we shall see; but the most common was the *actio furti nec manifesti* (the claim for non-manifest theft). It went right back to the Twelve Tables. Its *formula* is preserved almost complete because Gaius, at G.4.37, happens to use it to illustrate the use of a fiction of citizenship against a non-citizen defendant. Even so there are some difficulties. But the main lines are clear:

If it appears that theft of a golden plate, worth such and such a sum or more, was committed against Aulus Agerius by Numerius Negidius or with the help of Numerius Negidius, for which matter Numerius Negidius ought-at-civil-law to settle the loss as a thief,
for the value of that thing when the theft was committed, in money and doubled, let the judge condemn Numerius Negidius to Aulus Agerius.
If it does not appear, let him absolve.

The next four sections of this survey will be concerned with that part of the allegation in the first clause which can be cut down to this outline: If it appears that theft of a golden plate was committed by Numerius Negidius (*Si paret a N°. N°. furtum factum esse paterae aureae*). That omits all reference to helping and to the plaintiff. Those matters can come back in later.

Chance might have made the allegation different. In particular, instead of saying *furtum factum esse*, it might have broken down the notion of *furtum* into its ingredients. It could have run: 'If it appears that Numerius Negidius fraudulently carried off...' That would have had the effect of settling the shape of the discussion, if only by fixing the vocabulary. The questions for the jurists would have been as to the meaning of 'fraudulently' and 'carried off', but that these together constituted theft would have been beyond dispute. The formulation which was used, simply Had theft happened?, left the whole shape of *furtum* to the jurists. There was room for disagreement and development as to the very nature of theft and the main terms of the proper analysis.

2. Paul's Definition

When an English or Scottish judge offers a definition of a legal figure his words, however happily chosen and often repeated, have a quite different status from those of an Act of Parliament. The text of a statute contains the very words of the law. All interpreters must start from them even if they end by saying that 'black' on this occasion was used to mean 'white'. The judge's words are just an attempt to capture the essence of the matter. They can be paraphrased and qualified, added to and taken from, if the underlying thought is thereby better attained.

It is the same with a definition proposed by a jurist. However useful it is there is no obligation to pretend that it is final and no ban on improvements. But that is not to say that it may not be very useful indeed, very hard to improve upon and very hard to escape.

Towards the end of the classical period Paul advanced a definition of theft to which Justinian later gave great prominence. In the Digest it was moved from its natural place. The text in which it was embedded has been made to open the title *De Furtis*. It is D.47.2.1.3 (Paul, 39 *On the Edict*):

Furtum est contrectatio rei fraudulosa lucri faciendi gratia vel ipsius rei vel etiam usus eius possessionisue.

Theft is the fraudulent contrectation of a thing for the sake of making a gain whether from the thing itself, from its use or from its possession.

So this in Paul's view, provided it has not been tampered with, was the position to which the classical law had attained on *furtum factum esse*. Even though it is not a statutory text and was not a *datum* for the earlier jurists it provides a stable base from which to consider the ingredients of theft and to reflect on their development.

The words divide according as they do or do not have reference to the thief's intent. They describe the intent as 'fraudulent' and later 'for the sake of making a gain from, *etc*'. By contrast the conduct in which this theftuous intent manifests itself is described as 'contrectation of a thing'. The discussion cannot omit one 'non-intent' matter which Paul's words do not include. Suppose I take your cycle. I think you do not consent. In fact you do. Must you be objectively, i.e. independently of my belief, unwilling (*invitus*)? These then are the matters which will occupy the next three sections: intent, act and absence of consent.

One more thing must be added about Paul's definition. It recurs in Justinian's Institutes but with some words missing. Nothing is said of *lucri faciendi gratia*. The result is that the trichotomy at the end has to be carried back and made to depend on *contrectatio* which already has one 'of a thing' to itself. This is at J.4.1.1: 'Theft is the fraudulent contrectation of a thing, whether of the thing itself, its use or its possession'. This is clumsy. Moreover if contrectation implies physical handling it cannot be done of use or possession but only of the thing itself. There is controversy. It is rather unlikely that 'for the sake of making a gain' was cut out on purpose.

3. The Intent

In the core case, that central image in which the thief carries away another's goods, the intent attributed to him is, permanently to deprive the victim of the goods. Or, one might say, to treat them as though he were their owner. The whole point about a core case is that it satisfies all requirements in the strongest and most indisputable manner. The question always is, whether the law accepts anything less. Is there a weaker case out on the periphery but still just within the concept? So here, was it necessary that the defendant should have intended permanently to deprive the victim of the *res* itself?

It was not. Gaius, who does not cleanly sever his comments on intent and act, says at G.3.195: 'Theft is not committed only when someone removes a thing of another's with intent to have it for himself (*intercipiendi causa rem alienam amovet*) but quite generally when someone contrectates a *res aliena* without the owner's consent.' He then gives examples. The depositee is a thief if he uses the thing. So also the borrower if he uses it for a purpose other than he said, as where he borrows a horse for one journey and rides him on another or into battle. In these cases there is an intention to return the *res*. But that does not prevent the liability for theft from attaching. In the terms of Paul's definition there is an intention to gain by the use.

Even an intent to make off with a *res* which belongs to another is not sufficient in itself to constitute *animus furandi*, the intention to steal. Take an extreme case. I stuff your cake into my shopping bag. I intend to eat it. But I think it is my cake. To support my assertion, there, sitting by the till after I have gone, is the one I paid for. The same story can happen with umbrellas. I am leaving the station with yours. Mine is still on the luggage rack in the train. I have mistaken yours for mine. The point is, to be theftuous my intent must be dishonest. The word in Paul's definition is '*fraudulosa*'. It is an adjective, qualifying the act, *contrectatio*, but it expresses the requirement of a dishonest mind. Gaius, at G.3.196, says '*Furtum sine dolo malo non committitur* (theft is not committed without wicked deceit).' *Dolus malus* always causes trouble in translation. In this context 'dishonesty' is all right. 'Wicked deceit' is just a genuflexion to the difficulty.

What is dishonest intent? It nearly always comes down to this: when you form the intent in relation to the *res* you know that your conduct will be considered wrongful unless you have the consent of a given person, usually the owner, and you nevertheless propose to proceed without that consent. Honesty is genuine belief that the necessary consent is forthcoming. Dishonesty is the absence of that belief. This is not a general definition. It is a guide to the qualification 'dishonest' applied to an intention to deal with a *res*. Thus, what Gaius says as he leads up to the statement in G.3.187 that *dolus* is essential is:

> But it has been decided that, where people use borrowed things for purposes different from those for which they received them, they only commit *furtum* if they know that they are acting without the owner's consent (*invito domino*) and that he, had he been told, would not have consented. But if they believe that he would have consented, the decision is that they are outside the scope of a charge of *furtum*. This is an excellent distinction. For without *dolus malus* theft is not committed.

If one had to sum up Gaius's treatment of theftuous intent in the Institutes, it could be put in three points. Negatively, there is no need to find an intent to have the thing for good. Positively, there must be dishonesty. By way of explanation, dishonesty is the want of genuine belief in the owner's consent. In nine out of ten, perhaps even ninety-nine out of a hundred, cases, that will be sufficient guidance.

What problems can arise in the hundredth case? In other words, what deficiencies can be shown up in Gaius's three point analysis? Suppose I plan to tip your cargo of tea into the sea. Or to destroy a painting worth a fortune. Here I do intend that you shall be permanently deprived and I have no belief in your consent. But is this a theftuous intent? If it is, then many cases of intentional damage are going to count as theft. And that is especially true for a system in which the physical conduct deemed sufficient for theft is a good deal less than carrying away. Not only damage. Suppose I propose to give your slave a good shaking. Is that going to be theft? My intention is to mistreat your slave without your consent. Is that a plan for *furtum usus*?

The need to differentiate between *furtum* and other wrongs requires some refinement of the conception of theftuous intent. There is a great danger of overkill. Suppose that there must be a dishonest intent to have for oneself a thing or its enjoyment. That might exclude the cases just mentioned but it would also threaten to exclude cases which ought to be kept in. I plan to get your ring for my girlfriend. I could argue that that is not theftuous. Planning to give to another is different from having for oneself.

This accounts for the phrase *lucri faciendi gratia* in Paul's definition, and also for the hesitations about it which many scholars have expressed. *Lucrum* is the opposite of *damnum*, as 'gain' is the opposite of 'loss'. When the words 'for the sake of making a gain from the thing itself, its use or its possession' are put in, cases of spiteful loss and other harm are removed from the scope of *furtum*. My intent to dump your tea in the sea is not theftuous. It is an intent to cause loss, *damni dandi* not *lucri faciendi*. Perhaps to wound your feelings too.

The worry about this refinement of *animus furandi* is whether it does not cause this. Does it knock out the case of taking to give to another? A takes a book from a shop without paying, to give B a present. The law is perfectly clear that that is theft. The question is whether it remains theft only by ignoring *lucri faciendi gratia*. One should never have to play fast and loose with the terms of a definition. Paul was too good for that. The words do not have to be pressed too hard to reach the case of A's book. 'For the sake of a gain to be made', there is no indication who is to gain and no reason why the words should not be construed simply in contrast with their opposite 'for the sake of loss to be inflicted'.

It is not easy to see how early or how steadfastly this differentiating refinement of theftuous intent was achieved. I give you my slave whom you suspect of crime. You are to interrogate him. You immediately hand him over to the magistrate to be killed as one caught red-handed. Pomponius records the opinion of Proculus, or possibly Sabinus, that this was theft 'because he used another's thing knowing he did so without the owner's consent or that the owner, if he knew, would not consent'. That is D.12.4.15 (Pomponius, 22 *On Sabinus*). There is no insistence upon a redistributive as opposed to an extinctive intent. It is not completely clear from the text that Pomponius approved the earlier decision.

Someone who steals a book from a library may later, in revulsion from the daily reminder of his guilt, tear it up or throw it in the river. He may do it five minutes after getting away, suddenly coming to his senses. This is different from the case in which from the start he intends only destruction. He does commit *furtum*. His intent is theftuous when he does the act. Later his intent changes. He commits a separate delict by spoiling the book. That is *damnum iniuria datum* under ch. III of the *lex Aquilia*.

Malicious intent to inflict loss or pain without material gain to anyone is wicked. The point is that it has not quite the right shade of wickedness for theft. There are other cases which cause trouble for the three point analysis in Gaius. The defendant may try to say that although he knew that he was acting against the plaintiff's will yet his intent was such that it did not require the plaintiff's consent in order to be purified: irrespective of the plaintiff's view the plan was too honourable or humane to be characterised as dishonest. We have already absolved from theft those who poured tea into the sea, because it was not done *lucri faciendi gratia*. They might claim to be exonerated on another ground. If they did it by way of protest, for a political purpose, they might say that this high motive must exclude *dolus malus*. Similarly Robin Hood, who stole from the rich to give to the poor. Compassion motivated him, not avarice. So say all dissidents. And morally we value them as we value the system which they reject. There are two other cases. An animal-lover, I cannot bear to see the cruel way in which you keep your bull or your bear. I let them go and they are never seen again. It is the same case if my pity extends to your chained slave. Rather different and perhaps less reputable, you lend me your *ancilla* (slave girl) for a week while I have guests. You complain that what followed was *furtum usus*, but I say it was love.

I do not think there is any sign that the law regarded an unworldly motive as capable of negativing *dolus malus*. If you took my goods knowing that I did not consent and with the redistribution or re-allocative intent indicated by the liberal construction of *lucri faciendi gratia*, it would not help you to say that you took them for the poor and needy. In law Robin Hood was in the same case as A who took a book in a shop for B. On the other hand some unworldly motives would eliminate the redistributive intent. It was essential to the motives of the Boston tea party that the participants should pour away, not pocket the tea. Similarly, compassionately letting go your animal or slave, I manifest no intent either to have or to re-allocate your wealth. The texts on intercourse with *ancillae* are not at all easy. One possible view is that the intent which went with love or libido, if that was all there was to it, had nothing to do with wealth or material gain. Even if one knew her owner did not consent one nevertheless could not be said to intend a gain within any construction of *lucri faciendi gratia*. It would be different if the lover intended to keep the girl entirely to himself, hiding her away from her owner altogether. That, *furtum rei*, would be aimed at her entire economic value. Never mind that the motive for wanting it was love.

The shortest summary of this part goes thus: *animus furandi* did not suppose an intent permanently to deprive; subject to that, the earlier classics may have been content to think in terms of dishonesty without further refinement; difficult cases did, however, require some finer tuning to be done; that was achieved in the phrase *lucri faciendi gratia*, not without some danger that, construed in too narrow a spirit, it might cause more problems than it solved.

4. The Act

We have seen that D.47.2 (*De Furtis*) is made to start with an excerpt from Paul, 39 *On the Edict*. It contains his definition. But it does not start with it. It starts with the etymology, and within a few lines it has made the link between *furtum* and carrying off: *furtum* from *ferre*, and the text adds *auferre* for good measure. The prefix emphasises removal, motion away. Having established this image the text immediately uses it as a reason for a rule. *Inde sola cogitatio furti faciendi non facit furem*, thence merely thinking about committing a theft does not make you a thief. It is a good thing for most of us that the practical problems in the way of imposing liability for mere intent are never likely to be overcome.

How far did theftuous intent have to be manifested in conduct before liability could attach? At what point in the story did the law say that the theft had actually happened? What was the necessary and sufficient act? These three are all the same question, put in slightly different ways.

The words used in the definition are *contrectatio rei*, contrectation of a thing. We can assume for the moment that we know what a *res* is. Contrectation is more difficult. That is why it is anglicised rather than translated. The requirement of *contrectatio* is strongly and confidently asserted. Not only in Paul's definition. At D.47.2.52.19 (Ulpian, 37 *On the Edict*), Ulpian says:

> You cannot commit theft by word or by writing. For this is the law we use, that *furtum sine contrectatione non fiat* (theft does not happen without contrectation).

And we have already seen that Gaius had previously affirmed, at G.3.195:

Theft is committed not only when someone removes another's thing for the sake of keeping it *sed generaliter cum quis rem alienam invito domino contrectat* (but, generally, when someone contrectates something belonging to another without the owner's consent).

So *contrectatio* was for these jurists the necessary and sufficient act. The question is, What did it mean? If we confine that to these high classics, there are two other questions about the history. What did *contrectatio* mean later to Justinian who preserved its use? Was there an earlier period in which the act was differently denominated or understood?

i. What did contrectatio *mean to the high classics?*

In the dictionary *contrectare* can be seen to be a strong word for handling, something like 'to get to grips with'. 'Touching' would be on the weak side. It therefore looks as though a statement such as '*furtum sine contrectatione non fiat*' means 'without handling there can be no theft.' That is the starting point. The question is whether they meant to take 'handling' literally. The alternative is that they might have meant it loosely, in a sense such as 'meddling' or 'addressing' or 'interfering', senses in which physical contact ceases to be necessary in every case.

There is room for prolonged argument. I start from the point that the stricter meaning is more likely. If *contrectatio* means, in ordinary usage, 'handling', it would seem to be rather remarkable to assert 'You have to have handling' while meaning that something less would do. Still, that is only a starting point. But there are some cases strongly in support.

Gaius, at G.3.202, gives examples of people who do not themselves commit theft but are liable to the *actio furti* for helping. The examples then work two ways. They are examples of complicity, also of not committing theft. Among them are the case of knocking coins out of a man's hand or driving away his animals. Neither involves handling but both entail a looser notion of contrectation, meddling or interfering with the *res*. There can only be two reasons why on such facts the defendant has not himself committed theft, a deficiency of intent or a deficiency of act. If the reason is the latter, then the sufficient act must be handling. So can there be a deficiency of intent? Gaius says the acts are done 'so that another might make off with the *res*', and a line or two later he turns to the case in which there is no intention that a theft should be committed (*non data opera ut furtum committeretur*). If I shin up a drainpipe, enter a window and throw down a silver cup for you to make off with it there is no question of saying that I do not myself commit theft. Because an intent to reallocate to another is a species of *animus furandi* and I have handled the cup. To say otherwise would be to re-open the Robin Hood question, already discussed. The point is, you never need to reach questions about 'helping' against someone who has himself satisfied all conditions of liability as a principal, not even if the substantial relationship between the two is that the 'principal' is really the helper. As, for example, if in the case just given I did my part for a small payment the whole purpose being that you should have the cup. Applying this to the coins and the beasts, it becomes virtually impossible to explain the non-liability except in terms of a deficiency of act. *Semble*, therefore, that when Gaius uses *contrectare* he means what he seems to say. There has to be handling.

It might be objected that he says '... *non solum cum* ... *amovet sed generaliter cum* ... *contrectat* (not only when he removes but also, generally, when he contrectates)'.[1] The argument would be that there is *amovere* even if there is not handling of the coins and animals. That, in my view, mistakes the effect of the 'not only ... but also' whose rôle is to contrast the lay view with the version selected by the law. What is the meaning of *generaliter*? I think it is 'generically' in the sense of 'right across the whole category'. As we might say 'categorically' or 'definitively'. Its effect, if that is right, is to reinforce contrast between layman's and lawyer's version.

The next case is *The Peacock*. It comes from Pomponius, a bit earlier than Gaius. It is D.47.2.37 (Pomponius, 19 *On Sabinus*):

> My tame peacock flew from my house. You chased it *quoad is perit* (till it got lost). I shall be able to bring an *actio furti* against you provided that someone (*aliquis*) has begun to possess the bird.

This is not without difficulty, but as it stands it contains a proviso which can only be explained on one or other of the bases mentioned in relation to the last text. Why are you not a thief as soon as you chase? Either because mere meddling short of handling will not do or because your intent is wrong for theft. Nothing is said of your intent

[1] G.3.195.

but the case is so much like those of Gaius I just discussed that we are entitled to incline to the view that the same point is in issue. Further if you lacked theftuous intent it is difficult to see that you should incur liability even after the intervention of *aliquis*. On the whole, the text supports the view that meddling was not enough.

The next case is *The Filched Pedigree* from Ulpian. It is D.47.2.52.20 (Ulpian, 37 *On the Edict*). Someone drives his mares to another's stallion to be served, or the stallion to the mares. Modestinus, who was Ulpian's pupil, wrote from Dalmatia asking whether Ulpian thought that was theft. Ulpian answered in the form 'only if...'. The condition which we now see is 'only if there was *animus furandi*, theftuous intent.' That is too banal. He would never have said, especially not to his brilliant pupil, 'Do remember that acts in themselves are neutral, till cumulated with the right intent.' It is obvious enough that the point of the operation was to avoid paying the stud fees. So why did Modestinus write? The case must have been interesting, interesting enough to do justice to their intellectual relationship. The clue comes from the nature of the facts and their location immediately after the assertion that there can be no theft without *contrectatio*. A case is always interesting if it puts common sense and technical doctrine in conflict. The doctrine comes under pressure. Will it adjust? The same phenomenon can be observed in other fields. The Pope's every utterance on divorce and contraception is analysed acutely. The reason is that the doctrine is seriously out of accord with the moral perceptions of many laymen. Will it adjust? In the same spirit Modestinus's case was one of which most people would agree that it was theft. But was it? It was a dishonest plan whose end could be achieved without handling. I think Ulpian's answer was 'Only if there was *contrectatio* of the horse.' In other words he preferred precision to common sense and held the technical line. In its present position the text is placed to illustrate the general proposition about *contrectatio*. It is the best possible kind of illustration, one which immediately answers the question which always comes into a lawyer's mind on reading a general rule: Is it to be taken literally or subject to all kinds of artificial distortion? It was to be taken literally. No theft without handling.

What violence, if any, does this do to common sense? To make handling the necessary and sufficient act is to say in effect that the moment at which theft is committed is when it begins to be committed. The central image has the thief leaving the house, getting the thing and carrying it back with him. The law had to choose when in that story the liability attached. It could not have chosen 'leaving home' because that would have landed it in all the problems of *sola cogitatio*, liability for mere intent. Hence the range of choice was in reality narrowed down to the part of the story after the thief's conduct had actually manifested his theftuous intent in relation to the *res*. 'Handling' is the choice of the beginning of that part of the story. 'Carrying away' comes next. Later still 'arriving home with his *res*' or 'arriving at the place where the *res* is to be put'.

So far there is no obvious affront to common sense. The trouble arrives because thefts can begin in different ways. Most do begin in handling. But animals, which move themselves, can be driven away without contact. That is, the thief can get past the moment normally marked in the story by handling without ever getting to grips with the *res*. The donkey can be lured with a carrot, chickens can be whooshed along, and so on. And we have just seen how to filch a pedigree. Sometimes the same can be said of inanimate things. If you drop your ring and I see it lodge in a hole or crevice I can take an effective step by putting my shopping down over the place where it lies. If I have it in mind to get the coins which you are holding or some of them the first act may be to make you spill them on the floor. So I knock your hand. One can think of other examples. There is one which might seem to qualify but does not. Suppose I lengthen my arm by using a stick or a net or monkey or a young child. There are extensions of different kinds but I think that none of them get the theft under way without my touching the thing. At least, if a defendant tried to argue that when the stick or monkey touched he did not touch I would expect the law to have no trouble in saying he had.

There is therefore some difficulty in the fact that in some cases a theft may have advanced beyond the handling stage without any handling actually happening. I rush out and catch him while he is driving off my cow. It is obvious to everyone that he has not yet touched her at all. He has a technical defence. Caught too soon. This is offensive to common sense. But the number of cases in which the technical defence will actually work is minute. Forensic realities will take over. If you got my donkey home you will find it easy to persuade the judge of the rule that touching is required but difficult to convince him that you operated only with a carrot. So in practice the sacrifice of common sense is small. And the gain in precision is considerable. Notions such as 'meddling' or 'interfering' are vague. And besides being of doubtful scope they work back into the field of *sola cogitatio*. 'Handling' is clear and precise. It is also a reasonably unequivocal manifestation in conduct of a theftuous intent which has gone beyond reflection and temptation.

ii. What did contrectatio *mean to Justinian?*

The Digest and Institutes continue to denote the act as *contrectatio*. However, there is some ground for saying that the compilers were inclined in this area to strike a different balance in the competition between precision and common sense. Another example will be given later, in *The Loyal Slave*, a case on the owner's consent.

The Filched Pedigree now says that the owner of the mares will be liable for theft provided only that he had *animus furandi*. We have already observed that that ruling is banal, doubly so when given in answer to a star pupil. How can the text be explained in its present form? I think the point is that Ulpian's insistence on handling gave the defendant a very technical defence and that Justinian's team just would not tolerate his getting off. That is why they said 'If there is theftuous intent then on these facts he will be liable.' And there almost always would be. The switch to *animus* implies that Justinian was no longer insisting on a handling. Something less would do.

Further evidence consists in the preservation in the Digest of early authority concluding for theft even in the absence of any handling. That is one of the best ways to make one's position respectable: revive old authority. If Justinian had decided to adopt the rigorous requirement of handling he could have cut out all traces of a contrary doctrine. The fact that he did not shows that he wanted to loosen up the developed position by recurring to an earlier truth. We will see this when we get into the next question.

iii. Was there an earlier doctrine and nomenclature?

There almost certainly was. The word *contrectatio* was only established as the technical term for the act during the Principate. Under Tiberius, Sabinus used the verb *adtrectare*,[2] which seems to have the same meaning though with, no doubt, some slightly different nuance. Possibly the two words were used side by side for a while. Suppose we go back before Sabinus. Can we say anything about the Republican period?

[2] Aulus Gellius, *Noctes Atticae*, 11.18.20.

Nearly everyone says that the starting point must have been asportation. That is, the original requirement was that the *res* must have been taken away. There is no evidence for that at all, except the etymology from *ferre*, 'to carry'. The etymology tells us the central case. Nobody will deny that carrying away is and always has been the first picture to come to mind. From this, however, it does not follow that asportation was ever required by the law as something without which theft could not be said to happen. The law has an extra task, which laymen never have to face. It is, to say when a plan to carry away can be said to have been sufficiently put into action for liability to attach. Unflinching commitment to the central image still does not exclude the selection of a moment very early in the story. Put the other way about, acceptance of carrying away as the paradigm case does not entail the proposition of law that theft does not happen till the carrying off is complete.

One other factor should be borne in mind. It is an attribute of a developed system, with a well-organised and stable body of authority, to be able to draw firm technical lines at points not easily settled by common sense. The question when a theft happens does not have a common sense answer. A system still without an accumulated body of authority must be expected to handle it intuitively, from case to case. There will not be any precise generalisation.

Asportation, if it ever was a requirement, put the moment of liability rather late in the story, a stage further on than the classical *contrectatio*. One factor suggests that the moment of liability will always, right from the Twelve Tables, have been earlier. Roman law dealt more severely with the manifest thief, as we shall see. Worse consequences attached if you were caught red-handed. A system which does that can hardly insist on asportation. For to do so would give a technical defence to one caught just before he had moved the *res* away. Quite apart from the fact that the early system is unlikely to have the muscle to be technical, 'caught too soon' can never have gone down well when more severe consequences attached to earlier catching. I catch you with your hand on my jewel-box, red-handed. I am not going to be impressed by any attempt you may make to tell me that you have not yet physically removed it.

Another factor exerts a contrary force. It is probable that from earliest times it was true that, as in the *formula* of the *actio furti*, a plaintiff would have to name the *res* stolen. If the heavier consequences of red-handed theft suggest an early moment of liability this custom of pleading imposes a limit. You will have to have manifested your intent in relation to some specific thing.

So what was required by way of act in the earliest period? One widespread view says asportation. The other, which I favour, says that the plan must have been put into action sufficiently to enable the plaintiff to name the *res* and substantiate the allegation thus advanced that 'by Numerius Negidius theft was committed of a golden plate . . .'. On this second view the act is not named or otherwise specified. In a more amorphous way, it can be described as the *initium furti*, the beginning of the theft, with the acts varying according to the nature of the *res* and plan.

The first view has to suppose that the moment of liability was advanced from asportation to contrectation. Mommsen suggested that the aim was to penalise more thieves, there being no liability for mere attempts.[3] The other view does not need to see any real change in the moment of liability, always very early in the story. *Contrectatio* on this view will have been hit on as a way of naming and making more precise the loose notion of the *initium furti*. Settling on a single description will have bought precision at the cost of some sacrifice of common sense.

Paul reports, and Justinian preserves, the case of *The Mules*. It is D.47.2.67.1 (Paul, 7 *On Plautius*). Someone dishonestly (*dolo malo*) calls a mule-driver off to court. His mules are lost in his absence. The old jurists (*veteres*) held in *responsa* that that was theft on the part of the *in ius vocans*. There is no handling. Yet the conclusion is for theft. The preservation of this old ruling is part of the evidence that Justinian did not want a strict insistence on handling. If the *veteres* are the jurists of the Republic the case appears to tell us that at that time *contrectatio* had not become a requirement. Those who start from asportation have either to explain the case away or to accept that the moment of liability was not moved from asportation straight to *contrectatio* but rather from asportation to *initium furti* to *contrectatio*, with the last step representing a retrenchment. That seems to be the view of Thomas.[4] For him there was an intermediate phase in which theft was very wide indeed, deliberately made so in order to make good remedial deficiencies in the area of loss. On the other view *The Mules* fit in very easily. The

[3] Theodor Mommsen, *Römisches Privatrecht* (Leipzig: Duncker & Humblot, 1899), 735.

[4] J. A. C. Thomas, '*Contrectatio*, Complicity and *Furtum*', 13 *IVRA* (1962), 70, 86ff.; Thomas, '*Animus furandi*', 19 *IVRA* (1968), 1, 12.

starting point is the *initium furti*. As the law grew up you would expect some case law illustration of the beginnings of thefts. *The Mules* would belong there, before the classics settled on *contrectatio* as the single sufficient act.

There are one or two other cases of similar kind, some explicable as including a *contrectatio*. Sabinus has one, *The Toga*. It is not preserved in the Digest but by Aulus Gellius. He reports that a *iudex* condemned a man who had been sued for theft of a fugitive slave because he had, by stretching out his toga, hidden him from his searching master's view.[5] It is not clear whether Sabinus referred to this with approval or anecdotally. It does fit the picture of Republican and even early classical theft as lacking a firm description of the *actus reus*. And again the explanation may be deliberate enlargement from a requirement of asportation or illustration of the original idea, exemplification being the first juristic advance from an intuitive approach.

There are thus two versions of the pre-classical development in relation to the sufficient act. In one asportation gives way and the moment of liability is moved earlier in the story, probably to an unnamed *initium furti* rather than straight to *contrectatio*. In the other the crucial moment is all along the beginning of the theft identified just intuitively and then by case-law illustration. The two versions meet up when, in the classical period, the decision is made to insist on a single description, *contrectatio*. Later Justinian diluted the precision of *contrectatio* by not insisting absolutely on immediate physical contact between the thief and the *res*.

The discussion has assumed that *res* required no exposition. That is not quite true. There are three points to be made. First, the *res* had to be movable, for land could not be stolen. That is implicit in the image of a carrying away. However, the selection of an early moment of liability opens the possibility of debate. Since liability is to attach before the carrying off is achieved, why adhere to the logical implications of the entire image? Thoughts of this kind may have influenced Sabinus's unsuccessful heresy that land could be stolen. Secondly, things *divini iuris* could not be stolen. There was the crime of sacrilege for those who committed the equivalent of *furtum* against the gods, as from temples and burial grounds; also the praetorian *actio sepulchri violati*, for violation of a tomb. In the same way those who stole from the state, *res publicae*,

[5] Aulus Gellius, *Noctes Atticae*, 11.18.14.

were guilty of *peculatus*, not liable for *furtum*. Thirdly, going back to a time when little or no distinction was made between patriarchal power over free dependants and ownership of property, there could be theft of sons, daughters and wives *in manu*. Gaius also mentions theft of judgement debtors and bonded gladiators (*auctorati*). To what extent actions for free dependents were actually brought can only be guessed. Justinian at J.4.1.9 still repeats what Gaius says at G.3.199, deleting only the wife *in manu* long obsolete.

5. The Absence of Consent

This is the ingredient of theft omitted in Paul's definition. It is an objective requirement. That is, it does not relate to the intent of the defendant. We have already seen that belief in consent, as opposed to the fact of consent, is relevant to *animus*. The finding that the defendant did or did not believe that he had or would have consent will generally control the crucial issue of dishonesty. Here we are concerned with the fact of consent or its absence, not with belief. It is important to observe the distinction. At the same time it is true that in most cases the issue as to belief will swamp the other. In this way: if he believes he has or would have consent he will not be liable, so that further questions cease to matter; if he does not so believe he will be guilty of *dolus malus* and in nearly every case it will be true objectively that there was indeed no consent. Hence, though analytically independent in all cases, the issue as to the fact of consent will in practice only become important in the case in which the dishonest defendant is mistaken. That is, where the defendant contrary to his own belief does have consent.

The requirement is illustrated by *The Loyal Slave*, discussed by Gaius at G.3.198 and given a very different treatment by Justinian at J.4.1.8. Gaius starts by stating the rule:

> But even if a person believes that he is contrectating a thing without its owner's consent, it is held that no theft is committed.

Then he puts *The Loyal Slave*. A would-be thief, Titius, asks my slave to bring something of mine out to him. The slave tells. To catch Titius, I order the slave to go through with it.

Will Titius be liable to me in a trial for theft or for corruption of a slave [a praetorian wrong] or in neither? *Responsa* have held that he will be liable in neither. Not for theft, on the ground that he did not contrectate without my consent. Not for corruption of the slave, on the ground that the slave was not corrupted.

This is a fascinating case. You can use it as a litmus test, to find out what kind of lawyer you are. You will either be impatient of its technicality and formalism or what have you, standing in the way of substantial justice; or you will be excited by its determination to impose intellectual order on the chaos of common sense. Thanks to the Fascists order of all kinds has become unfashionable. Not the least injury inflicted by them on the human spirit. For myself, I think lawyers become dangerous when their urges for right answers are not curbed by the discipline of meaning what, after due consideration, they have chosen to say. It is a big subject. And there is no need to be an extremist either way. Justinian's preference was different from mine. He says that *The Loyal Slave* was presented to him as a case for ancient hesitation and dispute, with the learned divided between those who would allow neither action and those, not mentioned by Gaius, who would consider the *actio furti*. He settled the doubts. Faced with obvious wickedness, meaning what you were accustomed to say was less important than making the villain pay. This is what he says in the Institutes, at J.4.1.8:

To deal with this kind of cunning we provided by our determination [*decisionem*– this was one of the *Quinquaginta Decisiones*, Fifty Determinations or Settlements] that not only the *actio furti* but also the *actio servi corrupti* should be allowed against him.

At this point we can pick up the words of the *decisio* itself, at C.6.2.20:

Although the slave was not at all corrupted, yet the intention of the corruptor was directed to the subversion of his good character. And just as he is made liable for theft on account of his dishonesty, notwithstanding that according to the rules of law no theft has been committed, in that theft is understood to happen only in case of a *contrectatio rei* against the will of the owner, so the action for corruption may without aberration be extended against him on account of his own vice, so that the penal action may be brought to bear upon him as though by the attempt itself the slave had been corrupted, lest escaping scot free in this way should encourage him to put another, corruptible slave to the same test.

A legislator can get away with this. On the whole it is better for him to do it by a spare and brutal incursion into the interpretative logic. This falls between two stools, both interrupting and trying to satisfy the juristic requirements. Especially in 'as though by the attempt itself the slave had been corrupted'. That is typically the utterance of an interpreter struggling with a requirement of actual corruption, not of a legislator dispensing with it.

The Loyal Slave exemplifies the case in which the defendant believed he was contrectating *contra domini voluntatem* but actually had the owner's consent all along. The facts are freakish, but the conflict between the objective consent and the rogue's belief is straightforward. There is another kind of case where the conflict is more complicated.

Here the rogue is again dishonest. He knows that he has tricked the victim, whose consent is therefore vitiated by the deception. The victim so far as he is aware of the facts believes that he has consented to the *contrectatio*. The question is, Will the law regard the consent as operative or as nullified? If operative, the *actio furti* is excluded because the victim is taken to consent to the *contrectatio*. The extra complication arises because of the doubt, eternally troubling even to philosophers, whether a consent obtained by deception counts as consent at all.

The broad answer is that it depends how comprehensively the victim was deceived. If fundamentally, his consent will be nullified and the *actio furti* will lie. If not, he will be taken to have consented. With the *actio furti* excluded the victim can fall back to the *actio doli*, the praetorian remedy for fraud. Which deceptions fall on which side of the line? There is no sure guide. It is not surprising, given the metaphysical nature of the problem.

Suppose you misrepresent your qualities as a good person to lend money to. You say you are well off, about to embark the money in trade, will find good guarantors or will repay immediately. Or being a slave you say you are free, or a *paterfamilias* when you are still in power. In none of these cases do you steal what you get. So Ulpian at D.47.2.43.3 (41 *On Sabinus*) and D.47.2.52.15 (37 *On the Edict*). The same when you get money by selling what does not belong to you (D.47.2.52.17 = Ulpian, 37 *On the Edict*).

By contrast if you borrow money by misrepresenting your identity you are a thief. You pretend to be the Titius to whom I intend to lend.

That is Ulpian at D.47.2.52.21,[6] also at D.47.2.43.3.[7] Similarly if you use false weights to get more than you pay for, D.47.2.52.22.[8] Suppose you get your ring back from a pawnbroker by saying you are just going to pay and then once you have your hands on it you throw it out to a friend and dash off. Pomponius says that you are a thief (D.13.7.3 = 18 *On Sabinus*). Scaevola at D.13.1.18 (4 *Questions*) seems to regard it as axiomatic that where a payor hands over a sum which he believes he owes to you, if you know the money is not due you will commit theft.

These examples serve to show the nature of the problem. They barely touch on its complexity.

Who is it whose consent matters? It is easy to slip into the habit of referring to the consent of the owner. The Roman texts do the same. The usual phrase is *invito domino*. It is not always the owner. For example, an owner can steal from a pledgee as we have just seen. He consents but his consent is irrelevant. The pawnbroker is the man who matters on those facts. Again, an owner can steal from a *bona fide possessor.* And third parties can also steal from these non-owners. Hence 'owner' is no more than a convenient shorthand. The full statement is clumsy. We ought to say 'without the consent of the person whose interest is being infringed'. It is quite enough to say it once.

6. Liability for Helping

The formula asked the judge whether theft had been committed by Numerius Negidius or with the help of Numerius Negidius. And Gaius, at G.3.202, says:

> Sometimes a man is liable for theft who himself has not committed theft. The one who falls under this head is the person by whose help the theft is committed.

The first observation is that the theft must have happened. The judge has to say whether a theft was committed by or by the help of the defendant. It follows that there is no liability for helping a theft which

[6] Ulpian, 37 *On the Edict.*
[7] Ulpian, 41 *On Sabinus.*
[8] Ulpian, 37 *On the Edict.*

fails to come off. That is, which never reaches the point of *contrectatio*. This does not mean that there must always be a principal thief who is capable of being made liable to the *actio furti*. Take the case of *furtum domesticum*, domestic theft. This was a matter left to the private jurisdiction of the *paterfamilias*. If a son or a slave or a free servant stole within the household, no *actio furti* could be brought. Suppose then that the son was helped by an outsider. The proposition in the *formula* could still be substantiated. Because the question between the *paterfamilias* and the outsider was whether a theft had been committed and, if so, whether by the outsider's help. There was nothing about the liability of the principal thief.

Two questions arise. What nexus, if any, was required between the helper and the thief? What counted as help within the rather difficult Latin phrase which that too crudely translates?

What nexus? Centrally, we think of pre-complicity. That is, of the case in which the helper plots in advance with the other, so that a rôle in the action is assigned to each. The helper will drive the cows off, the other will collect them round the corner; the helper will dig the tunnel, have transport ready and so on, the other will go in and get the diamond. But there are less obvious cases capable of falling within the words of the *formula*. It only requires the theft to have been committed by the help of the defendant. Three cases can be constructed which might conceivably fit despite the absence of pre-complicity. Starting at the most extreme, I am mending your roof and for the job I have a set of ladders on your premises. At night thieves come. They use my ladders. I have done nothing unlawful but I have helped the theft. In the next case I break into your house. I smash down the door. I have no thoughts of theft. It is anger which makes me do it. Or once again love. Later, because your door is broken, thieves find easy access. Again I have helped. This time by an unlawful act but one unaccompanied by theftuous intent. In the third case, still short of pre-complicity, I want a theft to happen. I leave open the door of your house hoping that a thief will enter, and perhaps I broadcast the fact in the pub that evening. Or I drive off your cows knowing and hoping that someone will get them. Or I knock your hand so that your money goes into the crowd. If I were to throw your money into a crowd I myself would do the *contrectatio* and whether my motive was a grudge against you or compassion for the masses I myself would commit the theft. The difference in these cases is that intending to re-allocate your wealth I myself avoid handling it. Others dishonestly contrectate it, but

I help both unlawfully and with *animus furandi*. There is another version of this third case. Here there is a pre-complicity between me and X. I will drive off the beasts. He will collect them. Something goes wrong. He fails to be in his place. Y makes off with the animals instead. Y's theft has been committed by my help though I knew nothing of him.

Where did the law draw the line? All these cases are capable of being brought within the proposition of the *formula*. It would be difficult to accept that the first one was. It would be a dangerous world of liability for theft attached because a thief happened to avail himself of your lawful and everyday acts, driving off in the car you parked nearby, arming himself with the milk-bottle on your doorstep. We know the first case was excluded, because the second one was too. It is clear that one did not become liable for helping merely because one did an unlawful act which happened to help. Ulpian puts the case of *The Prostitute's Door*. It is D.47.2.39 (41 *On Sabinus*). A man broke into a prostitute's house. He did it *libidinis causa*. Thieves then entered and stole things from the woman. The man was not liable for theft. Again Gaius, at G.3.202, contemplates one who drives off cattle. He will be liable for helping theft if he did it to enable another to take; but if he did it for fun the only liability which Gaius suggests is for causing loss: 'It will be a question whether an *actio utilis* should be given since under the *lex Aquilia*, passed to deal with loss, even *culpa* (fault short of *dolus*) is punished.' This ignorant townie chasing sheep on his day in the country can, objectively, help theft happen. But as soon as it is given that he acted *non data opera ut furtum committeretur* (not bending his efforts towards the commission of a theft) the inquiry into a liability for theft falls away.

We can conclude with reasonable confidence that the defendant could not be liable for helping unless he intended a theft to happen. There is no inconsistency in saying that it would make no difference if that intent was itself motivated by a non-theftuous intent, as where I want your animals stolen because I hate you or I decide to help people steal from you because they are my friends. So Gaius says, at D.47.2.55.4 (13 *On the Provincial Edict*):

Someone who knowingly lends a jemmy to break a door or a chest, or knowingly lends a ladder for climbing up, is liable to the *actio furti*. It does not matter that no intent of his was bent principally on the commission of the theft (*licet nullum eius consilium principaliter ad furtum faciendum intervenerit*).

If we say that the helper must have had theftuous intent, must he also have been in league with the person who committed the theft? Was there a requirement of pre-complicity? Almost certainly not. This is partly established from silence. It is never said that this is a requirement. Then, the *formula* does not require it. Finally, the person committing the theft is not infrequently designated by an indefinite *aliquis* or *alius*, 'someone' or 'another person'.

What counted as help within the phrase used in the *formula*? The Latin is *ope consilio*, probably in apposition without any *et*. They are not easy words even taken one by one. Ulpian says, at D.47.2.50.3 (37 *On Sabinus*) that *consilium dare* means to persuade, incite and draw up a plan while *opem ferre* means to provide service and assistance for the carrying off. It is easy to say that *consilium* refers to mental and verbal contributions while *ops* covers physical assistance. However, it is not clear that any problem is solved by splitting the combined *ope consilio*.

It does seem clear that incitement and encouragement is not enough. But it is not safe to say therefore that *consilium* on its own will not suffice. Because drawing up a plan for the theft, which Ulpian attributes to *consilium dare*, must ground the liability without more. Justinian at J.4.1.12 says:

> Certainly a man is not liable to the *actio furti* if, giving no help to the commission of the theft (*nullam operam ad furtum faciendum adhibuit*), he merely offers advice and encourages its commission (*consilium dedit atque hortatus est ad furtum faciendum*).

This should not be construed as doing more than drawing a line between incitement and help. That is it should not be taken to require physical aid such as carrying ladders and breaking doors. In the first part of this section we simply used the word 'help', and that seems as safe as it is simple.

7. Claiming the *Res*

I see you beginning to drive away my cow. As I rush out you are pushing the animal into a cart. You are liable for theft.

But you now abandon your booty in order to escape. I have my cow again. This does not mean that I cannot bring the *actio furti* against you.

Because that action is not conceived as having a reipersecutory aim. That is, not as asset-recovering. On the contrary it is conceived to be penalty-recovering (*poenam persequens*). The money obtained by the victim through the *actio furti* punishes the defendant for the wrong. Therefore once you have committed theft the fact that I have recovered the thing is neither here nor there. I can still go for the penalty.

Suppose I have not recovered the *res*. You still have it. The logic still holds. I can vindicate it as well as claim the penalty. The *formula* of the *vindicatio* says 'If it appears that the cow which is the subject of this action belongs at civil law (*ex iure Quiritium*) to Aulus Agerius' and goes on to direct the judge to condemn in money. So my *vindicatio* will give me the value of the cow. But the *actio furti* asks whether you should settle as a thief, and that is taken to mean, pay for the wrong of stealing. The *vindicatio* leaves that untouched.

Suppose that I have not recovered the *res* but you, the thief, no longer have it. You have either eaten it or parted with it to someone else. The *vindicatio* will not lie against you. If the *res* still exists in the hands of a third party it will lie against him. If it has ceased to exist, the *vindicatio* died with it. But an owner has another reipersecutory action against the thief which is indifferent to the question whether he does or does not still possess the stolen good. This is the *condictio*. Against a thief it is called the *condictio furtiva*.

The *formula* of the *condictio* is abstract. It never reveals on its face the ground or cause of the plaintiff's claim. That only comes out in the facts which the plaintiff puts before the judge to substantiate his abstract proposition. He affirms 'The defendant ought-at-civil-law to give me the cow Daisy which is the subject of this action.' And the *formula* puts that into a conditional clause, 'If it appears that Numerius Negidius ought-at-civil-law to give (*dare oportere*) to Aulus Agerius the cow Daisy which is the subject of this action.' Gaius says that the word for 'give' (*dare*) does not denote the physical act of handing over but rather that giving which transfers ownership. Hence 'ought to give' means 'ought to convey' or 'ought to transfer title'. It follows that the proposition of the *condictio* cannot be substantiated by showing that, or indeed if it emerges that, the *res* in question belongs to the plaintiff. This is Gaius at G.4.4:

The boundaries between actions being so drawn, it is certain that we cannot claim our property (*rem nostram*) from another by this pleading: 'If it appears that he ought-at-civil-law to give'. For what is ours cannot be given to us, in that something is understood to be given to us when it is so given as to become ours, and a thing ours already cannot be made more so.

When a thief steals he obtains possession at best. He does not acquire title. The stolen Daisy remains mine. That is why I can use the *vindicatio*. It follows that the *condictio* against the thief, except where Daisy has ceased to exist, is a claim in respect of 'a thing which is ours already' and which cannot therefore be 'given'. So it should not lie at all. It is exceptional. Gaius goes on (G.4.4, continued):

Clearly it is from hatred of thieves, and to make them liable to more actions, that it has been accepted that, in addition to double and quadruple penalties, they should also be made liable, under the head of asset-recovery, to this action which says 'If it appears they ought-at-civil-law to give.' And this notwithstanding the fact that there also lies against them the action in which we assert that the *res* is ours.

The thief faces claims for penalties and claims for recovery of the thing. Success in the one aim does not exclude the other. But within each success cannot be multiplied. If I have succeeded in the reipersecutory aim by one means I cannot do it again by another. Hence the *vindicatio* and the *condictio furtiva* are alternative, and both are excluded if, as in the example at the beginning of the section, the thief never gets away with the *res*, or if he gives it back without litigation.

8. A Variety of Penalties

We have got this far with hardly a mention of the fact that there were a number of different actions for theft. And we are not going to be able to do justice to the concentration of legal history behind the family of claims.

The most important distinction is between manifest and non-manifest theft. We must be supposed to have been speaking all the while of non-manifest theft, for which the Twelve Tables laid down a *poena* of double, *duplum* or *duplio*. That double penalty was retained in the formulary action, as we saw earlier. The penalty for manifest theft under the Twelve Tables was what Gaius, at G.3.189, calls *capitalis*. It affected your *caput*, your person and personal status. The manifest thief was flogged and adjudged to his victim, into a state of slavery or near-slavery. If he was already a slave he was flogged and killed, by being thrown off the Tarpeian rock. All these consequences could be bought off. In the same way retaliation for bodily injury could be settled in money. In historical times the action was for a fourfold penalty. The praetor's edict was the basis of that. Having set out the old regime Gaius goes on (G.3.189, continued):

But later the harshness of the penalty was disapproved, and an action for fourfold was set up by the praetor's edict both for the case of the slave and the free thief.

It would be rash to think of this as a simple substitution of the one *poena* for the other. The *praetor* probably could not withdraw people's decemviral rights overnight. In some way what he offered was better, more attractive to plaintiffs than the old regime. And in some way the mysterious *lex Aebutia* helped.

To us 'manifest' means 'obvious' or 'indisputable'. It would be good to know whether, given that 'obviousness' comes from 'held in the hand', it was the hand-holding of the thief which originally mattered or his hand-having the stolen thing. There is always going to be debate on the original meaning.

Very oddly the classics seem to have been in doubt how to draw the line in their own day. Oddly, because there is nothing difficult about it. Just a question of making a choice. There are two questions. What has to be done in relation to the thief? And, how soon? The verb used for what has to be done is *deprehendere*. It signifies physically arresting, as opposed to merely seeing. We use 'catch' to cover both. However there are some signs of dilution from *deprehendere* (detain) to *videre* (see). And in the end Justinian seems to admit 'seen' as well as 'detained'. In the Digest, at D.47.2.7.1–3 (Ulpian, 41 *On Sabinus*), there is this passage:

In the same book [19 *ex Sabino*] Pomponius neatly wrote *deprehensione fieri manifestum furem* [To capture the neatness, perhaps one has to translate this, exaggerating the image, 'by hand-holding a thief becomes hand-held', but at all events it means 'It is arrest which makes a thief manifest']. So, if in fear of death you ran away while I was pilfering your house, even if you saw the theft happen, yet that is not manifest theft. 2. But Celsus adds this to 'deprehension'. You saw him taking the thing and ran at him to detain him but then he threw the thing down and fled. He calls that manifest theft. 3. And he thinks it does not matter whether the owner or a neighbour or some passer-by does the catching.

In the Institutes, at J.4.1.3, Justinian sets the limits of manifest theft thus:

Further, manifest theft is to be extended in this way: so long as the thief is *visus vel deprehensus* (seen or detained) *rem tenens* (holding the thing) whether in public or in private and whether by the owner or by someone else, provided he has not yet reached the place where he had decided to take the thing and set it down. Once he has reached his destination, he is not a manifest thief, even if he is detained carrying the thing.

This passage takes us into the second question. He must be seen or detained. How soon? Before arrival at his destination. This is what Gaius had said, at G.3.184:

Some say manifest theft is one which is caught *dum fit* (while it is being committed); others go further, saying that it is one caught *ubi fit* (in the place where it is being committed) so that, for example, when the theft is of olives from an orchard or grapes from a vineyard the thief is manifest so long as he is in the orchard or vineyard, or, if the theft is done in a house, so long as he is in that house; others go on again: whenever the thief is seen carrying the thing. That view has not found favour. But even another opinion has been disapproved, namely the view of those who thought the thief was manifest if caught before reaching his destination. The reason for the disapproval is the doubt whether a limit of one day or more is to be put to that test. And it matters, since thieves often plan to carry things stolen in one town either to another town or to another province. Hence one or other of the two earlier opinions is approved. Most prefer the second [i.e. *deprehensio ubi fit*].

Why was this doubt allowed to persist? The range of controversy should not be exaggerated. Gaius rejects all but two views, between which there would be little difference. All the same Zulueta may be right in suggesting that plaintiffs did not bother to bring the *actio furti manifesti* for the fourfold penalty.[9] They would have more to prove, and rarely much hope of recovery. For thieves are not often solvent. If the action had been frequent, the question would have been often asked and in a way which would have required a crisp answer.

[9] Francis de Zulueta, *The Institutes of Gaius*, vol. 2 (Oxford: Clarendon Press, 1953), 199.

No other mechanism concentrates the mind. Hence only Zulueta's solution accounts for continuing academic vacillation.

The Twelve Tables provided for one other case of manifest theft. Search after an invocation of divine help. This prompts Gaius to an interesting observation on the limits of legislative power. Can an Act of Parliament enact contrary to nature, making men women, lions tigers? This is what Gaius says, at G.3.194:

The fact that the *lex* makes this manifest theft causes some to divide *furtum manifestum* between 'natural' and 'statutory'. This being the statutory type; the natural, that which we have just discussed. But the truth is that there is only natural *furtum manifestum*. For a *lex* cannot turn a non-manifest thief into a manifest thief any more than it can turn into a thief one who is not a thief at all, or into an adulterer or murderer one who is neither. But certainly a *lex* can do this: it can make someone liable to a penalty just as though he had committed theft, adultery or homicide notwithstanding his having committed none of these.

His account of the ceremonial search shows him fascinated by the past but quite unsentimental about it. G.3.192–3:

192 . . . The *lex* just provided that one who wanted to search should do so in the nude *licio cinctus, lancem habens* (wearing a *licium*, holding a *lanx*). If he found anything in that way the *lex* ordains it manifest theft. 193. The question has been asked, What is a *licium*? The truth is likely to be that it is a cloth of some kind used to cover the private parts. The whole thing is laughable. For someone who forbids you to search clothed is likely to forbid it nude too. All the more so when a greater penalty attaches if something is found in that way. Then, there are two explanations of the requirement for holding a *lanx* (a dish). The one says it is to keep the hands occupied to prevent planting, the other that it is to receive what is found; but neither works for the case in which the thing sought is not of a size or kind to be either planted or placed on a dish. Certainly there is no argument but that the *lex* is satisfied whatever material the *lanx* is made of.

We are not quite in a position to understand the force of the remark about prohibiting nude and prohibiting clothed. Because we have departed from Gaius's own order to take this with *furtum manifestum*.

Recent scholarship confirms the picture which readily comes to mind of a search assisted by divine help. The *licium* and *lanx* are the routine emblems of religious ritual. The *licium* appears to be in the nature of a ribbon worn around the head. Which supposes the ancients less sensitive than Gaius's prudish explanation. The *lanx* is a bowl used in libations.

Aulus Gellius tells us that the search *lance et licio* was one of the antiquities which fell out of use after the passing of the *lex Aebutia*.[10] We learn that that statute prospered the praetor's formulary procedure. But its mechanism remains obscure. Its effects were certainly profound. If it prospered the *formula*, which it did, that comprehensible consequence sprang from a not so easily understood regulation of the relationship between the ancient civil law and this newer practice of the praetor's court.

A last question on the distinction between *furtum manifestum* and *nec manifestum*: Why were the penalties different? It is crude to say that greater certainty of guilt justifies greater punishment. Ten years in prison if we are sure you did it; five years if we are nearly sure. We would not say such a thing. And we should not lightly suppose it of the ancients. One explanation is this.

In the beginning the consequence was always the same as that which the Twelve Tables kept for *furtum manifestum*. But composition in money was usual, the rates being dictated by the threat of the primary sanction. Perhaps the extensive power of that threat was curbed a little by customary morality. But where guilt had to be proved by human means in court the severity of the primary sanction, mixed with the routine uncertainty of all human decision-making, was oppressive to the defendant, intimidating even the innocent and thus distorting the decision whether to defend. For that case the Twelve Tables therefore cut down the uncertainty by fixing the ransom at double the value, as perhaps custom had previously indicated. With the *poena* fixed, defendants could know what they faced and would not be stampeded into composition by fear.

In the case of *furtum manifestum* there were no innocent defendants. The rate of ransom could be left to negotiation without the special danger of terrorising the innocent into submission. The imminence of the physical sanction meant that the rate of composition ran high, higher than the double fixed for *furtum nec manifestum*. When the praetor introduced the next reform he had to make his action

[10] Aulus Gellius, *Noctes Atticae*, 11.18.9.

advantageous to plaintiffs. So he could not ignore existing practice. Hence the decision to impose a quadruple penalty, as good at least from the plaintiff's point of view as he could expect by way of ransom from the 'capital' sanction of the Twelve Tables.

This is guess-work. Even if it is right it only explains the beginning. The rest is inertia. Helped, just possibly, by the fact that plaintiffs did not bring actions for *furtum manifestum* anyhow.

8

Rapina (Robbery)

This (G.3.182) is how Gaius makes the transition to delict:

Transeamus nunc ad obligationes quae ex delicto nascuntur, veluti si quis furtum fecerit, bona rapuerit, damnum dederit, iniuriam commiserit; quarum omnium rerum uno genere consistit obligatio cum ex contractu obligationes in IIII genera diducantur, sicut supra exposuimus.
Now let us turn to obligations which are born of delict. As where someone commits theft, seizes goods, causes loss, inflicts contempt. And the obligation from all these events belongs in a single category, though obligations from contract divide into four categories, as we explained above.

Four delicts. All in one class. One of the four, *bona rapere,* seizure of goods, lit. 'to seize goods'. Gaius was a wonderfully clear-thinking lawyer. And in his scholarship he did not cheat. That is, he was not after effect but truth. But did he put in *bona rapere* for the sake of symmetry? Four kinds of contract and then, though only one kind, four species of delict. Justinian's Institutes do sometimes make you wonder whether truth has succumbed to beauty. Perhaps there are too many fours. But it is not like Gaius to be seduced. And yet the first problem with *rapina* is to see why it is not just a degree of theft, an aggravation of *furtum* much in the same relation to the central concept as is *furtum manifestum.* Nor does Gaius himself do anything to help us see why he promoted it to independence. When he comes to it, this is all he says (G.3.209):

Qui res alienas rapit, tenetur etiam furti (One who seizes another person's property is also liable to the action of theft). For who more clearly *alienam rem invito domino contrectat* (commits a *contrectatio* of another's property without his consent) than does someone who *vi rapit* (by violence seizes it)? And so it has quite rightly been said that such a person is a doubly disgraceful thief (*improbus fur*). But the praetor has introduced an action specially for this delict. It is called the *actio vi bonorum raptorum* (the action for things seized by violence). And it lies within a year for quadruple damages, but after a year is up for single damages. And the action is available even if the defendant seizes only one thing, even a very small one [*scilicet* despite the plural in the name: *bona, actio vi bonorum raptorum*].

If we could sit Gaius down and ask him why this has a place of its own he might only answer that violence (*vis*) is an extra fact which takes the matter beyond theft. An extra fact in the defendant's behaviour and therefore in the ingredients of the wrong itself. Whereas, in *furtum manifestum*, you are talking about the same wrong, exactly the same behaviour, but caught earlier. If so the next thing to ask him would be whether this second delict would better have been called *vis* than *bona rapere*. But this imaginary conversation gives us too much licence. There are three questions I would like to put to him: What justifies the separate heading? If you bring in this praetorian wrong (into what is otherwise a list in which everything has a *ius civile* root), how can you omit other edictal wrongs such as *dolus* (fraud) and *servi corruptio* (corruption of a slave)? For this is another difficulty for the fourfold list: if this *bona rapere* is genuinely distinct, other marginal wrongs are too. And finally, within this delict itself, what is the point of that *simplum* (single damages) after one year has passed? It is very odd that a plaintiff who can have an *actio furti* for the *furtum* which is contained within the *rapina* is offered an alternative action in which for proving more, *vis* as well as *furtum*, he gets less, *simplum* instead of *duplum*.

I do not know what the answers are. And the trouble is that this figure is too small to spend much time on here. Things are made worse by demonstrable interpolation in D.47.8, *Vi bonorum raptorum et de turba*. The picture is definitely more complex than Gaius reveals. For one thing the edict in question was not concerned only with violent theft but also with violent losses of other kinds. The shortest way to convey the outline of the classical picture is to give Lenel's reconstruction of the relevant edict.

Si cui dolo malo hominibus armatis coactisve damni quid factum esse dicetur sive cuius bona vi rapta esse dicentur,

If any kind of loss shall be alleged to have been done to anyone when with evil intent men have been put in arms or collected into a gang, or if anyone's goods shall be alleged to have been seized by violence,

in eum qui id fecisse dicetur, in anno quo primum de ea re experiundi potestas fuerit in quadruplum, post annum in simplum iudicium recuperatorium dabo.

against him who shall be said to have done it, I will give a trial before *recuperatores* for quadruple damages for one year from the time when it is first possible to bring an action about that matter, and for single damages after that year.

Item si servus familiave fecisse dicetur in dominum iudicium noxale dabo.

Also, if a slave or household shall be alleged to have done it, I shall give a noxal trial against the owner.[1]

Nearly all private actions went before *unus iudex*, a single lay judge. This one goes to *recuperatores*, recoverers. There may be an advantage in that for the plaintiff. Possibly, and unlike the ordinary *iudex*, the *recuperatores* would take active steps to see the plaintiff obtained his due. The *iudex* would give judgement, but to levy execution you would have to go back to the *praetor* and even then you would get authorisation to take certain steps but no state help.

Immediately after this edict there followed two more, closely related to the theme of public order. Crowd violence and looting are their concern. In this kind of context it is necessary to recall that, however much the events in question bring crime to mind, these actions are civil, not criminal. That means they lie for the victim to obtain redress from the wrongdoer. The events are contemplated as putting the defendant under an obligation to the plaintiff, binding him to make some performance in favour of the victim. They are not contemplated as exposing the wrongdoer to a liability to suffer state-punishment.

We cannot know whether Gaius meant his short reference to the action for goods seized by violence to include also these next two:

(i) *De Turba*

Cuius dolo malo in turba damni quid factum amissumve quid esse dicetur, in eum in anno quo primum de ea re experiundi potestas fuerit in duplum, post annum in simplum iudicium dabo.

[1] Lenel, §187.

On Crowd-Violence
If anyone shall be alleged to have inflicted any loss or caused anything to go missing by malice in a violent crowd (*turba*), I will give a trial against him for double damages within the year from when it is first possible to bring an action on that matter, and for single damages thereafter.[2]

(ii) *De incendio, ruina, naufragio, rate nave expugnata*
In eum qui ex incendio ruina naufragio rate nave expugnata quid rapuisse recepisse dolo malo damnive quid in his rebus dedisse dicetur, in quadruplum in anno quo primum de ea re experiundi potestas fuerit, post annum in simplum, iudicium dabo.
On Looting (lit. On fire, collapse, wreck, disabled boats and ships)
If anyone shall be alleged to have seized or received anything with wicked intent from out of a blaze, collapse, wreck or incapacitated boat or ship or to have inflicted some loss in any of these circumstances, against him I shall give a trial for quadruple damages within the year from the time when it is first possible to bring an action on that matter, for single damages thereafter.[3]

All three of these edicts are concerned with *damnum* (loss). Depending on what was meant in *De Turba* by 'making things go missing', either the first and third or all three are also about misappropriation. In this sense they both look back at *furtum* and forward to *damnum iniuria datum* (loss wrongfully caused) which is Gaius's next delict. They have in common the element of disorder. Perhaps the explanation of Gaius's treatment is that although the three together do arguably make a coherent unity distinct from *furtum* and *damnum iniuria datum*, yet 'aspects of disorder' is not a very happy heading in a list of otherwise neatly named wrongs. 'Theft, aspects of disorder, loss wrongfully caused and contempt' goes very soggy at second place. Possibly he meant to catch all three by using *bona rapere* as a representative. But that is a guess.

[2] Lenel, §188.
[3] Lenel, §189.

9

Damnum Iniuria Datum (Loss Wrongfully Caused)

1. The Shape of the Delict

Damnum means 'loss', though it is often still found incorrectly translated as 'damage'. In fact this delict is largely about damage, but the *damnum* is the loss which arises from the damage, as opposed to the killing, burning, breaking, bursting and so on. *Iniuria* is used here in the ablative case and means 'by a wrong' or, moving safely to an adverb, 'wrongfully'. And *datum* means 'given' or 'brought about'. So at a high level of generality the delict is simply 'loss wrongfully caused'.

The shape of the delict is dictated by the fact that it is based on a statute, the *lex Aquilia*. The juristic interpretation of the *lex* left the demand for further remedies still unsatisfied. The praetor therefore gave actions which overrode the technical limitations of the statutory remedy. These *actiones in factum* can be contemplated as clustering around the area covered by the *lex* itself. Thus whenever one has to analyse a disaster which looks as though it may give rise to a liability for loss wrongfully caused, it is necessary to ask first whether it falls within the statutory core and then, if it does not, whether it finds a place in the praetorian periphery of the delict.

2. The Statute

The *lex Aquilia* was actually an enactment of the *concilium plebis*. So technically it was a plebiscite and not a *lex*. But that strict usage was departed from. We know that plebiscites were made to bind the whole people, rather than just the *plebs*, by the *lex Hortensia* in 287 BC. On rather slender evidence it has been thought that the *lex Aquilia* was passed as a result of the same social disturbances, almost immediately after the *lex Hortensia* itself. More recently Professor Honoré has argued for a slightly later date, around 200 BC.[1] One argument in favour of that date is that it was then that the currency got into trouble as a result of the inflation brought about by the war with Hannibal. The relevance of that is that one of the provisions which the *lex Aquilia* displaced was the rule of the Twelve Tables relating to the fracture of a slave's bone. The early code provided for payment of a fixed sum, 150 *asses*. Inflation brings down the real value of redress which is fixed in that way. Because of the war with Hannibal there would have been a need for reform. So 200 BC may be our best estimate of the date. If we were brutally honest we would have to say that it must have been passed after the *lex Hortensia* and before the middle of the second century BC when we find Brutus commenting on it. So between 287 and 150, with 200 most probable. Some people believe that the statute as we have it was built up over a period of time as different legislative sallies were made into the field of loss wrongfully caused.

We know something of three main sections or chapters of the *lex*. I shall briefly mention the second first, in order to get it out of the way.

Ch. II was early obsolete. We do not know its words. It was passed, like the other, *de damno*, concerning loss. But the loss was of a highly specialised kind. The chapter dealt only with the case of an *adstipulator* who in fraud of the *stipulator* released a debt owed by the promisor. An *adstipulator* is a co-promisee to a promise made by stipulation. He is in a position to release the obligation either artificially or by accepting payment. It is not completely clear whether the statute contemplated only artificial release. Probably it contemplated both. Gaius tells us, at G.3.216, that the contract of mandate would serve to regulate relations between the principal and the subsidiary promisee. But he notices that the *lex* lay for a double penalty against one who denied liability, and one would have thought that that would have kept the section alive.

Chapters I and III are both about loss arising from damage of various kinds. The immediate task is just to set out their wording. Matters of interpretation will be dealt with in the next section.

[1] A. M. Honoré, 'Linguistic and Social Context of the *Lex Aquilia*', 7 *Irish Jurist (NS)* (1972), 138, 145ff.

> Ch. I
> If anyone wrongfully kills another person's male or female slave or four-footed herd-animal, let him be condemned to pay to the owner as much money as at the highest that thing was worth in the preceding year.[2]
>
> Ch. III
> In respect of other matters [besides slaves and herd-animals killed], if anyone causes loss to another by burning, breaking or bursting wrongfully, let him be condemned to pay to the owner as much money as that matter is worth in the nearest thirty days.[3]

These translated versions gloss over points of detailed dispute but nothing of substance is lost which cannot be recovered in the later discussion. Ch. III has caused a good many headaches. It is difficult partly because its opening words seem to attach directly to ch. I, whereas on the day when the *lex* was passed ch. II had not yet fallen into disuse and could not be ignored by the draftsman of ch. III, and partly because the words which quantify the amount to be paid seem to contemplate full value for small and partial losses, as where you chip my plate or burn my slave's arm. Apparently you might as well have killed him, since the difference between valuation over a year and over a month will rarely have been great and never wide enough to discriminate between a burned slave and a dead one.

These considerations have led to some radical suggestions to the effect that the text of the chapter was originally much more restricted in scope than it now seems. Jolowicz proposed that it must have been concerned only with total destruction of inanimate things, so that all three chapters would have been about the extinction of items of wealth.[4] Daube on the contrary maintained that the chapter was about wounding, rather than killing, chapter I objects, slaves and herd-animals.[5] Between these two radical approaches Daube has much the better of the argument. However, though some difficulties remain, the pendulum has swung back towards accepting the text as it stands subject only to the elimination of the words in brackets which in Latin are awkward and, in either language, read like an explanatory

[2] D.9.2.2 *pr.* (Gaius, 7 *On the Provincial Edict*).

[3] D.9.2.27.5 (Ulpian, 18 *On the Edict*).

[4] H. F. Jolowicz, 'The Original Scope of the *Lex Aquilia* and the Question of Damages', 38 *LQR* (1922), 220, 221ff.

[5] David Daube, 'On The Third Chapter of the *Lex Aquilia*', 52 *LQR* (1936), 253, 253ff.

gloss. Professor Honoré takes this less drastic line. He thinks that 'in respect of other matters', when standing alone, can follow on from both preceding chapters; and his later date here helps since the word for 'thing' (*res*) has more time to become abstract.[6] So far as the measure of ch. III damages is concerned, it is too much in dispute to be allowed to control one's view of the substantive scope of the early *lex*.

3. Interpretation in the Statutory Core

One ought to separate the treatment of the two chapters but for brevity's sake they can be taken together. The measure of recovery which constitutes a major difference can be severed and dealt with later.

The matters to be considered are covered by two large questions: Has the plaintiff suffered a disaster which is *prima facie* within the *lex*? And, Is the defendant liable for that disaster? These two questions can be broken into smaller ones, so that in the end one has three for the first and two for the second. Thus: (i) Has the plaintiff suffered loss (*damnum*)? (ii) Did that loss arise from a thing spoiled (*res corrupta*)? (iii) Did that spoiled thing belong to the plaintiff (*res actoris*)? If these are all answered in his favour the plaintiff has suffered a disaster within the *lex*. Then, (iv) Did the defendant do the spoiling with his own bodily force (*corpore suo*)? and (v) Did he do it wrongfully (*iniuria*)? If these last two are answered against the defendant then he must pay.

The form of some of these questions anticipates the discussion, but they will become clear.

*i. Has the plaintiff suffered loss (*damnum*)?*

This requirement is not mentioned expressly in ch. I. It is virtually impossible to construct a set of facts in which a plaintiff whose slave or beast is dead will not have suffered loss. In chapter III the first condition is, expressly, 'If anyone causes loss to another . . .' Not every bump or bruise will do so. Suppose the reaction of a hypothetical buyer. A scratch on a polished table will reduce its value, the same thing on the outside wall of a house will not affect the price. Similarly with living tissue. An ordinary black eye spoils a slave's looks but unless there is some evident risk of complications will not take down his value.

[6] Honoré (n. 1), 144–5.

Ulpian reports a famous example given by Vivianus.[7] Successful castration of a slave-boy would actually raise his value. Hence there could be no Aquilian liability.

All these examples assume that the verbs, bumping, bruising, scratching, amputating, would be within, and indeed they are within, the range of the statutory trilogy, *urere, frangere, rumpere*, one aspect of which is considered next.

*ii. Did that loss arise from a thing spoiled (*res corrupta*)?*

Under the *lex* itself the action described by one of four verbs had to happen. Each has an active and a passive aspect. At this point we are concerned only with the passive aspect. This means that we are not yet interested in the question whether the defendant did, say, the burning but whether the plaintiff suffered a thing burned.

Under chapter I it is evident that the plaintiff had to have suffered a slave or herd-animal killed. The words 'thing spoiled' do not arise under that chapter but clearly *servus etc. occisus* is within the notion of *res corrupta*.

Under chapter III there has to be a *res usta fracta* or *rupta*, a thing burned, broken or burst. The translation of this last word as 'burst' is conventional but not very good. 'Damaged' would be better though the trilogy would run less well if deprived of its alliteration. '*Rumpere*' is a very wide word, much less specialised than 'burst'. '*Frangere*' is rather narrower, for dry breaks as of bones, plates and pencil-leads.

Defendants would naturally try to escape by arguing that the consequences of their action could not be brought within one of the verbs. Suppose that I have poured out your wine onto the floor. You sue me and I say that this is certainly not within *occidere, urere* or *frangere*. It must be *rumpere* or nothing. And what have I smashed or damaged? Ulpian tells us that the *veteres*, the old jurists, put a stop to this tactic by giving *rumpere* its widest possible sense. The word *rumpere* was understood in the sense of *corrumpere*. Much as though we said 'damage' must be taken as 'spoil'. That reached the spilled wine clearly enough. One could not argue that it was not 'spoiled' or 'ruined'. This interpretation of *rumpere* as *corrumpere* meant that *urere* and *frangere* were really redundant. Ulpian reports Celsus as saying that he was bound to admit that the first two verbs—*fractum* and *ustum*—were contained within *corrupti appellatione*, the description of something as having been spoiled. But it was nothing

[7] D.9.2.27.28 (Ulpian, 18 *On the Edict*).

new, he said, for a statute to follow special words with some general catch-me-all. Gaius says that the interpretation as *corruptum* meant that *ruptum* would reach not only things *usta aut fracta* but also *scissa et collisa et effusa et quoquo modo vitiata aut perempta atque deteriora facta*: burned, broken, torn, crushed, spilled, vitiated in any way, destroyed or made worse.[8]

It has long been held that there could not be said to be a *res corrupta* where something was destroyed in the course of its proper use. It is certainly true that I cannot be liable under the *lex Aquilia* for eating your food or drinking your wine, but the reason is not likely to be found under this head. It is hard to say that there is no *res usta* when I burn your logs, just because logs are for burning. And when I eat your walnuts I must *frangere* their shells and *rumpere* the nuts within. There is no evidence that the interpretation as *corrumpere* did other than extend the statutory words. To exclude these cases under this head one would have to suppose it capable of restricting as well as extending.

The dynamic interpretation of *rumpere* had its limits. Moth, rust and wrongdoers can corrupt most things, but not all. Precious stones and metals are unaffected by immersion in the sea or in a river. Suppose I throw your silver cup into the sea or your ring into the Tiber or knock your coins down a drain. There is no *res corrupta* and so no liability under the *lex*. There is one indication that Sabinus was prepared to stretch this point presumably on the ground that total disappearance could be regarded as a type of destruction. However, that view, objectively incorrect, seems not to have prevailed. There are other examples, besides precious metals and gems, of things which can be made to vanish without damage. If you trap an animal and I let it back into the woods you suffer *damnum* but there is no *corpus laesum*. Perhaps nearer the line is the case in which I sow weeds in your corn. You get less yield but no *res* is actually *corrupta ac mutata*.

It seems therefore that under the *lex* there had to be at least some corporeal deterioration, some internal change for the worse. As we shall see the praetorian actions could go further.

*iii. Did the spoiled thing belong to the plaintiff (*res actoris*)?*

In ch. I the slave is described as *alienum alienamve*, belonging to another. There is nothing parallel to that in ch. III so far as concerns the words which describe the delict. But in the words laying down the measure of

[8] G.3.217.

damages, in both chapters, the plaintiff is described as 'owner'. For it is to the owner, probably the *lex* used the old word '*erus*', that the defendant must pay the value. Hence only an owner could sue, and only in respect of a *res corrupta* owned by him.

This restriction was inconvenient in two different ways, both of which made work for the praetor. First, there were people other than owners who suffered by the commission of the delict. The usufructuary, the *bona fide possessor*, the pawnbroker come immediately into view. Secondly, it meant that there was no Aquilian remedy for injuries to a free man. For *nemo dominus est membrorum suorum*: no-one owns the parts of his body. We will see that a free man could have the *actio iniuriarum*, but only for intentional injury. There could also be other problems. One's family would refer to 'our vault' or 'our tomb' but if people had been buried already 'our' would be inaccurate. Such places belonged only to the gods below. Again fixtures could pose questions. If I smash down your aqueduct running over my land, 'your' will not stand up in court. The fixture is mine by accession to the land. The materials which I have released are yours, but are not damaged.

iv. Did the defendant do the spoiling 'corpore suo'*?*

We now turn to the defendant's liability. The first aspect is the active element in the verbs. He must have 'killed' the slave or animal or inflicted loss 'in that he burned, broke, burst'. As a defendant seeking to escape, he will say that, though you have a dead slave or a spoiled bushel of corn, yet he did not do the killing or did not do the spoiling. The question is, When can a man be said to have 'done' something, as here 'killed' or 'spoiled'? And this has to be answered not just reasonably but in the teeth of all the unreasonableness which the defence can muster. Suppose I put poison in your slave's bedside drink. In the middle of the night he wakes and, feeling thirsty, drains his glass. I shall say that he killed himself. I did not do the killing, even though in a sense outside the statute I did cause his death. What the *lex* says is '*Si quis servum . . . occiderit*',[9] not '*Si quis servo . . . mortis causam praestiterit*'.[10]

This is a real problem. And there is a complicating factor. As we shall see the *lex* was not confined to cases of deliberate damage. Our question, Did he kill, burn and so on?, is more difficult to answer if it

[9] i.e. 'if anyone kills a slave'.
[10] i.e. 'if anyone provides the cause of the slave's death'.

has to be answered without reference to the defendant's intention. In short, it is easier to say he killed if he planned the death. In the example just given it is because I did intend to poison the slave that my defence looks very artificial. Suppose instead that the slave died of typhus. I was, innocently, a carrier of the disease. When I put his drink ready I infected it wholly without my knowledge. Unwilling cause of his death, did I kill him? Suppose again that your field of corn has burned down. I made a bonfire half a mile away and the wind carried the sparks. Did I burn the corn? I never thought about it, far away from my garden and my mind. It is difficult to say I burned it. You were my enemy. I waited till the wind was right. And then I lit my fire, willing the sparks to carry. Easier now to say I burned the corn. Samson tied torches to foxes' tails. The foxes burned the Philistines' corn.[11] But he wanted it burned and got the credit for it.

Because the *lex* was understood to create a liability even for unintentional harming, this problem could not be solved in terms of intent. It had to be looked at in terms only of forces, of physical causation.

The test which was adopted was this: the defendant must have brought about the damage *corpore suo*, by his body. Gaius, at G.3.219, says 'But it has been held that the action based on that *lex* lies only where someone *corpore suo damnum dederit*, caused the loss by his body.' Three points need to be made about this solution to the problem.

First, it is not primitive. 'Primitive' in this kind of matter is to have no answer at all, to leave the question to unpredictable intuition. To say that a man only kills or spoils when he does so *corpore suo*, you need both to have thought about the problem and to have mustered the authority to impose an artificial solution.

Secondly, it certainly does not mean that the defendant must have come into bodily contact with the *res* damaged. That would, at the most extreme interpretation, rule out even wounding with a sword, smashing with a stick. Your slave is transfixed by a javelin. I threw it from some seventy yards' distance. Your cart is crushed by a block of marble. On a scaffolding fifty feet above, I, a mason making ready to use it, let it drop. These are clear cases, centrally within the 'with his body' test.

'*Corpore suo*' is better translated with the addition of an extra word, 'by his bodily force'. The idea is easy enough to capture in general

11 Judges 15:4–5.

terms. The passive aspect of the verb, which we have already looked at (*occisum*, *ustum* and so on), must have been the immediate result of the defendant's bodily force. Or, the defendant's body must have been the last kinetic force to operate, the last source of movement. It is worth remembering at once that in the ancient world gravity was not a force. That is to say, if I dropped a lump of marble or took the brake off a cart at the top of a hill it was my force which sent it into your slave's head or over his toe, not the unseen hand of gravity.

Thirdly, even though the general idea of the test can be made out, its detailed application is inescapably difficult. There is nothing new in this. Often a test which is necessary and useful is difficult to apply to the facts. In the English case of *Scott v. Shepherd*[12] the defendant had thrown a firework into a market. Several stall-holders knocked it on away from themselves until when the fuse had burned it blew up in the plaintiff's eye. The action was in trespass *vi et armis*. English law had reached a test remarkably similar to the Romans' *corpore suo*. The question was, whether the plaintiff's eye had been injured by a direct and unlawful act of force on the part of defendant. Agreed on the test, the court divided on its application. The majority thought that the injury had been done directly. Quite apart from the inherent uncertainty of the formula to be applied, opinions will be affected by extrinsic factors. For example, the colour of the question will be different according as the choice is between liability and no liability at all or between liability under one head and liability under another. Substantial justice may be in issue in the first case, only clarity in the other. Again, the hardship to be inflicted on a particular, and especially deserving, plaintiff may enter into the decision. Among those who decide some are willing to lean more heavily than others.

These tensions are present in the Roman texts. It is wrong to look for perfect consistency, even in the same jurist. Consistency in application, that is. It would be shocking to find different tests in play. In classical law, when the praetorian supplementary actions were regularly available, there was less pressure for a liberal interpretation of *corpore suo*. The main thing then was a clear line round the action under the *lex* itself, the statutory core of the delict.

Some cases are quite easy. I lock your slave up or impound your cow and then give no food, so that death follows by starvation. There is no bodily force involved in the death. I send your slave up a tree and he

[12] 3 Wils KB 403; 96 ER 525 (King's Bench 1773).

falls, or down a well and he fails to return to the surface. Again, it would be difficult to argue that his death or injury happened *corpore meo*. These examples are given in Gaius, 3.219. My example of the poisoned drink is clearly outside the test. If I held the slave down and made him drink, that would be on the other side of the line. Similarly with poisoned ointments rubbed. Or hyperdermic application. If I cut a rope, I damage it *corpore meo*. If the boat attached to it then floats off and is driven by wind and wave onto a rock, its destruction is caused by me but not done by my bodily force. If I puncture a cistern of wine the hole is made directly. I have damaged the container within the meaning of ch. III. Suppose, however, that the wine pours or seeps out and spills on the ground. That happens indirectly, not *corpore meo*. That may be the least clear of these examples. What squeezes out the wine is gravity, and gravity is not supposed to count. But even we think of the weight of water as an independently identifiable force.

There are many more troublesome cases. The common characteristic of all difficult facts is that more than one force, or more than one body, is involved. Suppose a slave knocked into a river or into the sea. He drowns. At G.3.219 Gaius says this is outside the *lex* but he raises his eyebrows and admits that one might as easily say the opposite. Justinian, at J.4.3.16, does say the opposite. There was a dispute and, strictly but very inconveniently, the cases should have been divided. If he bobbed around and, struggling, was eventually overcome, the river killed him, not me. If he went down once and for all or, more clearly still, if he broke his neck on impact, I killed him, *corpore meo*. Again, suppose I set my Alsatian to bite you, adding length and strength to my arm. Have I done it? Julian said, only if I kept hold of the dog; but a more liberal view had prevailed earlier.[13] Finally, suppose you push me and I thus injure the plaintiff's slave. For example, you kick a ball. It strikes my elbow. I, a barber, am shaving the slave. I cut his throat. Have I wounded the slave? At one point Proculus seems to have no difficulty in saying that I have;[14] at another the mere intervention of my body seems to make it impossible for him to say that I did the injury *corpore meo*.[15] That may be unfair. In this kind of issue one often needs

[13] D.9.2.11.5 (Ulpian, 18 *On the Edict*).

[14] D.9.2.11 *pr.* (Ulpian, 18 *On the Edict*).

[15] D.9.2.7.3 (Ulpian, 18 *On the Edict*). Birks appears to have mixed up the parties in his manuscript; the text of this paragraph was altered so as to reflect what he most plausibly meant to say.

more facts than the texts give us. In the second case perhaps your intervening body was not helplessly inert, or not to the same degree as the barber's arm struck by a flying ball.

There is nothing mysterious about this section. The statute said that a man was liable if he killed, if he burned, if he broke and so on. The jurists held that he could be said to have done these things if he had done them *corpore suo*, with his body. It was not to be expected that they would all agree all of the time as to what facts satisfied the test. If someone brought the action under the statute the defendant would very likely run an argument under this head. The *iudex* would have to decide.

*v. Did the defendant do the harm wrongfully (*iniuria*)?*

The point we have reached is this. The plaintiff has suffered a disaster within the *lex*. The defendant has done it. If the *lex* had imposed strict liability, that would be the end of it. But it did not. More accurately, it left room for argument, and the decision was that it did not. The *lex* did not say 'If someone *dolo malo* kills another . . .' or 'If someone *negligenter* causes loss . . .'. The word it used, in both chapters, was *iniuria*. This, in the ablative case, is the noun made from the negative particle '*in–*' and the word for 'right' or 'law' which is '*ius*', as though we would say 'un-right'. So in the case of our defendant the question after the *lex* was passed was whether he had done his *occidere*, *urere* and so on 'unrightfully'.

That wording is neutral on the question of the kind of fault to be required, if any. All it implies is that there are some cases which are not wrongful, some which are. The content of right and wrong is not given. We do not know exactly the steps by which that vacuum was filled but we can consider the choices.

A. 'Wrongfully' becomes 'by malice or by fault' It is a natural human instinct, when faced with an accusation of damage and injury, to say, if there is room for the plea on the facts, 'Oh, it was only an accident.' A child does it almost automatically when a cup is broken or milk spilled. It is meant to avert responsibility. 'You cannot be cross with me' becomes in an adult and in a court 'You cannot punish me or make me pay.' An accident is like the measles. As victim you must complain to God, not your fellow man. Insurance has been provided as a means of material solace. After all, it is not clear why anyone should suffer any loss if a means can conveniently be found to save them. Certainly it is not a reason against the other means of relief that no fellow human is answerable for your disaster. Because it was an accident.

There is a trace of this plea already in the Twelve Tables: 'If the weapon flew from his hand rather than he threw it, let him offer a ram.'[16] The idea is evident and familiar. In the case of accident the principal burden of responsibility is averted. But something remains, just for causing the disaster or perhaps just for being involved in it. The token offering puts the matter straight.

'Accident' is itself a notion which requires the law to make choices. The child says, 'It was an accident. I didn't mean to do it.' 'Accident' there is everything which happens unintentionally. But the parent may still get angry: 'You are old enough to know better.' Or, 'You could at least have been more careful.' Here 'accident' is the disaster which happens without blameworthiness or fault, the premise being that there can be fault without deliberate intent. Lines can be drawn at different places, using different words and concepts, but these two are the most easily marked. The child's position is that liability should be for *dolus* only, that is, for intentional harm, with everything else classed as *casus*, accident. The parent's view is that liability is for *culpa*, with *casus* covering only what happens entirely without fault.

We must get back to the statute. It said the act must be done wrongfully. Someone was bound to say sooner or later that an accidental *occidere* or *rumpere* could not be regarded as wrongful. These were the choices: accept the argument or reject it entirely; if accept, either on the basis of the wider or of the narrower notion of accident. The law's choice was to accept that accident exonerated but, like the parent above, to narrow its scope to the case in which there was no fault at all.

That is a re-construction of the process by which a *lex* which imposed liability for what was done 'wrongfully' came to be understood as basing the liability on *culpa*. It is not easy to say how quickly this interpretation was completed. It seems to be already in place in all our sources. Alfenus Varus, pupil of Servius Sulpicius and contemporary of Augustus, handles Aquilian problems in terms of *culpa*.[17] That is two hundred years after the *lex*. There is no reason to think the *culpa* approach was not achieved much earlier.

16 Twelve Tables 8.24a.

17 D.9.2.29.4 (Ulpian, 18 *On the Edict*); D.9.2.52.1 (Alfenus, 2 *Digest*).

The developed position is summed up by Gaius at G.3.211:

A person is understood to kill *iniuria* if the result is brought about by his *dolus* (malice) or *culpa* (fault). Loss which happens *sine iniuria* (without wrongfulness) is not brought within any other statute. And so no liability is incurred by a person who inflicts loss without fault or malice by some mischance (*sine culpa et dolo malo casu quodam damnum committit*).

There is another rather different picture of the development which I will mention in section (c). For the moment it is more convenient to look at the content of *iniuria* understood as *dolus* or *culpa*. What facts would and would not amount to 'malice or fault'?

B. The content of iniuria *(=* dolo aut culpa*)* It is safe to contemplate this in two parts. In the first the defendant's claim to be exonerated is based on *casus*; in the second on some other ground.

Where the defendant relies on *casus*, necessarily he will not have intended harm to the plaintiff's property. The question is, What exactly is an accident? We have already said that the commitment to *culpa*, rather than *dolus* alone, is acceptance of a narrow defence of accident as an event which happens without fault. At this point we have to add some detail. In judging fault a high standard is taken. One text talks of *levissima culpa*, the slightest fault, as being sufficient. The expression may not be classical but the thought is right.

Suppose the defendant was not conscious of any want of care on his part. As a matter of fact he did not appreciate that there was any risk, was therefore not aware of taking one. He was pruning a tree in a field. From time to time he threw down branches. Getting on with his work he forgot there was a path below. He crushed a slave. He now says that he not only did not intend harm but also took no risk that it might happen. That is no answer. He ought to have foreseen the danger. It counts as *culpa* under the *lex Aquilia* to omit precautions which might have been taken. The question is not whether he was consciously at fault but whether he did all that could have been done to avoid the harm. Suppose he burned off the stubble in his field and the fire escaped and destroyed my crops. It is not enough for him to say that he thought he had done everything necessary. The question is whether in fact he had done everything which ought to have been done. We would turn immediately to the reasonable man. What is the standard behind 'ought to have done' or 'ought to have foreseen'? We say that people should foresee harm which a reasonable man would foresee and take such precaution to avoid it as a reasonable man would take. The Romans do not restate *culpa* in that way. Yet many of their conclusions correspond to those of the reasonable man, and one text comes close to putting the matter in our way: 'It is *culpa* not to foresee what a painstaking man (*diligens*) would have been able to foresee.'

Another defendant may say that not only did he not appreciate the risk but that he personally was incapable of doing so. He did his very best, but he could not measure up to the standards attainable by the best of men. He too is caught by the approach described in the preceding paragraph. Suppose his point is that he himself is not very intelligent. He cannot foresee or judge as others do. The only allowance which the law makes is for exceptional categories at so to say the extreme end of the spectrum. There are people who are relieved of all responsibility, *furiosi* (madmen) and young children. Everyone else is assumed to be equally capable for the purpose of legal responsibility. That does not mean that lawyers could not make moral distinctions, only that for practical reasons the law did not.

A third defendant may say that he did as well as the best man possibly could but that he lacked some special skill. His case is that people should be judged by a standard of general knowledge without assuming special training such as only some ever get. I ride my horse into you. I do everything that could be done by a careful man. My trouble is only that I am but a beginner in horsemanship. I bought the horse yesterday and today when I failed to hold him back I was learning to ride him. My argument is that I should not be judged as one who had acquired the special skill of riding, only by the standard of an ordinary unskilled man doing his best to avoid damage. Or, suppose your slave is bitten by a snake. I cut into him and cause a disaster. I did what the best of laymen would have done, but a doctor would have done something different. He would have known that for this kind of snake a day's rest was all that was needed. Again I want my conduct assessed from the standpoint of general knowledge, assuming an absence of special skills. I am prepared to be measured by a high standard but not as a rider or a doctor when in fact I am neither. The law's blunt answer is: *imperitia* (want of skill) counts as *culpa* (fault). If I engage in an activity which requires a special skill I must answer for loss which happens because I lack that skill. There is room for argument in cases of urgency. If the fault consists not so much in lacking the skill as in embarking without it on an activity which requires it, then I may be free of fault in cases in which there was no possibility of getting in an expert at the time when

I entered on the task. If the snake-bite happened miles from anywhere and death seemed imminent, I may be free of *culpa* even though a layman.

This discussion has been designed to show that *culpa* does not require conscious risk-taking, it is not judged by the particular defendant's own, perhaps limited, ability to appreciate the consequences of his conduct, and is not excluded by the fact that something more than general knowledge would have been needed to avert the disaster. The question is not, Did he foresee the damage? or even, Could he have foreseen it? Rather, Could he have foreseen it as a *paterfamilias* of sound judgement and intelligence possessing the skills necessary for the proper conduct of the operation in question?

The second part of the inquiry into the content of *iniuria* here, i.e. of *dolus* and *culpa*, concerns those cases in which the defendant did intend the *occidere* or *corrumpere* but claims to have been justified by the particular circumstances. The word 'justified' exactly matches the word *iniuria*. It means 'made right'. This is about cases in which the damage is done *iure* despite being done on purpose. Again I do not think there is any conflict between the word *iniuria* and the notion of *culpa* in these cases. What is deliberate but justified in the eye of the law is *sine culpa*, without blame or fault. I shall deal only with some examples.

The simplest case is this. Under the early law, by a provision of the Twelve Tables,[18] it was lawful to kill a thief caught by night. It is evident that this right was whittled away by juristic interpretation so as eventually to be assimilated to self-defence. However, at all stages of its development it provides a good model of a defence by way of justification. The same is true of magisterial authority. Suppose that an official acting within his jurisdiction kills or flogs your slave. Clearly he acts *iure* and cannot be said to be guilty of *culpa*.

The most important justification is self-defence, limited to force necessary to prevent the harm anticipated to oneself. The justification does not extend to measures which exceed this limit of proportionality, as for instance blows struck in revenge. Self-defence is a species within the wider genus 'necessity'. In the case of self-defence the danger is generated by the threat to one's body. There is no need to distinguish that from danger to one's family. But danger to property is more problematical. Am I justified in causing injury or damage in order to

[18] Twelve Tables, 8.12.

protect my own property? The answer is that in appropriate circumstances I am, but the details of the picture are not clear. If the wind blows my ship into your fishing nets so that extrication is otherwise impossible I may cut your nets. May I knock down your house to stop fire reaching mine? The answer is not clear. Perhaps the question is whether, like the nets, your house was already certainly lost.

Finally, one curiosity. If I eat your food or burn your logs I am not liable for *damnum iniuria datum*.[19] The reason is that proper user is regarded as rightful. It is specifically the *rumpere* which must happen *iniuria*; and when the particular *rumpere* is exactly what the thing is for, the classics hold that there is no *wrongful* breaking etc. It may be theft and it may be a contempt-*iniuria*. But these other elements of wrongfulness do not allow the actual chewing, burning or what have you to be regarded as wrongful for the purpose of this delict. One way of putting this is to say that even if there is fault there is not faulty chewing, swallowing and so on. The chewing is impeccable, despite being by the wrong person. There are other examples: wearing, and wearing out, someone else's shoes, quarrying rocks from his hillside, pressing his grapes when ripe to make wine.

There are two more sections to be considered under 'the content of *iniuria*': (c) an alternative picture of the development, and (d) a comparison between *culpa* and *negligence*. Both of these must be done rather briskly.

C. *An alternative picture* The key according to what has been said in the previous section is an equivalence between *iniuria* and *culpa*: What happens 'unrightfully' is what happens blameworthily or faultily. And that equivalence is seen as something initial or, more accurately, something worked out from the beginning as the interpretation of *iniuria* was built up. The other picture assumes that *culpa* was an innovation of early classical law into a picture first settled on different lines.

On this view *iniuria* was first interpreted on the basis that all *occidere*, *rumpere etc.* was *prima facie* wrongful. Within that assumption were worked out certain situations in which there was a right to do the killing or damage. And these situations were described somewhat stiffly, not with the sensitivity to particular facts which characterises the approach through *culpa*. Thus, it was right to kill a thief by night and right whatever his mien, whether violent or submissive. And,

19 D.9.2.30.2 (Paul, 22 *On the Edict*).

perhaps, it was right to do whatever you wanted on your own land so that you could not be liable for dropping a branch from your tree on to my slave unless he was on a public way overhung by your branches.

The best evidence of this stiff, typified approach actually comes from the wrong end of the *lex*'s history. Justinian's Institutes seem to use it. Thus at J.4.3.4, if you are a soldier using a javelin on a military field and you transfix a slave then, so long as you did not do it *dolo malo*, you are free of *culpa*; otherwise if you are a civilian, or a soldier on other land. This is stiff in that it ignores the careless soldier and the careful athlete. At J.4.3.5 a similar analysis seems to be used of the pruner's case, which is made to turn on presence of a road or path below and apparently rules out liability in any case in which there was no right to walk beneath the tree.

In such a picture the rôle of *culpa* would have been to bring flexibility, sensitivity to the particular facts, now relieving a liability (as of the careful athlete), now extending a liability (as of the careless soldier).

There are two main difficulties. First, it is a picture which can hardly accommodate the defence of accident. A typified notion of accident would have to be expressed in terms of superior force. You escape liability only if your precipitation into the plaintiff's *res* was due to an overwhelming force, a whirlwind or a flood. Not an impossible approach but not one which is securely evidenced in the texts. It is an approach which has an additionally complicating element in that it runs very close to the issue of causation making 'it was an accident' almost the same as 'I did not do it'. But again that is not a decisive argument against it.

The other objection is that the most convincing evidence is of the kind given in Justinian's Institutes from the wrong end of the development. This evidence can be explained as giving an unintentionally misleading picture. It can happen that when one cites facts to illustrate a proposition which dictates a different conclusion as the facts change—that is to say, precisely when one's aim is to illustrate the flexibility of the concepts in question—that one's illustrations can seem to be too starkly opposed. Thus, I believe that Justinian's Institutes fall into this trap. They intend to show the *culpa* conclusion varying with the facts but give the impression of excessive typification. In favour of this way of understanding them is the fact that in the Digest's versions of these same cases there is no sign of the indiscriminate approach.[20]

[20] D.9.2.9.4 (Ulpian, 18 *On the Edict*); D.9.2.31 (Paul, 10 *On Sabinus*).

The *culpa* question is, Was the defendant at fault on the particular facts? The possibility exists, though I am not convinced, that at some time the Romans dealt less sensitively with typical sets of facts, not immediately with the actual facts which happened.

D. Culpa *and negligence* The Roman equivalent of the modern tort of negligence is to be found within *damnum iniuria datum*, and in particular within the *culpa* interpretation of *iniuria*. One might say that nine times out of ten '*culpa*' means 'negligence' in the sense of the modern tort. However, it is dangerous to make that translation a habit. 'Fault' is better, even though the fault is nearly always negligence.

The Roman delict comprises both intended and unintended harm. That has an important impact on the meaning of *culpa*. Take the case of one who wounds in self-defence. We cannot explain his non-liability by saying that he is not guilty of malice (*dolus*) or negligence, but we can say he is not liable because neither malicious nor at fault. The point is, he is not guilty of negligence because he meant to harm and he is not guilty of *dolus* because he meant to harm for a good motive. So the first statement lacks explanatory force. The second says that he is free of both bases of blame, malice and fault. Suppose he exceeds the measure of proportionality. He is liable. Unless the excess is extreme I doubt whether we can say that he is guilty of *dolus* but we can say he is at fault. He was 'unreasonable' but not negligent. On these facts there is no question of unreasonable failure to foresee. We cannot explain his liability by saying he was negligent when he lunged with his sword. He was at fault. The difference is between unreasonableness and unreasonable failure to foresee. Suppose the case of a cruel teacher. If he flogs the slave-apprentice for bad learning and the slave dies—that is, something goes wrong and there is an unintended escalation of consequence—you might analyse his liability as based on negligence. But for the flogging itself, always supposing it is bad enough to inflict *damnum*, negligence will not do. The master is conceded a right to chastise. The easiest analysis of his liability is to say that his excessive punishment is unreasonable. He is guilty of 'fault', what good men condemn, even though on the facts there is no question of his failing to foresee what they foresee.

Even in cases in which *culpa* does refer to fault in relation to unintentional harm and where it does bear the sense of modern 'negligence' there are technical differences. First, modern law is always concerned to ask whether there was on the facts any duty of care, and

Roman law does not worry about that question. The reason is that Roman law limits itself to physical damage *corpori* (*res corrupta*) *corpore* (done by his bodily force). Excursions beyond that are controlled by praetorian discretion. The modern duty of care is a controlling mechanism to prevent liability running wild. It is needed because there is in principle no limitation to damage to physical property. If there were, the duty to take care to avoid such harm could be taken for granted in every case. Secondly, there is no habitual reliance on the reasonable man. Whether there was or was not *culpa* was a question for the *iudex*. He had what might be described as negative assistance from the corpus of juristic utterance. It was not an exonerating factor that one was unintelligent nor uninstructed in a skill. But the texts do not contain evidence of a positive test in habitual use. And one feels the lack. 'Reasonableness' though uncertain in content is an invaluable guide.

4. The Praetorian Periphery

Juristic interpretation of the statute sometimes produced results which failed to satisfy plaintiff demand. Such demand is, of course, not everything. It does not in itself justify reform. But if in addition the praetor could be persuaded that, judged by principle higher than the words of the *lex*, the particular stopping point was or had become unnecessary, he would allow the plaintiff a remedy. In time these praetorian extensions of the statutory core settled down, in such a way that a plaintiff would not have to regard himself as a pioneer breaking new and uncertain ground.

The praetorian periphery can most easily be surveyed through the five questions used to consider the statutory core.

*i. Has the plaintiff suffered loss (*damnum*)?*

Here there is no extension. A plaintiff who had not suffered loss would be out of range not only of the *lex* but of the principle, however stated, which the *lex* reflected. Praetorian extension of this liability is essentially a matter of giving remedies for more kinds of *damnum*.

*ii. Did that loss arise from a thing spoiled (*res corrupta*)?*

Here there are extensions. It is an area which raises the issue which we refer to as 'economic loss', the central problem of which is that there is a danger of ramifying and unlimited liabilities and hence a need to go carefully.

It is necessary to distinguish two types of case. First there is the disaster in which the absence of spoiling is no more than technical or even freakish. There is something tantamount to damage or destruction. Coins have gone down the drain irrecoverably. A diamond has been thrown over the side of a ship. An animal has been allowed to escape. These cases do not really raise the problems of 'pure economic loss', for the *damnum* still arises from a necessarily limited and finite event, the reduction (albeit not by spoiling) of the plaintiff's corporeal wealth. This type of case has to be contrasted with the other, in which the *damnum* consists solely in expenditure or loss of profits. Suppose that I negligently spread a rumour that plague has broken out in the district. A hundred or more substantial merchants evacuate their families and close their businesses; a thousand or more suppliers to those merchants lose contracts; and so on. Or suppose I give bad advice on investment opportunities. There is a bubble; and then it bursts. Thousands who relied on my tip come knocking at my door. This is pure economic loss, *damnum* not anchored to diminution of corporeal wealth.

How far did the *praetor* go? There is no doubt that he would give an action in the first case. There is a hint, perhaps not reliable, that Sabinus was even willing to fudge the issue of *res corrupta* and allow the action under the *lex*.[21] It has been thought that at least Justinian extended this extension so as to provide a general remedy for economic loss, but that is doubtful.[22] Classical law, one may be almost certain, did not venture beyond the first kind of case. For economic loss caused by deliberate trickery there would be an *actio doli*, for fraud. Otherwise it would be a question of asking whether the plaintiff could make out a cause of action in contract. Did he pay the defendant for advice so as to make it *locatio-conductio operis faciendi* (investment opportunity to be analysed)? Or was he commissioned by the defendant to lay out his money to support the now failed business, so as to give him an *actio mandati*?

*iii. Did the spoiled thing belong to the plaintiff (*res actoris*)?*

We saw that the *lex* gave the damages only to the *erus*, i.e. to the *dominus ex iure Quiritium*. The praetor allowed claims by others with

[21] D.9.2.27.21 (Ulpian, 18 *On the Edict*).
[22] J.4.3.16 *in fine*.

interests in the thing, the *bona fide* possessor, the usufructuary and the pledge-creditor. Also, though his obstacle was more comprehensive, the foreigner outside the *ius civile* was early given an action based on a fiction of citizenship.

The praetor also gave an action for injury to a free man's body, a thing not owned, also for the injury or death to members of his family in his paternal power (*in potestate*). In early law *dominium* and *potestas* may hardly have been distinguished. One writer, J. M. Kelly, believes that free children were intended to be within the *lex* itself.[23]

iv. Did the defendant do the spoiling 'corpore suo'*?*

It is difficult to see how the jurists could have done away with this test once adopted. What could they have put in its place? Yet there was plainly a need to reach defendants who were responsible for bringing damage about but had not actually done it. If I cause your slave to take poison or put a log in his way so that he rides into it I should not escape just because the statute happened to contemplate only the case in which I did the killing or injuring. There is no need to repeat the earlier discussion. The praetor did give actions for bringing about these consequences.

That is not the end of the difficulties. The restriction to corporeal causation had the effect of putting a very tight lid on questions about the infinite chain of causes. We all know that if we journey back in time we must at all costs not step on so much as a butterfly, lest the whole of history change. I cause a car to slow down as I dash across Princes Street. If I had not done so it would not two minutes later have been in position to run over a dog. Have I caused the dog's death? One way of handling this problem is to ask whether the death of the dog was within the risk which I created by my dash. That kind of question is one which moves the issue from causation to fault. Was I blameworthy in respect of the dog's death? The Romans must have followed that line, putting the burden on *culpa*. But there is no discussion explicitly on this problem. That is to say the texts do not directly address the issue of remote causation which lies behind the '*corpore suo*' test.

*v. Did the defendant do the harm wrongfully (*iniuria*)?*

This question is of the same order as the first, about *damnum*. You could not well extend the liability to instances of harm done *iure*, rightfully.

[23] J. M. Kelly, 'The Meaning of the *Lex Aquilia*', 80 *LQR* (1964), 73, 76–7.

And in fact no sorties were made by the praetor into the field of strict liability; that is, liability for causing loss without *culpa*. So far as I know the only trace of such liability in the field of this delict is the special vicarious liability imposed on *nautae*, *caupones* and *stabularii* (keepers of ships, inns and stables) for losses inflicted on users by members of their staff. We will encounter this figure again under the heading of quasi-delict.

Under these five questions we have considered the range of the praetor's satellite actions. A word must be added on his modes of innovation and the vocabulary used to describe them.

A plaintiff who could bring his case within the statutory core was said to claim by the *actio directa*. The word '*directa*' has nothing to do here with direct as opposed to indirect causation; it simply means 'directed' or 'laid down' or 'established'. An *actio directa*, in any field, is 'an established action'. A plaintiff who could not bring the *actio directa*, because his facts fell outside the statutory core and would therefore not serve to substantiate the proposition advanced by the established action, might urge the praetor to uphold a pleading different from the *actio directa*. He might ask that the pleading should be settled in any one of the ways familiar to the praetor as means of reform and innovation. Thus, he might ask for a fiction to be inserted to knock out a single requirement of the established action or he might ask for a *formula* which simply recited the facts which he alleged to have happened. The one case would produce a *formula* drafted *in ius*, based on the proposition of law in the *actio directa*, but *ficticia*, with a fiction. The other, a *formula* drafted on the facts, on the event which had happened. The *formulae* going on to the judge would thus be differently composed. But whichever adapted pleading he wanted the plaintiff's *actio* was said to be *in factum*. There is a difference between *actio* and *formula* in this respect. The plaintiff's *actio* is *in factum* as soon as he bases himself on his own story as opposed to the story covered by an *actio in ius*. But the business of *agere in factum* might lead to a praetorian *formula* of more than one pattern, depending on what was thought most suitable and convenient.

Sadly we do not know enough about the Aquilian actions. In particular we do not know the patterns of the *formulae* used by the *actiones in factum* which extended the statutory delict. We do know that a fiction was used to extend the liability to and for a non-citizen. Whether anything other than *formulae in factum* were used in other cases we cannot be sure.

So far at the level of *actio* we have only two terms, *actio directa* and *actio in factum*. You do not need any more vocabulary to cover the facts on the ground. Yet there is one more term, *actio utilis*. This adds nothing except an element of organisation. Thus, an *actio utilis* is an *actio in factum* re-named to express its relationship to the *actio directa*, in the following way. The spirit, higher principle or policy of the *lex* is called its *utilitas*, its social usefulness, its expediency. An *actio in factum* related to an *actio directa* in being dictated by the latter's policy or spirit, though outside its letter, could be called 'a policy action'—meaning 'a policy-as-opposed-to-letter action'. We turn nouns easily enough into adjectives: a policy action, a confrontation situation and so on. It would be risky to change to the adjective and say 'a politic action' because the adjective has its own specialised senses. If we did switch to 'politic' we would have to keep warning ourselves that it meant 'policy-motivated', not 'astute in a manner befitting a statesman'. The Romans did switch to the adjective. The '*utilitas*-motivated' actions were *actiones utiles*. But *utilis* must not be translated as 'useful' or 'usable' or 'expedient'. An *actio utilis* is an *actio in factum* upheld to implement the *utilitas*, the general policy or principle, of the *lex*.

This discussion, which suppresses a good deal of doubt and controversy, assumes that the two terms *utilis* and *in factum* are virtually synonymous. Not quite. For it leaves the possibility of there being an *actio in factum* which is so to say a spontaneous creation, not related to the *utilitas* of any other *action* but simply needed in its own right. With that in mind we can approach the difficult lines with which Justinian's Institutes close their discussion of the *lex Aquilia*, at J.4.3.16:

But it has been held that there is only an action under the *lex* if someone has caused loss immediately with his body (*corpore suo*). And so if one has caused loss in another way the practice is to give *utiles actiones*. [Examples are then given of loss arising other than by the defendant's bodily force.] If the loss was not caused *corpore* and in addition no *corpus* has been damaged but loss has in some other way affected someone, then, since neither the *directa* nor the *utilis* Aquilian action lies, it has been held that the person responsible is bound by an *actio in factum*. For example, if someone moved by pity frees someone else's slave from chains so that he escapes.

Here the contrast between the *actio utilis* and the *actio in factum* is puzzling. Nowhere else is a line drawn explicitly between them. There are two possible explanations. One is that Justinian is using language which by his time was old-fashioned, without much regard for earlier usage, simply to convey the idea of an extension upon an extension. The other is that the idea is deliberately meant to be conveyed that the sphere of the *lex* is damage leading to loss, not simply loss. When phrasing the policy or *utilitas* of any rule one has to pick one's level of generality. It would be possible to say that the general principle of the *lex* was that people should have a remedy for wrongful loss; but no less sensible to affirm, at a slightly lower level, that its principle was that one should have a remedy for wrongful damage. If one pitched the level of generality at damage, actions for loss *sine laesione corporis*, without physical harm, would be set outside the statute's *utilitas* so described. They would then be *actiones in factum* without being *actiones utiles*. That may be what Justinian meant.

The reason for pausing on *actiones in factum* and *actiones utiles* is that, though specially well illustrated in the Aquilian field, they have a wider importance. They give us an opportunity to see how the praetor worked and how the jurists organised the product of his innovative practice. *Actio in factum* expresses the potentiality of the system for growth outside and between *actiones directae*. *Actio utilis* is a systematising notion whose effect is to enable jurists to create compound molecules centred on direct actions.

5. The Measure of Recovery

This is the last major topic. Its place offends against the system used so far in that we have left the statutory core and must now return to it. We know very little about the measure of recovery under the praetorian actions, though we are entitled to assume that it was the same as in the *actio directa*, at least unless there are arguments to the contrary.

i. Lis crescit *(the suit enlarges)*

Under both main chapters the action gave double damages against a defendant who contested his liability. That is a fierce rule which probably has a historical explanation: in the *legis actio* system of procedure the defendant would have been subject to *manus iniectio*, physical seizure against which there was no defence unless a *vindex* came forward to throw off the claimant's hand. The third party defender brought the action on himself, for double the damages. Hence a *vindex* would not lightly take up the defence.

If the defendant admitted liability the action was called *confessoria*. You might think that there would be nothing to litigate about if the defendant confessed. But in the *actio confessoria* he would still contest the *measure*; and without incurring the doubling he was allowed to show that the event had not happened at all. The slave supposed to have been killed was actually alive and well. Confession precluded only argument on the issues of liability, *corpore suo* and *iniuria*.

It has been suggested, though the matter is not clear, that there was no doubling of damages in the praetorian actions.

ii. The original measure

Doubling does not tell us the unit to be doubled. What did the statute intend to be the *simplum*? Under ch. I the answer is straightforward. The original measure was the highest value of the now dead *res* during the preceding year. The words of the *lex* are clear. The condemnation is to be *plurimi*, for the greatest value, *in eo anno*, in that year. The retrospective calculation is best explained as a means of overcoming seasonal fluctuations. It was a technique which would eliminate doubts in the plaintiff's favour, leaning against the defendant because of his *culpa*. Sometimes the logic produced odd results, which were, however, not rejected. Suppose you killed my slave. Six months earlier he had lost a leg. You pay the value he had before he was crippled, and I recover more by far than you have caused me loss.

The measure under ch. III causes endless trouble. We know two things for certain. First, there was no mention of 'highest' value, because it was on the authority of Sabinus that the word '*plurimi*' was implied into ch. III to balance its presence in ch. I. Gaius reports this at G.3.218. Secondly, the period of time mentioned was not a year but thirty days.

Daube argues that the measure was meant to work quite differently from that under ch. I. What was intended was that there should be a delay of thirty days to see how the matter developed.[24] The defendant could get the loss as calculated after a month had passed. The point was that wounds need to be waited for in that way, being unpredictable. The words in Latin will more than bear that interpretation: *in diebus*

[24] Daube (n.5), 256ff.

triginta proximis is, literally, 'in the nearest thirty days', which could be prospective. And it is not impossible that the verb was *erit*, in the future: 'as much as *ea res* shall be worth over the next XXX days.'

This is attractive. The measure is very suitable for wounds, not crazy for other kinds of damage (though Daube himself thought inanimate damage was not at first included).[25] The trouble is that the ch. III provision does seem to have been interpreted symmetrically with ch. I at least from Sabinus onwards. That is, at least from the beginning of the classical period. The XXX days were thrown backwards, and *plurimi* was read in. Why would it have been turned round? It was better as it was. If it started with a prospective delay, there was no obvious need for the change.

Jolowicz thought the measure had from the start been substantially the same as for ch. I, the value of the thing in the previous month.[26] That really is a mad measure for wounding and other partial destruction: full value for a cut or a chip, even if the depreciation was slight. So Jolowicz said the early substantive scope of the chapter was originally confined to destruction of non-ch. I objects.

Kelly suggested that the XXX days was not a period for valuation but a period for payment, later converted into a period for valuation on the model of ch. I.[27] That is very attractive. I incline to the view that it may be right. The *lex* may have wanted the loss to be paid within one month, the means being *ea res*, the matter, i.e. the loss-causing disaster: let him pay its value within a month.

These difficulties are interesting and probably insoluble. It probably remains true that all the classics took the ch. III provision to be retrospective, working, with the help of Sabinus's *plurimi*, exactly as that of ch. I except with XXX (30) instead of CCCLXV (365) days.

iii. Full value under chapter III?

The uncertainties of the very early period oblige us to accept a base for ch. III some 200 years after the enactment: highest value in XXX retrospective days. Wounds were certainly included. Do we assume that I recovered 100 per cent for a wound depreciating a slave or cow by 1 per cent? Probably the 'highest value' calculation was only to

[25] Daube (n.5), 260–1.

[26] Jolowicz (n.4), 255ff.

[27] J. M. Kelly, 'Further Reflections on the *Lex Aquilia*', in *Studi in Onore di Edoardo Volterra* (Milan: Giuffrè, 1971), 235, 239ff.

provide a base from which to work. The penal nature of the *lex* cannot explain such gross disparity. The safest assumption is that full value so calculated was the *prima facie* measure of recovery, subject to a deduction of the injured *res*'s surviving value. You recover 100 but if he was depreciated by only 1, you must be taken to have received 99 already.

iv. The measure in high classical law

There was evidently a move away from value and to *interesse*. That is, away from asking how much the dead animal would have been worth on the market, or the injured one depreciated in terms of its market value before and after, and towards asking what the plaintiff's interest was in the safety of his *res*. In the end it seems that the defendant was to put him back so far as money could do it *in statu quo ante*, into his position as it would have been without the delict. It is not easy to say how this development was related to the words of the statute. And there are difficulties about remote losses which the texts do not answer. Most of what we know relates to ch. I.

There seem to have been two stages. In the first, one recovered the basic sum, the highest value, in every case; but one might get more if one could show that one had lost more. This is the 'more but not less' stage. You kill my slave. He was part of a team. I recover his value plus the loss from the depreciation of the team as a whole. Or he was just about to enter an inheritance which had been left to him. I can have the value of that too, which would have been mine if he had been able to enter. This is shortly described in G.3.212.

However, Ulpian seems to have gone further. He was apparently willing to switch so completely to the *interesse* principle that he could contemplate displacing the statutory measure altogether. If his *interesse* was less than the value the plaintiff would therefore get less than his statutory entitlement. That is a difficult way of putting it, but the steps in the interpretation are no easier. For an example, suppose this case. Among my slaves is X the illegitimate son of my cousin, Titius. Titius dies. Under his will X is to be heir if I free him, in which case I shall receive from the huge estate a legacy of ten times his market value. If X fails to take the inheritance for any reason other than my refusal to manumit, I am myself to be heir. You now negligently kill X after Titius' death but before I can manumit him. My interest in his survival is zero since I shall acquire more by his death than the legacy, itself greater than his market value. Retrospectively there was a time when

(a) he had a calculable market value and (b) that value was enhanced by the legacy attached to him. But Ulpian will give no award.[28] A century before, Julian would have allowed me to recover the market value as a minimum beyond which I could not fall.

Details under ch. III are obscure but two observations are worth making. First, consequential losses could sometimes be recovered by a separate action. I cut a rope. The ship on the other end floats off and hits a rock. There is an *actio directa* for the rope, an *actio in factum* (here also undoubtedly *utilis*) for the ship. If you could, did you have to divide in this way in classical law? I think the answer is that you did. You could not recover the value of the ship just as part of your *interesse* in the rope. This then raises a more alarming supplementary question: what if the consequential loss was of a kind not independently actionable? Because you injure my slave I fail to get my olives to market on a day when there is still a short supply; on the next market day there is a glut. So I lose profits. This question cannot be securely answered. It would be odd to allow some consequential losses to be reached by the *actio directa* while still insisting that those recoverable by *actio in factum* should be separately pursued.

The second observation is that a measure of recovery based on depreciation does obliquely reach many common consequential losses. Suppose a horse injured. The value before the disaster was 100. A vet will have to be called. The first item of depreciation from the standpoint of a notional buyer contemplating the fresh injury is the vet's bill, say 20. Hence, the horse, as is, goes down to 80. Then there is an imperfect recovery factor: if he gets better will he be as good as he was at 100? And a risk factor: will he pull through at all? The reductions attributable to these factors will depend very much on the nature of the injury. The essential point is that the vet's bill enters into the depreciation. If a plaintiff were allowed depreciation plus medical expenses he would be getting double recovery with respect to that item. It is easier to see with repair costs of inanimate objects. Suppose you break my Grecian urn. One way to work out my loss is to say that I shall have to pay out 20 to get it mended and that even then it will be worth 20 less than the original 100. Total loss = 40. Another way is to say, looking at the pieces, that the depreciation is 40, since a buyer would pay 60 for

[28] D.9.2.23 *pr.* (Ulpian, 18 *On the Edict*).

them as they are knowing that laying out a further 20 would give him an object worth 80.

It is difficult to prove but this 'depreciation' approach seems to me to fit the classical law best for ch. III. Was the *res* depreciated by the disaster? You look at it from the standpoint of a notional buyer bidding after the disaster. The plaintiff gets the difference between the highest price in the preceding XXX days, and the price which the notional buyer, anticipating repair work and so on, would give after the disaster (presumably one should say, immediately after the disaster).

Notice two similar cases. I am fond of my slave and I get a doctor to look at the black eye which you have given her. The bill is 20. But an unsentimental buyer would have taken nothing off: 'She'll soon be over that.' No expenses anticipated, no risk factor, *ergo* no depreciation. Hence I recover nothing. Ulpian is made to say the opposite at D.9.2.27.17,[29] but the text survives also in the *Collatio* at 12.4. There he does deny recovery. Suppose therefore that I insist on getting repaired something which you have broken very badly. Here there is depreciation but I spend more than is reasonable. For the sake of the friend who gave it I spend twice its value repairing a quite ordinary cooking pot. What would Ulpian have awarded? The notional buyer would have given me nothing on the ground that it would cost more to repair than to replace. His advice would have been to throw the pieces away. I think Ulpian and his predecessors would have given only the market price, not the actual repair bill. In 1981 the National Gallery in London restored a painting by Bryan Organ of Diana Spencer. It was said that the cost of making good the vandal's attack was greater than the cost of commissioning a new portrait. Let us accept the assumption that a second commission was possible, at £x. It does not follow that the Gallery unreasonably spent £x + 1 repairing the first portrait. Each painting is unique. Getting another means getting a different item by way of substitute. Possibly the value of the first version was £2x and the anticipated value of the repaired version still greater than £x + 1. Sentimental expenses, which the market will not contemplate, are only those which exceed the value which they can restore.

[29] Ulpian, 18 *On the Edict.*

10

Iniuria (Contempt)

The main Roman delicts divide the field in this way: *furtum* and *damnum iniuria datum* have to do with wealth. *Furtum* is concerned with wrongful redistribution of wealth and *damnum* with wrongful waste. *Iniuria* by contrast protects the human personality. That is a generic and abstract way of encompassing the many different aspects of life in which people need respect and consideration from others. Their bodily integrity, their personal freedom, their sexuality, their privacy, their good name. Different cultures have different approaches and emphases. The Roman way was to bring the various interests together in a single right, to an equality of respect: one free man ought not to belittle the individuality of another. The idea is too rarefied for a court to apply directly to the facts of everyday life. It is also too modern. The jurists themselves did not much theorise about what their law was doing, or how. They just got on with it.

There is not a definition of this delict, nor a statutory text to analyse. It forms a looser category, more a list of known cases held together by a principle and not closed. *Furtum* and *damnum* are much easier to get to grips with. Another complication is that one's view of how the category should be handled is to a certain extent controlled by the story of its development, how it was handled in the past. And that history is controversial. It is a mistake to allow those controversies too large a rôle. The approach which I use is to concentrate first on the law of the mid second century, Gaius's law, based on the edict as tidied up by Julian. After getting a view of the thing in its developed state there will be time to run to the pattern of its growth. It will be impossible to separate the history absolutely. It always is.

1. The Name of the Delict

We have already encountered the word '*iniuria*' in the *lex Aquilia*, where it was used in the ablative with adverbial effect: 'by a wrong' and hence 'wrongfully'. Here the noun stands alone as the name of one delict, albeit one whose content is not homogeneous. Just as interpretation gave the Aquilian *iniuria* a specialised sense, so here 'un-right' was also refined. But in a different way. I am going to postpone consideration of this specialisation. There is a danger of giving the impression that it was known or at least sensed all along. It probably was not.

It is a puzzle to know how such a general word could ever come to denote a single category of liability. It is not obviously better fit for specialisation than 'delict' itself. But this kind of thing can happen in any number of unplanned ways. The common law uses 'tort', the French word for 'wrong', to do the work of 'delict' as the generic term for actionable civil wrongs. That is because its first generic word, trespass, was pushed into specialised service: 'Forgive us our trespasses.' Back in the fourteenth century, when the common law was being built up, nobody thought that a trespass was or would be something narrow and technical. With a different fall of the evolutionary dice 'Tort' might be 'Trespass' now.

In fact it is extraordinarily tempting to translate '*iniuria*' as 'trespass'. That would convey the right impression of a wide word for 'wrong' used in an artificially narrow sense. The drawback would be that it would suggest a coincidence between the two technical senses. That would be misleading.

Even though the delict is called '*iniuria*', the use of the plural is strikingly prominent. The edictal rubric is '*De iniuriis*' (Concerning wrongs). So also the title of Justinian's Institutes. The Digest title is '*De iniuriis et famosis libellis*' (Concerning wrongs and written defamations). More importantly the action is the '*actio iniuriarum*' (the claim for wrongs). This use of the plural is an indication of variety within, even of variety not in perfect unity.

2. The Action

The *actio iniuriarum* had a *formula* which directed the trial court to assess the defendant's conduct according to a standard of decency and fairness. The crucial words were *bonum aequum*. The plaintiff had to say what *iniuria* he had suffered. He did that in a 'whereas' clause. It was called the '*demonstratio*' of the *formula*. Later on, in the part called the *condemnatio*, he had to put in his own valuation of the damages which he ought to be awarded. That would operate as a maximum. The programme for the trial would emerge from the proceedings *in iure* looking like this:

Whereas [here would follow a factual description of the wrong alleged to have been suffered by Aulus Agerius], which matter is the subject of the action,
in whatever sum of money it shall on that account seem decent and fair (*bonum aequum*) to the judge for Numerius Negidius to be condemned to Aulus Agerius,
for so much money, to a maximum of—, let the judge condemn Numerius Negidius to Aulus Agerius;
if it does not appear, let him absolve.[1]

This is slightly simplified. Also it evades some problems. Two should certainly be mentioned. First, at least some *iniuriae* were sent for trial not by *unus iudex* but by a bench of 'recoverers' called '*recuperatores*'. Secondly, and much more important, it is not absolutely clear whether both actionability and quantum were tested by the standard *bonum aequum*, or only quantum. This depends on whether in describing the wrong in the *demonstratio* the plaintiff was obliged to insert a word or phrase referring to some other standard. The obvious choice would be '*iniuria*' itself, in the ablative. Suppose you had pushed me off the pavement. Slipping for convenience into the second person, did I have to say 'Whereas you wrongfully pushed etc.', which would make actionability turn on 'wrongfully', or did I say enough if I simply alleged 'whereas you pushed etc.'? That would leave actionability and quantum to *bonum aequum*. You want to say the pushing was done in self-defence, also that the event was not very grave anyhow. The first statement goes to actionability, the second to quantum. Were they or were they not both taken under *bonum aequum*? This is important because the standard which the *formula* directed to be applied affects our whole understanding of the delict. That is, of the facts which

[1] For the Latin, see Lenel §190.

would and would not come within it. Sadly we cannot eliminate all doubt. Lenel, unsurpassed on this kind of question, inclined to the view that all the work was done by *bonum aequum* and no other standard was mentioned in the *demonstratio*.[2] If that is right, and I think that it is, very great weight was borne by the clause 'in whatever sum of money it shall on that account seem fair and decent to the judge for Numerius Negidius to be condemned to Aulus Agerius'. From what angle should he approach his assessment? That takes us straight to the measure of recovery, which is the matter to which the words are most obviously directed.

3. The Measure of Recovery

I know that we have not even reviewed the kinds of conduct for which the defendant might face an *actio iniuriarum*. It is odd to go straight to the plaintiff's measure of recovery. However, if we have the structure of the action right, there is no doubt that settling the angle of approach to quantum would be crucial in determining the scope of actionability. So far we have an action for wrongs which are to be assessed in money on the basis of *bonum aequum*. All very vague. Once you determine the angle of assessment, however, you will begin to know what wrongs are in question.

The critical statement is negative. The evaluation is not of *damnum*. It is not about loss. That is the province of the *lex Aquilia*. When loss is seen to be taken out by that statute, not much choice of angle is left. The non-economic interest more or less has to be solace for pain and suffering. That itself offers choices. There can be a limit to physical pain or a larger view can be taken so that pecuniary solace is extended to wounded feelings, in the sense of outrage, affront, humiliation. That was the line which was taken. Negatively the condemnation was not to be concerned with *damnum*, positively it was to be directed at contempt, *contumelia*, the outrage felt by the plaintiff. If you have your face slapped there is some physical pain. But you burn inside. The psychological pain is much worse than the physical. You feel outraged, belittled, held in contempt. That is *contumelia*, ultimately the hallmark of this delict.

[2] Lenel §190.

How early was it settled that the *condemnatio* was to be a solace for *contumelia*? It is difficult to say. The negative proposition that it was not about *damnum* was probably understood by as early as 100 BC. Capturing the precise positive angle probably came later, perhaps in the early Principate.

Gaius wrote about AD 160. By his time all this had long been known and understood. But even his treatment contains evidence that *contumelia*, contempt, worked its way into the delict from the measure of recovery. In dealing with the substantive scope of the liability, the conduct which would trigger it, he gives no prominence at all to *contumelia*. He mentions it once, obliquely. This very low profile which *contumelia* has in Gaius is concealed in translation if *iniuria* is rendered as 'contempt' or, as in Zulueta, 'outrage'.[3] But Gaius's treatment of the measure of recovery takes the *contumelia* basis of the award for granted. He explains the system whereby the plaintiff names his own sum by way of maximum and then goes on, at G.3.224–5, to deal with the special case of *atrox iniuria* (aggravated wrong). Here, if you name the same sum in your *formula* as the praetor fixes for *vadimonium* (security for re-appearance), the *iudex* will in practice not go below that sum. What is *atrox iniuria*? Gaius divides the aggravations between *ex facto*, where there is a serious wound or flogging, *ex loco* where the deed is done in public, *ex persona* where the wrong is offered to a magistrate or to a senator by a humble person. If no other case suggested it, *atrocitas ex persona*, aggravation by personal status, would make quite plain the assumption of a *contumelia* base for the award.

In the Digest Ulpian is recorded as asserting confidently that the specialised sense of *iniuria* as an independent delict is *contumelia*.[4] Justinian's Institutes 4.4, *De Iniuriis*, begin with a similar assertion, rather insensitively expressed.[5] We will come back to that. What I have been suggesting is that the engine driving that specialisation was the need to understand how to approach the quantification of damages under the words *quantum pecuniam ... bonum aequum videbitur ... condemnari*. If the award of money was designed to solace wounded self-respect, *contumelia* not *damnum*, that would necessarily work back into the substance of the action. It would shape and limit the conduct actionable. The *iniuriae* within the *actio iniuriarum*, wrongs

[3] Francis de Zulueta, *The Institutes of Gaius* (Oxford: Clarendon Press, 1946), vol. 1, 227.
[4] D.47.10.1 *pr.* (Ulpian, 56 *On the Edict*).
[5] J.4.4 *pr.*

within the action for wrongs, would become the contempt-wrongs, the ones with the effect of wounding self-respect.

4. The Edictal Provisions

In the Edict as settled by Julian *De Iniuriis* is Title XXXV. It contains eight provisions.The last four can safely be described as adjective or procedural: 194, *Of* iniuriae *committed against slaves*; 195, *Of the* actio iniuriarum *in noxal form*; 196, *If an* iniuria *shall be said to have been committed against one who is in another's* potestas; 197, *Of the counter-* iudicium *for* iniuria.[6] For the substance of the category it is the first four which matter: 190, *The general edict*; 191, *Of* convicium; 192, *Of affronts to sexual propriety*; 193, *Let nothing be done to cause infamy*.[7] The last three are about conduct easily described. I will sketch in their scope before coming back to the general edict.

i. Of convicium *(shouted invective)*

Convicium is shouted invective. Not every *maledictum* but the malediction *cum vociferatione*, with vociferation. Suppose that I stand outside your house and yell out complaints against you: 'You're a cheat and a liar!' Or, more specifically, 'Just because you own half the town you think you need not pay your bills.' These are *convicia*. There is no need to multiply examples.

If I did these things I would quickly enough have a crowd around me, and very likely I would prefer to mount the demonstration with some friends rather than in lonely isolation. A case can be made that a crowd, a *coetus*, is an essential element of a *convicium* or that it was so at one time. There is a very good reason why that cannot be decided finally. *Convicium* was just a part of *iniuria*. Nothing turned on its exact definition. Certainly not in developed law.

The edict promised a trial (*iudicium*) against anyone who perpetrated or brought about the perpetration of a *convicium contra bonos mores*, meaning 'against decent standards of behaviour'. Its presence shows that some *convicia* were thought allowable, even when directed at a specific victim. According to the standards of our time demonstrations

[6] See Lenel §§194–7.
[7] See Lenel §§190–3.

are allowable. The marchers shout their demands or complaints. A demonstration of that kind is a good example of an allowable *convicium*; but it is rarely directed against a specific person and can therefore be removed from the area of liability on that ground alone, without relying on *contra bonos mores*. Reasonable heckling of a particular politician may do for a modern example of a *convicium* allowable according to prevailing standards despite its having an identified victim. There is some suggestion that in Roman society *convicium* was a recognised mode of self-help, an extra-judicial mode of seeking one's rights or registering disapproval of a wrongdoer. The typical allowable *convicium* was probably shouting out a justified complaint, a complaint which one was prepared to justify before the *iudex*: He really was a debtor, oppressor of the poor, adulterer and so forth.

We do not know whether, when one supposed oneself victim of a *convicium contra bonos mores*, the *formula* would allege the matter generally as a *convicium* or would recite the specific vociferation: 'Whereas Numerius Negidius shouted against Aulus Agerius that he was an extortionate and corrupt landlord.' Nor do we know whether the words '*contra bonos mores*' would be inserted or had to be. I think the probability is that the allegation was specific, not general, and that the words *contra bonos mores* were usual but not necessary. If they did appear they constituted a reference in the *demonstratio* to a standard apparently distinct from *bonum aequum*. On closer inspection the two standards would tend to merge in that, under the different words, consonance with prevailing standards must correspond with what a judge thinks decent and fair. Nevertheless, even if the standard was the same in both formulations, the double mention would have the attraction of allowing a formal separation of issues of liability from issues of quantification.

ii. Of affronts to sexual propriety

The Latin rubric is '*De adtemptata pudicitia*'. It is not easy to translate. *Pudicitia* is the sense of restraint and propriety in sexual matters which is sometimes referred to as 'modesty', though the usage has become old-fashioned. 'Chastity' is not quite right. 'Of modesty affronted' is probably the safest literal rendering.

The edict envisaged three cases: a) *Comitem abducere*, removing a companion from a woman, a girl or a boy. The idea is better conveyed by substituting 'chaperone' for 'companion'. The adult male is tacitly supposed to be the hunter, these others the prey. Left alone by the *abducere* they are exposed to impropriety, threatened, endangered. b) *Appellare*. This is seduction, urging or soliciting sexual intercourse. c) *Adsectari*. This is following around after the object of one's desire, dogging their footsteps. It is a familiar enough way of pressing attention on another. In the case of *appellare* and *adsectari* the edict again used the phrase *contra bonos mores*. What was said in relation to *convicium* applies here too. There were allowable versions of these activities, honourable or even just light-hearted.

The texts are not quite steady on the question whether the gist is affront to feelings or damage to reputation, a narrower base. But I think the classics would certainly have said it was affront.

iii. 'Let nothing be done to cause infamy'

Ne quid infamandi causa fiat. We do have a specimen *demonstratio* for this but unfortunately it is crucially incomplete. It is given in a text from Paul in *Collatio*, 2.6.5. Daube's reconstruction goes in effect 'Whereas Numerius Negidius wore sack cloth and ashes against Aulus Agerius for the sake of infaming him.'[8] Only sack cloth and ashes is the Biblical, not the Roman, manifestation of grief and mourning. The Roman version is 'going unkempt', with your hair unbrushed and beard untended. This case is conspicuous both in Digest texts[9] and Seneca the Elder.[10] By traipsing around after someone in mourning clothes one could, according to the other prevailing circumstances, raise an innuendo about that person. So, if my father has died, I might, by mourning pointedly, manage to implicate you in his death. A silent version of Hamlet's play. The other reconstruction is less interesting but might still be right: 'Whereas Numerius Negidius sent off a writing (*libellus*) to a third party for the sake of infaming Aulus Agerius.'

Both examples have in common that they involve conduct other than spoken words, *facta* not *dicta*, aimed at bringing infamy on the plaintiff: *infamandi causa facta*, things done to bring an infamy.

The praetor did not promise a *iudicium*. He simply said '*animadvertam* (I shall look into it)', and we are told that this meant there would be a more active than usual inquiry *in iure*. It is easy to see why. In principle

[8] David Daube, '*Ne quid infamandi causa fiat*. The Roman Law of Defamation', reproduced in David Daube (David Cohen and Dieter Simon, eds.), *Collected Studies in Roman Law* (Frankfurt am Main: Vittorio Klostermann, 1991), vol. 1, 465, 465.

[9] D.47.10.15.27 (Ulpian, 77 *On the Edict*).

[10] Seneca the Elder, *Controversiae*, 10.1 (Lugens Divitem Sequens Filius Pauperis).

the edict could be offended by almost any conduct, however lawful on its face, if only a defendant was ingenious enough to make it convey a message about the plaintiff. There is always an argument about the floodgates of litigation, especially when the liability in question is not tied down to a specific type of conduct. The promise to look into the matter before sending it on to trial is probably an answer to that fear.

Daube says that there was another limiting factor.[11] The edict was concerned with only very serious forms of defamation. 'For the sake of infaming' did not mean just 'for the sake of damaging reputation' but 'for the sake of bringing on civil disabilities'. Magistrates could impose disabilities on those who were *infames*, had incurred *infamia*, depriving them of citizen rights, as to make a will, to represent and be represented in court. Daube's view is that the edict intended to remedy only attempts to bring on that technical infamy. However his argument is fragile and has not found support.

The gist is damage to reputation even if not in the aggravated way which Daube maintains. It is useful to recall how defamation and affront relate. Defamation is narrower. One who defames me affronts me, but one who affronts me does not necessarily defame me. If he calls me a liar and a cheat I shall be upset, outraged and so on, even if he does not tell anyone else or let them hear. The reason for recalling this relationship is to make it plain that a figure which deals in defamation is not necessarily out of place in a group concerned with affront or contempt.

iv. The general edict de iniuriis

This came before the other three. They have been discussed first only because their content is easily captured. The *edictum generale* made no reference to any specific type of conduct. The only qualification to be put on that is this: the specimen formula under the edict necessarily did recite a concrete case. Its *demonstratio* described a slap or similar blow on the plaintiff's cheek: 'Whereas Aulus Agerius was struck on the cheek by a fist . . .' Hence we know that physical blows fell within this area. But in itself, the example tells us nothing about the limits, about what did not fall within it.

The edict itself contained instructions about how to plead: 'Anyone who maintains an *actio iniuriarum* must say for certain what by way

11 Daube (n.8), 470ff.

of *iniuria* has been done and must insert a *taxatio* (i.e. a maximum award) not less than the sum fixed for *vadimonium* (security for reappearance)'.[12]

There may also have survived in Julian's redaction of the edict a clause on the lines: 'If anyone has suffered an *iniuria* I will appoint *recuperatores* to assess an award of damages.' For Aulus Gellius tells us in *Noctes Atticae* that the praetors stated by edict that they would give *recuperatores* for the estimation of *iniuriae*.[13]

At least in the classical law this category included many more types of conduct than physical blows. That is to say, not only did the general edict embrace and include the other three special edicts, but also it reached many types of wrongful conduct other than, on the one hand, the blows illustrated in its *formula* and, on the other hand, *convicia*, *adtemptata pudicitia* and *infamandi causa facta*. The classical delict is made up of these four segments, three of which are finite while the fourth, though containing physical injuries, is open-ended. The scope of this compound delict in the classical law is the subject of the next section.

5. The Scope of the Classical Delict

This is Gaius's first paragraph on *iniuria*, at G.3.220:

> *Iniuria* is committed not only when someone is struck by, say, a fist or a stick or even beaten up, but also if a *convicium* is perpetrated against someone, or if someone advertises a person's goods to be sold off to pay debts knowing that that person owes him nothing, or if someone writes a pamphlet or poem defaming another, or if someone follows around after a woman or a boy, or in short in many other ways.

Having already looked at the edict, we are in a position to see this list as something more than a rambling miscellany. What it obviously does is to work through the rubrics which we have met. First, physical injuries within the example used in the specimen *formula* of the general edict, then *convicium*, then two cases of *infamandi causa facta* and finally one of *adtemptata pudicitia*. There is a change from the edictal order, probably

[12] *Collatio* 2.6.1.

[13] Aulus Gellius, *Noctes Atticae*, 20.1.13.

in order to bring *convicium* into juxtaposition with *infamandi causa facta*. After the list of edictal examples, comes the devastating phrase 'and in short in many other ways'. He gives no guidance, and the list does not obviously reveal any principle upon which further illustrations might be constructed. How would Gaius himself have explained what facts would and what facts would not fit under this very open-ended phrase? That is the key question. Both limbs of it are important. A boundary is only defined if one can say which cases fall each side of it. With *iniuria* the question which receives little attention is the negative one, What conduct will *not* be actionable under this head?

The quantum of doubt should not be exaggerated. Gaius's edictal examples pin down most of the delict's content. The Digest title 47.10 follows the same pattern, still working through the main edictal heads. Given a set of facts a classical jurist would certainly have started by asking himself whether they could fit under one of these edictally established cases. Only if they could not would he have to face the inquiry into the principle which controlled the delict as a whole and hence its capacity to reach novel cases. And with luck his case even outside the Gaian list of examples would not be novel but would already have been considered under the general edict in, so to say, the gap between the blows illustrated in its *formula* and the special cases within the three other edicts. We know for example that already by the beginning of the classical period entry uninvited into another's home or onto his land would be an actionable *iniuria*. So also preventing him from using his own property, as when you somehow refuse me access to my own ship or bar my exercise of a right of way over your land which you find irritating. Similarly, depriving another of his enjoyment of public rights, as by denying him access to a public street or public bath or by forbidding him to fish in the sea off your island. Hence, if we ask how Gaius himself would have handled the open-endedness of the general edict, we must keep in mind that the principle which he had to apply was supported by examples outside the strictly edictal list and also that, because the general edict included the special edicts, the list of examples supporting the principle included the cases falling under them too.

We have already seen that *contumelia* was the specialised sense which *iniuria* acquired as the name of this delict. 'Contumely' is not a good translation. For us it tends to mean no more than 'abuse', though the adjective 'contumelious' is wider. I have been using 'contempt'.

Whatever the word, the underlying idea is of attaching so much importance to oneself, blowing oneself up to such a size, that one can belittle others. Queue-jumping is a good example. You have been waiting at the bus-stop for half an hour. I sweep in at the front of the line. If you do no more, you think 'Who does he imagine he is?' Or take talking during a play. 'Don't they think there is anyone else here?' Or hitting. The reaction 'How dare you?' is not about braving retaliation. It is about arrogance. The Greek word was '*hubris*'.

The question of the limits of the classical delict can be restated: Would the jurist faced with novel facts merely ask whether they amounted to a contempt? Suppose two modern examples. A owns a shop. When B comes in, A orders him to leave. The altercation reveals that the reason is simply that A hates B. There is no suggestion that B is a thief or a debtor or the carrier of an infectious disease. A simply cannot stand him. Then, X is going to marry Y. X happens to be the most famous person in the land. Overnight the hitherto private Y is dragged into the light. She is hounded by the press. Without putting a foot on private land Z pulls off the ultimate coup, a photograph of Y in the nude. Has A or Z committed an *iniuria*?

Both will want to object that they have done nothing *contra ius*, unlawful. Z will in addition feel able to say that he intended no contempt of Y. He was a journalist, just doing his job, he had no feeling against Y. In fact he thought she was marvellous in every way.

Let us deal with Z's additional argument first to put it aside. Liability in *iniuria* does not necessarily require a specifically contemptuous intent. Contempt is usually an inference from deliberate wrongfulness. If I hit you in the face on purpose it is no good my saying that I never heard or thought about *hubris*. Similarly the too persistent lover when he oversteps the mark with his *appellare* or *adsectari* may say that he intended no contempt. Far from it. His libido was simply on fire. The answer is, *contumelia* is an inference drawn by a notional bystander, the court itself. Who does he think he is? Who does he think he is, treating her like that? A specific intent to contemn is not necessary where the conduct is intentional and wrong.

Unlike Z, A did intend to contemn B. His conduct was contemptuous in intent and in effect. The bystander sees B humiliated and that is what A wanted. But A says that he has done nothing wrong. Does his *contumelia* suffice in itself?

We know that right and proper acts (mourning one's dead father) can be made unlawful when done *infamandi causa*.[14] If A ordered B out of his shop to defame him, he would be guilty of *iniuria*. It would then do him no good to say that he could choose who should and should not enter his shop, just as lawfully as he could prefer to drink with his friends rather than his enemies. So we know that one intent, intent to defame, could make conduct unlawful. But could general hatred or spite do the same? This is as much as to say, Is intended *contumelia* enough in itself?

Without answering that for the moment, let us look at Z's case. We have dealt with his argument about intent. His other point is that in taking the photo he did nothing unlawful. Sophisticated equipment saved him the trouble of leaving the public road outside Y's house. It is not unlawful, he says, to take photographs across private land. The other examples given earlier, invading a man's land, forbidding him the use of his own property or the exercise of a public right, are different precisely in being demonstrably unlawful without relying on the workings of this delict. The answer to this is that contravention of positive law is not required. If it were, the delict would ossify, or very nearly. But evidently the standards in question are *bonum aequum* and *boni mores*, not positive law but prevailing reasonableness. As the edict expressly says in the case of *convicium* and *adtemptata pudicitia*, the question is whether Z has acted *contra bonos mores*. Judged by that standard, is his conduct *quod licet* (what is allowed) or *quod non licet* (what is not allowed)?

A Roman *iudex* deciding this case, or jurists contemplating it, would find it difficult. We have brought him to Scotland, in 1982, and he must decide according to the *mores huius civitatis*, the standards of this society. This society, however, is rather unclear on the line between allowable and not allowable in relation to public figures. Let us suppose that he decides Z went too far. What he did was not permissible, *non licet*. Then there is Z's point about not intending disrespect. There is nothing in that. He intentionally did what was not permissible. Contempt is inferred, and he must pay.

Now back to A. He says, accepting that the standard to be applied is social morality not positive law, that you must be able to show independently of intent, just as you can in Z's case, that what was

[14] Above, 228.

done was impermissible. That must be wrong as a general proposition. *Infamandi causa facta* prove it. B who was ordered out of the shop builds on from *Ne quid*. He says that anything at all, however lawful and proper in appearance, becomes impermissible when done out of hatred or spite. That must be wrong too. If it were not I should have to give good reasons for not voting for your membership of a club, for not employing you, for not trading with you.

The truth lies in the intermediate position. The judge must find that the conduct complained of, as a whole taking acts with intents, was impermissible according to the standards of the time and place. Let us add a new fact to the case of A and B. A is an anti-Semite, and he thinks B is Jewish. Now he is certainly liable to the *actio iniuriarum*. Even if the *mores huius civitatis* in general allow A as a shopkeeper arbitrarily to exclude anyone whether white, black, male, female, protestant, catholic or jew, they do not allow exclusion of anyone *because* they are white or Jewish or gentile and so on. Some intents *moribus improbant* are condemned by current standards; others, even some that are not laudable, are allowed. 'No coaches', 'No trippers', 'Nobody without a coat and tie', 'No football supporters'—these exclusions are probably on the safe side of the line. 'No blacks' or 'No protestants' are not. Those certainly do offend, and not merely the feelings of the victims. They offend the standards by which we now divide what, even if unkind, is allowable from what is downright impermissible.

6. The Classical Scope Re-Stated Summarily

There was a long list of examples, some mentioned in the edictal provisions, others not. The list was open-ended. The generic conception of the whole category was this: taken as a whole the conduct had to be (a) *non iure* in the sense of contrary to accepted standards of behaviour, and (b) such as would support the inference of *contumelia* to the plaintiff. Where the conduct was improper on its face without reference to intent, that meant only that it had to have been done intentionally; where the conduct could be said to be proper on its face the plaintiff-victim would have to show a specific intent against him such as would turn the whole event from proper to improper, as for example an intent to damage his reputation. *Contumelia* is the essence of the matter but it is not quite able to stand on its own. The reason is that in some contexts spite and malice are acceptable even if not laudable. Hence the need to determine whether the event as a whole was one *quod non licuit*, not allowable by the standards of the time.

7. Requirements in Relation to Intention

Intention needs some lines to itself. It is always difficult. In this delict, especially. The bald statements that *iniuria* requires intent or cannot be committed unintentionally are true but not simple.

Every would-be plaintiff in an *actio iniuriarum* has suffered some material or psychological harm. That is what he wants to complain about. Sometimes the defendant has not intended the act or omission which the plaintiff claims to have caused the harm. He was struck in the face by my arm but my arm was pushed by a third party; or, driving all night, I fell asleep and was carried into him. Where the defendant did not intend the act in question there is no possibility of liability for *iniuria*. Sometimes the defendant has intended the act but has not intended the harmful consequence. I swung my golf-club intending precisely the curve which it followed. I did it again, but you have come up behind me. It cost you two teeth. There I intended no harmful consequence at all, though I intended all the movement of my body and the club. There is another version. A schoolmaster is teaching a boy whose work is badly done. The master, holding a biro, intends to accompany his reproof with a jab to the back of the head. At the crucial moment the boy turns round and takes the biro in his eye. The master intended the act and some small harm but not this blinded eye. I shall come back to the schoolmaster. In the third type of case the defendant has intended the act and the harmful consequence but can say that he would not have intended them if he had known some fact which he did not know. That is, if he had not been labouring under a mistake. This is the case of Oedipus. He intended to sleep with Jocasta, not his mother. He intended to kill the stranger who barred his way, not his father. Had he known the woman was his mother and the man his father, he would not have formed the intentions which he did form in relation to them. There are different versions of this too. Here I am, beating you up or shouting dreadful allegations outside your door. My mistake is, I have got the wrong man. You are N. I thought you were M with whom I have a quarrel. I would not have done these things to you. However, if I had done them to M I would have been guilty of an *iniuria* to him. In the other version my mistake is such that, had my view of the facts been right, I could not have been guilty of an *iniuria*. When I struck you I thought you were attacking me. Actually you were lunging at a poisonous snake behind me. I bundled you off my land. I did not know you had a right of way. I thought you had not paid your debts. When I shouted 'Pay up, you scoundrel' after you, you had already paid the money at my shop while I was out. In the first of these versions, where the deed would have been an *iniuria* anyway, the mistake does not exonerate. In the second one has to proceed more cautiously. It is certain that honest belief in the truth of defamatory allegations did not exonerate. In other words the defendant took the risk of his mistake. Whether this can be generalised to all cases in this category is more doubtful. The right answer may be that the notion of *bonum aequum* and *boni mores* could vary the incidence of risk according to the case. It should be noticed that if I write a story depicting a fictional character or a real Q and people understand the story to apply to P, my facts with respect to P fall with the golf swing category, not with Oedipus.

All the cases considered so far have involved defendants who could plausibly say that they had not intended the harm to the plaintiff, albeit in the Oedipus case that has to be rewritten as 'would not have intended if'.

A defendant may say that he did intend the harm but for a laudable reason. Will his excellent ulterior purpose exonerate him? The answer is, it will if the event as a whole is then transformed into one of which the law and *boni mores* approve. This is the obverse of the point made previously that some wicked intents can transform what is *prima facie* allowable into what is not allowed. The teacher strikes a boy with his hand or gives him a jab with a biro. It is done *monendi ac docendi causa*, to educate. The number of people who believe violence educates has become less. The Romans thought *levis castigatio* acceptable. Hence within the limits of light chastisement the intention to hit for the purpose of teaching would prevent liability for *iniuria*. Suppose a teacher who after the mistakes in a week would chop off a little toe or an ear: however much his intention was to teach, and however good his results, he would not escape liability. Pursued to the length of this *saevitia* the desire to teach does not make the blows consonant with *boni mores*. Again, suppose we fight together *gloriae ac virtutis causa*, that is allowed; but if for the sake of a more resounding victory I lay you out as you are in the act of giving in, my quest for glory will not save me. The approved motive fails to purify the means. Similarly an intent to marry would not justify refusal to leave an unwilling girl in peace.

8. The History

The story can be divided into two parts. At a quite early date, probably about 200 BC, the praetor made his first excursion into the field with his edict announcing that he would have *iniuriae* reckoned up in money awards adjusted to the particular case. From then on we are in the delict's edictal phase. The earlier part can be called 'decemviral', from the *decemviri* who drew up the Twelve Tables, or simply 'pre-edictal'. Doubts and difficulties multiply as one goes back. It is easier, and wiser, to take the edictal phase first.

i. The edictal phase

The single question which matters is the relationship between the general edict and the three special edicts. We know that by the early Principate the three were within the one, just special cases identified in a longer list. Labeo is the authority.[15] Had they always been? Or were they in origin separate wrongs which were brought within the *actio iniuriarum* by a synthesising jurisprudence? It is obvious that the choice between these two possibilities bears directly on the original nature of *iniuria* itself, the entity to which, back in 200 BC, the praetor first directed his attention. The very same choice can be re-stated. Was *iniuria* at first a narrow category dealing with some quite specific type of objectionable conduct? Or was it from the start wide, loose and comprehensive?

There is much to be said for both views. The argument is long and complex. My own preference is for the picture in which *iniuria* is always wide, and the special edicts always inside it. Most scholars would say the opposite.

The dominant view is that *iniuria* starts as physical injury, possibly as physical injuries less than wounding. The blow to the face used in the specimen *formula* thus exemplified the only kind of conduct envisaged by the new estimatory machinery. Then, at some date no later than the

[15] D.47.10.15.26 (Ulpian, 77 *On the Edict*).

early first century BC, *convicium* and *adtemptata pudicitia* were recognised as being *iniuriae* despite being founded on separate edicts. That is to say, it was recognised that assaults on the body, vociferated abuse and affronts to sexual propriety had something sufficiently in common to make one category. The bond between blows and *convicium* may have been made earlier than that between those two and sexual affronts. Then, later in the first century *infamandi causa facta* were also grafted on. That provided the take-off point. The same understanding of the category which let *infamandi causa facta* in formed the basis of the classical delict. In a very brilliant paper, Daube argued that a demonstration debate written up by the father of the philosopher-statesman Seneca preserves the discussion of the question whether *iniuria* could absorb the edict *Ne quid infamandi causa fiat.*[16]

There is one thing strongly in favour of this account. In building on an original equation between *iniuria* and physical assaults, it ties in with the most easily supported view of the pre-edictal content of the delict. As we shall see, there are acute difficulties in accepting the pre-edictal *iniuria* in any other shape.

Also in its favour is that this pattern of growth is better able to account for the birth of the special edicts. If *convicium* and the others had always been actionable within the *actio iniuriarum*, would the praetor ever have needed to pronounce on them? However, this is less strong. In the case of all three special edicts, there is a problem arising from the *prima facie* lawfulness of at least some of the conduct in question. The use of the words *contra bonos mores* in two of them show this. Take *adtempta pudicitia*. You can hear people laughing at the thought of an action for courting. If damages had to be paid for following a girl about, no-one would be safe. The serious implication in this is that the bad case cannot be reached without catching the good too. The edict puts paid to that. It affirms that a line can and will be drawn by the judge's perception of decent standards. Even if the whole story was going on inside the *actio iniuriarum* this kind of problem would still have needed this kind of solution. Also, Labeo actually said that the edict *Ne quid* was unnecessary.[17] And he does not seem to mean that it became unnecessary, with the passing of time and aggrandisement of the *edictum generale*.

[16] Daube (n.8), 484ff.

[17] D.47.10.15.26 (Ulpian, 77 *On the Edict*).

Without forgetting that the pre-edictal history may possibly carry this account over all its difficulties, we can say without unfairness that all the other evidence runs the other way, in favour of a category always broad. It can be condensed into five points: (a) The name '*iniuria*' and the plural of '*actio iniuriarum*' become more mysterious the narrower is supposed to be the actual content of the category. An 'action for grievances (wrongs, complaints, trespasses)' does not suggest a category confined to blows. The edict's injunction to 'say for certain what *iniuria* had been done' reinforces the impression that the content of the action was contemplated as very various. (b) The *Rhetorica ad Herennium* of about 80 BC tells us that poets reviled from the stage had already in the second century BC been allowed to bring *actiones iniuriarum*.[18] (c) The same book gives a definition of *iniuria* which makes it include blows, *convicia* and any turpitude violating another's life, an expression much wider than *adtemptata pudicitia*.[19] (d) Servius Sulpicius, praetor in 65 BC and murdered in 43 BC, gave an *actio iniuriarum* against one who sold a pledge to infame another who owed him nothing.[20] (e) The Augustan orators and advocates reported by the Elder Seneca appear in their debate not to be discussing Daube's issue, whether actionable *infamandi causa facta* could be counted as *iniuriae*, but rather whether conduct ostensibly lawful and indeed duty-bound, mourning a father, could be actionable at all if done to defame.[21] They seem to know nothing of *Ne quid*. In debating whether lawful conduct can be actionable, the only head they have in mind is the *actio iniuriarum*. I mourn my father. I happen to choose to do it wherever you are. I wonder who killed him. This conduct is done *iure*. How can it give rise to a liability for *iniuria*? All the indications are that the debate points to the need for *Ne quid*, as yet not introduced, not to the elision of *iniuria* and a separate wrong already long familiar. We should infer that *Ne quid* was Augustan, introduced to clear up a doubt. In the opinion of some, Labeo amongst them, unnecessary.[22]

One general consideration can be added to these five points. The other view has to suppose 'blows' expanding to capture other wrongs. It is difficult to find a practical reason why that should have been

[18] *Rhetorica ad Herennium*, 2.26.41.
[19] *Rhetorica ad Herennium*, 4.25.35.
[20] D.47.10.15.32 (Ulpian, 77 *On the Edict*).
[21] Above, 228.
[22] Above, 238.

necessary. Reduction of entities is a good in itself, simplifying and enlightening. But it is a good sought by jurists given to reflection and organisation. The end of the second century BC is the wrong time for that kind of jurisprudence. Hence some practical reason for the assimilation of categories has to be found. It is not obvious what it might be. Nor is it clear why the scope of *iniuria* would have been expanded piecemeal. If, for example, the Greek notion of *hubris* had caught the juristic imagination of this early age, one would have expected the re-alignment of old categories to happen all at once.

So, this is the picture which I make out. The praetor said you could sue for damages for any grievance. The question whether you would get anything was measured by *bonum aequum*, the standard of decent fairness in the *formula*. Working out the measure of the award put focus on wounded self-respect and this gave shape and direction to the category. The special edicts were introduced to eliminate doubts and difficulties. They were, so to say, reinforcements inside the one category, not accessions deprived of once independent existence.

The weakness of this view is the strength of the other. The decemviral law must now be considered.

ii. The pre-edictal phase

The Twelve Tables are reported to have contained a tariff of responses to blows. It was in Table VIII:[23]

Against one who has injured another's body, if no agreed settlement is reached, let there be retaliation. [The Latin for this deed is *membrum rumpere*. Its meaning may have been narrower than in this translation.]
Against one who has broken a bone let the *poena* be 300 *asses* where the victim was free, 150 *asses* where he was a slave. [This is *os frangere*; notice these Aquilian verbs.]
Against one who *iniuriam alteri faxsit* (has committed an *iniuria* against another) let the *poena* be 25 *asses*.

There is no doubt that the jurists later regarded the third of these provisions as including minor blows. Labeo is reported by Aulus Gellius as having explained the praetor's intervention by means of a

[23] Twelve Tables, 8.2–4.

story of one Lucius Veratius.[24] With inflation, the fixed penalty became derisory. Lucius amused himself by slapping faces and immediately paying out the decemviral *poena.* His game pointed up the need for awards adjusted to the case. Hence the praetor's estimatory machinery. Nobody else mentions Lucius Veratius, but Gaius, in a paragraph which understands inflation solely as growth in real wealth, paints the same picture. It is G.3.223:

> The *poena* for *iniuriae* under the text of the Twelve Tables was, for *membrum rumpere*, retaliation, while for a bone broken or crushed it was 300 *asses* if it was done to a free man and 150 if to a slave; for other *iniuriae* (*propter ceteras vero iniurias*) a *poena* of 25 *asses* was set up. Those paltry money *poenae* (*istae pecuniariae poenae*) seemed suitable enough in that age of extreme poverty.

It is nowhere made clear either expressly or by secure implication that the classical jurists thought that the *iniuria* provision of the Twelve Tables was confined to physical attacks. It is only certain that they thought it included them. However, the restriction is imposed by another consideration. The character of the decemviral provisions is such that one cannot reasonably accept that they would have embraced a wide variety of conduct in a single term. So, if *iniuriae* included blows, they included nothing else. Bad cases, *membrum rumpere* and *os frangere*, were taken out and dealt with specially. All other bodily attacks were visited with the *poena* of 25.

If this is right, the 'steady state' account of the edictal phase must be wrong. The edictal *iniuria* must have been an expanding category, beginning from the narrow decemviral category which the praetor first reformed. Is it right?

The mystery of the nomenclature persists. The earlier the date the less time and scope there is for a technical accident to happen to 'un-right'. It is not the easiest act of faith to believe that in the mid-fifth century BC 'un-right' would suggest itself to the legislator as a suitable word for 'body blow'. It is not impossible though. If it were, scholars would never have accepted the equation.

It is impossible to take what at first sight seems the easiest way out. That is, knock out the assumption that the *decemviri* would never have dealt with a variety of conduct under one label. That would mean

[24] Aulus Gellius, *Noctes Atticae*, 20.1.12–13.

believing that they offered 25 *asses*, in value supposed to equal two and a half sheep, for any wrong suffered, any wrong not visited more severely elsewhere in the code. The difficulty of fitting that vague and abstract provision into the character of the Twelve Tables is too great.

There is one other way. It is possible that, looking back as we might to a period before James VI and I, the jurists themselves did not know with certainty what the old *iniuria* provision was about. They may have reconstructed its meaning by reference to the specimen *formula* under the edict *de iniuriis* and to any other scraps of information. If that happened the continuity between the edictal *actio iniuriarum* and the *iniuria* provision of the Twelve Tables may be imaginary, the invention of a later age. This kind of thing does happen. The English action on the case, matrix of the modern common law, was found an origin in ch. 24 of the Statute of Westminster, 1285. Everyone believed it. Till Plucknett showed that the story could not quite be made to knit together.[25]

There is a different reconstruction which I have proposed.[26] It focuses on *os frangere*. The Twelve Tables fixed *poenae* for breaking bones. What if someone retaliated in kind, ignoring the fixed sums? That would be wrong but less so than an act of first aggression. For *membrum rumpere* it remained the proper course, in the absence of agreement. It is possible that the *poena* of 25 was intended to cover the case of wrongful retaliation. This version would still have room for Lucius Veratius, albeit one less debonair. When the bronze *as* lost its value, a victim would be found who would tender the 25. That way, threatening immediate retaliation, he stood some chance of getting more than the no less depreciated 300 which the statute offered for his broken leg.

This too may be fiction. But so also may be the other story. It is a question whether the obscure pre-edictal history ought to be allowed to mould our impression of the edictal period. If it is discounted altogether, the steady-state account of the run-up to the classical law is preferable. If it is not, the other may be better. My own view is that it

[25] Theodore F. T. Plucknett, *A Concise History of the Common Law* (5th ed., London: Butterworths & Co, 1956), 373.

[26] Peter Birks, 'The Early History of *Iniuria*', 37 *Tijdschrift voor Rechtsgeschiedenis* (1969), 163, 178ff.

is not. I do not believe that the *actio iniuriarum* was ever 'the claim for bodily attacks'.

9. Some Ancillary Features

i. Recollections in tranquillity

At home after a long day you might be able to recall a dozen *iniuriae* which caused you a moment's irritation, or might have done if you had the time and inclination. X barged past you, Y said you and your party were unfit for office, Z made jokes about your personal life which cut too near the bone. The rule was that you could not revive *iniuriae* once you had let them go: *postea ex poenitentia remissam iniuriam non poterit recolere* (J.4.4.12). We do not know enough to be able to say exactly how this worked. It probably meant that you had to reveal your intention not to overlook the matter as soon as you could reasonably be expected to do so. Suppose outrageous allegations at a dinner party. If you struggled through with a stiff upper lip and sent a message next morning, that would probably keep your rights alive.

The rule is summed up in these words: *Haec actio dissimulatione aboletur*, this action is extinguished by dissimulation. What exactly is the dissimulation envisaged? You smart, but you pretend not to be angry. As at the dinner party just mentioned. That would often be the proper course. To penalise that difficult *dissimulatio* would encourage a lack of restraint. The pretence which the rule aimed at was more likely that induced by the recollection of an opportunity to claim damages. The temptation would be, to pretend that one had not been indifferent or complaisant.

ii. A year to sue

The defendant could, and no doubt would if there was room on the facts, get an *exceptio annalis* inserted in the *formula*. It would make the order to condemn conditional on there having been less than a year since the action could have been brought. According to the words of his *exceptio*, the time runs not from the event but from the *potestas experiundi*, the possibility of suing. This can be tied into *contumelia*, with the last rule just discussed. Genuine contempts are not usually left slowly burning. Also, the evidence is by nature ephemeral in many cases. It is not clear whether the *actio iniuriarum* was always *annalis*.

*iii. The counter-*iudicium

The *actio iniuriarum* was itself a means of bringing infamy on the defendant. If he was condemned he became officially *infamis*. That was right enough. But if the plaintiff lost, the defendant would have suffered some preparatory dishonour. Before the praetor he could ask to have attached to the plaintiff's *formula* a further clause requiring the judge to condemn the plaintiff, if he did not win, for one tenth part of the amount he had claimed. This was only one of a variety of measures which a defendant could use against vexatious or foolhardy litigation.

iv. The lex Cornelia de iniuriis

This was one of Sulla's criminal statutes. It allowed a person guilty of certain grave *iniuriae* to be charged before a *quaestio*, a criminal court. There were three cases: *verberare*, *pulsare*, *vi domum introire*. The first two are varieties of beating up, the line being none too easy to draw between them. The third is violent intrusion into someone's home. The exact relationship between the *lex* and the ordinary *actio iniuriarum* is not clear. It has been suggested that the *lex* displaced the *actio iniuriarum* from its three cases, but Gaius certainly does not think so, since his first examples are types of beating and he never says that the plaintiff could only complain under the *lex*.[27] In the Digest the exposition of the *lex* is incorporated into his exposition of *iniuriae*.[28] It may be that the statutory action was not criminal in any sense, except that it was heard by the *quaestio*. That is, just an *actio iniuriarum* with procedural modification and reinforcement.

v. Dependent persons

(a) Iniuria *to children* in potestate *(in paternal power)*. Suppose that someone made improper advances to your daughter or struck your son. The normal rule was that they could not sue themselves. You had to sue, as *paterfamilias*. However, a special edict provided that in the absence of the *paterfamilias* and any general agent of his with authority to act, the praetor would examine the case and give the *iudicium* to the immediate victim.

[27] G.3.220.
[28] D.47.10.5 (Ulpian, 56 *On the Edict*).

(b) Iniuria *through children* in potestate. There is nothing artificial in saying that an attack on your children is an attack on you too. You suffer, and not vicariously. Mistreatment of a daughter for example is as much an *iniuria* to the father himself as would be for instance a violent entry into his home. There is no comparison intended here between the home and the girl: the point is that the *iniuria* is equally direct in both cases. So the *paterfamilias* here has an action *filiae nomine* and another *suo nomine*, one for his daughter and one for himself. Whether the two counts could be combined in the one *formula* I am not sure.

Suppose an emancipated son finds that his parents have suffered an outrage. Their home has been broken into and they have been mistreated. Can he sue for the outrage to himself? Sons do suffer in such circumstances. So also wives when husbands are attacked. The answer is that nature is not given full reign. The law imposes artificial restrictions. Subject to one exception, only the *paterfamilias* can sue under this head. The exception is the husband where his wife, not being in his *potestas*, is wronged.

My daughter is married to Titius. He is *sui iuris*. She is still in my *potestas*. She was married *sine manu*. She suffers a wrong. There is the count for herself. I must deal with that, as her *paterfamilias*. And I have a count for myself. So I have two. Then Titius, her husband, has a claim for himself. He is *sui iuris*. He brings that himself. The wrongdoer pays three awards.

(c) *Iniuria to slaves*. All issues of economic loss are taken care of under the *lex Aquilia*. They can be ignored here. Then, many events which would be *iniuriae* to free persons are permissible in relation to slaves. That is in the nature of the institution. If you shout at my slave or if you strike or poke him you do not offend standards of decency and fairness. He is only a slave. He has to put up with animal-like treatment, even from someone other than his owner. But there were limits. There would be a point at which your treatment offended *boni mores*.

The edict contained a special provision. It promised a *iudicium* against anyone who flogged another's slave *contra bonos mores* or put him to torture without the owner's consent. Further, for anything else done to a slave, the praetor would send it on to trial if that seemed the right course after examination of the case. It is this edict which gives Gaius the occasion for his one explicit reference to *contumelia*. According to his analysis the action under this edict is to be regarded as *domini nomine*.

It is the second of the two things discussed in relation to children.[29] There is no such thing as an *iniuria* to the slave himself and therefore no action *servi nomine*. The passage is G.3.222:

To a slave himself no *iniuria* is held to be committed. The wrong is understood to be committed to his master through him. The modes by which this can happen are not the same as those which result in one suffering *iniuria* through our children and wives. Instead, only when something rather grave is done, of a kind to be clearly in contempt of the master. As where someone flogs another's slave. For that case there is a published *formula*. But there is no such published *formula* for shouting at or punching a slave. Nor is one lightly given to a plaintiff who petitions for one.

On this analysis the edict has nothing to do with any vestigial humanity of the slave. It is not protecting him at all, except fortuitously. The outrage is to the master, a usurpation of his right to decide how his slaves shall be punished.

There is another case in which the slave is not made to suffer, or not unduly, but is made the vehicle for an attack on the master. Episodes of this kind would usually fall under *Ne quid*, deeds done to defame. Suppose the slave is compelled to behave absurdly in public or commanded not to go about the business on which he has been sent. Such antics can be used to make it plain that the master is a person of no account. Similarly, a *convicium* directed in substance at the master might be uttered at his slave. In such cases there would be no need for the special edict.

[29] Above, 245.

PART III

Miscellaneous Other Categories

11

The Quasi Categories

Back at the beginning, in the section on the conceptual map, we noticed how Gaius divided obligations into two categories.[1] They arose either from contract or from delict. And then he found that this simple dichotomy would not quite do. There were obligations which arose from neither of these two events. Almost as soon as he made his division between contract and wrongs he encountered the obligation to repay money paid by mistake. Paying and receiving a sum mistakenly supposed to be due did not necessarily involve either a contract or a wrong. It was an event of a third kind. So in another book Gaius made room for whatever would not fit within his two-term classification. He added a third class, essentially an unnamed miscellany. And in that way he produced this three-term classification: obligations arise from contracts or from wrongs or from other events (G.3.88–91; D.44.7.1 *pr.* = Gaius, 2 *Nuggets*).

Residual miscellanies of the kind which Gaius uses here are devices to protect categories which have been successfully identified. There is not necessarily any need to give up contracts and wrongs as useful, coherent and manageable classes just because, contrary to first impressions, it turns out that there are obligation-triggering events other than these two. 'Others' allows the ground which has been gained to be held despite the set-back. It admits that there is some unmapped territory beyond what has been reduced to order. But it also constitutes a challenge. Nobody is going to be happy for long with leaving territory unmapped. Attempts will be made to map it. That is, people

[1] Above, 17.

will look into the miscellany to see whether another useful category of events can be taken out of it, so as to leave a smaller unruly residue. Or, even better if it can be done, they will try to divide the whole miscellany into named classes, so as to make the map complete. For those with the right cast of mind the challenge is irresistible. And there is a temptation to cheat. That is, one may settle for the appearance of order without achieving the reality. Perhaps this is what Justinian does (J.3.13.2):

The next division puts obligations into four species: *aut enim ex contractu sunt aut quasi ex contractu aut ex maleficio aut quasi ex maleficio* (for they are either from contract or *quasi* from contract or from wrongdoing or *quasi* from wrongdoing).

This statement certainly purports to eliminate the miscellany altogether. It divides the entire category of 'others' between *quasi ex contractu* and *quasi ex maleficio*. But at first sight this does not look very promising. Because the names are not informative. They do not tell us anything positive about the unities which are supposed to have been identified. We usually anglicise the *quasi* categories to 'quasi-contract' and, ignoring the change from *delictum* to *maleficium*, 'quasi-delict'. But these terms should not be allowed to encourage the belief that the Latin words mean anything as positive as 'sort of contract' and 'sort of wrong'. Their message is almost entirely negative. *Quasi ex contractu* means 'as though from contract (*scilicet* when in reality there is no contract)' and *quasi ex delicto* means 'as though from delict (*scilicet* when in reality there is no delict)'. So the first message in this terminology is the negative one, that the named event (contract, delict) is *not* present. Beneath that, there comes an implication which is positive but uncertain in content: although there is no contract (or delict), yet there is something unidentified which makes 'as though from contract' suitable for some and 'as though from delict' suitable for others. This suggestion of an unidentified resemblance to one or other of the main categories has its source not in the *quasi* phrases individually but solely in the fact that there are two *quasi* categories. If the whole miscellany had been renamed *quasi ex contractu*, there would have been no suggestion of resemblance to contract but only a negative assertion that the category-three obligations arose as though from a contract, though no contract was made. But, because some of the miscellany is attributed to one and some to the other *quasi* category, we have to infer that there is some similarity to justify that distribution.

We cannot really go further without knowing what specific events were placed in each *quasi* category. But there is one question which ought to be put first. Was it Justinian's commissioners who invented the *quasi* categories, or was it Gaius himself? It is a question which cannot be finally answered. In the Digest it appears from excerpts from the *Nuggets* that Gaius not only modified the dichotomy by introducing the third miscellaneous category, but that he also described some members of the miscellany as arising *quasi ex contractu* and others as arising *quasi ex maleficio* (D.44.7.5 = Gaius, 3 *Nuggets*). It is almost certain that this passage has to some extent been tampered with. And it is possible that the interpolations include the insertion of the *quasi* labels. My own view is that that is unlikely. There is considerable evidence that Gaius enjoyed and attached importance to accurate classification. It is consistent with this that he would himself have tried to do something with the miscellany. But it is not possible to be sure.

1. The Content of the Quasi Categories

This is most easily taken straight from Justinian's Institutes. Quasi-contractual obligations are considered at J.3.27, quasi-delictual at J.4.5:

On Obligations *Quasi ex Contractu* (J.3.27)

We have finished examining the types of contract. Let us turn to those obligations which cannot properly be said to arise from a contract but which can however, in that they do not owe their substance to a delict, be understood as arising *quasi ex contractu*. 1. [INTERVENTION IN ANOTHER'S AFFAIRS (*negotiorum gestio*)] Thus, when someone intervenes in the affairs of another when he is away (*absentis negotia gesserit*) actions arise in each direction between them called the *actiones negotiorum gestorum* (the actions for intervention in another's affairs). The person to whom the affair belongs (*dominus rei gestae*) has the direct action, and the intervener (*gestor*) has the counter-action for intervention. It is obvious that these actions do not properly arise from any contract. For they come into being in the very case in which anyone puts himself forward to conduct another's affairs without being given any mandate to do it. It follows that those whose business is done come under an obligation even when unaware of what is happening (*etiam ignorantes*). And this was established as good public policy (*utilitatis causa*) to stop the affairs of the absent running to ruin if some sudden urgency drove them to leave without entrusting to someone the management of their interests. Certainly nobody would look after them without an action to recover his outlay. But, just as an intervener who has usefully conducted the business holds the other to whom it belongs under an obligation to him, so *vice versa* he himself must also render an account of his management. And for that case he is obliged to answer to the highest standard of diligence (*ad exactissimam diligentiam*). And it is not enough for him to show such attention as he usually shows in his own affairs if it happens that another more attentive person would have conducted the intervention more successfully. 2. [GUARDIANSHIP (*tutela*)] Furthermore guardians made liable in the trial arising from guardianship also cannot properly be understood as coming under an obligation by virtue of contract (for there is no deal at all contracted between guardian and ward). But, since a guardian's liability is certainly not delictual, he is taken to become liable *quasi ex contractu*. Here too the actions are reciprocal. For not only does a ward have the action on guardianship (*actio tutelae*) against his guardian, but also the guardian from the other side has the counter-action on guardianship against the ward for the case in which he has spent anything in the ward's interest or incurred an obligation for him or charged his own property to the ward's creditor. 3. [INVOLUNTARY COMMON OWNERSHIP (*communio incidens*)] Again if some asset is shared between people who have not agreed to be partners (*sine societate*) as where it is bequeathed or given to them both equally, each is liable to the other in the action for division of shared property (*actio communi dividundo*) as, say, because he alone took the fruits of the thing or because his *socius* bore the burden of necessary expenditure upon it. This obligation cannot be understood as properly deriving from contract in that no terms are agreed between them. Yet, in that the liability does not come from delict, it seems to arise *quasi ex contractu*. 4. The same legal analysis applies where someone comes under an obligation to a co-heir on similar grounds in the action for division of an inheritance (*actio familiae erciscundae*). 5. An heir also cannot be understood as incurring a properly contractual obligation to pay legacies. For the legatee cannot rightly be described as having concluded any deal either with the heir or with the deceased. But because his obligation is not born of wrongdoing his debt is understood to arise *quasi ex contractu*. 6. [PAYMENT OF SOMETHING NOT DUE (*indebitum solvere*)] Again the person to whom a payment which is not due is mistakenly made is taken to incur a debt *quasi ex contractu*. To such an extent is it true that he does not properly come under a contractual obligation that if we stuck to a more logical analysis we might rather say, as was mentioned earlier, that his obligation arises *ex distractu*, not *ex contractu* [from discharge rather than from contract—but the word-play cannot be reproduced in English: 'from un-contract rather than contract']. For one who gives money with the intention of performing a duty appears to give it for this purpose, namely to untie rather than to tie up a transaction. Yet despite this the recipient comes under an obligation just as though a loan (*mutuum*) had been given to him. Which is why the *condictio* lies against him. 7. In some cases it is not possible to recover a payment mistakenly made when not due. Thus the older jurists made it a maxim that wherever denial doubled liability (*ex quibus causis infitiando lis crescit*), in those cases there would be no recovery of what was paid when not owed, as for instance under the *lex Aquilia* and under legacy. But those older jurists applied this to only those legacies which were left to someone in exact certainty by the imposition of an obligation on the heir (*quae certa constituta per damnationem cuicumque fuerant legata*). However, our enactment has made all legacies and trusts by will into one kind and has applied this increase of liability to all such legacies and trusts but not in respect of all recipients. The rule now applies only where the legacy or trust is to holy churches or other sacred places endowed for the sake of religion and piety. Such gifts once paid cannot be recovered if they turn out not to have been due.

On Obligations Arising *Quasi ex Delicto* (J.4.5)

[THE JUDGE WHO MAKES A CASE HIS OWN] If a judge 'makes a case his own' (*si iudex litem suam fecerit*) he does not appear to come under an obligation which is properly *ex maleficio* (from wrongdoing). But his obligation is also not contractual and he is certainly seen to have incurred some blame even through want of knowledge (*et utique peccasse aliquid intellegitur licet per imprudentiam*). For these reasons he seems to become liable as though from wrongdoing. And he will have to bear such penalty as the conscience of the court deems fair on the facts of his case. 1. [THINGS THROWN OR POURED FROM A DWELLING] Again if something is thrown down or poured down from a dwelling in such a way as to harm someone, the person whose dwelling it is, whether he owns it, hires it or lives there free, is taken to come under an obligation as though from wrongdoing. And the reason why he is not properly said to incur an obligation from wrongdoing is that frequently his liability arises from the fault (*culpa*) of someone else, perhaps of a slave or a child. [THINGS DANGEROUSLY PLACED OR HUNG] Similar to his case is that of the man who, in a place where people commonly pass, has something placed or hung in such a way that if it fell it could harm someone. For that case a penalty of ten *aurei* is laid down. On the other hand, for something thrown or poured an action is given for double the value of the loss caused, while in the case of a free man there is a penalty of fifty *aurei* if he is killed and an action for as much as seems fair to the judge on the facts if he survives but is injured. And the judge should take into account the fees paid to a doctor and all the other expenses of the cure as well as the earnings lost or to be lost because of the faculty which has been impaired. 2. If a son in power lives separately from his *paterfamilias* and something is thrown or poured from his dwelling or he has something placed or hung so as to be dangerous if it falls, Julian held that there is no action maintainable against the father but that the suit must be brought against the *filiusfamilias* himself. The same applies in the case of a *filius* who is a judge and makes the case his own. 3. [SHIPS, INNS, STABLES (*adversus nautas, caupones, stabularios*)] Again where any fraud or theft is committed in a ship, inn or stable the owner running the business (*exercitor*) comes under a liability *quasi ex maleficio*, so long as the *maleficium* is in fact not his own but that of one of the people through whose labour he manages the ship, inn or stable. The reason this is *quasi ex maleficio* is that the action given against him for this case is not based on contract and yet he is to a certain degree blameworthy in relying on the service of bad men. The action for these cases in *in factum* and is available to the heir of the person to whom the claim accrues but not against the heir of the person against whom it accrues.

According to these accounts in the Institutes there are therefore five quasi-contractual events and four quasi-delictual events. Quasi-contractual are (1) intervention in another's affairs, (2) becoming a guardian, (3) becoming a co-owner (where that is thrust upon you willy-nilly), (4) receiving an inheritance subject to legacies, (5) receiving a mistaken payment wrongly supposed to be due. Quasi-delictual are (1) as a judge, making the case one's own, (2) a throwing or pouring from a dwelling occupied by the defendant, (3) a dangerous placing or hanging on premises occupied by the defendant, and (4) theft or fraud in a ship, inn or stable run by the defendant.

So far as concerns the quasi-contractual events the list is the same, subject to one exception, as that attributed to Gaius at D.44.7.5. *pr.*-3.[2] The one difference is that the Digest list is shorter by the omission of the co-ownership case. No other events are anywhere called quasi-contractual. Do any others count as falling under the same label? Almost certainly mistaken payment is meant to stand for the whole

[2] Gaius, 3 *Nuggets*.

non-contractual spectrum of events giving rise to the *condictio*. This needs a short explanation.

We have encountered the *condictio* many times. It was the action which claimed a *ius civile* duty to give a *certum*, either a fixed thing (Daisy) or fixed quantity (50 kilos of corn) or a fixed sum (£20). The legal category formed by the action was based on a unity of content or type of claim (*certum dare*), not on a unity of event at any level of generality (sale, contract, *furtum*, delict). The modern category of 'debt' is similar. Indeed it is all but completely safe to translate *condictio* as 'action for debt'. Such categories cut across unities of event. Any event can give rise to the *condictio* so long only as it triggers an obligation *certum dare*. So when the division between contract, delict and other events was held up against the much older legal category of the *condictio* its effect was to break up the *condictio*, at least in the sense that some of the *condictio* events then seemed to live in one compartment as contracts and others not. We have seen that three *condictio*-events (or, as one might say, three causes of indebtedness) rested on agreement and could be seen as contracts. These were *stipulatio* (for a *certum dare*),[3] *expensilatio* (the contract by written transcriptions)[4] and *mutuum* (the contract of loan for consumption, as opposed to loan for use and return).[5] These three events constitute the contractual part of the spectrum of *condictio*-events.

The mistaken payment supposed to be due is the most prominent member of the non-contractual part of the spectrum. The rest of it is notoriously difficult to divide and name with satisfactory precision. The Digest uses the following heads. D.12.4 is called *De condictione causa data causa non secuta* (On the *condictio* in respect of things given on a basis, which basis fails to sustain itself). This covers two types of cases which show signs of being distinguished but may not need to be. Either I pay on account of a state of affairs which you, the recipient, are to bring about, as for instance because you are going to marry my daughter or because you are going to free such and such a slave, or I pay simply on account of a state of affairs which is nothing to do with you but is merely essential to my intention that you should receive the payment, as for instance 'because I am dying'. And then you do not marry my girl, do not free the slave or I do not die. So the basis of my

[3] Above, 53.
[4] Above, 39–40.
[5] Above, 131–2.

giving falls away. It fails to materialise or fails to sustain itself, as the case may be.

D.12.5 is *De condictione ob turpem vel iniustam causam* (On the *condictio* for what is given for a disgraceful or unlawful cause). This covers the case in which the *causa* of the payment may well have been sustained but where it was disgraceful or unlawful for the recipient to take anything on that account. He is paid not to commit theft. He does not commit theft. So it cannot be said that the basis fails. But it is *turpis* to take money not to steal. Whence the *condictio* for recovery. A distinction is drawn between cases where the taint is shared or on the giver's side alone, in both of which restitution is refused, and where it is on the recipient's side only, which is when restitution is allowed by means of the *condictio*. If I give money to corrupt a judge there is no question of recovery, because the turpitude is shared between briber and bribee.

Then D.12.6 is *De condictione indebiti* (Concerning the *condictio* in respect of what is not due). The *indebitum* is the case with which we are already familiar. There is room for much argument as to whether it is analytically distinct from or rather a special case of *causa data causa non secuta*. It is certainly true that in some cases a payment mistakenly supposed to be due can be analysed as a payment on a basis (for discharge) which fails to materialise (because there is no debt to discharge). But it may be that there are sound reasons for keeping the two distinct. One may be that you can recover an *indebitum* without having to show that you specified (i.e. communicated to the other) the intended basis of the payment whereas under the other head you did have to communicate the reason if you were afterwards to complain of its failure. But this is uncertain.

Then D.12.7 is *De condictione sine causa* (On the *condictio* for what is given without a basis). The words *sine causa* are probably better translated 'on a basis which is void'. Without this ground a wrong conclusion sometimes seems inescapable. Wrong in the sense of undesirable. If I pay because I have lost your clothes at my laundry and then a week later the clothes turn up I cannot say I did not owe. And the basis of my payment (the discharge of my liability) does materialise and sustain itself, for undeniably I was liable and do remain discharged. But we can (just about) say that the discovery of the clothes makes nonsense of the basis on which I paid and nullifies it. Or again if a dowry is paid by a woman to a man within the prohibited degrees, resting recovery on nullity—that a dowry is a legal impossibility in such circumstances—

may serve to outflank arguments which the man might use against a *condictio causa data causa non secuta*. As for instance that though the basis had failed (no marriage) nevertheless the failure meant that she became party to the crime of incest and thus became barred from recovery: for *in pari delicto potior est conditio defendentis* (In shared guilt the defendant's position is stronger: *cf.* D.12.7.5). He wants to say that she cannot recover because she cannot be heard to complain of the failure of any incestuous marriage. To which she says that she is not complaining of the failure on that basis but only of the initial nullity. With goodwill, it is possible to accept the distinction. But nobody can pretend that the *condictio* for a void cause is easy.

D.13.1 is *De condictione furtiva* (On the *condictio* for what is obtained by theft). This is the anomalous case in which the claim is allowed against the thief 'that he ought at civil law to give the *res* to the plaintiff' even though the *res* already belongs to the plaintiff and cannot, according to the interpretation of *dare*, therefore be given to him. G.4.4:

> And with actions thus distinguished, it is certain that we cannot claim what is ours from someone else by this form of words: 'If it appears that he ought-at-civil-law to give'. For what is ours cannot be given to us, it being understood that something is given to us when it is so given that it becomes ours. And what is ours already cannot become more so. It is plainly from hatred of thieves, in order to make them liable in more actions, that the law has accepted that they should be liable, in addition to the penalties of double and quadruple, also even to this action: 'if it appears that they ought-at-civil-law to give'. This is allowed to enable an owner to recover his asset (*rei recipiendae nomine*) and even despite the fact that the action in which we claim that something is ours is available against them as well.

The last case is D.13.2 *De condictione ex lege* (On the *condictio* based on statute). This is a title with only one fragment, which affirms that if a *lex* imposes an obligation and says nothing about the action, nevertheless the *lex* is taken to authorise an action. And from that we have to infer that in classical law the *condictio* was given for all statutory claims so long as they had the *condictio* content (*certum dare*). So this stands for a miscellany of statutory events triggering impositions, fees and other dues.

This survey allows us to put together a view of the non-contractual part of the spectrum of *condictio*-events: receipts for a basis which fails, receipts disgraceful to the recipient, receipts of mistaken payments not due, receipts on a basis which is void, receipts by theft and miscellaneous statutory impositions. The proposition from which we started was that, probably, the receipt of mistaken payments was meant to stand in the quasi-contractual category to represent all these. Probably. The list may never have been closely examined. There is room for a long argument on the question whether receipts by theft (for which the event is *furtum*) can belong in quasi-contract as well as in delict.

In the category of quasi-delict the four named figures are, so far as we know, the only ones intended to belong to it. None is there merely as the representative of a family in the way that the *indebitum* is probably meant to represent the other non-contractual *condictio*-events in quasi-contract. Furthermore it is obvious that the quasi-delictual figures are much less important than the quasi-contractual. No system can do without law on uninvited interventions, mistaken payments, legacies and so on. Special liabilities of occupiers, innkeepers (though possibly not of judges) are optional, even quirky.

The one quasi-delict which does need some explanation is the judge's idiomatic *litem suam facere*. The idiom conceals the thumbnail sketch which names usually convey. And unfortunately the texts do not allow us a clear picture of the judicial failing involved. Bias comes first to mind. It is not only the typical judicial fault but also matches up with the idea of 'making a case one's own'. For partiality involves taking sides, joining in, not remaining on the sidelines. Texts which speak of malicious refusal to apply the law, as by ignoring a statute, are compatible with that starting-point. But there is a difficulty. The passage given earlier says that the judge can become liable *per imprudentiam*, and *imprudentia*, whether it means in this context simple lack of malice (negligence rather than *dolus*) or specifically lack of legal learning, is a cause of wrong judging which is incompatible with bias. It is not impossible that there was a division within *litem suam facere* such that for some failings liability would attach only on proof of malice (getting his law wrong), and for others (ignoring the instructions in the *formula*, not turning up) either no malice or perhaps even no fault at all had to be proved. At all events a general liability for incorrect decisions is implausible if extended beyond malice. It would have made the office of *iudex* too dangerous. Disappointed litigants would have been for ever re-opening the question by suing their judge.

2. The Ideas behind the Quasi Categories

Whoever it was who organised the residual miscellany into the two quasi categories, it is not easy to see what unities he had perceived or why he thought they could best be captured in this quasi terminology. The underlying ideas are not obvious, neither in the two categories taken one by one nor in the contrast between them. Austin, the nineteenth-century jurist, said roundly that there was no rational justification for the division and that if it was thought useful to explain the miscellany in terms of a fiction, 'as though from one of the nominate events', one fiction would have sufficed: you could have called all the miscellaneous obligations quasi-contractual.[6] The difficulty of penetrating the original thinking is greatest with quasi-delict. It is puzzling on two fronts. Why are the quasi-delicts different from quasi-contracts? And why are they different from delicts?

In relation to quasi-contract the first necessity is to eliminate a non-Roman distraction. Nowadays making our own exploration of the miscellany beyond contract and tort the unity which we think we can discover within it and thus remove from it, narrowing the uncharted residue, is the class of event generically describable as unjust enrichment at the expense of another. Mistaken payments are a species of that genus, which is recognisable whenever the law imposes an obligation, independent of the recipient's consent, to give up wealth received at the expense of another. This category of law, the law of unjust enrichment, is often hung on a Roman peg. For in D.50.17, which is 'On various long-standing legal principles', there is this fragment from Pomponius, D.50.17.206 (Pomponius, 9 *Various Readings*):

Iure naturae aequum est neminem cum alterius detrimento et iniuria fieri locupletiorem
By the law of nature it is fair that nobody should be enriched through loss and wrong to another.

Torn from its context, this is vague and meaningless except, and the exception is real and important, as a principle of the same open-textured kind as *pacta sunt servanda* (agreements should be kept) or *sic utere tuo ut alieno non laedas* (so use your own property as not to harm another's). Such principles provide a child's-eye view of areas of law.

[6] John Austin, *Lectures on Jurisprudence* (5th ed. by Robert Campbell, London: J. Murray, 1911), vol. 2, 911ff.

'Open-textured' is the fashionable language for them, but 'over-simplified' might be better if the honesty did not, wrongly, suggest that their work was of no importance to grown-up lawyers. Masses of cases and statutes thrown together without attention to any child's-eye view of what is going on lose their coherence. The first sign is that the area in question becomes very difficult to learn, except by heart. So the generality of Pomponius's principle does not mean that it is useless. But from that alone we cannot infer that the Romans did use it. For different systems can put to conscious use different open-textured principles. And really there is no evidence that the Romans did create and organise a legal category under the principle against unjust enrichment. They had a great deal of law and litigation about the phenomenon of enrichment-to-be-reversed. The *condictio* proves it. But in the divisions which they chose to make, 'unjust enrichment' did not find an independent place. Otherwise we might have expected to find some such statement as this: every obligation arises from a contract, from a wrong, from an unjust enrichment or from some other causal event. There is no such statement.

It is certain that the Roman category of quasi-contract included many figures which do belong in the category of unjust enrichment if that unity is once perceived and used. But it also includes other matter. For example the man who intervenes in the affairs of another (*negotiorum gestor*) is under a duty to perform his intervention carefully and must pay for loss which is attributable to want of that care. The *actio negotiorum gestorum directa* lies to enforce that duty. The *actio negotiorum gestorum contraria* lies to allow him to obtain reimbursement of his expenses. This counter-action, taken alone, might be referred to the event consisting in the enrichment of the beneficiary of the intervention. But the obligation enforced by the direct action has nothing to do with enrichment. The *gestor* is not enriched by his decision to mend his neighbour's roof, milk his cows, pay his creditor and so on. There is no question of making him disgorge any wealth. It is a matter of protecting the other by keeping the intervener to a given standard. The same can be said of the guardian in the *actio tutelae*.

So the Roman category of quasi-contract is not the category of unjust enrichment under another name. This is simple enough. But we make it very difficult for ourselves by using the term 'quasi-contract' as an unexamined synonym for unjust enrichment. In other words we borrow the Roman phrase to denominate a category of our own. But, worse still, all this is done without the clarity which comes from close attention. For the land beyond contract and delict is not much visited.

All this has been negative. Whatever our usage of the noun made from *quasi ex contractu*, the Romans did not see this category of obligations as generated by unjust enrichment. How then did they see it?

The difference from contract is the absence of agreement. These obligations are not incurred voluntarily, by being undertaken. They are imposed willy-nilly when the event happens. In that point they resemble delictual obligations. But they differ from delictual obligations in that the events which trigger them are allowed or even encouraged, not forbidden. So, the quasi-contractual events are those which are lawful but bring into being involuntary obligations.

That is not quite all there is to it. It is also true that for each quasi-contractual event there is, in terms of its consequences a close analogy to one of the contracts in the Roman scheme. This analogy can in the majority of cases be identified as something more specific than an unanalysed impression or feel. It is a matter of a shared actional regime. Thus *negotiorum gestio* and *tutela* not only look like *mandatum* in a loose, impressionistic way (a commission to manage the affairs of another without the crucial commission itself, *quasi ex mandato*) but also rest on classical actions of the same *bonae fidei* type. And the similar actions in the formulary system meant that the packages of obligations developed by interpretation and exposition of the *formulae* retained a structural similarity even after the formulary system itself gave way to *cognitio* procedure. In the same way the *condictio*-events in the non-contractual part of the spectrum shared the same action, the *condictio* itself, as *mutuum*, *stipulatio* and *expensilatio*. A payment by mistake can in a loose way, from an external point of view, be analogised to loan. But, more precisely, the actional consequences are exactly the same. And that makes crisper sense of 'as though upon a contract'.

In the case of the other two, involuntary common ownership and legacy, it is impossible to assert that they share an action and an actional regime with a nominate contract. But the legatee's *actio ex testamento* (on a will) is a close cousin to the *condictio*. And common ownership, though giving rise to actions different in structure from the action on partnership, can claim an analogy to partnership of the less technical kind and one which is underpinned by Gaius's account of the history of *societas* as an imitation of joint heirship.[7]

[7] G.3.154a.

So the members of the category share the qualities of lawfulness and involuntariness with respect to the obligation. But to justify the name '*quasi ex contractu*' there is also an analogy to a contract in the list of contracts. The analogy does not make the quasi-contractual events into 'sort of contracts'. It is an analogy of consequence: although there is no contract at all, nevertheless once the thing is under way there is either or both a loose factual or behavioural similarity and, at least in three cases, a close actional similarity, or indeed identity, to a named contract.

As was said earlier, if it were not for the contrast between the two different quasi categories you probably would not look for these similarities. It is because some of these miscellaneous obligations are *quasi ex delicto* rather than *quasi ex contractu* that you are driven to justify the name. Otherwise *quasi ex contractu*, or *quasi ex delicto*, would suffice to explain all cases neither contractual nor delictual. Or, more accurately, suffice to conceal by means of a fiction the absence of explanation.

Two small points are worth adding. First, a guardian or intervener incurs liability for bad management. Hence his case clearly offers the classifier a choice. Shall he be classified on the basis of the lawful act of becoming a guardian or intervening in another's affairs or on the basis of the wrong of bad management or bad intervention? The choice of the former is not quite an accident. We know that in classical law the model *formulae* of these actions recited the entry on task, not the default after entry: 'whereas he intervened', not 'whereas he managed badly'. According to the structure of the *formulae* the obligations were contemplated as flowing from the primary, not the secondary event. The choice was made, therefore, when the *formula* settled down, not when the business of classifying was done.

Secondly, it ought not to escape notice that among the non-contractual *condictio* events in the family behind mistaken payment there are some which encounter difficulty with the word 'lawful'. The *condictio* given after theft and that given on account of disgraceful behaviour by the recipient are both difficult to explain as quasi-contractual if lawfulness is essential, as it seems to be. There are two ways out. Either to say that it is after all no accident that the list of obligations *quasi ex contractu* does not expressly consider every event in the *condictio* family. Or to say, by a refined but not impossible argument, that these apparently unlawful events can be admitted on the ground that, though they do involve unlawfulness, it is not *qua* forbidden acts that they trigger the *condictio*. Alternative legal analyses of fact-situations are not uncommon. A story which has one consequence as a fraud can have another as a mistake, and to the second consequence it can be quite irrelevant whether the mistake was induced by fraud or not. The argument for keeping the *condictio furtiva* and *condictio ob turpem causam* within a category of quasi-contract to which lawfulness was essential would have to follow these lines.

That leaves quasi-delict. Nobody has ever come up with a view which commanded universal acceptance. There is a difference from quasi-contract. All the quasi-delicts are events which the law forbids: no *litem suam facere*, no pouring or throwing from houses, no placing or hanging above public ways, no stealing in ships, inns and stables. But, if this suffices to make the line between the quasi categories, the next question is, Why are these figures not delicts? What is 'quasi' about them?

The judge tends to spoil almost every attempt to answer this question. The other three all show a number of features which could provide the distinction. They are all cases in which the liability is vicarious, the occupier, innkeeper and so on being made to answer even for the acts of others. They are all cases of liability without personal misfeasance, liability which can extend to pure omissions. They are probably all cases of liability without proof of any fault in the defendant himself. Attempts have been made to fit the *iudex*, at the head of the list, into conformity with one or other of these features. It is difficult to make his liability look vicarious, except where he wrongly absolves. In that case, but not in wrongful condemnation, he can at a stretch be seen as substituted for another, the party whom he let off. Again, if you look hard you can find evidence that the *iudex* could be liable for not doing. That is, one means of *litem suam facere* was failing to turn up.

Stein has argued that strict liability does provide the answer, even for the *iudex*.[8] This is in one way much the best suggestion. It gives a convincing picture of the line between quasi-delict and delict. The two together form one super-category of unlawful events triggering involuntary obligations. Within that there are events involving fault, or blameworthiness, and events which if they happen impose liability independently of fault. Delicts involve fault, quasi-delicts entail strict liability. That is attractive. Because there really is some difficulty in treating events of strict liability as 'wrongs'.

[8] Peter Stein, 'The Nature of Quasi-delictal Obligations in Roman Law', 5 *RIDA* (1958), 563, 563ff.

But this probably will not work. Partly because Justinian seems to lean over backwards to find and point to traces of blame even in the three figures other than the judge. He would hardly do that if the whole point of the category was that it was based on no-fault liability. And partly because it is difficult to restrict the content of the judge's wrong in such a way as to make a no-fault liability plausible. Strict liability for wrong judgements is unimaginable. Nobody would do the job.

One feature which is common to the quasi-delicts is that they all involve defendants in special positions. You have to become a *iudex* before you can *litem suam facere*, and so on. They all involve breaches of duties imposed not just on people generally but specifically on judges, occupiers, innkeepers. At first sight this seems to have no jurisprudential weight. In short, so what?

However, I think the answer does lie in this direction. The business of elegant classification is delicate. The classifier may have been worried about the special positions as having some potential for de-stabilising the category of delict. An argument could be made that they could and should be classified according to the first, lawful event (becoming a judge, becoming an innkeeper), not according to the second event, the *litem suam facere* or the inn-theft. A separate category for special-position-wrongs would effectively isolate them and anticipate all possible attempts at such destabilisation.

If this is right the law of obligations was intended to be divided according to obligation-creating events, in this way. On the one hand lawful events, themselves divided between undertakings (contracts) and other events not connoting voluntary acceptance of the obligation (quasi-contracts). On the other hand, unlawful events. These might have been left in one class or might sensibly have been divided between events involving moral blame and events of strict liability. But in fact they seem to have been divided between forbidden events which anyone could commit (delicts) and forbidden events which could be committed only within the context of a special relationship (quasi-delicts). This classification has influenced both civilian systems and common law systems, though Austin did not like it and warned the common law against it.[9] Contract and delict remain, under some critical pressure, dominant categories of our legal thought. The miscellaneous residue is still troublesome, still not much understood. The quasi categories have certainly not settled the way in which it should be seen.

[9] Austin (n.6), 769ff.

Extracts from Gaius's and Justinian's Institutes

Translated by the author

Gaius

Institutes, book 3

88. Now let us move on to obligations. Of these the main division distinguishes two species. For every obligation is born either from a contract (*ex contractu*) or from a delict (*ex delicto*).

89. And first let us look into those which are born *ex contractu*. This time the division is into four *genera*. For the obligation is contracted either *re* or *verbis* or *litteris* or *consensu*.

90. An obligation is contracted *re* as, for example, by the giving of a *mutuum*. The giving of a *mutuum* happens, properly speaking in relation to the sort of things which are dealt in by weight, by number or by measure. Coined money is of this kind, as also oil, corn, bronze, silver and gold. With such things, when we either count or measure or weigh them out, we give them with the intent that they should vest in the receiver and that any later render back to ourselves should be, not of the very same things, but of others of the same kind. This is how *mutuum* gets its name, because what is given by me to you in this way does become *ex meo tuum*.

91. An obligation *re* is also incurred by one who has received something not due from one who has paid by mistake. In fact he can be sued by the *condictio*, with its pleading which says 'if it appears that he ought at civil law to convey (*si paret eum dare oportere*)', just as though he had received a *mutuum*. For this reason some hold that a *pupillus* or a woman to whom, without the guardian's authority, something not due has been given by mistake is not bound by the *condictio*, no more than by reason of the giving of a *mutuum*. But this species of obligation does not seem to exist by virtue of contract because he who gives with the intention of paying off a debt (*solvendi animo*) has it in mind rather to undo a deal than to do one up (*magis distrahere uult negotium quam contrahere*).

92. An obligation *verbis* is created by question and answer, as in this way:

Dari spondes? Spondeo.
Dabis? Dabo.
Promittis? Promitto.
Fidepromittis? Fidepromitto.
Fideiubes? Fideiubeo.
Facies? Faciam.

93. But this obligation *verbis* in the form *Dari spondes? Spondeo* is confined to Roman citizens. Yet the others are *ius gentium*. As such they are valid between all men, whether Roman citizens or aliens, and even if put into Greek, as in this manner:

Doseis? Doso.
Homologeis? Homologo.
Pistei keleueis? Pistei keleuo.
Poieseis? Poieso.

These are also valid however even between Roman citizens, provided only that they are able to understand Greek. And, *vice versa*, even if Latin is used the obligations are nonetheless valid between aliens, so long as they understand Latin. But that obligation *verbis* in the form *Dari spondes? Spondeo* is so restricted to Roman citizens that it cannot properly be found an equivalent in Greek, even though the verb is said to be derived from Greek.

94. In this connexion it is said that in one case it is possible even for an alien to be put under an obligation by this word, as where our emperor questions the leader of an alien people about peace, thus: *Pacem futuram spondes?* Or where the question is put to him in the same form. But this example is too clever by half since if anything is done against the peace treaty no action *ex stipulatu* arises but the matter is pursued by the law of war.

95. There is a doubtful question whether, if someone . . . [Illegible lines create a gap, and then the text relies on somewhat conjectural reconstruction through 95a and part of 96].

95a. There are also other obligations which can be contracted by words spoken without any question being put beforehand, as where a woman declares a dowry either to her fiancé as a wife to be or to her husband after marriage. This applies as much to movables as to land. And in this obligation not only can the woman herself be bound but also her father and her debtor if at her behest he declares as dowry the debt he owes to her. Nobody else can incur an obligation in this way. Therefore, if anyone else does want to promise a dowry for a woman he must bind himself according to the ordinary law. That is, he must promise in response to a stipulation by the man.

96. Again an obligation is contracted by unilateral speech, with a promise made to the other without any question put, where a freedman has sworn that he will render his patron a gift or service or labour. This, however, is the single case in which an obligation is contracted by means of an oath. Certainly there is no other case in which men incur obligations through oath-taking, at least so long as the inquiry is confined to the law of the Romans. As for the question as to the law applicable among aliens, we will find, if we look into the laws of different citizenships, that different rules prevail from one to another.

97. Suppose that the thing which we stipulate to be given (*dari*) is such that it cannot be given. The stipulation is then ineffective. Examples are where one stipulates for the giving of a free man in the belief that he is a slave or for the giving of a dead man in the belief that he is alive or for sacred or religious land in the belief that it is governed by human law.

97a. Again, if someone stipulates for a thing which in the nature of things cannot exist, as for instance a hippocentaur, the stipulation is equally ineffective.

98. Again, if someone stipulates subject to a condition which cannot be fulfilled, as for instance 'on condition that he touches the sky', the stipulation is ineffective. Yet in the case of a legacy left under an impossible condition, our teachers hold it to be due exactly as though left unconditionally. The supporters of the other school think the legacy ineffective, just as with the stipulation. And it is certainly true that a satisfactory reason can hardly be given for any distinction.

99. Besides these, a stipulation is also ineffective where someone stipulates for a thing to be given to him which, unknown to him, is his already. This is because what belongs to a man cannot be given to him.

100. Next, the stipulation is ineffective if someone stipulates for a giving in this way: *Post mortem meam dari spondes*? Or in this way: *Post mortem tuam dari spondes*? Yet this form of stipulation is valid: *Cum moriar* (when I am dying) *dari spondes*? So also this: *Cum morieris* (when you are dying) *dari spondes*? The point is that these forms have the effect of triggering the obligation during the last moments of the life of the stipulator or promissor. For it was perceived as awkward (*inelegans*) to have an obligation come first into being with the person of the heir. Moreover, we cannot stipulate thus: *Pridie quam moriar* (the day before I die) or *Pridie quam morieris* (the day before you die) *dari spondes*? For there is no way of discovering 'the day before someone dies' other than by waiting for him to be dead. And then, once the death has happened, the stipulation is pushed back into the time before. It is tantamount to saying: *Heredi meo dari spondes* (Do you promise a giving to my heir)? And there is no doubt that that is ineffective.

101. What we have said of death must be taken to apply also to *capitis deminutio* (status-loss).

102. The stipulation is also ineffective where someone fails to answer to the question put, as where I stipulate for 10,000 sesterces to be given by you and you promise 5,000. Or where I stipulate absolutely, and you promise conditionally.

103. Again, the stipulation is ineffective if we stipulate for a giving to someone to whose rule we are not subject. Suppose therefore that someone stipulates for a giving both to himself and to someone to whose rule he is not subject. There is a question then to what extent the stipulation is valid. Our teachers hold it wholly valid and say that the full amount is due to the stipulator alone, just as though the outsider's name had not been mentioned. But the supporters of the other school think that half is due to him, and that the stipulation is ineffective so far as concerns the other half.

103a. It is a different case if I have stipulated thus: *Mihi aut Titio dari spondes* (Do you promise a giving to me or Titius)? Here it is agreed that the full sum is due to me and that I alone can bring an action on that stipulation. Yet you can discharge yourself by paying Titius.

104. Again, the stipulation is ineffective if I stipulate from one who is subject to my rule, or he from me. In fact a slave, a person *in mancipio*, a daughter in power, and a woman *in manu*, cannot be put under an obligation to anyone at all, let alone to a person to whose rule they are subject.

105. It is obvious that a mute cannot stipulate or promise. The same has been accepted for the deaf, since the stipulator and the promissor ought to hear each other's words.

106. A madman (*furiosus*) cannot transact any deal at all, because he does not understand what he is doing.

107. A *pupillus* can properly transact every deal, subject however to his getting his guardian's authority where necessary, as where he himself is put under an obligation; for he can put someone else under an obligation to himself even without his guardian's authority.

108. The law is the same for women who are under guardianship.

109. But what we have said about a *pupillus* is properly speaking only true of one who already has some understanding. In fact infants and those very close to infancy scarcely differ from madmen in that pupils of that age have no understanding. But for the sake of convenience the law in relation to such *pupilli* has been less drastically interpreted.

110. But we can join another person to a stipulation made by ourselves. He then stipulates for the same performance. The common name for such a party is 'adstipulator'.

111. The action then lies for him just as well as for ourselves. And payment can as well be made to him as to us. But he will be compelled to make over to us whatever he obtains, this duty being enforced by the *actio mandati*.

112. Moreover, the adstipulator can use words other than those which we ourselves have used. Thus if, for example, I have put the stipulatory question in the form, 'DARI SPONDES?', the adstipulator can still say, 'IDEM FIDE TUA PROMITTIS?' or 'IDEM FIDEIUBES?' Or *vice versa.*

113. Again the adstipulator can demand a lesser performance. He cannot demand a greater. Hence, if I stipulate for 10,000 *sestertii* he can demand 5,000, but he cannot ask for more than that. Again, if I make an absolute demand, he can demand conditionally. But not the other way about. Here 'more' and 'less' are applied not only to quantity but also to time; for it is 'more' to give immediately, 'less' to give after an interval of time.

114. This area of law reveals some legal oddities. For the adstipulator's heir acquires no action. Again a slave's adstipulation achieves nothing whereas in all other cases he acquires a right for his owner through his stipulation. The same view has prevailed of persons *in mancipio*, who are in a position equivalent to that of a slave. He who is in the power of his father does achieve something acting as adstipulator, but he acquires nothing for his parent even though in other cases he does acquire for him by making a stipulation. Yet even in his own case, no action lies for him unless he leaves his father's power without suffering a *capitis deminutio* (status-loss), as by the father's death or by himself becoming a *flamen Dialis*. The same results must be taken to apply in the case of a daughter in power or woman *in manu*.

115. On the other side it is also usual for extra people to be obligated on behalf of the promissor. These we call either *sponsors* or *fidepromissors* or *fideiussors*.

116. The question to a *sponsor* is, *Idem dari spondes*? To a *fidepromissor* it is, *Idem fidepromittis*? To a *fideiussor* it is, *Idem fide tua esse iubes*? There is a question what name can be given to people who answer to, *Idem dabis*? or *Idem promittis*? or *Idem facies*?

117. We often take *sponsors*, *fidepromissors* or *fideiussors* as a means of making sure that we are provided with better security. On the other hand almost the only case for using an *adstipulator* is where we stipulate for something to be given after our death. For since by making such a stipulation we ourselves achieve nothing, an *adstipulator* is attached so that he can sue after our death. Then, if he obtains anything, the trial for *mandatum* (commission) binds him to restore it to my heir.

118. The legal positions of *sponsors* and *fidepromissors* are similar; but *fideiussors* stand markedly apart.

119. For the first two cannot be attached to any obligations other than those *verbis*. The qualification is that the obligation *verbis* sometimes is not binding on the actual promissor, as where a woman or *pupillus* promises without the guardian's authority or where someone promises a giving after his own death. It is debated, however, whether a *sponsor* or *fidepromissor* is bound if a slave or alien is principal promissor by the word *spondere*.

119a. A *fideiussor*, by contrast, can be added to all sorts of obligations, that is to say whether the obligation is contracted *re*, *verbis*, *litteris* or *consensu*. Nor does it even matter whether the principal obligation is civil or natural. It can even be a slave for whom the guarantor by *fideiussio* becomes liable, and the stipulator who takes the guarantor for the slave can be an outsider or even the slave's own owner seeking a guarantee of what is owed to himself.

120. Next, the heir of a *sponsor* or *fidepromissor* is not bound (unless we think of an alien *fidepromissor* whose *civitas* uses a different rule). But in the case of a *fideiussor*, the heir is bound.

121. Next, *sponsors* and *fidepromissors* are discharged after two years by the *lex Furia*; and, whatever their number shall be at the time when it becomes possible to sue for the money, in that many parts the obligation is shared between them and each will be called for his share only. By contrast, *fideiussors* are liable without limit of time and, whatever their number, each is obligated for the full amount. Hence, it is up to the creditor to sue whichever he wants. However, a letter (*epistula*) of the deified Hadrian now compels the creditor to sue for a share from each of them who is solvent. The rule of this letter differs from that of the *lex Furia* in this: if any *sponsor* or *fidepromissor* is insolvent his burden does not accrue to the others; with *fideiussors*, however, even if only one is solvent he must carry the burden of all the others.

121a. But the *lex Furia* applies only in Italy and the effect of this is that in other provinces *sponsors* and *fidepromissors* are, in the same way as *fideiussors*, bound without limit of time and are each under an obligation for the full amount, unless they too derive assistance as to part from the letter of the deified Hadrian.

122. The next aspect of the matter this: the *lex Appuleia* introduced a kind of partnership (*societas*) between *sponsors* and *fidepromissors*. In fact if one of them paid more than his share the *lex* established an action for him against the others in respect of the overpayment. This *lex* was passed before the *lex Furia*, when each was under an obligation for the full amount. The question thus arises whether the right (*beneficium*) given by the *lex Appuleia* survives the passing of the *lex Furia*. There is no doubt that outside Italy it does survive. For the *lex Furia* only applies in Italy, while the *lex Appuleia* applies also in other provinces. But there really is room for debate whether the Appuleian right survives in Italy too. On the other hand, to *fideiussors* the *lex Appuleia* does not apply. Hence if a creditor obtains the whole sum from one *fideiussor* the loss is his alone, at least if the principal for whom he stood surety is insolvent. However, as is clear from what was said above, one who is sued for the whole sum by the creditor can now plead that under the terms of the letter of the deified Hadrian the action should be given against him only for his share.

123. Next, it was provided by the *lex Cicereia* that someone taking *sponsors* or *fidepromissors* should openly say so in advance and declare both the matter in respect of which he is taking security and the number of *sponsors* and *fidepromissors* he is about to have. And if he does not make this announcement the *sponsors* and

fidepromissors are permitted to ask within thirty days for a declaratory judgement (*praeiudicium*) to answer the question whether the statutory declaration was made. And if it is declared that it was not made they are thereby discharged. Under this statute no mention is made of *fideiussors*. However the practice is to give the statutory notice even when we take *fideiussors*.

124. The *lex Cornelia*, on the other hand, introduced a control (*beneficium*) common to all guarantors. By this statute it is prohibited for any person to bind himself in any one year to any one creditor on behalf of any one debtor for a sum of 'credited money (*creditae pecuniae*)' greater than 20,000 *sesterces*. Then, even if the *sponsors*, *fidepromissors* or *fideiussors* have bound themselves in a full sum of, say, 100,000, nevertheless their liability is limited to a maximum of 20,000. We define 'credited money' as including not only money which we give on credit (*eam quam credendi causa damus*) but also every sum which is certain to be owed at the moment at which an obligation is contracted—that is, money which is unconditionally subjected to an obligation of payment. Hence, if we stipulate for money to be paid on a certain day, that sum comes within the definition, because it is certain that the money will be owed even though the suit is postponed. Moreover the term 'money (*pecunia*)' in this statute includes all things (*omnes res*). Hence, if we stipulate for wine or corn or a farm or a slave, the statute must be applied.

125. The statute does however allow unlimited guarantees in some cases, as for dowry or for what is owed to you under a will or a guarantee given by judicial order (*iussu iudicis*). And, further, the *lex* on estate duty at 5 per cent provides that the *lex Cornelia* shall not apply to guarantees required under its provisions.

126. Another rule common to all, that is to *sponsors* and *fidepromissors* and *fideiussors*, is that they cannot incur an obligation such that they owe more than is owed by the person for whom they take on the guarantee. And, the other way round, they can bind themselves to owe less, as we said in relation to *adstipulators*. For as in the case of the *adstipulator*'s right, so here the obligation of these guarantors is an addition (*accessio*) to the principal obligation. And it is impossible for there to be more in the addition than in the principal matter.

127. In this next rule too, all are in the same case, namely that if they pay anything on the principal's behalf they have an *actio mandati* against him for its recovery. And, beyond this, *sponsors* have an action of their own under the *lex Publilia* for double recovery (*duplum*). That is called the *actio depensi*.

128. An obligation is created by writing (*litteris*) as for example in cross-written debts (*in nominibus transcripticiis*). Now a cross-written debt is something which happens in two ways. It happens either from a thing to a person (*a re in personam*) or from one person to another (*a persona in personam*).

129. A cross-entry is made from a thing to a person when, for example, I enter as paid out to you that which you owe me as the result of a purchase or a hiring or a partnership.

130. A cross-entry is made from one person to another when, for example, I enter as paid out to you, that which Titius owes to me. That is to say, so long as Titius has offered you to me as a substitute debtor (*te pro se delegaverit mihi*).

131. It is a different case with the debt-entries called 'cash-box entries'. For with them the obligation arises *re*, not *litteris*. The reason is that they only take effect if the money is actually paid out. The paying out of the money makes an obligation *re*. And we therefore rightly assert that cash-box entries (*nomina arcaria*) do not create any obligation but rather provide evidence of an obligation already created.

132. It follows that it cannot correctly be said even that aliens are put under obligations by cash-box entries, since it is not by the entry itself (*non ipso nomine*) but by the payment out of the money (*numeratione pecuniae*) that they are obligated. And that kind of obligation belongs to the *ius gentium*.

133. It is a good question, by contrast, whether aliens incur obligations by cross-written debts. For that kind of obligation is arguably *ius civile*. Nerva so held. Sabinus and Cassius took the view, however, that even aliens are bound by a cross-written debt from a thing to a person but not by a cross-writing from one person to another.

134. Beyond this, an obligation appears to arise *litteris* through the use of cheirographs and syngraphs. That is to say, where a person writes that he owes or that he will give, in circumstances in which no *stipulatio* is made on that account. That kind of obligation is peculiar to aliens.

135. Obligations are created *consensu* (by agreement) in *emptio-venditio* (sale), *locatio-conductio* (hire), *societas* (partnership) and *mandatum* (commission).

136. The reason why we say that in those ways the obligation is contracted *consensu* is that no formality of words or writing is required but, on the contrary, it suffices that the parties to the transaction have come to an agreement. Hence such deals can be contracted even *inter absentes*, as by letter or messenger, whereas by contrast an obligation *verbis* cannot be created *inter absentes*.

137. Again, in these contracts the parties come under obligations to each other on the basis of that which each ought to make good for the other in decency and fairness (*ex bono et aequo*), whereas by contrast in obligations *verbis* one party stipulates and the other party promises, and in cross-entries by the entry of the payment out one party binds and the other is bound.

138. Yet, even though an obligation *verbis* cannot be contracted with a person who is absent, the entry of a payment out can be effected with a party not present.

139. *Emptio-venditio* (sale) is contracted when agreement is reached on price. This is so notwithstanding the fact that the price may not yet have been paid and not even any *arra* may have been given. For what is given by way of *arra* is evidence of an *emptio-venditio* already contracted.[1]

[1] An alternative translation reads: '*Emptio-venditio* is contracted when agreement is reached on the price. It does not matter that the price has not been paid or that no *arra* has even been given. For what is given by way of *arra* is evidence of an *emptio-venditio* already contracted.'

140. The price must, however, be definite (*pretium autem certum esse debet*). For, on the other side of the line, if we come to an agreement that a thing be bought at Titius's valuation (*ut quanti Titius rem aestimaverit, tanti sit empta*), Labeo held that the deal had no effect whatever. And Cassius approves Labeo's opinion. Ofilius thought that even that was *emptio-venditio*. And Proculus followed Ofilius's opinion.

141. Next, the price must consist in counted money (*pretium in numerata pecunia consistere debet*). There is, to be sure, a hot debate whether the price can consist in other things, as for example whether the price of something can be a slave or a toga or a parcel of land. Our teachers think that the price can consist in something other than money. Hence follows their regular tenet that an exchange of things makes a contract of *emptio-venditio* and is indeed the oldest form of *emptio-venditio*. By way of evidence they cite the Greek poet Homer, who at one place says this:

> There the long-haired Achaeans bought wine,
> Some with bronze, and some with shining steel,
> Some with ox-hides, some with the very oxen,
> And some with slaves [Iliad, 7.472–5].

The masters of the other school disagree. They say that *permutatio* (barter) is one thing and *emptio-venditio* is another and that it is not otherwise possible to settle the issue, when things have been exchanged, which thing should be seen as sold and which as given by way of price. Then, following on from there, they hold it absurd to count each thing as both sold and given by way of price. However, Caelius Sabinus says that if you have something on offer for sale, as for instance a farm, and I give say a slave as its price, the farm has clearly enough been sold and the slave given as price for the purpose of acquiring the farm.

142. *Locatio-conductio* is formed on similar principles. Thus, if no fixed reward (*certa merces*) is determined, no contract of *locatio-conductio* is made.

143. And from this arises the question whether *locatio-conductio* is formed when the reward is left to the decision of a third party, as where it is set at 'as much as Titius' valuation comes to'. For this reason it is a question whether a contract of *locatio-conductio* comes into existence where I give clothes to a cleaner to be cleaned or treated or to tailor for mending and I do not immediately fix any reward but instead intend to give whatever we later agree.

144. Again if I give something to you to use and in return receive from you another thing to use, there is a question whether that amounts to a contract of *locatio-conductio*.

145. The closeness between *emptio-venditio* and *locatio-conductio* is such that in some cases there is a standing debate as to which of the two contracts is made. For example, suppose a thing is located without limit of time (*in perpetuum*) which happens in relation to municipal estates, which are located on the express terms that so long as the public ground-rent (*vectigal*) is paid they will not be taken away from

either the *conductor* himself or from his heir. The prevailing view does make this *locatio-conductio*.

146. Next, suppose I deliver gladiators to you on the express terms that I will get 20 *denarii* for the sweat of each one who comes off harmless but 1000 *denarii* for each one killed or maimed. Is that *emptio-venditio* or *locatio-conductio*? The prevailing view is that there seems to be *locatio-conductio* of the ones who come off harmless but *emptio-venditio* for those killed or maimed. Events determine one classification, as though there is a conditional sale or hire of each one. For there is no longer any doubt that things can be sold and hired subject to conditions.

147. Again there is a question whether *emptio-venditio* is contracted, or rather *locatio-conductio*, where I agree with a goldsmith that he will make for me from his gold some rings of specified form and weight in return for, say, 200 *denarii*. Cassius holds that on the one hand there is *emptio-venditio* of the material while on the other there is *locatio-conductio* of the labour (*operarum*). But the view of very many jurists is that the contract is *emptio-venditio*. By contrast, if I give him my gold and a reward is fixed for the work, it is agreed that there is a contract of *locatio-conductio*.

148. It is usual to enter partnerships either of 'all wealth (*totorum bonorum*)' or of one line of business (*alicuius negotii*), as for instance in buying or selling slaves.

149. There was a great question whether *societas* could be formed on such terms that one party would take a larger share of the profit but a smaller share of loss. Quintus Mucius thought that that was contrary to the nature of *societas*. But Servius Sulpicius, whose view has prevailed, thought that such a partnership could be made, even to the extreme that, in his opinion, the contract could be entered on the term that one party should make no contribution at all to a loss but should take a share in profit, so long as his assistance seems so valuable that it is reasonable (*aequum*) for him to be admitted to the partnership subject to this agreement (*hac pactione*). In fact *societas* can also be entered, as is now accepted, on the term that one shall and the other shall not bring in capital, the profit nonetheless being shared. For often some person's support (*opera*) is as valuable as money.

150. And this is certain, that, if nothing is agreed about the shares of profit and loss, then both plus and minus must be shared equally. But if shares are specified in one or other, as for example in profit, while there is silence as to the other, then the shares on the omitted side will be the same as specified on the other.

151. The *societas* continues to exist just so long as the parties remain of the same mind. But if one party renounces, the partnership is dissolved. Yet it is clear that if the renunciation is made in order to secure some approaching profit exclusively for himself, the party will be compelled to share that profit. Take, for example, the case where my partner of 'all wealth' is left heir to some other person and then renounces the partnership to take the profit of the inheritance solely for himself. On the other hand, if some profit comes to him other than the one which he snatched at then that

goes to him alone. On my side, though, anything at all acquired after his renunciation of the partnership is attributed to me.

152. *Societas* is also dissolved by the death of a partner, because one who makes a contract of partnership chooses for himself a particular person (*certam personam*).

153. It is said that *societas* is also dissolved by status-loss (*capitis deminutio*), on the ground that according to the reason of the civil law (*civili ratione*) status-loss is made equivalent to death. Yet the truth is that, if the parties still maintain the intention to be partners, a new partnership is understood to be set in train.

154. Again, if the goods of a partner are sold up by the state or by ordinary creditors, the partnership is dissolved. Yet this *societas* of which we are speaking (i.e. that which is contracted by mere agreement) is part of the *ius gentium*. It operates by virtue of common sense (*naturali ratione*) among all men.

154a. There is, however, another genus of *societas* peculiar to Roman citizens. For in former times it was the case that when a *paterfamilias* died there arose among his immediate heirs (*sui heredes*) a kind of partnership which was at once statutory and natural. This was called *ercto non cito*, which is 'ownership undivided'. For *erctum* means ownership (*dominium*), whence *erus* is a word for 'owner'. And *ciere*, on the other hand, means 'to divide', whence also *caedere* (to strike) and *secare* (to cut).

154b. Other people also, if they wanted to have this same *societas*, could achieve it before the praetor by means of a set form of words (*certa legis actio*). In this partnership between brothers or between other people entering a partnership in imitation of brothers (*ad exemplum fratrum suorum*), a special feature was that even one of the partners could by manumission free a jointly-owned slave and acquire him as a freedman of all of them, or again that one partner by mancipating a jointly owned asset could transfer the property in it to the person taking through *mancipatio*.

155. *Mandatum* occurs when we give a commission, whether in our own interest or in the interest of another (*sive nostra gratia . . . sive aliena*). And, so, whether I commission you to do my business or someone else's business the obligation of mandate is contracted, and we will be bound to one another in that which in good faith I ought to do for you or you for me.

156. Now if I give you a commission on your own account (*tua gratia*) the mandate is quite without effect (*supervacuum*). For in respect of anything you are inclined to do on your own account you should rely on your own decision and not on my commission. And so if you have idle money at home and I exhort you to lend it out you will not have an action of mandate against me even if you lend it out as a *mutuum* to someone from whom you cannot get it back. Again, if I have encouraged you to buy something I will not be liable in an *actio mandati* even if it turns out to have been a bad bargain for you. This is carried to the length of raising a question whether a man is liable to the action of mandate if he commissions you to lend to Titius. Servius said not. In his view no obligation could arise in this case any more than in the case of a general mandate to lend out money. But we follow Sabinus's

contrary opinion based on the fact that you would not have selected Titius to give credit to, had it not been for the mandate given to you.

157. It is agreed that if someone gives a mandate for a performance which is *contra bonos mores* (against good standards of behaviour), no obligation is contracted, as for example if I commissioned you to commit a theft or a wrongful contempt (*iniuria*).

158. Again, if someone gives a mandate to me for something to be done after my death, the mandate is ineffective, on the ground of the general rule laid down that an obligation cannot begin in the person of the heir.

159. Also, even a mandate properly contracted dissolves if revoked before there has been any action in reliance about it.

160. Again, if one of the parties, whether the one who gave the mandate or the one who accepted it, dies before the mandate has been acted upon, the contract is dissolved. But for policy reasons (*utilitatis causa*) it has been accepted that if the person who gives me a mandate dies and I nevertheless perform the mandate in ignorance of his death, I can bring the *actio mandati*. Otherwise a just and demonstrable want of knowledge would cause me loss. This conclusion is similar to that in which, as many hold, a debtor is discharged by paying my cashier after and in ignorance of the latter's manumission. There, the strict logic of the law cannot explain this discharge since he has paid someone other than the person whom he was bound to pay.

161. If I give a mandate to someone and he exceeds the terms of the commission, I have an action of mandate against him to the extent that I have an interest in his performance of the commission, provided only that it was possible for him to fulfil it. But he cannot bring any action against me. Thus, if I have mandated you to, say, buy a farm for me for 100,000 sesterces and you have bought it for 150,000, you will have no action of mandate against me, even though you are willing to let me have the farm at the sum at which I mandated you to buy. Sabinus and Cassius were very strongly of that opinion. On the other hand, if you have bought for a lesser sum you will certainly have an action against me because one who commissions a purchase at 100,000 is obviously understood to commission a purchase for less if it be possible.

162. In conclusion we should note that whenever I give something to be done *gratis* in circumstances in which if I had fixed a reward a contract of *locatio-conductio* would have been made, then in those circumstances the action of mandate lies. Take, for example, the case in which I have given clothes to a cleaner for cleaning or some other treatment or to a tailor for mending.

163. That completes the exposition of the genera of obligation which arise from contract (*quae ex contractu nascuntur*). We must now take note that there is acquisition for us (*adquiri nobis*) not only through our own selves but also through those persons in our *potestas* (paternal power), *manus* (matrimonial power), or *mancipium* (patrimonial power).

164. There is also acquisition for us through free men and through slaves belonging to other people when possessed in good faith by us. But this occurs only in two cases. Those are, where they acquire *ex operis suis* (through their own labour) or *ex re nostra* (through our capital).

165. There is acquisition for us under the same two heads in the case in which we have a usufruct in a slave.

166. Now take the case of one who has the *nudum ius Quiritium* (bare Quiritary title, empty Quiritary title) in a slave. Even though he is 'owner' (*dominus*), yet he is understood as having less right in the thing even than the usufructuary or *bona fide possessor*. For it is the rule that there is no case in which the rights accrue to him. To such a length is this taken that some hold that, even if a slave expressly names him as the beneficiary of a stipulation or mancipation, still nothing is acquired for him.

167. There is no doubt that a slave in joint ownership acquires for his owners in the proportions of their ownership. The exception is that if he names one owner as the beneficiary of the stipulation or the mancipation he acquires solely for that named owner. As where he stipulates in these words: 'Do you promise (*spondes*) conveyance to Titius my owner (*dominus*)?' or takes my mancipation with this declaration: 'I say that this *res* belongs by Quiritary title to Lucius Titius, my *dominus*, and let it be bought for him with this bronze and these bronze scales (*Hanc rem ex iure Quiritium Lucii Titii domini mei esse aio, eaque ei empta esto hoc aere aeneaque libra*)'.

167a. This is a question: does the consequence which flows from naming one *dominus* also flow from a *iussum* (authority) given by one of the *domini*? Our teachers hold that an owner who gives a *iussum* becomes entitled exclusively in exactly the same way as where an owner is expressly named as the beneficiary of a stipulation by the slave or a mancipation to the slave. But the authorities of the other school hold that the entitlement accrues to each of them exactly as though no *iussum* had been given by any one of them.

168. An obligation is discharged immediately by the performance (*solutione*) of that which is owed. From this there arises a question. If something else is given instead with the consent of the creditor, is the debtor freed by automatic operation of law (*ipso iure*) as our authorities hold? Or, does he remain technically subject to the obligation at law with the effect that he must defend himself by an *exceptio doli mali* (defence of fraud) in the event of his being sued, which is the analysis of the authorities of the other school.

169. An obligation is also discharged by 'verbal release (*acceptilatio*)'. 'Verbal release' is essentially an imaginary performance (*solutio*). Suppose that I owe you something under an obligation *verbis*, and you want to let me off. It can be done by your allowing me to make this declaration: 'That which I promised to you, do you hold it in receipt (*habesne acceptum*)?' And then your answering, 'I do so hold it.'

170. By this means, as we have said, obligations *verbis* are discharged. But the rest are not. For there seemed to be a proper congruency in the rule that an obligation

created *verbis* should be capable of being dissolved *verbis*. However, it is possible to reduce anything owed on another basis into the form of a stipulation and then to effect a verbal release.

171. Though an *acceptilatio* is an imaginary performance (*solutio*) yet a woman cannot effect an *acceptilatio* without her guardian's authority, albeit she can accept an actual performance without his authority.

172. There is a question whether given that there can be partial discharge by partial performance of what is owed, there can also be an *acceptilatio* limited to part.

173. There is another species of imaginary performance. This is discharge *per aes et libram* (by bronze and scales). This too has been recognised only for certain cases, as where something is owing as a result of a transaction *per aes et libram* or under a judgement.

174. In the presence of no less than five witnesses and a *libripens* (scale-holder), the person being freed must make this declaration: 'Whereas I have been condemned to pay you such and such a sum of *sestertii*, with this bronze and these scales I now loose and free myself from you in that matter (*me eo nomine a te solvo liberoque hoc aere aeneaque libra*). I weigh out this pound for you as first and last, in accordance with the public statute.' Next he strikes the scales with the bronze piece and gives it to the person from whom he is obtaining the release, as though thereby making his performance (*veluti solvendi causa*).

175. In the same way a legatee releases an heir from payment of a legacy constituted *per damnationem*. There is then this variation. Whereas the judgement-debtor signifies that he has been condemned (*condemnatus*) the heir declares that he has been 'by will doomed' (*testamento damnatus*). However, an heir can only be freed in this way from legacies of things reckoned by weight or number and then only when their quantum is fixed. Some hold that the same extends also to things handled by measure.

176. The next way in which an obligation is discharged is novation (*novatio*), as where I take a stipulation from Titius for what you owe me. For with the intervention of a new person a new obligation arises and the old is discharged, merged into the new. This can go very far, as where it happens that the new stipulation is ineffective but nevertheless discharges the old one by novation: for example, where I stipulate from Titius that what you owe me will be given to me after his death or where I take such a stipulation from a woman or *pupillus* without the authority of their guardian. In such a case I lose out. The earlier debtor is released, and the later obligation is void. A different legal conclusion follows if I take the stipulation from a slave. Then the earlier obligation subsists just as though I had later taken a stipulation from no person at all.

177. Suppose it is the same person to whom I return with a later stipulation. In that case a novation only happens if something new is added in the later stipulation, as

for instance where a condition or a time or a guarantor (*sponsor*) is either added or removed.

178. Yet what we have said about a *sponsor* is doubtful, because the authorities of the other school hold that the addition or removal of a sponsor does nothing to work a novation.

179. And what we have said about novation occurring if a condition is added is to be understood as meaning that it happens if the condition is fulfilled. On the other hand, if it fails the earlier obligation survives. But the question must be put whether one who sues on it should not be defeated by a defence of fraud or of contrary agreement (*exceptione doli mali aut pacti conventi*). For the parties' intention would seem to have been that the claim should arise only if the condition of the later stipulation was fulfilled. The opinion of Servius Sulpicius was that there was an immediate novation even while the condition remained unfulfilled and, further, that if the condition failed no action could be brought on either ground, so that the matter was in that way lost. Following the same line, he gave a *responsum* that someone who stipulated from a slave for payment of what was owed to him by Lucius Titius did effect a novation and thus incur a loss, since no action can be brought against a slave. However, in both cases we employ a different rule; there is no more a novation here than if I stipulate from an alien for that which you owe me and, when he is outside the number of those people who share the word *spondere*, I put the question in the form '*spondes?*'

180. Next, an obligation is discharged by joinder of issue (*litis contestatio*), so long as the suit was through a *iudicium legitimum* (statutory trial). For in such a case the original obligation is discharged, and the defendant begins to be bound instead by the *litis contestatio*. Then, if he is condemned the *litis contestatio* is displaced and he begins to be bound on the basis of the judgement. This is the key to the writing of the old jurists to the effect that before *litis contestatio* the debtor ought to give; after *litis contestatio* he ought to be condemned; after condemnation he ought to satisfy the judgement.

181. It follows from this that, if I sue for what is owed to me through a *iudicium legitimum*, thereafter automatically (*ipso iure*) I cannot sue again for that matter, since my *intentio* will maintain in vain that he ought-at-civil-law to give. For with *litis contestatio* he ceased to be under that duty. It is different if I sue through a *iudicium imperio continens* (a trial based on magistral power). For there the obligation survives, and I can as a matter of technical law maintain another action later. But then I should be defeated by the defence that the matter has been decided or carried to trial (*exceptio rei iudicatae vel in iudicium deductae*). The difference between *iudicia legitima* and *iudicia imperio continentia* will be considered in the next book.

182. Let us now cross over to the obligations which arise from delict, as where someone has committed a theft, has seized goods, has inflicted a loss, or has been guilty of a contempt-*iniuria*. There is only one genus of obligation arising from these

types of conduct. By contrast, as we have set out above, obligations from contract divide into four *genera*.

183. But within theft (*furtum*) there are four genera according to Servius Sulpicius and Masurius Sabinus, namely; manifest theft, non-manifest theft, theft by receiving and theft by planting (*manifestum, nec manifestum, conceptum, oblatum*). According to Labeo there are two *genera*, namely manifest and non-manifest, since the others, receiving and planting, are really species of action emanating from theft rather than *genera* of theft. That certainly seems nearer the truth as will appear from the discussion below.

184. Manifest theft is, some have said, that which happens when the thief is seized while he is in the act (*dum fit*). Others, however, have gone further saying that it is enough that he is seized in the place of the theft (*ubi fit*); as for instance, if there is a theft of olives from a grove or grapes from a vineyard, the manifest stage would last so long as the thief remains in that grove or that vineyard, or, in the case of theft from a house, so long as he remains in that house. Others have gone even further and have said that the manifest stage lasts even so long as the thief is carrying the thing to the place to which he planned to take it (*donec perferret*). Yet others have gone even beyond this, making the theft manifest if and whenever the thief is seen carrying the thing (*quandoque rem tenens*). But this last opinion has been rejected. And the opinion of those who thought the theft manifest if the thief was seized while carrying the thing to the predetermined place (*donec perferret*) has also been disapproved, for the reason that it admits of a great doubt whether the test applies for only one day or for a number of days. This is an important issue since it is often the case that thieves intend to carry stolen goods from the district (*civitas*) of the theft to another district or province. Of the two other positions reported above each has its supporters, but most authorities incline to the second (i.e. *ubi fit*).

185. The definition of non-manifest theft can be inferred from what we have just said, since that which does not qualify as manifest is non-manifest.

186. Theft by receiving (*furtum conceptum*) is said to happen where a stolen thing is found with someone (*apud aliquem*) after a search in the presence of witnesses. For against such a person a special action is provided even though he may not be a thief. And the name of the action is *actio furti concepti* (action of theft-having-been-received).

187. Theft by planting (*furtum oblatum*) is said to happen where a stolen *res* is brought to you by someone and is received in by you, so long of course as there is the intention that it be taken in by you rather than by him who gave it to you. For a special action is provided for you, the receiver, against him, the planter, even though he may not be the thief. And the name of the action is *actio furti oblati* (action of theft-having-been-brought-in).

188. There is also an *actio furti prohibiti* (action of theft-having-been-prohibited) against a man who prevents one who wants to conduct a search from doing so.

[Note on translation of *furtum conceptum*. In this translation the verb *concipere* is taken in the sense of 'receive in', 'take in'. It is more usually (cf. Zulueta, 3.187) made to refer to the act of seizing done by the finder in his search, i.e. the *con-capere* is of the finder not of the person made liable. It is certainly true that 3.187 is easier to translate if the planter's intention is that the *res* be 'found on your premises': *apud te . . . conciperetur*. The translation above supposes that the planter must intend to find the thing a home with the receiver rather than with himself, i.e. the focus of the intention is his desire to keep his own premises clear.]

189. The penalty for manifest theft was capital under the Twelve Tables; that is, a free man was flogged and assigned to the victim of this theft—it was a question among the old jurists whether he was made a slave by such assignment or was put in the position of an *adiudicatus* (a judgement debtor)—while a slave was similarly flogged and then despatched. But later the severity of this punishment was disapproved and an action for quadruple damages was set up by the praetor's edict.

190. For non-manifest theft the Twelve Tables appointed a penalty of double damages, which the praetor also retains.

191. The Twelve Tables had a threefold penalty for *furtum conceptum* and *furtum oblatum*, and the praetor also retains those.

192. For *furtum prohibitum* the praetor introduced a quadruple penalty. Statute never provided any penalty under that head. It only provides that anyone wishing to conduct a search should so do naked save for a *licium* and should hold a dish (*lanx*). Under these conditions the statutory provision is that if the searcher finds something the theft is manifest.

193. There has been a question as to what a *licium* is. But the truth appears to be that it is a species of clothing to cover the private parts. All of which is wholly ridiculous. For anyone who wants to prevent a search will no less prevent a naked searcher than one who keeps his clothes on, all the more so if finding by a naked searcher leads to a higher penalty being imposed. Next, as between competing reasons for the *lanx*, either to keep the hands occupied to prevent planting or to receive the *res* when found, neither fits the case of a thing of such a kind or size as to be impossible either to plant or to put in the dish. At least no question is raised whether to satisfy the statute the *lanx* must be of some special material.

194. As a result of this provision that the theft is manifest in such a case there are writers who hold that there can be *furtum manifestum* either *lege* (by statute) or *natura* (by nature), statutory manifestness consisting in this case, natural manifestness in the case discussed earlier. But it is more true to say that there can only be natural manifest theft. For statute cannot make a thief who is non-manifest into a thief manifest, no more than it can make a person into a thief when he is not a thief at all or can turn someone into an adulterer or a murderer who is not an adulterer and not a murderer. What statute certainly can do is to make someone subject to the very

same penalty as if he had committed theft, adultery or murder even in a case in which in fact he committed none of these.

195. *Furtum* is committed not only when someone takes away a *res* belonging to another for the sake of having it for himself (*non solum cum quis intercipiendi causa rem alienam amovet*) but, taking the matter at its full width (*generaliter*), when someone handles something belonging to another without the owner's consent (*cum quis rem alienam invito domino contrectat*).

196. And so if someone uses a thing which has been deposited with him he commits *furtum*. Again if one borrows a thing for use and then transfers it to some other use one incurs the obligation from theft, as where one borrows silver with a view to entertaining friends to dinner and then takes it on a journey to another place, or where one borrows a horse for riding and takes it further, a point made by the old jurists in the case of one who took a borrowed horse into battle.

197. It has been decided, however, that those who use borrowed things for different purposes only commit theft if they know that they are doing it without the owner's consent and that he, if he knew, would not consent. But if they believe he would consent, they are outside the scope of a charge of theft. And this is certainly an excellent distinction because theft cannot be committed without wicked intent (*furtum sine dolo malo non committitur*).

198. But even if someone does think he is handling goods without their owner's consent, when in fact the owner happens to want him to do so, it is said that no theft is committed. Hence this problem: Titius approaches my slave to get him to remove goods of mine and take them to him. The slave tells me. Wanting to catch Titius in the very act of committing the delict, I permit the slave to take some things to him. Is Titius liable for theft or *servi corruptio* (corruption of a slave) or neither? The question has elicited this *responsum*: he is liable for neither, not for theft because it was not without my consent that he handled the *res* and not for corruption of the slave because the slave was not made worse.

199. Sometimes there can be theft even of free people, as of our children in power, a wife *in manu*, a judgement-debtor, or a bonded gladiator.

200. And sometimes a man can steal his own goods, as where a debtor removes the *res* given to a creditor as a pledge, or if I carry off from a *bona fide possessor* a thing of mine which he is holding. Whence it is held to follow that if one's own slave returns to one from someone who was holding him as a *bona fide possessor* then, if one hides him away, one commits theft.

201. Then there is an opposite case, where it is allowed to seize and usucapt someone else's goods without it being held that theft is committed, as for instance—but only in a case where there is no *heres necessarius* (automatic heir)—by taking estate goods of which the heir has not yet obtained. If there is a *heres necessarius* this *usucapio pro herede* is excluded. Again, a debtor who has parted with a *res* through a fiduciary

mancipation or cession-at-law in the way discussed in our earlier book can possess and usucapt it without committing theft.

202. Sometimes someone comes under a liability to the *actio furti* without himself committing theft. Such a person is one by whose 'help or plan' (*ope consilio*) a theft is committed. In the number of such people fall: one who strikes coins from your hand so that another can get then, or obstructs you so that another can remove something from you, or one who chases off your sheep or cattle so that another may take them. The example used by the older jurists in their writing was driving off a herd with a red rag. But if something is done like this for fun and not to have a theft committed (*per lasciviam et non data opera ut furtum committeretur*) the question is whether an *actio utilis* should be given since the *lex Aquilia*, which was passed to deal with economic loss (*de damno*), penalises even non-intentional fault (*culpa*).

203. The action of theft lies for someone with an interest in the safety of the thing even though not necessarily its owner. By the same token it does not even lie to the owner if he has no such interest.

204. Whence it is agreed that a pledge-creditor can have the action of theft for a pledge removed, even to the extent that if it is removed by the owner himself, that is to say by the debtor, still the action of theft lies for the creditor.

205. Again if a cleaner receives clothes for cleaning at a fixed price or giving them some other treatment, or if a tailor takes in clothes to be mended, loss of them by theft gives the cleaner or tailor the action of theft and not the *dominus*. The reason is that here the owner has no interest in their not being lost, since the trial under *locatio* (hire) will allow him to recover fully from the cleaner or the tailor, so long as the cleaner or tailor have sufficient means to make good the value of his property. If they are insolvent the owner, unable to recover from them, can maintain the *actio furti*, since on these facts the owner again does have an interest in the safety of his *res*.

206. What we have said about cleaners and tailors applies also to borrowers-for-use (*ad eum cui rem commodavimus*). For as the former must guarantee safe-keeping (*custodiam praestare*) by reason of receiving for a reward, so here the borrower must do so by reason of the advantage which accrues to him in the user of the thing.

207. But a depositee does not guarantee safe-keeping and is only liable if he himself does something *dolo malo* (with wicked intent). Hence if the *res* is removed from him, the *actio depositi* will not make him liable on such facts for restoration of it, with the further consequence that the interest in the thing's security does not attach to him. It follows that the depositee cannot use the *actio furti* and the owner can.

208. Finally we must notice that it has been a question whether a young person (*impubes*) commits theft by removing another's property. Most hold that, since theft is based on intention, an *impubes* can only be under an obligation from this wrong if he is very near to puberty and on that account able to understand that he is doing wrong.

209. Someone who seizes goods of another is also liable for theft. For who more obviously handles another's goods without his consent than one who seizes them with force? Hence it is rightly said that such a man is disgraceful even among thieves (*improbum furem*). But for this delict the praetor has introduced a special action whose name is *actio vi bonorum raptorum* (action of goods violently seized). It lies within a year for quadruple damages, thereafter for single damages. This action is capable of being used even where one *res* is seized, however small.

210. The action for wrongful loss is established by the *lex Aquilia*. That *lex* provides by section 1 that, if someone wrongfully kills someone else's slave, male or female, or quadruped within the category of *pecus* (cattle), he is to be condemned to pay the owner the value of that thing at its highest in the preceding year.

211. A person is understood to kill wrongfully (*iniuria* = lit. 'by a wrong') when the death happens by his evil intent (*dolus*) or fault (*culpa*). There is no other statute which sanctions loss caused without wrongfulness (*damnum quod sine iniuria datur*). Hence no liability is imposed on one who inflicts loss without fault (*culpa*) or evil intent (*dolus malus*) but by some accident (*casu*).

212. In the action under this *lex* the valuation is made not only of the body but also of any extra loss which the owner suffers by the death of his slave over and above his price, as where my slave, instituted heir by someone, is killed before he enters on the inheritance with my authority. There the valuation is not only of his price but also of the inheritance which has been lost. Again, suppose one of a pair of twins or of a team of actors or musicians is killed. The valuation is made not only of the one who has been killed but also, in addition, of the depreciation of the survivors. The same applies where one of a pair of mules or a team of horses is killed.

213. When someone's slave is killed, the owner has a free choice whether to make the killer the object of a criminal and capital charge or to pursue the remedy for loss under this *lex*.

214. When the *lex* says 'the value of the thing at its highest in that year', the effect is that, if a lame or one-eyed slave is killed who in that year was once whole, the valuation must proceed not as at the date of his death but as at the time in the year when his value was highest. From him it happens that sometimes one recovers more than one has suffered loss.

215. The second section of the *lex* provides an action against an *adstipulator* who discharges a debt in fraud of the *stipulator*, and it gives the action for the value in money of that matter.

216. It is obvious that this part of the *lex* is also about loss (*damnum*) and was introduced on that account, but the provision was not necessary because the action on mandate suffices for that purpose, unless one wants the doubling of damages which the *lex* allows in case of one who denies liability.

217. The third section provides for all other loss. Hence, if someone wounds a slave or quadruped in the category of *pecus* (cattle), or if someone wounds or kills a non-

pecus quadruped, such as a dog or a wild beast like a lion, an action lies under this section. In respect of all other animals and all inanimate things, loss wrongfully caused is remedied under this section. For the section establishes a remedy for anything *ustum*, *fractum* or *ruptum* (burnt, broken, burst). In fact the word *rumpere* (*ruptum*) would have covered all these cases. For by '*ruptum*' is understood any type of corruption. Whence the word includes not only burning and breaking but also tearing, bruising, spilling, and any kind of vitiation or destruction or deterioration.

218. By this section the award is not the value in that year but the value in the nearest thirty days (*in diebus triginta proximis*). That is what the person causing the loss must pay. Note that the word '*plurimi*' is not present. Some have therefore thought that the judge was free to make his valuation at the time in the thirty days when the *res* was at its highest value or when it stood lower. But Sabinus held that the word *plurimi* was to be implied into that part just as though it had been expressly added, the legislator having been content to make express mention of it only in the first section.

219. On the other hand it has been decided that the action on this statute lies only where someone has caused loss by his own bodily force ('*corpore suo*'). Hence where loss is caused in another mode *actiones utiles* (policy-actions) are given, as where someone shuts up a slave or beast and starves them to death; or drives a beast of burden so hard as to cause it to damage itself; or, again, persuades another's slave to climb a tree to go down a well so that in going up or down he falls and is killed or injured in some part of his body; or, again, if someone pushes another's slave off a bridge or river bank and he drowns (though here it would not be difficult to say that he inflicts the loss *corpore suo*, in that he pushed).

220. Contempt-*iniuria* is committed not only when someone is struck with a fist or, say, a stick, or when he is even flogged; but also when a *convicium* (a verbal abuse) is offered to someone; or where a person advertises someone's goods for a debtor's selling up, knowing that he owes him nothing; or when someone writes a book or a poem to bring infamy on another; or where someone hangs about after a lady or a youth; and in short many other ways.

221. We are understood to suffer contempt-*iniuria* not only in our own selves but also through our children in our power and through our wives. Hence, if you commit a contempt-*iniuria* to my daughter who is married to Titius you will be exposed to actions for contempt-*iniuria* not only on her account but also on mine and on his.

222. No contempt-*iniuria* is understood to be committed to a slave, but only to his *dominus* through him. However, the same things done to our children or wives which cause us to suffer contempt-*iniuria* do not have that effect when done to slaves, but only acts which are of an aggravated kind, which are clearly in contempt of the owner as the law sees them, as where one man flogs another's slave. And for this case a *formula* is proposed in the edict. But if someone offers a slave a *convicium*

(verbal offence) or strikes him with a fist, no pattern *formula* is provided and none is likely to be given to one who rashly seeks such a remedy.

223. The penalty for *iniuriae* under the Twelve Tables was: for *membrum ruptum*, retaliation; for *os fractum aut collisum*, 300 *asses* for a free man, and 150 *asses* for a slave; for all other *iniuriae*, 25 *asses* was the penalty established. And it seemed in those times of great poverty that those pecuniary penalties were sufficient.

224. But now the law we use is different. The praetor allows us to put our own value on the *iniuria*, and then the judge condemns either for the sum which we have fixed or for less, as seems right to him. But since the praetor customarily sets the value of aggravated *iniuriae* himself, if once he has set the sum for bail (*vadimonium*) we then put the same sum in our *formula* as the *taxatio* [the clause specifying the maximum], the *iudex*, though he can go lower, will generally out of respect for the *praetor*'s authority not be so bold as to reduce the condemnation below that figure.

225. Aggravated contempt-*iniuria* are so qualified either *ex facto*, as where someone is wounded by someone or beaten up or struck with clubs, or *ex loco*, as where the contempt-*iniuria* is committed in the theatre or in the forum, or *ex persona*, as where a magistrate is the victim or a senator suffers a contempt-*iniuria* from a commoner (*ab humili persona*).

Justinian

Institutes, 3.13.2

The next division puts obligations into four species: *aut enim ex contractu sunt aut quasi ex contractu aut ex maleficio aut quasi ex maleficio* (for they are either from contract or *quasi* from contract or from wrongdoing or *quasi* from wrongdoing).

Institutes, 3.27: On Obligations Quasi ex Contractu

We have finished examining the types of contract. Let us turn to those obligations which cannot properly be said to arise from a contract but which can however, in that they do not owe their substance to a delict, be understood as arising *quasi ex contractu*.

1. Thus, when someone intervenes in the affairs of another when he is away (*absentis negotia gesserit*) actions arise in each direction between them called the *actiones negotiorum gestorum* (the actions for intervention in another's affairs). The person to whom the affair belongs (*dominus rei gestae*) has the direct action, and the intervener (*gestor*) has the counter action for intervention. It is obvious that these actions do not properly arise from any contract. For they come into being in the very case in which anyone puts himself forward to conduct another's affairs without being given any mandate to do it. It follows that those whose business is done come under an obligation even when unaware of what is happening (*etiam ignorantes*). And

this was established as good public policy (*utilitatis causa*) to stop the affairs of the absent running to ruin if some sudden urgency drove them to leave without entrusting to someone the management of their interests. Certainly nobody would look after them without an action to recover his outlay. But, just as an intervener who has usefully conducted the business holds the other to whom it belongs under an obligation to him, so *vice versa* he himself must also render an account of his management. And for that case he is obliged to answer to the highest standard of diligence (*ad exactissimam diligentiam*). And it is not enough for him to show such attention as he usually shows in his own affairs if it happens that another more attentive person would have conducted the intervention more successfully.

2. Furthermore guardians made liable in the trial arising from guardianship also cannot properly be understood as coming under an obligation by virtue of contract (for there is no deal at all contracted between guardian and ward). But, since a guardian's liability is certainly not delictual, he is taken to become liable *quasi ex contractu*. Here too the actions are reciprocal. For not only does a ward have the action on guardianship (*actio tutelae*) against his guardian, but also the guardian from the other side has the counter-action on guardianship against the ward for the case in which he has spent anything in the ward's interest or incurred an obligation for him or charged his own property to the ward's creditor.

3. Again if some asset is shared between people who have not agreed to be partners (*sine societate*), as where it is bequeathed or given to them both equally, each is liable to the other in the action for division of shared property (*actio communi dividundo*) as, say, because he alone took the fruits of the thing or because his *socius* bore the burden of necessary expenditure upon it. This obligation cannot be understood as properly deriving from contract in that no terms are agreed between them. Yet, in that the liability does not come from delict, it seems to arise *quasi ex contractu*.

4. The same legal analysis applies where someone comes under an obligation to a co-heir on similar grounds in the action for division of an inheritance (*actio familiae erciscundae*).

5. An heir also cannot be understood as incurring a properly contractual obligation to pay legacies. For the legatee cannot rightly be described as having concluded any deal either with the heir or with the deceased. But because his obligation is not born of wrongdoing his debt is understood to arise *quasi ex contractu*.

6. Again the person to whom a payment which is not due is mistakenly made is taken to incur a debt *quasi ex contractu*. To such an extent it is true that he does not properly come under a contractual obligation that if we stuck to a more logical analysis we might rather say, as was mentioned earlier, that his obligation arises *ex distractu*, not *ex contractu* [from discharge rather than from contract—but the word-play cannot be reproduced in English: 'from un-contract rather than contract']. For one who gives money with the intention of performing a duty appears to give it for this purpose, namely to untie rather than to tie up a transaction. Yet

despite this the recipient comes under an obligation just as though a loan (*mutuum*) had been given to him. Which is why the *condictio* lies against him.

7. In some cases it is not possible to recover a payment mistakenly made when not due. Thus the older jurists made it a maxim that wherever denial doubled liability (*ex quibus causis infitiando lis crescit*) in those cases there would be no recovery of what was paid when not owed, as for instance under the *lex Aquilia* and under legacy. But those older jurists applied this to only those legacies which were left to someone in exact certainty by the imposition of an obligation on the heir (*quae certa constitute per damnationem cuicumque fuerunt legata*). However, our enactment has made all legacies and trusts by will into one kind and has applied this increase of liability to all such legacies and trusts but not in respect of all recipients. The rule now applies only where the legacy or trust is to holy churches or other sacred places endowed for the sake of religion and piety. Such gifts once paid cannot be recovered if they turn out not to have been due.

Institutes, 4.5: On Obligations Arising Quasi ex Delicto

If a judge 'makes a case his own' (*si iudex litem suam fecerit*) he does not appear to come under an obligation which is properly *ex maleficio* (from wrongdoing). But his obligation is also not contractual and he is certainly seen to have incurred some blame even though want of knowledge (*et utique peccasse aliquid intellegitur licet per imprudentiam*). For those reasons he seems to become liable as though from wrongdoing. And he will have to bear such penalty as the conscience of the court deems fair on the facts of his case.

1. Again if something is thrown down or poured down from a dwelling in such a way as to harm someone, the person whose dwelling it is, whether he owns it, hires it or lives there free, is taken to come under an obligation as though from wrongdoing. And the reason why he is not properly said to incur an obligation as though from wrongdoing is that frequently his liability arises from the fault (*culpa*) of someone else, perhaps of a slave or a child. Similar to his case is that of the man who, in a place where people commonly pass, has something placed or hung in such a way that if it fell it could harm someone. For that case a penalty of ten *aurei* is laid down. On the other hand for something thrown or poured an action is given for double the value of the loss caused, while in the case of a freeman there is a penalty of fifty *aurei* if he is killed and an action for as much as seems fair to the judge on the facts if he survives but is injured. And the judge should take into account the fees paid to a doctor and all the other expenses of the cure as well as the earnings lost or to be lost because of the faculty which has been impaired.

2. If a son in power lives separately from his *paterfamilias* and something is thrown or poured from his dwelling or he has something placed or hung so as to be dangerous if it falls, Julian held that there is no action maintainable against the father but that the suit must be brought against the *filiusfamilias* himself. The same applies in the case of a *filius* who is a judge and makes the case his own.

3. Again where any fraud or theft is committed in a ship, inn or stable the owner running the business (*exercitor*) comes under a liability *quasi ex maleficio*, so long as the *maleficium* is in fact not his own but that of one of the people through whose labour he manages the ship, inn or stable. The reason this is *quasi ex maleficio* is that the action given against him for this case is not based on contract and yet he is to a certain degree blameworthy in relying on the service of bad men. The action for these cases is *in factum* and is available to the heir of the person to whom the claim accrues but not against the heir of the person against whom it accrues.

Questions

Chapter 1 (Obligations: The Conceptual Map)

1. What is an obligation?
2. What is the metaphor which is heavily relied upon in the language of obligation? (Cf. Fr. *lier*; Eng. 'liable'; Lat. *ligare*, giving 'ligature', 'ligament' etc. And cf. J.3.15 *pr.*: *Obligatio est iuris vinculum quo necessitate adstringimur alicuius solvendae rei secundum nostrae civitatis iura.*)
3. 'Now let us move on to obligations.' From what? How do obligations fit into the institutional picture of the law?
4. What is the difference between obligations and other 'incorporeal things'?
5. Gaius uses a two-fold classification of obligations. What kind of classification is it?
6. What is wrong with Gaius's two-fold classification? What was done to try to remedy its defects?
7. What classification does Justinian use? In what *two* respects does it differ from that of Gaius?
8. What, in brief, is meant by 'contract', 'delict', 'quasi-contract' and 'quasi-delict'?
9. What was the *condictio*?
10. Considered as a legal category, what unity did the *condictio* have?
11. What was the effect on the *condictio* of the decision to divide obligations by the events by which they were created (contract, delict, etc.)?
12. Why does Gaius examine discharge of obligations *between* contract and delict (cf. G.3.182)?
13. Why do we say that 'delicts' as discussed by Gaius are not 'crimes' but civil wrongs?
14. How is the law of delict divided? Are there any delicts which Gaius and Justinian omit from the Institutional exposition?

Chapter 2 (The Organisation of Roman Contract)

1. How does Gaius classify contractual obligations?

Chapter 3 (The Contract *Litteris* and The Rôle of Writing Generally)

1. What is the distinction between dispositive and evidential use of writing?
2. The name of the contract *litteris* in Gaius's time is *expensilatio*. How was the contract made?
3. To what action did *expensilatio* give rise?

4. What purpose did *expensilatio* serve?
5. What is meant by 'novation'?
6. What combination of rules allows Justinian to say that in his time the contract *litteris* still existed?
7. Why did Justinian preserve the category of contracts *litteris* at all?
8. What signs are there that writing, technically only evidential according to Roman theory, in practice played an enormously important role in contract?
9. What did Justinian do, stopping short of breaking with classical theory, to recognise the importance of writing in Hellenistic law and practice? In relation to *stipulatio*? In relation to other contracts?
10. What was *arra*? And what was its use in classical law?
11. To what special use did Justinian put the '*arra* rule' in relation to his reform of contracts *in scriptis*?
12. Did Justinian's reforms in relation to writing leave the consensual contracts even theoretically intact?

Chapter 4 (Contracts *Verbis*)

1. How was a contract of stipulation made?
2. What role, if any, did writing have in relation to *stipulatio?*
3. Why did 'declaration of dowry' and 'freedman's oath' not require the question and answer form?
4. The word '*dari*' recurs many times throughout Gaius's and Justinian's treatment of the *stipulatio*. What is the ordinary meaning of the word and what is its technical legal signification?
5. What are the main causes of invalidity of *stipulatio* which Gaius enumerates? Distinguish between the effects of 'initial' and 'subsequent' impossibility.
6. Is there any good reason why a stipulation for the benefit of a third party should be regarded as void?
7. Are stipulations post-mortem merely a particular example of invalidity arising from want of privity?
8. What is the difference between a stipulation for conveyance to me and Titius and a stipulation for conveyance to me or Titius?
9. What incapacities are peculiar to contracts *verbis*?
10. What is the effect of a stipulation made by (a) a slave, (b) a *filiusfamilias*, (c) a young man whose *paterfamilias* has already died?
11. Why did *stipulatio* not provide the basis for a 'general' law of contract, avoiding the need for a law of specific contracts?
12. What is the difference between 'real security' and 'personal security'?
13. Where in the Institutional scheme does the law of real security belong?
14. What types of personal security does Gaius mention? Were there any other types?

15. How is the length and detail of Gaius's treatment of personal security to be accounted for?
16. In what way is the law of personal security more simple in the time of Justinian?
17. Suppose the guarantor has to pay. How, if at all, can he recover from the principal debtor?
18. What provisions were made to share the burden between a plurality of guarantors?
19. Was the creditor compelled to demand or sue for his money from the principal debtor before turning to the guarantors?
20. What was *litis contestatio* and what was its principal consequence?

Chapter 5 (Contracts *Consensu*)

1. What is meant by the term 'consensual contract'?
2. To what actions (forms of pleading) do the consensual contracts give rise? Do any other contracts or events give rise to similar pleadings?
3. Why were the consensual contracts necessary given that sales, hirings and so on could easily be arranged by stipulation?
4. Gaius omits from his introductory treatment of sale many of the matters which were in practice of crucial importance. Can you enumerate the principal omissions?
5. Upon what aspect of the law of sale does Gaius concentrate?
6. In terms of the actions (*actio ex empto* and *actio ex vendito*) what is the key to Gaius's exposition?
7. How did Justinian approach the problem of valuation by a third party?
8. Suppose an agreement to buy and sell 'for as much as you think reasonable' or 'for as much as you bought it for'. Would a sale have been concluded?
9. What would the Proculian school have made of the common modern transaction in which a customer obtains a new car from a garage by 'part-exchange'?
10. What is the strength of the Proculian view that 'the price must be in money'?
11. Did the decision to classify barter (*permutatio*) as a separate contract mean that parties to such a transaction were deprived of all recourse to the courts?
12. Suppose I accidentally agree to sell a priceless statue for a trivial sum. If sued, could I challenge the *demonstratio* of the *actio ex empto* (i.e. deny that I had sold)?
13. Gaius does not discuss requirements of certainty in relation to the *res*. If you agree to let me have two dozen bottles of Falernian wine for 500 *denarii*, can I plead 'Whereas I bought, etc.'?
14. In classical law what were the seller's obligations in respect of title?
15. And in respect of legal defects such as adverse servitudes?
16. And in respect of substantial defects?
17. How did Justinian change the law in relation to the seller's liability for substantial defects?
18. At what moment does ownership pass from seller to buyer?
19. Does 'risk' pass at the same moment?

20. What do the words *locare* and *conducere* mean? Does payment of the *merces* proceed from the *locator* or the *conductor* or sometimes from one and sometimes from the other?
21. In what ways is *locatio-conductio* wider in scope than the contract which we call hire?
22. Is it possible to define *locatio-conductio* in such a way as both to establish its unity and to differentiate it from all other nominate contracts?
23. What exactly are the problems of differentiation between *locatio-conductio* and other contracts in relation to (i) *emphyteusis*, (ii) the gladiators and (iii) the goldsmith?
24. Could the reward (*merces*) in the contract of *locatio-conductio* be in kind rather than in money?
25. What are the principal obligations within the *actio ex conducto* (i.e. what 'ought a *locator* to give or do *ex fide bona*')?
26. What are the principal obligations within the *actio ex locato* (i.e. what 'ought a *conductor* to give or do *ex fide bona*')?
27. Gaius does not define partnership (*societas*). What definition should we supply?
28. Was a Roman *societas* a legal person (like a modern company)?
29. Were the *socii* (the partners) agents for each other in the conduct of partnership business? For example, if partner A ordered 5000 *amphorae* of wine at 10 *denarii* each and failed to pay, could the seller sue partner B?
30. What is meant by the statement that partnership was concerned solely with the 'internal relations of the partners'?
31. What was the typical scope of *societas* (G.3.148)? What partnership provides the background to Cicero's speech *Pro Roscio Comoedo*?
32. Was it necessary to fix the shares of profit and loss before a *societas* could be said to have come into existence?
33. According to G.3.149, what was the difference of opinion between the pre-classical jurists Quintus Mucius (consul in 95 BC) and Servius Sulpicius (praetor in 65 BC)? What was *societas leonina* (partnership with a lion)?
34. What were the principal events which would bring a partnership to an end?
35. What was the object of bringing an *actio pro socio*?
36. How did the species of *societas* peculiar to Roman citizens differ from ordinary consensual *societas* (G.3.154a–b)?
37. How do the relations created by the contract of mandate differ from those entailed by modern 'agency'?
38. How are the contracts of *locatio-conductio* and *mandatum* to be differentiated (cf. G.3.162)?
39. Why is there no contract if the mandate is *tua gratia* (for the sake of the *mandatarius* only)? What is the difference between a mandate 'Lend out your money' and another 'Lend out your money to X' (G.3.156)?
40. What were the consequences of the mandatary's going outside the terms of the mandate (G.3.161)?

41. What were the principal obligations demanded within the *actio mandati directa* (the mandator's action) and the *actio mandati contraria* (the mandatary's action)?
42. The contract of mandate supplied one part of the piecemeal Roman law of agency. Another was contributed by the *actiones adiectitiae qualitatis* (liability-extending actions). But the picture cannot be fully understood without the third and perhaps most important part, namely the employment of slave agents. What was the effect of a slave's contract?
43. What was the consequence if the slave who made the contract was owned by X but was possessed by Y in the belief that he was owner? And what would happen if the slave, owned by X, was subject to a usufruct in Y (G.3.165–6)?
44. A slave might be owned by, say, three brothers, Seius, Lucius and Titius. What would the consequence be if he purported to contract solely for Lucius (G.3.167–167a)?
45. In the treatment of, for example, *societas* there are many references to events which bring the contract to an end. How many modes of discharge does Gaius enumerate? How should one explain Gaius's selection, in this specialised discussion, of these particular modes of discharge?

Chapter 6 (Contracts *Re*)

1. What is meant by 'contracts *re*'?
2. How does the category of contracts *re* differ in Justinian's Institutes, compared to Gaius's?
3. Differentiate between the four 'real contracts': *mutuum, depositum, commodatum* and *pignus*. What grounds are there for saying that *mutuum* is a cuckoo in this nest?
4. What is the effect of an agreement between creditor and debtor that money lent shall not be repaid or shall be repaid only as to one half the capital sum?
5. What is the meaning of the concept used in G.3.206 called '*custodiam praestare*' (safety-guarantee)?
6. What is the content of the obligation *custodiam praestare* in relation to *commodatum*? What kind of people come under this *custodia* liability?

Chapter 7 (*Furtum*)

1. Between G.3.182 and G.3.194 Gaius is talking about different measures of theftuous liability. How many such measures were there in his time?
2. From G.3.195 to G.3.201 Gaius is talking about the elements of theft. What elements does he identify?
3. The definition of theft given by Paul in D.47.2.1.3 is this: '*Furtum est contrectatio rei fraudulosa lucri faciendi gratia vel ipsius rei vel etiam usus eius possessionisve*' (Theft is the fraudulent contrectation of a thing for the sake of making a gain from the thing itself, from its use, or from its possession). Does Paul's definition introduce elements absent from Gaius's discussion or omit elements present in Gaius's discussion?

4. In G.3.202 Gaius discusses liability for 'helping' theft. What was necessary in order to make a man liable for theft '*ope consilio*'?
5. What is the point of Gaius's mention in G.3.202 of the case of a herd driven away '*per lasciviam*' (for fun)?
6. Who is allowed to bring an *actio furti* (action of theft)?

Chapter 8 (*Rapina*)

1. What was *rapina* and why did the praetor provide an additional action for it?

Chapter 9 (*Damnum Iniuria Datum*)

1. When was the *lex Aquilia* passed? Was it technically a *lex*?
2. What is the relationship between the Aquilian delict and *furtum*?
3. In developed law, was the scope of the Aquilian delict (*damnum iniuria datum*) controlled solely by the *lex* itself?
4. The outline of the delict is carried by the name '*damnum iniuria datum*'. What does each word mean?
5. From the plaintiff's viewpoint, what kind of loss-causing disasters fell with chapter I and chapter III of the *lex Aquilia*?
6. What must be true of the defendant in order to make him liable for those disasters?
7. What was the measure of recovery for *damnum iniuria datum*?
8. What were the main praetorian extensions of the statutory liability under the *lex Aquilia*?

Chapter 10 (*Iniuria*)

1. The delict rendered in these lectures as 'contempt-*iniuria*' is in Latin merely '*iniuria*'. Can you account for a delict having such an extraordinary name? Are there any parallels in modern law?
2. The content of 'contempt-*iniuria*' is very diverse. Does the category have any unity? Is it possible to frame an abstract definition of the delict?
3. Gaius, at G.3.223, is concerned with the early history of the delict *iniuria*. What in outline was the story of its development?
4. What problems arise in relation to these three delictual events: (a) negligent injury to a free man, (b) kicking a slave, (c) sexual harassment of an *ancilla*?
5. Would the Roman jurists have classified racial discrimination as contempt-*iniuria*?
6. Can the measure of recovery for contempt-*iniuria* be called 'compensation'?

Chapter 11 (The Quasi Categories)

1. Where did the two quasi categories come from? Do they appear in Gaius's Institutes?
2. What events fall in the category *quasi ex contractu* according to J.3.27?
3. Does the phrase '*quasi ex contractu*' mean 'implied contract' or 'sort of contract'?
4. What is the factor common to all events in the category of quasi-contract?
5. What, if any, connexion is there between quasi-contract and 'unjust enrichment'?
6. Should any events other than those listed in J.3.27 be counted as quasi-contracts?
7. Should the term 'quasi-contract' be replaced and abandoned?
8. What events are listed in J.4.5 as belonging to the category *quasi ex delicto*?
9. What theories have been advanced to explain why it was thought necessary to have a category of quasi-delict?
10. If we could start again with a clean slate, what classification of obligations would we use? Would quasi-delict (or an equivalent category differently named) have any place in the scheme?
11. In the exercise of classifying obligations the ones which cause difficulty are always those which are both (a) imposed irrespective of the consent of the person subjected to the obligation, and (b) not explicable in terms of fault on that person's part. What explanations of such obligations have been relied on in the past?

Further Publications by Peter Birks

The list below contains other publications by the author concerning the Roman law of obligations and also some more jurisprudential topics, like taxonomy, which feature in the present Lectures.

Translations

1. Translation of books 12 and 13 in A Watson (ed), *The Digest of Justinian*, vol. 1 (Philadelphia: University of Pennsylvania Press, 1985), 357–414. Reprinted in the 1998 revised English-language edition
2. (tr with G McLeod) *Justinian's Institutes* (London: Duckworth and Ithaca, NY: Cornell University Press, 1987)

Obligations in General

3. 'Obligations: One Tier or Two?' in PG Stein and ADE Lewis (eds), *Studies in Justinian's Institutes in Memory of JAC Thomas* (London: Sweet & Maxwell, 1983), 18–38
4. 'Introduction' in P Birks and G McLeod (tr) *Justinian's Institutes* (London: Duckworth and Ithaca, NY: Cornell University Press, 1987), 7–28
5. 'Definition and Division: A Meditation on *Institutes* 3.13' in P Birks (ed), *The Classification of Obligations* (Oxford: Clarendon Press, 1997), 1–36

Delict

6. 'The Concept of a Civil Wrong' in D Owen (ed), *Philosophical Foundations of Tort Law* (Oxford: Clarendon Press, 1996), 29–52

Furtum

7. 'A Note on the Development of *Furtum*' (1973) 8 *Irish Jurist (NS)* 349–55
8. 'The Case of the Filched Pedigree: D. 47.2.52.20' in *Sodalitas: Scritti in Onore di Antonio Guarino* (Naples: Jovene Editore, 1984), 731–48

Damnum iniuria datum

9. 'Other Men's Meat: Aquilian Liability for Proper Use' (1981) 16 *Irish Jurist (NS)* 141–85
10. 'A Point of Aquilian Pleading' (1985) 36 *IVRA* 97–107

11. 'Cooking the Meat: Aquilian Liability for Hearths and Ovens' (1985) 20 *Irish Jurist (NS)* 352–77
12. 'The Model Pleading of the Action for Wrongful Loss' (1992) 25–27 *Irish Jurist (NS)* 311–28 [=*Liber Memorialis John M Kelly*]
13. 'Wrongful Loss by Co-Promisees' (1994) 22 *Index* 181–8
14. 'Doing and Causing to be Done' in ADE Lewis and DJ Ibbetson (eds), *The Roman Law Tradition* (Cambridge: Cambridge University Press, 1994), 31–53
15. 'The Edictal Rubric "*Ad Legem Aquiliam*"' in R Pérez-Bustamente (ed), *Estudios de historia del derecho europeo: homenaje al professor Gonzalo Martínez Díez* (Madrid: Editorial Complutense, 1994), vol. 1, 81–9
16. 'Ulpian 18 *ad Edictum*: Introducing *Damnum Iniuria*' in R Feenstra et al. (eds), *Collatio Iuris Romani*, vol. 1 (Amsterdam: Gieben, 1995), 17–36
17. 'Can we get nearer to the text of the *Lex Aquilia*?' in BCM Jacobs and EC Coppens (eds), *Een rijk gerecht: opstellen aangeboden aan prof. mr. P. L. Nève* (Nijmegen: Gerard Noodt Instituut, 1998), 25–41

Iniuria

18. 'The Early History of *Iniuria*' (1969) 37 *Tijdschrift voor Rechtsgeschiedenis* 163–208
19. 'Lucius Veratius and the *Lex Aebutia*' in A Watson (ed), *Daube Noster: Essays in Legal History for David Daube* (Edinburgh et al.: Scottish Academic Press, 1974), 39–48
20. '*Infamandi Causa Facta* in Disguise' (1976) *Acta Juridica* 83–104
21. 'Harassment and Hubris: The Right to an Equality of Respect' (1997) 32 *Irish Jurist* (NS) 1–45 [revised version of *Harassment and Hubris: The Right to an Equality of Respect, Being the Second John Maurice Kelly Memorial Lecture* (Dublin: University College Dublin, Faculty of Law, 1996)]

Miscellaneous Other Causes

22. 'The Problem of Quasi-Delict' (1969) 22 *CLP* 164–80
23. 'A New Argument for A Narrow View of *Litem Suam Facere*' (1984) 52 *Tijdschrift voor Rechtsgeschiedenis* 373–87

Index

The manufacturer's authorised representative in the EU for product safety is Oxford University Press España S.A. of El Parque Empresarial San Fernando de Henares, Avenida de Castilla, 2 - 28830 Madrid (www.oup.es/en or product.safety@oup.com). OUP España S.A. also acts as importer into Spain of products made by the manufacturer.
Printed and bound by CPI Group (UK) Ltd, Croydon, CR0 4YY
14/09/2026
02216307-0014